Praise for Reynold Feldman's *Wisdom*

"*Wisdom* is an invaluable resource and guide for strengthening, developing, and accessing our own inherent wisdom nature."

Angeles Arrien, PhD, cultural anthropologist and author of *The Four-Fold Way and Signs of Life*

"If there were a formula for gaining wisdom, Reynold Feldman has it. Focusing upon daily reflection and practice – meditation and action – he provides day-after-day challenges that move us toward the elusive, deeply desired goal of deepening our selves: getting wisdom."

John D. Maguire, president emeritus, Claremont Graduate University, and social-justice advocate

"This book of reflections on wisdom quotations from world cultures, spiritual traditions, and perceptive authors increases our depth of vision and quality of life. Creative ideas for keeping a personal wisdom journal open the way to life enrichment."

Roland Seboldt, editor and publisher

"Reynold Feldman knows how to use his extensive experience of teaching, counseling, and meditation to present the 'way to wisdom' in daily nuggets that challenge as much as they inspire, probe, and ask more of us each day. Rewarding if you stay with it!"

David Burrell, CSC, Hesburgh Professor of Philosophy and Theology, University of Notre Dame

"Having a daily inspirer to dip into when at your God space is a blessing. Reynold Feldman has produced such an ecumenical-transdenominational soul friend."

Rabbi Zalman M. Schachter-Shalomi, coauthor of *From Age-ing to Sage-ing*

WISDOM

WISDOM

Daily Reflections for a New Era

by

Reynold Feldman

Saint Mary's Press
Christian Brothers Publications
Winona, Minnesota

The publishing team included Michael Wilt, development editor; Laurie A. Berg, copy editor; Brooke E. Saron, production editor; Cären Yang, designer; pre-press, printing, and binding by the graphics division of Saint Mary's Press.

Cover painting by Laure Heinz

Author photo by Mark S. Anderson, Ideal Images, Honolulu

The acknowledgments continue on page 381.

Printed in the United States of America

Printing: 9 8 7 6 5 4 3 2 1

Year: 2008 07 06 05 04 03 02 01 00

ISBN 0-88489-637-4

Genuine recycled paper with 10% post-consumer waste.
Printed with soy-based ink.

For

Bapak Muhammad Subuh Sumohadiwidjojo
(1901–1987)
who opened me to
the Source
of all
wisdom.

–R. F.

Wisdom is the principal thing;
therefore get wisdom. . . .

–PROVERBS 4:7, KJV

Facts bring us to knowledge, but stories lead to wisdom.

–RACHEL NAOMI REMEN, MD

CONTENTS

In his 1973 book *Survival of the Wisest*, Dr. Jonas Salk, discoverer of the first polio vaccine, argued that world survival depends on wisdom. Wise people, for him, were those who made decisions that over the long term yielded positive rather than negative consequences. Unless enough such individuals emerged, he didn't extend the planet much hope.

As a physician Dr. Salk had a public-health model for global wellness. Every organism contains healthy and diseased cells. If the former predominate, the result is wellness. If the latter predominate, the result is illness and death.

As the turn of the millennium approached, some people expected imminent disaster. Others predicted the Last Days, the Second Coming, the Rapture. Still others saw paradise unfolding with each new technological breakthrough. To judge by the movies, the pessimists have it. Most of Hollywood's aliens these days are bad.

Whatever the case, the end of the world lies ahead for each of us. Eternal life in these bodies is unlikely. The need for wisdom – for deciding what to do during our limited stay on earth – begins with this realization.

The present collection of daily reflections is meant to provide insight into what wisdom is. This is not a theoretical or academic book, however. Each day begins with a quotation from the riches of world cultures. (A basic principle of wisdom, I believe, is that we can – and *should* – learn from everyone.) I then briefly discuss what the passage means to me, sometimes in a very direct way, other times in a more elliptical fashion. Finally, there is an exercise in which I ask you, the reader, to reflect on some aspect of your life in light of the reading and to write your thoughts down in a Wisdom Journal.

Now a Wisdom Journal is no more, but no less, than a blank notebook of your choosing. Unless you really get into your writing, limit yourself to ten minutes. Very important! This is not a mid-term exam. Review of spelling and grammar is neither required nor desired. Just write freely and leave the spellchecker – and internal critic – at work. Your Wisdom Journal is intended for you and you alone.

Nor is this book meant to add another burden to already overbusy lives. Each page can be read and reread quickly. Devote twenty minutes – before or after breakfast, before going to sleep – to wisdom. I increase my Chinese vocabulary by devoting that amount of time each day, so I am confident we can all increase our "wisdom quotient" with the same commitment. A Yugoslav proverb has it right: "Grain by grain, a loaf; stone by stone, a castle."

A final word. This book is part of a larger undertaking, the World Wisdom Project. We plan a world gathering of wisdom-seekers in Hawaii in 2001, to kick off a series of activities to nurture and sustain individual and community wisdom worldwide. Are you interested? See *www.worldwisdomproject.org* for details.

WISDOM

THE WISDOM OF NEW BEGINNINGS

Today is the first day of the rest of your life.

–A CONTEMPORARY AMERICAN SAYING

Happy New Year and welcome to a yearlong exploration of personal wisdom. For today is not only the first day of the year, it is also the first day of the rest of your life. What you do or don't do today will affect who, where, and what you are, not only tomorrow but all the tomorrows thereafter. Welcome to a world of possibilities where you are author, protagonist, and chief beneficiary.

Life's small changes might not seem important. But from them grows individual, family, even global transformation. Take the film many of us see yearly: *It's a Wonderful Life.* Jimmy Stewart's character, George Bailey, is an ordinary person running a small savings and loan office in Small Town, U.S.A. When his father died, George gave up plans for a life of travel and took over the family business. Years later the town Scrooge, Mr. Potter, plays a trick on George – a trick that will put the bank out of business. George, bereft, contemplates throwing himself from the bridge. His life, he concludes, has been a waste. Enabled by his guardian angel to experience what the town would have been like had he never lived, George prays for another chance and finds that his many friends have raised enough money to save the bank, and that, as his brother puts it, he is "the richest man in town."

On a road trip in 1981, my wife, younger daughter, and I stopped by the Yale campus. I had been a student there and hadn't been back for years. I pointed out a second-floor window to our ten-year-old. "You should be grateful to that room," I said. "Why, Daddy?" she asked. "Because that's where I took first-year German. Had I taken any other language to fulfill my requirement, I never would have gone to Heidelberg for my junior year or ever met Mommy. So, except for that room, you would never have been born!"

For the first exercise in your Wisdom Journal, write freely for about five minutes on some small choice you have made that has had a major impact on your life. Happy journaling!

KNOWING WHEN TO FOLD

Ah! I intended
Never never to grow old . . .
Listen: New Year's bell!

-A HAIKU BY JOKUN

The up side of a new year is all the possibilities it brings. The down side is, we are another year older and, maybe, deeper in debt. One thing is certain. Every passing year means one year less in which to do, learn, and be things. You can't turn back the clock. Each year brings us closer to the stage Shakespeare described so well in *As You Like It:* "Sans teeth, sans eyes, sans taste, sans everything" (II, vii, 166).

None of us, I imagine, intends to grow old. My wife and I, seeing people who look the age of our parents as we remember them, think of those people as old. Ironically they are sometimes younger than we are. Our inner voice doesn't seem to age either. Yet we look in the mirror and see our father or mother.

I remember when I turned fifty-five. To celebrate, my wife and I went to a local restaurant that gave senior discounts. I proudly ordered my first senior meal. Not many days later, we had a major snowfall in Saint Paul. After I had carefully shoveled out my driveway, the plow came by and closed it up. Furious, I started shoveling with a vengeance. For the first time in my life, my back went out. For the next three days, I had to walk with a cane and crawl into and out of bed. Now I was a senior all right!

The art of living has to be like the art of playing poker – knowing when to hold and when to fold. Timing is everything. Wisdom here has to do with respecting our changing capacity – and also trying, as we get older, to do what's really important while weeding out attitudes, behaviors, and activities that are harmful to ourselves and others. Time is limited, after all, as the calendar reminds us every New Year's Eve.

In your Wisdom Journal, briefly write about a time when you held on too long to some belief, habit, or activity. What lesson did you learn?

THE WISDOM OF REPETITION

Pray the Rosary for world peace.

–FROM A BUMPER STICKER

As I passed the RV with that bumper sticker, I was busy listening to and then repeating Japanese phrases from a "You Can Speak Japanese" tape. Repetition is well regarded as a memorization technique, but less highly thought of as a religious practice. It seems quaint, even medieval, to "say your beads." There are dozens of jokes about doing penance via twenty Our Fathers and ten Hail Marys. One is reminded of pre-1960s elementary classrooms in which faulty spellers would have to print the correctly spelled word 50 times on the back of homework papers, or "rattlers" like me would have to write "I will not talk while the teacher is speaking" 25 times on the blackboard. How stupid, mechanical, shameful!

Yet I'll wager that most continuing religious and spiritual practices are based on repetition. First you go to religious services on a recurring basis. Then the service format remains more or less the same week after week. Hymns contain choruses. Liturgies repeat the same intercessory phrases.

I have been to Baha'i, Buddhist, Christian, Hindu, Jewish, Muslim, and Sikh services. Repetition of words, phrases, gestures, and activities seem prominent in them all. Mystical practices are no different. When you meditate, for example, you keep repeating your *mantra*–or in centering prayer your "sacred word"–as a means to achieve a tranquil state. During the Ramadan fast, Muslims begin each day with a statement of intent and end it with a prayer of thanksgiving.

If you are reminded of the hypnotic effect of repetition, that's okay. The point is, repetition is a time-honored, still-effective way of helping us enter altered states. W. T. Stace remarked that the poet Tennyson could put himself into a trance by intoning his last name. Repetition, like Keats's Grecian urn, "teases us out of thought as doth eternity." And discursive thinking, we now know, is as much the enemy of the meditative state as it is of sleep.

Sit quietly. Think your first name with each breath. Do this sixty times. Then sit quietly for about ten minutes. Later, write about the experience in your Wisdom Journal.

THE WISDOM OF PLANNING

It's not the man, it's the plan.
It's not the rap, it's the map.

-OSSIE DAVIS, 1971

One of my favorite activities occurs every New Year's Day. I tabulate monthly income and expenditures for the year just ended, compare them with the year before, then set up my line-item budget for the year about to begin. In 1969–70, as intercultural activities officer at the East-West Center in Honolulu, I participated in my first formal planning exercise. The center had just reconfigured as a cluster of East-West problem-solving institutes. My assignment was to figure out how to integrate degree and nondegree students into the overall center plan, and how extracurricular activities might complement the degree and research activities of the new institutes.

In the late seventies and early eighties, as dean of program development at Northeastern Illinois University, Chicago, I worked on several more plans. First, with funding from a foundation, we produced a faculty development program and spent many hours with our faculty fellows devising how to renew both the institution and themselves. Second, I became cochair of Northeastern Illinois University's General Education Reform Task Force. Aided this time with a grant from the Society for Values in Higher Education, we joined thirteen other colleges and universities around the country to revise our general-education programs collaboratively. Recently I helped the nonprofit homeless charity I work for as development director complete a major exercise in financial, management, and marketing planning. My sense is that if we can successfully follow the plan, also funded by a foundation, we will avoid being forced out of business by inconsistent state funding and will become a strong, thriving organization.

Assessing where we have been and where we are going–what our vision, goals, and values are–and the best route to get from here to there, whether as individuals or organizations, is a wise thing to do. As Ossie Davis says, "It's not the rap, it's the map." Based on my experience to date, I agree.

Discuss in your Wisdom Journal how you use planning in your personal or professional life.

PARENTAL WISDOM

The most important thing that parents can teach their children is how to get along without them.

–FRANK A. CLARK, AS QUOTED ON THE INSPIRE LISTSERV, JANUARY 29, 1999

To hear the tales we tell about our parents, you'd imagine there were at most five sets of good parents out there, none of them in America. The reality is, there are many good parents. If not, the country would be in total chaos. Still, raising successful adults is far from easy, and the phrase *parental wisdom* may sound like an oxymoron.

Not all of us, to be sure, come from intact nuclear families. More and more are products of one-person, generally single-mother, families. The burden once carried by not just two parents but a close-knit network of aunts, uncles, grandparents, older cousins, and siblings must now often be borne by a single individual otherwise engaged in the struggle to make a living. Whether virtual villages have been assembled to help raise the new generation is a matter of debate. So far the smart money seems to be betting that they have not.

Whatever the case, successful human development seems to follow a pattern from dependence through independence to healthy interdependence. Once the fetus is delivered from the paradise of the womb, the infant moves to ever greater independence: from being carried to standing to being led to walking freely; from infancy to teenage rebellion to full growth to leaving home to financial and emotional self-reliance. Interdependence means, for instance, that even if we own our own business, we still have to rely on others to buy our goods or services. Being "self-made" can really be applied only to God. Our mission as parents, then, is to coach our kids to become emotionally and fiscally independent of us, to learn to rely on themselves as much as possible, and yet to be able to take part in larger mutual-support networks without losing their identity as individuals. Those networks will include us as prominent members. Wisdom here means learning how to become a good coach.

Discuss in your Wisdom Journal the pros and cons of how you were parented and (if applicable) what you are doing now to parent your children well.

RELIGIOUS WISDOM

Someone in the choir room whispered, "Who's religious? Anybody in here religious?" The huddled students started to pray, very, very quietly. "I was terrified on the outside," says Craig Nason, a junior. "But on the inside, God gave me peace. I felt like many others outside the school were praying for us."

–"SPECIAL REPORT: THE LITTLETON MASSACRE," *TIME*, MAY 3, 1999

When the going gets tough, the tough get going. Or so the saying goes. Clearly, though, a life-and-death situation will test our religious faith.

My wife, Simone, experienced such an ordeal when she was age fourteen. She, her mother (a trained Red Cross volunteer), and her eight-months-pregnant older sister were fleeing from the approaching Russian front in their native East Prussia. It was January 1945. First the German MPs didn't want to let her on the overcrowded hospital train. My mother-in-law argued and bribed them into it. Then the train just sat there. Word came back that the engine had broken down. At the time Simone didn't know if she believed in God. She was angry about the war and the human devastation accompanying it. But she joined the others in the car in prayer until, exhausted, she fell asleep. Suddenly she lurched forward. Hours had passed, but prayers had been answered. Among the wounded were former railroad engineers. They had cannibalized parts from nearby trains and had gotten their engine to start. After the war Simone was confirmed in the Lutheran church.

As I write, America is still recovering from the worst student-perpetrated school crime ever committed on American soil. The student quoted above got out safely, as did another young man named Craig. Craig Scott hid under a library table as the killers entered. He prayed for courage. When the shooters left for more bullets, God told Craig to run for it. Taking a wounded girl with him, he made it to safety. There he led others in praying for those still inside. Almost all the kids they prayed for made it out. Only his 17-year-old sister, Rachel, never did.

In your Wisdom Journal, describe a situation where prayer helped you through a critical situation.

AFFIRMATIONAL WISDOM

I dwell in the midst of infinite Abundance.
The Abundance of God is my Infinite Source.
The River of Life never stops flowing.
It flows through me in lavish expression.
Good comes to me through unexpected avenues.
God works in myriad ways to bless me.
I now open my mind to receive my good.
Nothing is too good to be true.
Nothing is too wonderful to happen. . . .
God provides for me in wondrous ways.
I am indeed grateful. And so it is.

–An anonymous poem of affirmation, distributed in Unity churches

The praying of affirmations is based on the belief that speaking of desired situations as already existing will hasten them into existence: *I am happy; I am in perfect health; I am in a mutually fulfilling relationship; I am wealthy.* When so many of us are unhappy, ill, in troubled relationships, and struggling financially, it is clear why affirmations have become a popular way of praying.

In conventional prayer God is like the owner of an infinitely endowed foundation with assets in happiness, health, wealth, and so on. I find myself in a deficit situation in one or more of these departments. So I ask God for a grant or loan. In the praying of affirmations, I already am happy, healthy, and wealthy, but because I don't have the eyes to see it, these states are prevented from manifesting themselves in me. Basically my lack of faith in a God flowing with abundance toward all of Creation gets in the way of my claiming the universal lottery I have already won.

The concept of affirmations makes sense to me, although at times it all sounds too easy – like winning a lottery. Let's face it. Lotteries have lots of losers and not too many winners. On the other hand, we often are our own worst enemy, preventing our own success. Maybe we should give affirmations a chance. Some people swear by them – at least twice a day.

Try the above affirmation for two weeks. Write about the experience and any results in your Wisdom Journal.

AQUARIAN WISDOM

A leaderless but powerful network is working to bring about radical change in the United States. . . . This Network is the Aquarian Conspiracy. . . . Broader than reform, deeper than revolution, this benign conspiracy for a new human agenda has triggered the most rapid cultural realignment in history. . . . Not even the Renaissance has promised such a radical renewal. . . . We create alternative scenarios of the future. We communicate about the failures of old systems, forcing new frameworks for problem-solving in every area. . . . Awake and alarmed, we are looking to each other for answers.

-MARILYN FERGUSON, *THE AQUARIAN CONSPIRACY*, 1980

When *The Aquarian Conspiracy* came out in 1980, it was a heady event. The book expressed what many of us had been feeling. At a time when the public-access Internet wasn't even a glimmer in anyone's eye, Marilyn Ferguson was talking about the various worldwide networks that were creating a global society while governments looked on unawares. The new Middle Ages were turning into the new Renaissance under our very noses. Everything was changing: family, religion, science, government. The Age of Aquarius was dawning, and it was more than a hippie folk opera. But too many of us were still asleep.

In 1978 my wife and I attended a conference with Dr. Jonas Salk and two dozen others at Farnham Castle, Surrey, England. Dr. Salk had been thinking and writing about Epoch A and Epoch B, roughly the old system and the New Age. For example, in Epoch A the focus was on antidisease (health) and independence (politics), whereas in Epoch B it would be on wellness and interdependence. He was convinced that global society was undergoing epoch-making changes and had established the Epoch B Foundation to explore them.

Were Marilyn Ferguson and Jonas Salk prophetic or merely misguided? A hundred years will give our descendants the proper perspective to judge.

Do you think we are entering a new age? Respond in your Wisdom Journal.

CONNECTED WISDOM

Mysticism and spirituality by themselves are not enough. Social action and therapeutic caring by themselves are not enough. Nor is it enough merely to reach for both at the same time. The lost element in our lives is the force within myself that can attend to both movements of human nature within my own being and can then guide the arising of this force within my neighbor in a manner suited to his understanding.

-JACOB NEEDLEMAN, *LOST CHRISTIANITY,* 1980

During the early 1970s, I was assistant director of a short-lived program at the University of Hawaii called New College. The brainchild of a senior history professor, New College quickly became known as the "hippie college." We probably lasted as long as we did – three years – because some of the "hippies" were children of other senior professors.

During the first two years, all students studied the same four interdisciplinary courses. In the last two years, they worked on independent projects for presentation to the student-faculty community for graduation. Top faculty taught and served as student advisors. Activities were housed in a leased mansion a block from campus. In monthly town meetings, everything was discussed, like whether or not pot might be smoked in the house even though drugs were banned from all university facilities. This being the early seventies, students and many faculty were into either the New Left or what I termed "the New East." Our director commented, "Put them together and you get 'the New Least.'"

Professor Jacob Needleman, at the end of the seventies, concluded that exclusive attention to either inner or outer concerns makes for inadequate religion and cannot satisfy our basic human need. We must find a way to live effectively in this world without forgetting our spiritual nature, and to develop our inner selves without neglecting our worldly responsibilities. This trick, he thought, requires tapping a particular "force" within. Not a simple proposition. May that Force be with us all.

How do you balance inner and outer concerns? Respond in your Wisdom Journal.

DESERT-PATH WISDOM

Did you know that the word for "mystic path" in Sufism – tariqah *– means the path in the desert that the Bedouin takes to travel from oasis to oasis? Obviously such a path is not clearly marked like a highway and isn't even a visible road. But it is there to those who know. To find your way in the trackless desert you need to know the area intimately. Sufis are those who know the area intimately.*

–A Sufi woman, quoted by Andrew Harvey in "The Perfume of the Desert," 1998

I once saw a documentary on the voyage of six traditional Polynesian sailing canoes from the Marshall Islands, in the South Pacific, to Hawaii. The program followed the building of the canoes, but the main focus was on training the navigators. All were of Polynesian background, and were relearning their ancestral art of navigating without recourse to instruments. In training runs they were taught to recognize stars, interpret winds and cloud formations, look for certain birds and fish, even refine their sense of smell to help them find land. The voyages were successful – three weeks after departure, all six boats arrived in Hawaii.

I imagine that navigating through a desert must require similar skills. Deserts, in fact, are often considered oceans of sand, with continents of arable land on all sides and oases scattered like islands throughout. With strong winds and sandstorms constantly shifting a desert's topography, one must truly know the area to find the next oasis, the next source of water and food. Survival depends on this knowledge.

I am reminded of "the Force," a key factor in the *Star Wars* movies. As I understand it, the Force will guide individuals to make right choices if they but surrender themselves to it. Mystics across cultures believe in something similar: an in-built spiritual homing device that enables sensitive human beings to find their way from island to island, oasis to oasis as they journey through life. It is heartening that people around the world today are making efforts to relearn this traditional, if forgotten, skill.

In your Wisdom Journal, discuss an experience of having been guided to an "oasis" during your life.

THE FOOLISHNESS OF CONVENTIONAL WISDOM

Conventional wisdom is life under the lordship of culture, which is both oppressive and alienating.

–MARCUS J. BORG, *MEETING JESUS AGAIN FOR THE FIRST TIME*, 1994

In religious (versus secular) societies, the priest ranks higher than the nobleman. In India, for example, the *brahmin* caste comes first, followed by the caste of *kshatriyas*, or warrior aristocrats. In medieval Christianity, the Pope crowned the Holy Roman Emperor, whom he also outranked. The reasoning is straightforward: Priests stand for the eternal verities of the spiritual realm while kings and queens, who receive their mandate from that realm, represent the temporal, the here and now. Eternity outranks time.

Conventional wisdom consists of customs and taboos: the way things are done and the way they are never done – except by heathens, communists, or the "great unwashed." In North American subcultures, the word *cool* has been around for several generations. Other words that express cultural approval, like *swell* and *groovy*, come and go. When I was an undergraduate at Yale, the equivalent word for cool was *shoe*. (As far as I know, this term was limited to New Haven and had to do with the fashionableness of white buckskin shoes.) I forget what our negative control words were – the equivalents of today's nerdy, geeky, or dorky. Maybe I am repressing them. How un-shoe.

There is nothing wrong with being cool – authentically so. Great jazz definitely is. But nothing is less cool than spending all one's energy aspiring to coolness. Nor sadder if the aspirant is over twenty-five. Being locked in a time warp of temporal values (conventional wisdom) to the exclusion of eternal ones (true wisdom) is one of the worst traps of materialistic cultures. It is as if an individual has never put off childish things and grown up. Dreiser's *An American Tragedy* and Fitzgerald's *The Great Gatsby* are classic case studies of this failing. For in seeking a superficial reputation, we lose the most precious thing of all: our selves.

In your Wisdom Journal, give an example of a cultural value that in your opinion keeps us from living according to true values.

FURBY WISDOM

Our job with Furby was that it had to have all the senses present: intelligence, emotion and life. Furby is a toy that can invoke a child's imagination. . . . Furby's physical movements and facial expressions create the cues that we have come to understand represent human emotions. Once those basics are covered, we are allowed to suspend our disbelief. . . . Our imaginations are then free to project all kinds of intelligence and emotions into [the] toy. . . . A child's imagination is the most powerful technology available to us.

–CALEB CHUNG, CREATOR OF FURBY, THE 1998 TOY OF THE YEAR

I do not (yet) own a Furby. No doubt the only reason I am writing about Furby here is that Caleb Chung and I belong to the same national entrepreneurs' association and I read an extended article on how Furby came about in our newsletter. The story is interesting.

Caleb got his start in the toy business in 1986, when he was hired to be a designer in Mattel's advanced research division. Caleb's dream was to do for the toy business what George Lucas had done for on-screen science fiction. Specifically, he hoped to create a whole line of interactive, "animatronic" pets. He started with dinosaurs, but they required too many motors and were therefore too expensive. After leaving Mattel, Caleb came up with an interactive sumo wrestler, and in February 1997, after visiting the New York International Toy Fair, he and his wife had the idea for Furby. The rest of the year was a blur of work. Today Tiger Electronics (since bought by Hasbro) is turning out a million Furbies a month.

There are several bits of wisdom here. It takes timing, faith, hard work, and luck to hit an entrepreneurial grand slam. Go and do likewise is easier said than done. Fundamental to Caleb's success, however, is his ability to remember his own childhood and to know that, like good radio, good toys invoke rather than supplant children's imaginations.

Spend a half hour playing with a child under the age of seven. Discuss the experience in your Wisdom Journal.

HOPI END-TIME WISDOM

There is a river flowing now very fast. It is so great and swift, that there are those who will be afraid. They will try to hold on to the shore. They will feel they are being torn apart and will suffer greatly. Know the river has its destination.

The elders say we must let go of the shore, push off into the middle of the river, keep our eyes open, and our heads above the water. . . . All that we do now must be done in a sacred manner and in celebration.

–Gary Gach from the Hopi Nation, Oraibi, Arizona, 1999

A related item, from Hopi elder Cho Qosh, states that now is no longer the eleventh hour. Now is *the* hour. Like the Y2K problem, the year 2000 is a human construction. Maybe all our thoughts and concerns about the end of the millennium caused eddies and swirls in the noösphere. Still, you never know. Did you lay in your supply of drinking water?

As I write, I am aware of turbulence in my life. Things that go bump in the night are going bump during the daytime. Often they are little things, like my computer freezing when I am trying to "save as." Or the garage door refusing to stay down. Both functions work fine most of the time. Then, typically when I am in a rush, they malfunction. Because this rush-reaction happens so frequently, I am beginning to think it has a message for me.

In response, I've been trying to go with the flow. Nowadays, when the glitch occurs or I have an attack of the clumsies or I simply can't find the raffle tickets I am supposed to be selling for charity, rather than freaking out–my reaction of choice–I laugh. After all, what does it matter? This, too, will pass. Being five minutes late beats having a stroke any day. So I don't know if the world is ending or not, but I'd love to take these special times–real, created, or imagined–and learn how to relax.

Have you learned alternate behaviors for times when you'd like to scream? Share them in your Wisdom Journal.

MAINTAINING WISDOM

The maintenance of wisdom throughout the life course and its restoration if it has been lost depends upon the continued immersion of the individual within a "wisdom atmosphere" that assists the individual in avoiding the extremes of too confident knowing and of paralyzing doubt. . . . The maintenance of wisdom and its restoration also depend upon a willingness to cultivate a certain detachment from the knowledge, success, power, and importance that represent threats or risks to wisdom. . . . To counter these risks, it becomes essential to . . . generate questions and doubts about the knowledge one has acquired . . . [and] to challenge the basis for one's own power and authority. . . . These challenges are . . . more easily carried out within a network of supportive interpersonal relations, in which the challenges . . . come gently from those around us.

-JOHN A. MEACHAM, "THE LOSS OF WISDOM," 1990

Dr. Meacham, a psychologist at SUNY-Buffalo, bases his article on the premise that wisdom is more likely to be present early in our lives and to be lost with time. He defines wisdom as keeping a balance between knowing and doubting. Children tend to be less sure of what they know and more open to learning. Moreover they are less given to intolerance stemming from established belief systems. It is the children, remember, who shelter and assist E.T. in the Spielberg film. Therefore, although one may be old and wise, wisdom, Dr. Meacham concludes, is actually the domain of children.

His suggestions for maintaining – or retrieving – wisdom make sense. First, if being wise means balancing knowing and doubting, we will be supported by a community that reinforces us through its example of wise practice. Second, if by becoming too sure of ourselves we put our wisdom at risk, we are well advised to have colleagues who tactfully remind us to stay humble.

I would simply add that we can find helpful companionship in books, art, music, and nature as well as people. If we sincerely wish to retain or increase wisdom, resources to do so abound.

Write in your Wisdom Journal ways you maintain or enhance your wisdom.

NOSTRADAMIC WISDOM

Under one shall be peace, and everywhere clemency,
But not for a long while, then shall be plundering
and rebellion,
By a denial shall town, land and sea be assaulted,
Dead and taken prisoner shall be the third part of
a million.

–NOSTRADAMUS (1503–1566), *PROPHECIES*, I, 92

Michel de Notredame, better known as Nostradamus, was born in San Remi, Provence, France. A physician and astrologer – the two professions could still be conjoined in the sixteenth century – he achieved initial fame for his treatment of plague victims in the south of France. Claiming the ability to predict future events, he published, at age forty-seven, 1,200 prophecies in the form of rhyming quatrains. One of those impressed by his ability was the queen of France, Catherine de Médicis, who called Nostradamus to Paris to cast horoscopes for her sons. When one of them became Charles IX, Nostradamus was appointed court physician. He probably did double duty as prognosticator royale.

The above quatrain, a faithful translation of the French, is fairly vague, to say the least. According to Henry C. Roberts, the translator, here is what these verses are predicting: "The sneak attack on Pearl Harbor by the Japanese ushered the United States into World War II, resulting in 350,000 American casualties." Now, I live ten miles from Pearl Harbor, and even that advantage doesn't help me to see the connection.

I have nothing against individuals who attempt to predict the future. Obviously Nostradamus must have gotten some things more right than in the above example. Otherwise why is he still a household word? Also, Mr. Roberts, not Nostradamus, is the one actually interpreting the elusive poem. Still, there are two different conceptions of what being a prophet means. One is Nostradamic: The person in question is skilled at predicting the future. The other is Biblic (and Koranic): The prophet speaks on behalf of God in order to bring the people back into conformity with the divine will. If I had to determine which of the two types were wiser, I'd go with the prophets in the Bible and the Koran.

Have you experienced an accurate future prediction? Share the story in your Wisdom Journal.

PERSONAL/PLANETARY WISDOM

When we connect with ourselves in love, we can connect with others and the planet in love. This gives us the power, the courage and the motivation to act in the common good because we experience the reality of oneness inside ourselves. This in turn gives us the capacity to perceive and be part of a global vision of peace and unity and enables us to act out of an inner consciousness and conviction that creates what we intend.

-RATTANA K. HETZEL, PHD, *INNER AND OUTER ECOLOGY*, 1992

To use a T. S. Eliot term, the 1960s saw a "dissociation of sensibilites" in Western culture. First of all were those who looked back with longing to the good old days of established and respected values. Over and against this conservative group were two very different sets of revolutionaries: political radicals and spiritual seekers.

Arthur Koestler called these the "kommissars" and the "yogis." Kommissars believed that significant social or environmental change could take place only through concerted political action. They were not wrong. Where would we be without the civil rights legislation of the sixties and seventies? Or the movement that culminated in outlawing leaded gasoline? Yogis, on the other hand, were spiritual seekers who believed that the real revolution had to take place within each individual person. To kommissars, yogis were escapists who refused to work for meaningful change. But the yogis were also right. What good was land reform if the peasants were still tenant farmers in their minds? Or civil rights legislation if a majority were still bigots?

In 1979 Theodore Roszak published *Person/Planet*, in which he argued for conjoining inner development and political reform. He made the commonsense point that you can't have one without the other. Two centuries ago Goethe wrote, "If to the infinite you would stride, / Begin with the finite on every side." Perhaps today he would substitute, "If to the infinite you would stride, / Begin with the infinite right there inside."

In your Wisdom Journal, discuss how you balance personal and planetary reform activities.

RUTH'S WISDOM

"You see," said Naomi, "your sister-in-law has gone back to her people and her gods; go back with her." "Do not urge me to go back and desert you," Ruth answered. "Where you go, I will go, and where you stay, I will stay. Your people shall be my people, and your God my God. Where you die, I will die, and there I will be buried. I swear a solemn oath before the Lord your God: nothing but death shall divide us."

-Ruth 1:15–18

Ruth is one of the shortest books in the Old Testament. It tells a story of loyalty and its resultant blessings. It is also a tale of crosscultural virtue, because Ruth from Moab is a foreign woman and a heathen. She marries one of the two sons of Elimelech and Naomi, Israelites from Bethlehem living abroad in Moab. Apparently Ruth does not convert to her in-laws' religion, since after Elimelech and his two sons die, Ruth speaks to Naomi of "your God."

Ruth is both the good Gentile and the ideal daughter-in-law. Released by her husband's death from her obligations to her mother-in-law, Ruth is determined to sacrifice home, country, and the chance to remarry in order to care for Naomi in Naomi's homeland. Ruth looks ahead to the New Testament figure of the centurion with the sick servant, a Gentile with greater faith, Jesus says, than he has found in all Judea. It is not meaningless that Ruth becomes the great-grandmother of King David and a direct ancestor of Joseph, Jesus' legal father.

My German wife left her homeland to marry me, a not-yet-baptized American Jew. We included a reading from Ruth at our Lutheran wedding service in hopes my parents would attend. They did. And after our first child was born, my wife's mother, Ruth, came to live with us. She stayed with us for eighteen years until her death. Our children are bilingual as a result. Loyalty has many blessings. Like Jesus, Ruth from Moab is a prime example of faithfulness unto death.

In your Wisdom Journal, tell a story from your experience in which loyalty paid off.

SERPENT WISDOM

Be ye therefore wise as serpents, and harmless as doves.

–Matthew 10:16, KJV

Some people like dogs and hate cats. Other people like cats and hate dogs. And still others like both cats and dogs. Few, however, like snakes. Every once in a while, you'll encounter someone who does. Come meet my pet boa constrictor, they say. You remember a pressing appointment. Weird, you think, as you hurry to your car.

Snakes have a bad reputation in Western culture. Satan, masquerading as one, got us booted out of paradise. Cleopatra, Serpent of the Nile, caused lots of trouble before killing herself with an asp. Snakes are quiet, sneaky, and slinky. They are literally cold-blooded, with small, beady eyes. Worst of all, they are frequently poisonous, and in all the movies, they attack without provocation.

But like their forked tongues, snakes have a double reputation. On the up side, they represent powerful medicine. Chemotherapy, for example, works by injecting patients with poisons which cure by killing the cancer. The ancient symbol of medicine, the caduceus, includes two intertwined snakes. In West Africa the circled snake with its tail in its mouth symbolizes continuity and eternity. Through its ability to slough off its skin, the snake also represents the virtue of transformation. Above all, snakes can stand for wisdom. Was not the biblical serpent found in the Tree of Knowledge?

A Hindu story tells of a snake terrorizing a certain village. One day it was about to bite a passing sage, but the mahatma's goodness caused the snake to reconsider. The holy man upbraided the snake, which vowed henceforth not to harm anyone. A few months later, the returning sage found the snake half dead. The villagers now teased and tormented the creature, which refused to fight back. "My friend," said the sage, "I told you not to bite. I never told you not to hiss." The lesson, clearly, is that while we should refrain from harming others, we should make sure they don't harm us.

How well do you balance your serpent and your dove? Respond in your Wisdom Journal.

SYMPHONIC WISDOM

Sometimes when I enter a familiar room or street, I think I see a past self walking toward me. She can't see me in the future, but I can see her very clearly. She runs past me, worried about being late for an appointment she doesn't want to go to. She sits at a restaurant table in tears of anger arguing with the wrong lover. . . . I used to feel impatient with her: Why was she wasting time? Why was she with this man? at that appointment? . . . But lately . . . I think: She's doing the best she can. She's survived – and she's trying so hard. . . . *We are so many selves. . . . What brings together these ever-shifting selves of infinite reactions and returnings is this: There is always one true inner voice. . . . Trust it.*

–Gloria Steinem, *Revolution from Within*, 1992

The puzzle is ancient. Are we one person or many? What about divinity? The answer to both questions, I believe, is the same. Each of us, in the image of our Creator, is a unitary being comprising many aspects.

In the case of human beings, problems occur when these aspects do not live in harmony. We can be outgoing at times and reflective at others. But when we fluctuate, helter-skelter, between the two states – now one, now the other – psychiatrists label us "bipolar." Or we may have many aspects to our personality, each showing up in an appropriate context. But when these aspects begin to assume a kind of independence and try to dominate the body they share with the others, we have multiple-personality disorder.

The "one true inner voice" Ms. Steinem refers to is like an orchestra conductor. It must correctly blend our inner forces, our aspects, to play the music of our soul. If this maestro is not strong enough and the instruments play without respect for the others, the result is cacophony and chaos. We are then possessed. Our name is Legion.

Do you recognize your "true inner voice"? Write about it in your Wisdom Journal.

TRADITIONAL VILLAGE WISDOM

Grandparents form the circle of the elders. They represent the world of knowledge and constitute the supreme council of the village. To avoid the anger of the ancestors, with whom they can communicate through rituals and divination, they are supposed to know all the prohibitions and how to remedy any violation of a social taboo. They are wise and move thoughtfully. They are walking books of know-how. They are the judges, lawyers, catalysts, negotiators, moderators, moralizers, critics, and counselors.

–YAYA DIALLO AND MITCHELL HALL, *THE HEALING DRUM*, 1989

Western culture prizes the individual. We talk about Michelangelo's "David" and Beethoven's "Ninth." We love Horatio Alger-type stories of individuals who, by dint of hard work and a little luck, have gone from rags to riches. We spend millions of dollars on self-help books. Moreover, when we think of wisdom, we focus on wise individuals.

As my associates and I began developing the World Wisdom Project, our individualistic bias soon became apparent. The first colleague to make a case for including "community wisdom" was a university nurse-educator whose training included an apprenticeship with a Native American medicine man. Kathy consults with rural municipalities on community self-care, whereby individuals share their wisdom on health and healing so that their small town can avoid spending money it doesn't have on expensive medical expertise and equipment.

A stunning example of community wisdom appeared in the March 30, 1998, issue of *Time* magazine. It told how, at age thirteen, a young man in Mozambique was abducted from his village by a rebel band and forced to rob, rape, and kill his own people. When he finally escaped, he sought out an elder to perform a three-day ritual cleansing. Later, his nightmares gone, he was able to return to his people, who were also able to embrace him. Commented *Time*, "Call it witchcraft if you like, but such rural healing is a major reason that nearly 95,000 demobilized soldiers and five million refugees have been absorbed back into society."

In your Wisdom Journal, discuss an example of community wisdom with which you are familiar.

WISDOM IN TIME

Dear God, here on earth you are constantly seeking to change us. At times we wish to flee into the wilderness to avoid you. But let us learn to love the lasting things of heaven, rather than the dying things of earth. We must accept that time always brings change; and we pray that by your grace the change within our souls will make us worthy of your heavenly kingdom, where all time will cease.

–Alcuin of York (c. 735–804)

I look into the mirror these days and see my father. At the supermarket I'm asked if I need help getting to my car. Young women hold doors for me. People tell me I look young for my age and ask if I'd like a senior discount. Talk about the changes wrought by time! Inside, of course, I feel as young as ever. I see elderly people and think of *them* as old.

Christianity, represented here by Alcuin of York, has traditionally placed greater value on the eternal life of the spirit than the temporary life of the body, on heaven than the earthly abode where moths corrupt and thieves break in and steal. This preference is seen in the cross, where the vertical post representing heavenly life is longer than the horizontal piece which stands for life on this earthly plane. The two intersect, but the vertical has more significance. Contrast this symbolism with that of the Star of David. There you have two same-sized equilateral triangles superimposed on each other. One has its apex downward, the other upward, demonstrating the covenantal relationship between humanity and its Creator. Divinity looks down and involves itself with us. We look up and involve ourselves with God.

Alcuin's prayer implies the need to put first things first and live in time as in eternity. We must accept God's transforming work within us as we would the coaching of a personal trainer. Our bodies, too, are crosses. If we spread our arms, the span from head to toe will be greater than that from fingertips to fingertips. May we grow in time to live in eternity, and live in eternity to grow in time.

What does time mean to you? Respond in your Wisdom Journal.

THE WISDOM OF AUTHENTIC LIVING

Too many of us consent, or are forced, to spend time doing things for which we have no heartfelt reason. . . . We do it to hold a job, to make a living, to satisfy the expectations of others, to fill our time, to evade the fact that we don't know what else to do – but not because the doing comes from inside us. When our action is dictated by factors external to our souls, we do not live active lives but reactive lives.

–PARKER J. PALMER, *THE ACTIVE LIFE*, 1990

"To thine own self be true." Easy to say – hard to do. Back in the sixties, we encouraged one another to do our own thing. But what is our thing? Or what happens if we are good at several things? Do we choose to do one at the expense of the others? What if we are unsure of our true talents? How do we identify them? Sometimes the process takes a lifetime – like the childhood game Cold, Warm, and Hot. You hide something, then ask someone else to find it. As they get closer to the object, you encourage them by saying, "You are getting warmer." But when they take a wrong turn, you say, "Whoops. Now you're getting cold."

To follow Parker Palmer's sage advice, we have to be, or become, sensitive to who we are, what we are good at, and what makes our hearts sing. Then we have to have the courage of our convictions. If we are not a Jones, trying to keep up with the Joneses will never make us happy – if we are not careful, we can spend our career doing things we don't like in order to maintain a lifestyle we do like.

Given this conundrum, our daily prayer should be: "O God, let me know the self you want me to be and grant me the strength to become that self fully. And please, God, if possible let me earn my living in ways that enhance rather than diminish my soul."

In your Wisdom Journal, write about your work. What steps must you take to do your "right work" more completely?

THE WISDOM OF DEFERRED GRATIFICATION

Manage with bread and salted butter until God brings something to eat with it.

–A MOROCCAN PROVERB

My friend Binh was a boat person. He left Vietnam with nothing but the clothes on his back. He was lucky. The Thais who intercepted his boat were not pirates. Binh spent the next months in a Thai refugee camp. Not the best place, but far better than his old hometown, now Ho Chi Minh City, where, as a young architect, he would have fared much worse. Before long an international organization secured his release and flew him to Vienna. He soon began learning German and working in an architectural firm as a draftsman.

I met Binh a year or so later in Chicago. He had immigrated to join his parents and seven siblings. His father, who had managed a district post office in Saigon, was now doing janitorial work, and his mother was sewing in a dress factory. The children had started brilliant careers in school; several were already in college. As soon as they could, they took part-time jobs. The family lived cramped together in a Near Northwest Side apartment. All the money was pooled. Nobody complained. Within a few years, the children were earning enough so that the parents could retire. In the meantime Binh was promoted up the ladder at a large architectural firm. Shortly before I left Chicago for Saint Paul, he had become site manager for a new skyscraper going up in the Loop.

Once I asked Binh when he planned to marry. (He was in his forties at the time.) "Not yet," came the reply. I understood. As the oldest responsible male after his father, he needed to wait until his last sibling completed college. That was how it was in his culture. Before long, though, he married an attractive young woman; then several sons arrived in short order. No one told Binh and his family that the American Dream was dead. They worked hard, pooled their resources, and deferred gratification. Before long everybody was doing well. It was an American success story, Vietnamese style.

In your Wisdom Journal, write about an example you know of deferred gratification leading to material success.

DEATH AND TRANSFORMATION WISDOM

What the caterpillar calls the end of life, the master calls a butterfly.

-Richard Bach

Tod und Verklärung – death and transfiguration. I remember the term from college. Is it the title of a Schubert song and string quartet? No. That's *"Der Tod und das Mädchen"* – "Death and the Maiden." Maybe I am thinking of Richard Strauss!

For many of us in the West, this is it – life as we know it. Better make the best of it. Death is the last stop, "All out!" Visions of Auschwitz without the possibility of Sophie's choice. No wonder post-World War II existentialists took the concentration camp as a symbol of life itself. Each of us is born to die. Life is a prison, and we are all on death row. No sentence will be commuted. The Latin-derived English word *terminal* is sanitized, scientific, official – like the Nazis' bureaucratic "final solution." The German equivalent of *terminal, Endstation,* comes closer to our feelings of fear and finality.

Yet there is a long crosscultural tradition of death not as end but as new beginning. In the Judeo-Christian world, the chief example, of course, is Jesus' Crucifixion and Resurrection. When Jesus restored a young girl to life, he explained to the distraught parents that their child was not dead but asleep. John Donne consoles us in his famous Holy Sonnet "Death Be not Proud" by saying that after the transitional sleep of death, "we wake eternally."

In addition to final death and resurrection is the mystical concept of little deaths and renewals. These can include major outer events like job loss, the end of a relationship, a natural disaster, a life-threatening illness. From the participant's perspective, all seems lost. Yet healing takes place when we focus on the transformation that can now occur. My own spiritual guide, who died in 1987, talked about forty-nine little deaths we must undergo to develop into fully realized human beings. Some of these we may be hardly aware of, while others will be full-blown life crises. In either case, unless we die as caterpillars, we can never become butterflies.

In your Wisdom Journal, discuss a "little death" and the resulting transformation.

DIVINE WISDOM

The LORD giveth wisdom.

–PROVERBS 2:6, KJV

When people learn that I am involved in the World Wisdom Project, the avowed goal of which is to raise the world's "wisdom quotient," their initial reaction is almost always, "But can people become wiser?" Implied is the sense that wisdom is inherited, like blue eyes or skinny legs. Sometimes my questioner admits the belief that wisdom never survived ancient times. Back in the time of Socrates and Jesus, there were miracles and sages. Nowadays we have science and charlatans. Wise guys you can find in abundance, they declare. But as for the truly wise, forget it! Then we have the romantics who find sages in the fantasy worlds of J. R. R. Tolkien or George Lucas – in Strider and Obiwan Kenobi – or in the "exotic" cultures of indigenous peoples or Tibetan Buddhists.

What about us garden-variety, middle-class, college-educated Westerners? We can become more credentialed, better skilled in a specialty, more highly paid for our work, more respected by our colleagues. However, can we become wiser? The quotation from Proverbs seems to take away any chance. After all, if wisdom is a divine gift, we may as well dream about winning the lottery. No amount of intention or study will make a difference.

To be sure, the Bible is also a book about moving mountains and raising the dead. Nor are these miracles the purview of Jesus alone. Doesn't he tell the disciples that they will do these and even greater things after he is gone? The ASK formula is a central tenet of Jesus' ministry: Ask, and what you request will be given. Seek, and what you need will be found. Knock, and the door to your destination will be opened. The Good News of the Gospels is that faith is the key to our salvation. God has provided us with everything we need to become as wise as Yoda. Why else should Proverbs 4:7 (KJV) say, "Wisdom is the principal thing; therefore get wisdom"?

Can people become wiser? Write and support your opinion in your Wisdom Journal.

EMPOWERING WISDOM

If you would feed someone for a day, give them a fish. If you would feed someone for a lifetime, teach them how to fish.

–A Chinese saying

Back in the sixties, Alfred Whittaker left the presidency of Bristol-Myer International to do something for the world's poor people. An entrepreneur, he was not interested in simply giving alms. Rather, he wanted to help destitute individuals help themselves. To do this he created Opportunity, International. In a recent five-year period, Whittaker's organization granted more than 100,000 small loans to would-be entrepreneurs. During that same period, he helped create 275,000 new jobs. By increasing the ranks of the middle class in developing countries, he intended to build a dam against poverty and give these countries a better chance for a secure future.

Microenterprise development has become a major strategy for assisting poor people all over the world. South Asia's Ganeen Foundation has a track record similar to that of Opportunity, International. Mr. Ganeen makes very small loans of, say, fifty dollars to rural women to purchase the equipment needed to open businesses such as roadside fast-food operations. The success rate is high – the local entrepreneurs typically go into businesses for which they know there is a demand – and the default rate is much lower than among qualified borrowers from commercial banks. Such community lending provides just enough of a boost to people otherwise considered uncreditworthy.

Oahu's Waianae Coast is among the most depressed areas in Hawaii. As I write, Angel Network Charities, a local nonprofit assisting homeless people, is opening Angel Outlet, a large resale shop. It will sell "recycled" goods and use the income to support its operations. Meanwhile a spin-off, Angel Enterprise Association, is developing a micro-enterprise incubator to be housed at Angel Outlet. A furniture-restoration business will fix up and resell items at higher prices in the outlet. Profits will go back to the enterprise. Charity is an important stopgap, and not everyone is meant to run a business. Still, to the extent possible, empowering people to help themselves is the way of wisdom.

Share in your Wisdom Journal the story of someone who "learned to fish."

KNOW-NOTHING WISDOM

The only thing that we can know is that we know nothing and that is the highest flight of human wisdom.

–Leo Tolstoy (1828–1910)

One problem with quoting something another person has quoted is that you don't know the original context. In the above case, is this a thought Tolstoy himself entertained, or is it the opinion of one of his fictional characters? I'll probably never find out. But for our purposes, the sentiment is what is important, and a pessimistic sentiment it is. We human beings can know nothing. Arriving at this "fact" is the ultimate reach of our wisdom.

Goethe's Faust comes to the same conclusion at the beginning of the play. He complains that despite all his study of philosophy, law, medicine, and theology, he feels he knows no more than when he started. His academic degrees are only useful for impressing his students. The degrees themselves mean nothing. For now he has discerned the truth: We mortals can know nothing.

Tolstoy and Goethe notwithstanding, human wisdom seems to come in two kinds: the worldly variety and the spiritual type. Lord Chesterfield, Benjamin Franklin, and Madame de Sevigné are well-known dispensers of the former; the great religious founding figures are fountainheads of the latter. Both kinds have their usefulness. To the extent that all of us must live in this world, it helps to know that a penny saved is a penny earned. But when it comes to transcendent questions of life and death, worldly wisdom remains earthbound and insufficient. Our efforts to solve deep mysteries of this kind on our own will lead us to a conclusion similar to that of Faust and Tolstoy. As my old Latin teacher used to say, "You don't know how much you have to know in order to know how little you know." Wisdom of the transcendent kind belongs to God. Fortunately God seems willing to share divine wisdom with the least of us, to the extent that we are able to humble ourselves and listen. In this regard, admitting our ignorance may be the first and most important step to gaining wisdom.

Have you ever felt that you know nothing? Write about the experience in your Wisdom Journal.

PROPHETIC WISDOM

I am Sir Oracle,
And when I ope my lips, let no dog bark!

—WILLIAM SHAKESPEARE, *THE MERCHANT OF VENICE*, I, I, 93

These words, spoken by the character Gratiano to Bassanio, are some of my favorite lines in Shakespeare. It was love at first sight when I was forced to read the play back in eighth grade. But to this day, I don't have the foggiest idea what Gratiano was talking about. Maybe he didn't either. Twenty lines later Bassanio comments, "Gratiano speaks an infinite deal of nothing, more than any man in all Venice: his reasons are as two grains of wheat hid in two bushels of chaff; you shall seek all day ere you find them; and when you have found them they are not worth the search."

During my junior year abroad, 1958–59, I took a fateful trip over spring break to Greece. My stomach was still not right after having eaten something bad in Spain a few months before. I came within an ace of not going. "Maybe Italy would be an easier destination," I thought, at least for my digestion. But then I thought: "Italy is the kind of place you visit when you are married. Better go to Greece now while you are single." And it is a good thing I decided to go, for on that three-week bus tour, I met my future wife. (Interestingly, she almost pulled out of the trip because of stomach problems of her own.)

Midway through the trip, we visited Delphi. Besides declaiming the first eighteen lines of the *Canterbury Tales* in the amphitheater, I joined my wife-to-be in leaning over backward, as required, and drinking from the Castalian Springs. The Pythia, better known as the Oracle of Delphi, drank this water regularly. It was the reputed source of her psychic ability. Now, since I have been doing spiritual training, I do have some low-level ESP: I often know, for example, how many children strangers have. A far better kind of prophetic wisdom, it seems to me, would be sensing the results of one's intentions and choosing one's actions accordingly.

Have you ever had a preview of later events? Discuss your experience in your Wisdom Journal.

THE WISDOM OF NO-FEAR

The world is a very narrow bridge. The main thing is not to be afraid.

–As quoted from a Hasidic rabbi by Ellen Kushner on WGBH's *Sound and Spirit*

The first thing biblical angels say to earthlings is, "Fear not!" I wonder how aliens, if they exist, greet humans. Creatures from out of this world, whether spiritual or material, are scary by definition.

But plenty of things this side of extraterrestrials require courage. Life itself is scary. Just getting up in the morning and going to work challenges us. Will I be able to finish that assignment on time? Will the boss yell at me? What happens if I blow my big presentation? Years ago when my spiritual guide was visiting Hawaii from his native Indonesia, I bragged that Hawaii had no snakes. He joked back: "In Indonesia, many snakes. Big ones like this," he demonstrated with his hands. "And the worst kind," his interpreter chimed in, "are the ones with two legs."

The world *is* a narrow bridge. It is made of wood–shaky, strung between two unequal cliffs, with a sheer drop of a thousand feet between them. Yet once here, we have little choice but to cross. It is thus not surprising that one of the greatest spiritual gifts, according to the Vietnamese Buddhist monk Thich Nhat Hanh, is the state of no-fear. It is the fruit of inner development. We have to work hard to attain it. But once attained, it indicates that we have come a long way.

Fear's first cousin, with a strong family resemblance, is worry. Focusing on the here and now, learning to live one day at a time, is an excellent practice to keep one's worry-o-meter low. As Shakespeare's Julius Caesar says, "Cowards die many times before their deaths; / The valiant never taste of death but once" (II, ii, 30). The main thing is to be in relationship with one's Higher Power. For if we know the Lord to be our shepherd, even a walk through the valley of the shadow of death will cause us to fear no evil.

Write in your Wisdom Journal about how close you are to the no-fear state. What steps might you take to get closer?

THE WISDOM OF SIGNIFICANCE, NOT SUCCESS

It's not the what; it's the so-what.

–Alexander McClaren Witherspoon

A doctoral dissertation is supposed to be a work of original research. In reality, when you write a dissertation, you are like the top cheerleader standing on the backs of your colleagues. Without them you have no place to go. I suppose there are original ideas. But to explain them in the context of different ideas, you have to use the work of others. The construction you create may be unique, but the building materials are derivative, like so many Lego pieces.

This thought occurs as I borrow a saying from my favorite professor, the late Alexander Witherspoon of Yale. The main idea of the saying – the preference of significance over success – is derivative itself. I have heard it before and since, most recently in an adult Bible study class. What I will do is to put significance and success side by side and see what happens.

Significance is the so-what of our lives. Success is the what. Untold books, magazines, and workshops counsel us on how to become successful. They generally have acquisition in mind. Do this and become rich. Do that and win the man or woman of your dreams. Do the other and have an incredible sex life. Now, I have nothing against wealth, a wonderful partner, or great sex, but all these attainments beg the next question. Wealth for what? Great sex and what else? Or, how should my partner and I spend our time together now that he or she has been won? In short, so what? What's the significance of my success?

Professor Witherspoon taught us freshmen the difference between book reports and book reviews. In the former you merely summarize the story or, in the case of nonfiction, the main points – the what. In the latter you quickly dispense with the summary to get to the work's significance, its so-what. Why is this writing meaningful? Does it have the power to transform us and, if so, why? Similarly, as we journey through life in our success-oriented culture, it might help to ask ourselves from time to time, "So what?"

In your Wisdom Journal, name two or three significant accomplishments to date and explain why you chose them.

"OLD, OLD STORY" WISDOM

I love to tell the story,
For those who know it best
Seem hungering and thirsting
To hear it like the rest.
And when, in scenes of glory,
I sing the new, new song,
'Twill be the old, old story
That I have loved so long.
I love to tell the story,
'Twill be my theme in glory
To tell the old, old story
Of Jesus and His love.

–Catherine Hankey and William G. Fischer,
"I Love to Tell the Story"

Florine was my first witness. When I was a little kid on Long Island, she would tune in to the "Bible Hour" (or whatever it was called) with George Beverly Shea. Now George Beverly – I always thought it was strange but cool that a man could also have a woman's name – had no idea, I am sure, that a black woman and a little Jewish kid would be sitting together in the kitchen in a red-brick house in Great Neck, New York, listening faithfully to his schmaltzy hymns and encouragement from the Scriptures. But there we were, hearing those old, old stories of Jesus and his love.

Talk about Jews for Jesus! In 1942 I was a Jew for Jesus before there were Jews for Jesus. Unless, of course, you include Saint Peter, Saint Paul, the rest of the Apostles, and most first-century saints.

It is a commonplace of music history that the worst poems make the best song texts. Goethe's Earl-King *(Der Erlkönig)* is usually trotted out as a case in point. My old poetry professors would die a thousand deaths or, more likely, roll over in their graves if they caught me quoting "I Love to Tell the Story." I can hear their mocking tones now. But the fact is, this old, old story I first heard from George Beverly Shea supplied some of the sturdiest two-by-fours in the bridge to my conversion. Jesus and his love, important to me then, remains important to me now. "Jesus Christ the same yesterday, and today, and for ever" (Hebrews 13:8, KJV).

In your Wisdom Journal, write about a hymn or anthem that is especially meaningful for you.

CAVE WISDOM

The philosopher Chuang-tze, awaking from a dream that he was a butterfly, asked himself, "Am I Chuang-tze, who dreamed he was a butterfly, or am I a butterfly dreaming it is Chuang-tze?"

–CHUANG-TZE, TAOIST PHILOSOPHER, 4TH CENTURY B.C.E.

Dreams are sometimes so vivid that we are glad to wake up. "It was only a dream," we reassure ourselves, relieved that the plane wasn't really crashing or the house burning. But what is base reality and what, only fantasy? Chuang-tze's famous question illustrates an issue that has puzzled many cultures and received a variety of answers.

Contemporary secular civilization considers our waking flesh-and-blood reality the sum and substance of human existence. While experts may debate about when an individual human life begins, agreement is widespread that no life exists before conception or after physical death.

Classical Hindu culture espouses a rather different position. Our physical life is illusion, *maya*. True life exists only in the spiritual realm. Physical life, despite its apparent substantiality, is but a shadow of the real. A significant strain of Christian theology would agree that the earth is not our home but a kind of home-away-from-home and our bodies, a sort of organic spacesuit allowing us to live here. When we die we leave our spacesuits behind and return to our home "planet," where we rejoin our Father.

Plato begins Book VII of the *Republic* with the famous Allegory of the Cave. Imagine an underground cave, Socrates says to the gathered philosophers, where prisoners are chained fast to a wall and their heads restrained so they can only see the wall in front of them. Assuming that torches above and behind them cast shadows on the visible wall of objects placed before the torches, while an unseen jailer names them, the prisoners will come to identify these shadows as reality. If one prisoner were released to the surface and then returns, having once seen "real" objects, to share what he has learned with his former cavemates, they will not believe him. Thus reality is what we take to be true, not necessarily what is.

What is "real"? Write for ten minutes in your Wisdom Journal.

CHIAROSCURO WISDOM

Help us to be the always hopeful gardeners of the spirit who know that without darkness nothing comes to birth as without light nothing flowers.

-MAY SARTON, *JOURNAL OF A SOLITUDE*, 1973

I took art history as a freshman. This yearlong overview covered the history of art from cave paintings to the present. Several hundred of us crowded into a large lecture hall twice weekly to see great works of art projected onto the large screen. Yale being Yale, we had the benefit of world-renowned scholars telling us about the painting, sculpture, and architecture of their respective periods. Then once a week we would meet in small groups with a junior faculty member who led us in discussions.

Later, as a professor myself, I learned that students remember the strangest things. For me it was generally foreign terms. So when we got to the Italian Baroque period, the term *chiaroscuro* stuck. It is one of those paradoxical Italian combination words like *pianoforte*, literally "soft-loud." In the case of *chiaroscuro*, the literal meaning is "light-dark." In painting it refers to an artist's somewhat stylized use of contrasting light and shadow.

We in the Western world tend to prefer *chiaro* to *oscuro*, the "yang" to the "yin." The light, sun, and day are good. On the other hand, darkness is scary, the moon is variable, and the night, a time for burglars and sinners. May Sarton's reflection is important because it reminds us that one day of twenty-four hours includes both day and night. We can't–or shouldn't–choose sides. The dark is as necessary to life and health as the light. Try sleeping with the light on. It's torture. We need the snug blanket of darkness to restore us for a new day of activity. Saint John of the Cross's dark night of the soul is the darkness of the womb, of the ground surrounding the seed. We have to break out of our seed casing before we emerge through the soil to the sun. We have to die to our selves in order to be reborn.

Have you experienced a dark night of the soul leading to rebirth? Write about the process in your Wisdom Journal.

DEATH-DEFYING WISDOM

Death, be not proud, though some have callèd thee
Mighty and dreadful, for thou art not so;
For those whom thou think'st thou dost overthrow
Die not, poor Death; nor yet canst thou kill me. . . .
Thou'rt slave to fate, chance, kings, and desperate men,
And dost with poison, war, and sickness dwell;
And poppy and charms can make us sleep as well
And better than thy stroke. Why swell'st thou then?
One short sleep past, we wake eternally,
And Death shall be no more: Death, thou shalt die.

–John Donne (1572–1631), "Holy Sonnet X"

Last week I hit my fifty-ninth-and-a-half birthday. Normally I don't count half birthdays, or at least I haven't since childhood. Back then every little bit brought you closer to being big, or at least bigger than the kid down the street. But I counted this particular half birthday because it meant I could now draw down tax-sheltered funds without triggering the ten-percent federal penalty for early withdrawal. When I started consulting full-time in 1991, I was not so lucky. Unfortunately my cash flow wasn't what it needed to be, so I found myself forced to liquidate one retirement account. The money was a godsend. I don't know what we would have done without it. But I hated giving that involuntary tithe to Uncle Sam.

Once you hit 50, you begin to learn the different measures for seniority. The American Association of Retired Persons greet you first and offer you membership. Some restaurant chains will give you discounts at 55. The next benchmark seems to be the one I have just crossed. Then come the Big Six-O, Social Security early retirement at 62, Social Security full retirement at 65, and generally forced retirement at the biblical age of 70. I am not too sure of the next major indicators until the century mark, immortalized by TV's Willard Scott.

With death and taxes the only commonly accepted certainties, I pray that as I age, my faith will stand the test of time, and that, with my fellow Christian John Donne, I can experience the life that transcends bodily death.

In your Wisdom Journal, share your thoughts about growing older.

THE LOVE DOCTOR'S WISDOM

Each day we are offered new means for learning and growing in love. Each day in which we become more observant, more flexible, more knowledgeable, more aware, we grow in love. Even the seemingly most insignificant thing can bring us closer to ourselves and therefore to others.

–LEO BUSCAGLIA, PHD, *LOVE*, 1972

Leo Buscaglia became well known in the seventies through his books and televised lectures. The former were offered as premiums during PBS pledge drives. I remember viewing one of his lectures. I was hooked. Making a pledge at the next opportunity, I requested a book.

A signature event after each lecture was his hug line. Virtually every person in a large auditorium would queue up to receive a bear hug from the master. During one program he returned to the podium after only about a dozen hugs. He asked people to stay in line. But something so important had just happened, he said, that he needed to share it. Apparently he had hugged an elderly widow who then broke down in sobs. When asked why she was crying, she replied, "My husband died twenty years ago, and this is the first hug I've received in twenty years!" Buscaglia's comment went something like this: "You have to ask yourself what kind of society we live in where someone can go for twenty years without being hugged!"

But love for the Love Doctor meant more than hugs. He told the story of going to Europe without his Italian-immigrant mother's blessing. Apparently she wanted him to finish school first and go later. He had some savings, so he decided to go anyway. In Paris, I think it was, he developed quite a circle by throwing parties. Before he knew it, his funds had run out, and his friends suddenly disappeared. Sending the least expensive telegram possible, he wrote his mother, "Mamma, Starving, Felice [his Italian first name]," to which she replied, "Felice, Starve, Mamma." From that experience he learned about listening, budgeting, and knowing who your real friends are. He also came face-to-face with what is called "tough love."

Write for five minutes in your Wisdom Journal on the characteristics of genuine love.

HOMING WISDOM

Be thou thine own home, and in thy self dwell. . . .
And seeing the snail, which everywhere doth roam,
Carrying his own house still, still is at home,
Follow (for he is easy pac'd) this snail,
Be thine own palace, or the world's thy jail.

-JOHN DONNE (1572–1631),
"VERSE LETTER TO SIR HENRY WOTTON"

We did not find the house. The house found us. We had moved to Saint Paul from Chicago four months earlier. We started out on the twenty-ninth floor of a downtown apartment building. The view was spectacular, and I was five blocks from work. In winter, moreover, I could get there without going outside by using Saint Paul's skyway system. The location was ideal.

Still, we wanted to buy. Neither we, nor our parents, had ever owned a home. With the payout of my Illinois pension fund, we now had the money for a down payment. But much as we looked, we never found anything we liked. Not even the expensive houses we saw attracted us. Then came the first day of May. It was the first nice Sunday, and we wanted to take Grandma for a stroll in her new wheelchair. On the way to River Boulevard, we stopped to look at a house. Again, nothing. When we got to our destination, we found we couldn't park on the Boulevard. Driving up the hill, we noticed an "open house" sign in front of an attractive house. Should we take a quick look? Leaving Grandma in the car, I ran inside with Simone and our teenaged daughter. The open house was just ending.

What greeted us was a beautiful stucco house surrounded by trees on a corner lot. Each of us got an expansive feeling in our chest. It had a real fireplace, lovely hardwood floors, and a huge family room with floor-to-ceiling windows. In the back was a deck with a gazebo – a little meditation temple. The following Thursday we made our offer, and not long after that, we closed the deal. Truly we didn't find this house. The house had somehow found us.

Have you ever been "guided" to something important for your life? Tell about the experience in your Wisdom Journal.

KARMA-YOGI WISDOM

Work like you don't need the money; love like you've never been hurt; and dance like no one's watching!

–Anonymous

Mahatma Gandhi described himself as a "karma yogi," that is, someone who works without attachment to the outcome of his or her actions. Does this mean that Gandhi didn't care whether his fellow Indians received justice from their British masters or whether India eventually got its independence? Obviously not. Caring about outcomes, however, is very different from being attached to them. This distinction is mirrored in the Serenity Prayer. Serenity comes from accepting the inevitable. But not everything is inevitable. Therefore our prayer is for the wisdom to discern what we can and cannot change, and to expend our efforts only on the former.

As the lead quotation suggests, we should work as if we don't need the paycheck. Our efforts should be motivated by love, not fear. Someone at Yale once told me that a small number of professors there served on the faculty for a dollar a year. Independently wealthy, they refused to take money they didn't need. They were all, in the words of the "Whiffenpoof Song," "gentleman scholars," though hardly off on a spree. Although they were trained professionals, they were *amateurs* in the best sense of the word.

Love may be eternal, but we are creatures who live moment by moment. Nothing is worse than souring the wine of the present with vinegar from the past. As a cat lover, I understand why mistreated cats run away from me just because I have two legs. Still, if we want to be happy, we have to find a way, through therapy or spiritual training, to keep the past from intruding upon the present.

I am such an extrovert–way off the Meyers-Briggs scale–that I always dance as if no one were watching, or rather, as if everyone were watching: a fact I glory in. A danger, of course, is becoming a show-off. Mostly, though, I am not thinking about who is out there, so intense is my relationship with the dance.

Read chapter 5 of the Bhagavad-Gita, then comment in your Wisdom Journal on the concept of "karma yoga."

MONOTHEISTIC WISDOM

One God, one law, one element
And one far-off divine event,
To which the whole creation moves.

–Alfred, Lord Tennyson, "In Memoriam," 1850

The number issue is a big concern for religions. To Jews and Moslems, strict monotheists, there is only one God, the creator of all things visible and invisible. There may be other spiritual powers, such as angels, but they are likewise creatures, not independent entities. Christians believe in a single God consisting of three Persons, the Father, Son, and Holy Spirit. This does not work for Moslems, who speak of Nabi Isa, the "Prophet" Jesus. For them the concept of God having a son is unthinkable. God by definition has no partners or relatives. The chief Islamic sin is to place anyone or anything on a par with Allah. A medieval Moslem mystic, El Hallaj, once spontaneously uttered the words, *"Ana el haq"*; "I am the Truth." Unfortunately, co-religionists overheard him, and he was put to death. "The Truth" is one of the ninety-nine names reserved for God.

I have never had a problem with polytheism or pantheism. To my mind, there are lots of gods and goddesses, elves and ogres, angels and monsters. I have always responded to the idea that the Divine Force inhabits everything, even rocks, sticks, and other supposedly dead things. I like the idea of having a much broader set of family relations than I once thought. But at base I am a monotheist: "Hear, O Israel, the Lord is our God, one Lord" (Deuteronomy 6:4). The universe is the universe because it pivots on a single axis. The globe contains many nations. Each nation contains many states. Each state contains many people. Each person contains many cells. Each cell contains many atoms. Each atom contains many moving forms of energy.

When Tennyson wrote his long elegy "In Memoriam," he was grieving the death of his friend Arthur Henry Hallam. During the poem the mood changes from despair to reconciliation. An understanding develops that the coming and going we call birth and death are ultimately but a part of the single divine event "to which the whole creation moves."

Write in your Wisdom Journal what the oneness of God means to you.

PURGATIONAL WISDOM

I was in my room [in Rome]. It was night. The light was on. Suddenly it seemed to me that Father, who had now been dead more than a year, was there with me. . . . The whole thing passed in a flash, but in that flash, instantly, I was overwhelmed with a sudden and profound insight into the mystery and corruption of my own soul. . . . And now I think for the first time in my whole life I really began to pray . . . to the God I had never known. . . . There were a lot of tears connected with this, and they did me good. . . . The morning that followed this experience . . . I remember how I climbed the deserted Aventine . . . with my soul broken up with contrition, but broken and clean, painful but sanitary like a lanced abscess, like a bone broken and re-set.

-THOMAS MERTON, *THE SEVEN STOREY MOUNTAIN*, 1948

The Seven Storey Mountain must rank among the most popular spiritual autobiographies written in English. Most educated Roman Catholics over forty have read it at least once. So have many non-Catholics interested in spiritual development or Thomas Merton's life.

Individuals familiar with *The Divine Comedy* recognize the mountain in the title to be Mount Purgatory. As Dante and Virgil trudge up its seven levels, they encounter the famous dead working off their venial sins in hopes of graduation into paradise. In Merton's book, purgatory symbolizes his life, especially from adolescence through his college years, as a skeptical intellectual who undergoes conversion to Catholicism and enters the Trappist order of monks. Mystics refer to this difficult sort of progression as the *via purgativa* – the way of purgation.

In our materialistic culture, value is placed on adding to our store: making more money, increasing our portfolio, buying more cars or shoes. Paradoxically, God often blesses us by taking away what we no longer need, like a dentist extracting a rotten tooth. Only then can we heal, learn the simple faith of children, and enter the Kingdom of heaven.

Recount in your Wisdom Journal an experience of remorse and the impact it had on your life.

WISDOM AS NOTHING SPECIAL

In zazen [sitting Zen meditation] what you are doing is not for the sake of anything. . . . But as long as you think that you are practicing zazen for the sake of something, that is not true practice. If you continue this simple practice every day you will obtain a wonderful power. Before you attain it, it is something wonderful, but after you attain it, it is nothing special.

–SHUNRYU SUZUKI, *ZEN MIND, BEGINNER'S MIND*, 1970

The early stages of spiritual practice are often like a honeymoon. You experience something unlike anything you can remember. You see lights with your eyes closed, you visualize golden Buddhas, you meet Jesus or Mary. You want to tell everyone about what happened. You do tell a few people. At least one of them is the wrong person to tell. You hear that you should sleep more, eat better, get more exercise, and maybe consider seeing a good therapist. They know just the person you should see. You are mortified.

Inner development and the heightened perceptiveness that goes with it are extraordinary only because they are minority experiences in our culture. They are fairly run-of-the-mill in places like India, Tibet, or Indonesia. It's a matter of what you are used to. My late friend and colleague Arthur Goodfriend Sr. spent a few years in Indonesia in the early 1950s. He once visited a remote area where the inhabitants had never experienced radio. When Arthur played his portable for them, they thought they had met the magician of the century. How in the world could he get people into that little box? But when they mentioned offhand that the spirits of their ancestors were sitting in the branches of some nearby trees taking in the meeting, it was Arthur's turn to be incredulous.

Spiritual practice is a paradoxical journey. You approach your destination when you relax and stop trying. When you arrive there, it is simple, ordinary, as familiar as home. The most special thing in the world turns out to be, as Suzuki says, "nothing special."

In your Wisdom Journal, discuss an experience where things worked out once you stopped trying.

THE WISDOM OF CIVIC TOLERANCE

When we came to the throne this our Kingdom was divided into several factions and many parts and our subjects beset by great trouble and peril. . . .

Our opinion is that a simple and sovereign law must be stated by the government by which all present and future conflicts in this sphere may be fully resolved.

Therefore . . . we in this perpetual and unbreakable Edict declare and order:

That the recollection of everything done by one party or the other during all the preceding period of troubles, remain obliterated and forgotten, as if no such things had happened. . . .

We desire here to append that all of the Reformed group as well as the Catholic shall be enabled henceforth to hold all public, Royal, and civil offices – and no oath save loyalty to the laws shall be demanded of them.

-FROM THE EDICT OF NANTES, FRANCE, 1598

When Henry IV assumed the French throne in 1589, the country had experienced three centuries of religious unrest. In the interest of national unity, Henry advocated a program, articulated in the Edict of Nantes, to balance the religious forces then dividing the country. Less than thirty years later, Cardinal Richelieu, while continuing to strengthen the monarchy, began to dismantle the religious and political toleration promulgated in Henry's Edict.

The development of civil and political rights has had a checkered history. There have been times when the whole enterprise has seemed to reverse course. When we see ethnic and religious disruptions today, we are reminded that, as a race, we have not yet matured. For all the Henrys, Lincolns, Susan B. Anthonys, Gandhis, Pope John the Twenty-thirds, Martin Luther King Jrs., and Mandelas, we still have a long way to go. Nevertheless we do live in a more tolerant world. In an increasing number of countries, citizens may worship God as they wish, vote, and express themselves freely in public. The Edict of Nantes four hundred years ago was an important step in this direction.

In your Wisdom Journal, suggest one thing each of us could do to make the world a more tolerant place.

THE WISDOM OF FREE-FORM PRAYER

Love entered the mosque and said: "O master and guide,
Tear off the shackles of existence – why are you still
in the fetters of the rug prayer?"

–JALALUDDIN RUMI (1207–1273)

Okay, I like it both ways. On my good days, I consider myself a universalist, able to go with the flow. On my bad days, I criticize myself for being wishy-washy, for never taking a stand on basic things like prayer.

As an undergraduate I used to date Catholic girls, in part to accompany them to church. This was pre–Vatican II, so most things were still in Latin. After four years of classical Latin at boarding school and two more at college, I loved to relax into the pre-Italian simplicity of church Latin. But what I really liked was the Gregorian chant. Later I bought myself a chant recording and would take occasional "chant breaks" between papers. Then, too, something in me liked showing off that as a non–Catholic, I understood the liturgical language better than many to the missal born. The old Adam dies hard.

There is something to be said for a universal prayer language. In pre–Vatican II Masses, for instance, every attendee the world over would hear the ordinary in the exact same words. You could be in Timbuktu or Toronto. *Agnus Dei* would be invariable. But I understand Rumi too. If prayer has to do with God talking to God through us, shouldn't what comes through depend to some extent on the intermediary? In a famous Rumi image, he implores God, "Let me be your flute; play me as you will." Now if Rumi is a flute and I am, say, a French horn, how God "plays" us will differ, as will the resulting sounds.

The reciting of written prayers seems appropriate for group worship. For those unaccustomed to speaking freely to God, printed devotionals make sense too. We are not all Tevyes or Zorbas. But when we die, we will be on our own. So maybe we should occasionally practice praying in our own words, from the heart.

For the next few days, make up all your prayers. Then write about the experience in your Wisdom Journal.

THE WISDOM OF JOB

I know that thou canst do all things
and that no purpose is beyond thee.
But I have spoken of great things which
I have not understood,
things too wonderful for me to know.
I knew of thee then only by report,
but now I see thee with my own eyes.
Therefore I melt away;
I repent in dust and ashes.

–Job's final response to God, in Job 42:2–6

In Bible study, Solomon is known for wisdom, Job for patience. Yet one can talk of Job's wisdom as well. His patience *is* his wisdom. Job is described as "the greatest man in all the East" (1:3), wealthy in both family and possessions. Moreover, he has lived a "blameless and upright" life (1:1). When God praises Job for his virtue before the heavenly court, where Satan acts as a kind of inspector general, the latter responds: Why shouldn't Job be God-fearing? He has everything: a loving family, regal wealth, good health, and a great reputation. Take away those benefits, and let's see how well he fares. "But stretch out your hand and touch all that he has," Satan tells God, "and then he will curse you to your face" (1:11). God accepts the challenge, and the famous story unfolds.

Job loses just about everything. It's not that he doesn't suffer. He simply refuses to "curse God and die" (2:10). He does complain, though. His three friends aren't much help. From their perspective – and his – the upright prosper while sinners suffer. He must have done something wrong! Job insists that he has not. And that is what really gets him. He never learns that all this is merely a test. When God finally responds, it is primarily by making clear who is the Creator and who is the creature. Job humbles himself in the lines quoted above and lives to see his health, wealth, family, and reputation restored. But, more important, by maintaining his ways in the face of extended suffering, Job is permitted to see God and live. Like Jacob, he has wrestled with God and won a blessing.

In your Wisdom Journal, give an example of a long struggle after which things finally worked out for you.

THE WISDOM OF NOT QUESTIONING

Much of life can never be explained but only witnessed.

–Rachel Naomi Remen, MD, *Kitchen Table Wisdom,* 1996

I have been following the same spiritual path for thirty-eight years. During this time I have done an active meditation twice a week. Each session lasts a half hour. Rather than sitting or lying down or focusing on a sacred word, I stand quietly in anticipation of whatever spontaneous activity I feel inspired to do. The point is to learn – in twelve-step talk, to "let go and let God." In this way one is trained to live from within, learning how it feels to be moved from a deep, inner place rather than from one's ordinary will or intentions.

In accordance with Jesus' advice, I try to judge all trees by their fruit. Clearly I must be getting something from my spiritual exercises. Why else would I drive an hour twice weekly to stand in a YWCA classroom for a half hour and wait to see what happens in the active meditation process? Recently I got an unexpected confirmation. One of our newer members told me he was having a lot of questions about his life, work, spiritual, and personal development. What struck me as I listened was how few questions I had about anything. I just got up and did what was in front of me. This has not always been so. One of the fruits of my spiritual practice seems to be an increased willingness to play the hand dealt me.

My spiritual guide, Muhammad Subuh, liked to tell a story about two sons of Adam, Said Anwar and Said Anwas. The first represented surrender to God's will, the second self-sufficiency. Anwar chose the way of mystery, or witnessing, to use Rachel Remen's term; Anwas opted for the way of mastery, or explanation. Secular culture and some spiritual practices are devoted to the latter. Religions and mystical paths based on surrender to the Divine will exemplify the former. We are taught in college to ask good questions. But in many life situations, I have learned, the best questions may be none at all.

How good are you at turning your will and life over to the care of God as you understand God? Respond in your Wisdom Journal.

THE WISDOM OF OPENNESS

The principle that guides the Teacher is be open to outcome, not attached to outcome. . . . *Wisdom is at work when we are open to all options.*

–ANGELES ARRIEN, PHD, *THE FOUR-FOLD WAY,* 1993

I agree with Dr. Arrien, but there is a problem. Teachers are usually guided by course syllabi specifying the items to be covered. If I am teaching nineteenth-century American fiction and all we read is *The Scarlet Letter,* the course has been misnamed, and the students will be right to protest. There must be truth in advertising.

Then there are learning goals. Exposure to certain books is not enough. I want my students to understand specific ideas and associate them with authors, books, and schools of thought. The same is true for writing styles and rhetorical techniques. Maybe there are issues of influence, like the effect on Hawthorne of the commune movement during his life. I also want my students to become familiar with the characters we meet, as word-portraits of true-to-life human beings. Not much time is available for ad hoc interests in a semester course.

On the other hand, I want to communicate my love of literature to the students. This is not always easy. First, grades get in the way. It is hard to instill love when you hold the power of the grade book. Second, not everyone in class chooses to be there. For some the course may be a requirement. Third, the tyranny of coverage makes it hard for everyone to spend time on issues that interest them.

As a college teacher, I always preferred fewer works and more time for exploration. True openness is modeled by the teacher willing to entertain student ideas in opposition to his or her own. The professor who publicly cedes his own position for one put forward by a student is ready for canonization. Making space in class for emerging student interests and ideas may not serve the short-term goal of coverage, but it can make the difference between someone becoming a lifelong reader or considering literature as yet another straitjacket for the soul.

How open to options were your best teachers? Respond in your Wisdom Journal.

THE WISDOM OF PRACTICING THE PRESENCE OF GOD

He had attained a state wherein he thought only of God. . . .
When he had outside business to attend to, he did not think of it ahead of time, but when it was time to take action in the matter, God showed him, as in a mirror, what he should do. . . . He gave no thought to those things he had finished with and almost none to those in which he was engaged; . . . after he had dined, he did not know what he had eaten; but all [things] were done very simply in such a way as to keep him in the loving presence of God.

–THE ABBÉ DE BEAUFORT ON BROTHER LAWRENCE OF THE RESURRECTION (1614?–1691)

Brother Lawrence, a French Carmelite lay brother, never wrote a book. He did develop a following for his everyday spirituality. After his death his abbot found some of Lawrence's letters, added the sage's favorite sayings and his own memories of conversations with Lawrence, and combined them in a slender volume that became known in English as *The Practice of the Presence of God.*

Lawrence, born Nicholas Herman in Lorraine, came from a religious family. After fighting in the Thirty Years' War, he served for a time as a footman in an aristocratic household. Soon he left for Paris to become a lay monk in the monastery where he stayed for the rest of his life. He worked first in the kitchen, then in the shoe shop. After ten inwardly difficult years, a peacefulness descended on him that remained with him until he died.

According to Henri Nouwen, prayer for Lawrence was not "saying prayers but a way of living in which all we do becomes prayer." Practicing the presence of God meant living in the present moment–following Jesus' advice to take no thought for the morrow. My cats are like that. They don't worry about getting fed and never fret about trips to the vet–until they are in the car. I am aspiring to follow Lawrence's example, and theirs.

Practice living in God's presence for a day. Discuss the experience in your Wisdom Journal.

THE WISDOM OF SELF-ENTERTAINMENT

So I unto my self alone will sing;
The woods shall to me answer, and my echo ring.

–EDMUND SPENSER (1552?–1599), "EPITHALAMION"

The film *Marty* contains a memorable dialogue between the hero and his buddy. It goes something like this: "What do you want to do tonight, Marty?" To which Marty replies: "I don't know. What do you want to do?"

Boredom, someone once said, is among the most important but least acknowledged factors in history.

I have been lucky in this regard. Life has always contained more things I wanted to do, more places I wanted to see, more people I wanted to meet than there was time. So I find it hard to understand people who are chronically bored – who sit around with time on their hands. In my case I'd be learning Russian, doing the Sunday *Times* puzzle, taking a nap.

In consequence I see the capacity to entertain oneself, to go through life without ever being bored, as one sign of a wise human being. It is also a trait, I think, that can be learned. One need only look at every situation as a chance for self-improvement. In 1960 and 1961, I worked for my father. I had just graduated from college, was 1-A in the draft, and was planning to go to graduate school in the fall. Because I insisted on telling interviewers the last two facts when I went on job interviews, I never got hired. So my father had me do clerical work for his one-person grain-brokerage business. There I was on the forty-second floor of the Board of Trade building, Chicago, with a grand view north along LaSalle Street. I improved my typing that year, strove to create aesthetically shaped contracts as I filled in the lines, and even learned a few things about the grain business.

Nowadays at parties I am so convinced that there are no boring people – that everyone has an interesting story if you listen actively enough and ask an occasional stimulating question – that I always end up having a good time. Besides, my listening skills can always stand improvement.

In your Wisdom Journal, describe the techniques you use to keep from being bored.

THE WISDOM OF SERVANT LEADERSHIP

If you cannot serve, you cannot rule.

–A Bulgarian proverb

In a time shadowed by the likes of Hitler and Stalin, it is hard to speak of servant leadership. Yet both probably thought they were doing right by their people – securing borders or getting rid of undesirables. Clever thieves, if asked, would probably argue that they benefited society by providing the police and members of the legal system with jobs. After all, if we had no crime, we would have no need for law enforcement. Hundreds of thousands in every country would suddenly be out of work!

Readers familiar with leadership literature will recognize the term *servant leadership* as the title of a book written some years ago by Robert Greenleaf. The concept goes back, of course, to the time of Christ, if not earlier. In Matthew 23:11–12, Jesus states for the disciples what might be called the Principle of Christian Leadership: "The greatest among you must be your servant. For whoever exalts himself will be humbled; and whoever humbles himself will be exalted." As you can see, we are some distance here from Hitler's self-description as the "Greatest Field Commander of All Time." When James and John asked Jesus if they might be seated next to him in heaven, he made a clear distinction between worldly leadership and what he advocated: "You know that in the world the recognized rulers lord it over their subjects, and their great men make them feel the weight of authority. That is not the way with you; among you, whoever wants to be great must be your servant, and whoever wants to be first must be the willing slave of all. For even the Son of Man did not come to be served but to serve, and to give up his life as a ransom for many" (Mark 10:42–45).

After two thousand years of Christianity, servant leadership is still a stretch for many of us. How else can we explain all the "mean boss" stories? Still, is there really a wise option to Jesus' advice?

In your Wisdom Journal, write about the characteristics of your best boss. Was she or he a "servant leader"?

THE WISDOM OF SHARING

We are united through sharing . . . our lives made meaningful . . . made new. "Take. Eat. This is my body," said Jesus when He broke the bread at the Last Supper. Then He gave His life for us. Behind all commu-nion is the knowledge that we must give our lives to each other, for each other. . . . In sharing, the meaning of our lives is given back to God.

–Gunilla Norris, *Becoming Bread,* 1993

My only sibling, a sister, is nearly nine years older than I am. When I arrived she was suddenly demoted from being the only child. Now she was merely the older sister of "the baby," who also happened to be the only son, an honored position in Jewish families. On the up side, at least she didn't have to share clothes with me. Moreover, once I figured out I was a boy and that boys didn't play with dolls, I left her playthings alone. Still, I think she never got over the unexpected loss of exclusive rights to her parents. Until our mother's death at age ninety-five, my sister always referred to her – in my presence – as "my" mother.

When it came to sharing, I was no paragon either. As the prince in the family, I was spoiled rotten. What I didn't get from my parents, I got from Florine, our housekeeper. It wasn't until my first summer camp experience at age seven that I began learning to share. Two other summers at camp plus scouting helped some too. When we went on overnight hikes, shared responsibility was essential, whether in putting up the pup tent, cooking the meals, or policing the area.

More lessons in sharing came at boarding school, which I started at age twelve and continued for four years until graduation. Having roommates from New Jersey, Venezuela, and Delaware – one Baptist, one Catholic, and one Methodist – meant having to adjust to different kinds of people and becoming able to share across cultures. All those experiences culminated in postgraduate studies in sharing: marriage. Thirty-six years later, I am still learning.

Discuss in your Wisdom Journal what the hardest things are for you to share and why.

THE WISDOM OF SPIRITUAL ELDERING

The difference between being an elder and an old person is that an elder is someone who has gained wisdom. They have distilled their life experience in such a way that their very presence becomes a witness to others. And originally this was what we had in a tribal society – that an elder was a repository of wisdom and awareness, and younger people would check with them and say, "Am I on the right track? Am I doing right?" I like to use the word as a verb – eldering – because it's a process; it's something that we begin to grow into. Sometimes you find that the elder begins to shine forth in young children – people speak of them as having old souls.

–"SPIRITUAL ELDERING: A CONVERSATION WITH ZALMAN SCHACHTER-SHALOMI," 1998

I first became aware of Rabbi Zalman as an undergraduate. He showed up one Friday night at the Sabbath service as speaker and "magician." In the latter role, he did more than pull rabbits from a hat. He made our sophisticated inhibitions disappear and even had us dancing in the aisles. He was dressed in a long, black cape trimmed with ermine; a big, black cap, similarly adorned; and shiny, black boots. Although he was a Jewish chaplain at a Canadian university at the time, he identified with his Hasidic mystical order and dressed accordingly.

My next Zalmanic encounter was in the mid-sixties at the meditation center I attended in New York City. Our spiritual guide was Muslim, but I was delighted to find this unique rabbi showing up in our midst. Three years ago I became aware of his spiritual-eldering work and wrote him a letter about my interest in wisdom. He called a week or so later.

At age seventy, Zalman explained, his interest had turned to helping individuals become old in more than body. Through his Philadelphia-based institute, he and his associates train seniors to become spiritual elders by learning to harvest wisdom from their years of living and sharing it with others. His goal: to get everyone on the path to spiritual eldering, a transformation he describes as going from "aging to saging."

In your Wisdom Journal, describe a wise elder you know.

THE WISDOM OF UNLIMITED CAPACITY

What do we teach our children? . . . We should say to each of them: Do you know what you are? You are a marvel. You are unique. . . . You may become a Shakespeare, a Michelangelo, a Beethoven. You have the capacity for anything.

–PABLO CASALS (1876–1973)

Now wait a minute! Shakespeare had the capacity to become Shakespeare and Michelangelo Michelangelo. But isn't it unfair to fill the minds of children with ideas like this? I mean, I had one of the best educations money can buy, but I never had it in me to become either of these geniuses. Let's face it. Short of alchemy, you can't make silk purses out of sows' ears.

Another problem is, the world just isn't big enough for dozens of Shakespeares and Michelangelos. Their uniqueness would be lost in a sea of prodigies. Who would ever have time to perform or see all their works?

Consider this: Children shouldn't be encouraged to become *whatever* they want. Rather, they should grow into the unique individuals they *are.* That person may turn out to be a skilled furniture restorer or a loving foster parent. Why always the president of the United States – or Beethoven?

Come to think of it, why do we equate a successful life with one's profession? Plenty of well-known individuals are unhappy with their lives and unpleasant to live with. Beethoven is a case in point. Musical genius though he was, he was reputed to be a holy terror to be around. A more recent example, by various accounts, is Pablo Picasso. Why should all the points go to being famous and none to a person's quality as a human being?

Okay, I know. What Señor Casals is really talking about is not foreclosing children's options. In former times and still today in some cultures, your potential was limited not by capacity but by society. If persons in your caste were merchants, you would have to be one too. In this regard I prefer the U.S. Army's slogan: "Be all that you can be."

In your Wisdom Journal, share how you think children should be encouraged concerning their future.

THE WISDOM OF YOGA

Yoga believes that the subconscious can be dominated by asceticism. . . . The psychological and parapsychological experience of the East in general, and of Yoga in particular, being uncontestably more extensive and better organized than the experience upon which Western theories of the structure of the psyche have been built up, it is probable that, on this point too, Yoga is right and that – paradoxical as it may seem – the subconscious can be known, mastered, and conquered.

–MIRCEA ELIADE, *YOGA: IMMORTALITY AND FREEDOM*, 1969

My first encounter with yoga was in the stacks of Sterling Memorial Library. As a Yale undergraduate, I soon discovered that my "accidental education" was often the best– finding books I wasn't looking for in the course of tracking down those I was. In this case I started leafing through a book on hatha yoga, the yoga of postures. I may have tried the half-lotus position in my dorm. With a half-dozen deadlines looming, however, yoga was soon forgotten.

After making my first East Indian friend, Kasi, I began reading more on the subject. I learned that hatha yoga was only the beginning. The word *yoga* comes from the same Indo-European root as *yoke*, an instrument that joins two draft animals and enables them to work as one. In Hindu thought our inner and outer selves approximate two such entities. Hinduism also understands that human beings come in all kinds. Therefore, the techniques leading to psychic integration must vary.

Among these techniques, bhakti yoga comes closest to Western religion. In it the yogi worships one of many personal gods. For intellectuals there is gñana yoga, the path of discrimination. Basically, after analyzing that no individual thing or idea is divine, you realize in a flash that everything is. For activists like Gandhi, you have karma yoga, the practice of taking action without attachment to actions' outcomes. Finally, there is raja yoga, the yoga of increasingly demanding forms of meditation. Each path, yogis say, can lead to Enlightenment. The trick is to pick the one right for you and persevere.

Skim a book on yoga, then write your reactions in your Wisdom Journal.

THE WISDOM OF YOUTH

What is youth? It is not only a period of life that corresponds to a certain number of years, it is also a time given by Providence to every person and given to him as a responsibility. *During that time he searches, like the young man in the Gospel, for answers to basic questions; he searches not only for the meaning of life but also for a concrete way to go about living his life. This is the most fundamental characteristic of youth.*

–Pope John Paul II, *Crossing the Threshold of Hope,* 1994

The final images of *East of Eden,* my favorite James Dean movie, stick in my mind. A patriarchal father has two sons. The "bad" son, who could never win his father's respect, finally decides to take revenge. When he tells his all-American brother the truth about their mother, that she is a prostitute, the "good" son gets drunk, enlists in the army, and is last seen half crazy in his troop train, about to leave for war. The father then has a massive stroke. In the final scene, Dean, the "bad" son, visits his now-paralyzed father to ask forgiveness. Who can forget the harrowing looks on their faces?

Unfortunately youth is sometimes the period when the mistakes of parents, especially the fathers, are realized in the actions of their sons. Such is the case in Steinbeck's novel and the movie made from it. Unrequited idealism, like unrequited love, can have dire results as well. Raskolnikov, the nineteen-year-old murderer in Dostoyevsky's *Crime and Punishment,* was young, abstract, and therefore given to being cruel. Any college student who has ever been subjected to the rigidities of graduate-assistant graders will nod. Even when the motivation is pure, youthful idealism can sometimes be misshapen into cultlike fanaticism.

Pope John Paul II is not wrong in his assessment. Youth *is* a time for searching. But it can also be a time of strong feelings, hard edges, fraternity rituals that go too far, and date rape. Adults, especially men, must be there for our youth; otherwise they may find it difficult to be there for themselves.

Spend a few minutes in your Wisdom Journal discussing your own youth.

NUMINOUS WISDOM

I arise from dreams of thee
In the first sweet sleep of night,
When the winds are breathing low,
And the stars are shining bright;
I arise from dreams of thee,
And a spirit in my feet
Hath led me – who knows how?
To thy chamber window, sweet!

–PERCY BYSSHE SHELLEY (1792–1822),
"THE INDIAN SERENADE"

I have always been superstitious. Now, though, thirty-two years after receiving my PhD, I call it *mystical.* Time may help me distinguish the true from the merely imagined.

Like a lot of kids, I was afraid of the unknown. I refused to look at the movie screen when The Thing made its appearance. Later, as a college student, I felt gratified to learn that the esteemed Samuel Johnson would take pains to avoid stepping on cracks in the road. Jack Nicholson's obsessive-compulsive character in *As Good As It Gets* followed the same regimen. Although this is not a practice of mine, I still knock on wood.

While these habits are silly and, in large amounts, pathological, I believe in the presence of numinous forces in and around us that go largely unnoticed in our culture. To be sure, angels are making a comeback, and the UFO industry is alive and well and landing in a backyard near you. I do think we human beings can receive guidance about what to do, and not to do, within, say, our limbs.

The Romantic writers had insight into this phenomenon. Henry Thoreau mentions how he practiced walking without a goal. He would then arrive at just the right place, as if his feet had been drawn there by invisible magnetic lines. Shelley, in his love song, similarly talks about "a spirit in my feet" that unaccountably takes him to the window of his beloved. Spirits can, of course, be demonic as well as divine. *The Exorcist* is a frightening portrayal of demon possession. Still, it may be wise to investigate these forces and, if they exist, allow ourselves to be guided by the good ones while learning to resist the bad, assuming we can tell the difference.

What is your experience with numinous forces? Write briefly about it in your Wisdom Journal.

AEROBIC WISDOM

Health is the vital principal of bliss,
And exercise, of health.

-James Thomson (1700–1748), "The Castle of Indolence"

I've just come in from a fast walk – 2.1 miles in 27:53. I try to follow this regimen three times a week, with one of the outings a bit shorter and a run. Lately I have been neglectful. The scale is my witness. Time to get back to my regular program.

In high school I played soccer in the fall, swam competitively in winter, and golfed in the spring. Although swimming helped me get my first job as a camp counselor, the daily workouts killed my love of swimming pools. Fortunately my wife and I have invented several games that make me more willing to join her in our pool. We play cooperative catch to see how many times we can throw the ball across the pool without dropping it. Our record to date is 250. In the other game, we sit on a little concrete shelf on one side of the deep end and see how long we can kick.

About twenty years ago, in Chicago, my doctor told me to lose thirty pounds and begin a regular exercise program. A runner himself, he suggested I try that. So I launched diet number 52, bought Jim Fixx's running book, and joined the early-morning joggers doing the two-mile circumference of the nearby park. About six months into jogging, my daughter's best friend's father asked if I wanted to play tennis. For a while I continued both exercises. Then the tennis bug bit.

Here in Hawaii I've gone back to running, or running mixed with walking. I exercise for health, of course, but that's not the only reason. Often the more immediate reason is that vigorous exercise takes the air out of the various worries oppressing me. I go out filled with some problem and return feeling great. Running seems to aerate my brain and make room for the part of me that knows everything is basically all right.

Profile your history of physical exercise in your Wisdom Journal. Then describe your current program or, if you don't have one, sketch out what you might do.

APPROPRIATE WISDOM

When the music changes, so does the dance.

–A Hausa proverb from West Africa

Our situation changes all the time. Sometimes we cause the change. More often, external factors do. Whichever the case, we need to respond appropriately. Different music, different dance.

Two issues immediately surface. One is our ability to hear the change in the music. The other is our familiarity with the new dance. Another African proverb states, "If you don't know the dance, sit down." So sometimes the way of wisdom is to stay on the sidelines until the music changes to a dance we can do. Sensitivity precedes suitability.

Some years ago public television presented a short film entitled "Who Am I This Time?" Based on a story by Kurt Vonnegut, it focused on a versatile young actor in a small town. As star, he took all the leading male roles during the season. One reason he was popular is that he identified completely with each character he played. Before long he discovered that without a role to play, he really had no identity.

I had a similar problem when I was young. Because I was a good mimic, I did well with foreign languages. Not only did I get the accents right, but people remarked that my facial expression and body language changed too. I began to wonder whether I had a central self that could act in different ways or if I was simply a chameleon by nature. In New York City I would fall into a New York accent. Back in Hawaii I would start speaking pidgin. Who was I anyway?

Following my spiritual practice has seemed to help me here. Over time I have gained the sense of an inner self, or core presence, which does not change. However, my outer demeanor automatically adjusts to outward circumstances. When I am with young children, I play. When I am at a party, I dance. When I am in the library, I study. But I no longer feel that I lack an essential self just because my behavior changes to fit the new situation. I am the same dancer as before. Only now I am doing a different dance.

How do you adjust to changing situations? Discuss this question in your Wisdom Journal.

ETERNAL-LIGHT WISDOM

In my grandfather's synagogue there was a light that never went out. All synagogues have such an eternal light. It signifies that the unseen presence of God is always in this place.

–RACHEL NAOMI REMEN, MD, *KITCHEN TABLE WISDOM*, 1996

Okay. I'll admit it. I was a Hebrew School dropout. After one year, paralleling my seventh grade, I told my parents I didn't want to go back. Too bad. Now, if I follow my plan to study biblical Hebrew as a retirement project, it will be much harder to learn.

I do remember a few words and phrases, though, even at a distance of nearly fifty years. One is *nair tamid*, "eternal light." When I read the above passage from Dr. Remen's book, I recalled the concept as well. Nowadays, in our secular world, the only light that stays on all the time says EXIT. I don't know if I want to explore the ramifications of this fact.

According to my mother, the first word I said – probably after "Mama" and "Papa" – was "light." Apparently I pointed to a lamp as I was saying it. When I was in my twenties, at the Vivekananda-Vedanta Temple on Chicago's North Side, the swami would intone in his deep voice, "Lead us from the darkness into the light." A few years later, when I became interested in Indonesian culture, I found that the early-twentieth-century Javanese feminist, Princess Kartini, entitled her memoir *From Darkness into Light*. And later still, I gained a sense of the mystical meanings associated by Sufis with the term *nur*, "light," the first cousin of the Hebrew *nair*.

In determining if I should have cataract surgery, the ophthalmologist I consulted shined a sharp, white light into my eye. The experience was not painful in the usual sense, like a headache or a pin prick. Still, I couldn't wait until the examination was over. The probing brightness made me feel ill. This contrasts with the "figure of light" frequently seen in near-death experiences, where the light is described as warm and welcoming. May our own journey from darkness lead us to the warm, welcoming, eternal light of God.

In your Wisdom Journal, write about the role of light in your life.

BEE WISDOM

It's not so much how busy you are,
but why you are busy.
The bee is praised.
The mosquito is swatted.

—MARY O'CONNOR, FROM THE INTERNET

It seems I am spending more and more time sorting through my e-mail. (Why are you nodding?!) Because online friends and family know I am working on this book, I get unsolicited maxims and saws almost daily. Some get deleted, some saved, and some – like Mary O'Connor's – get used.

In the Mary-Martha debate, I am definitely a Martha. That is, as much of a Martha as someone named Reynold can be. For those of you unfamiliar with the New Testament story, it goes like this: Jesus arrives in a village where a woman named Martha welcomes him into her house. As hostess, she is busy seeing to her guests. Her sister Mary, meanwhile, doesn't lift a finger but sits down at Jesus' feet to listen. Martha complains to Jesus that she, Martha, is doing all the work while that sister of hers, rather than helping, is acting as if *she* were a guest. Jesus' response is classic: "Martha, Martha, you are fretting and fussing about so many things; but one thing is necessary. The part that Mary has chosen is best; and it shall not be taken away from her" (Luke 10:42).

I relate to Martha but wish I were more like Mary. Not buzzing my life away in busyness but, in every situation, knowing the important thing to do and doing it.

Fortunately my wife, Simone, is helpful in this regard. Going to Kailua Beach Park is hardly equivalent to sitting at Jesus' feet, but knowing how I am apt to get glued to the computer, Simone will say something like: "Reinhold, it is a beautiful day. Could we perhaps go to the beach for an hour?" The point is that if I were going to be working all the time, we could have stayed in Saint Paul, where there is no Kailua Beach. We would have saved ourselves a bundle.

Are you a workaholic like me? Is this really how we should be spending our time? Think about it and write a little something in your Wisdom Journal.

THE TRUE PHILOSOPHER

To be a philosopher is not merely to have subtle thoughts, nor even to found a school, but so to love wisdom as to live according to its dictates, a life of simplicity, independence, magnanimity, and trust. It is to solve some of the problems of life, not only theoretically, but practically.

–HENRY DAVID THOREAU (1817–1862), *WALDEN*

Philosophers are professional lovers of wisdom. That's what the word means. And we doctors of philosophy have acquired that love, one assumes, and have a responsibility to pass it on. The tendency in today's university, however, is to have subtle thoughts and to pass *them* on. Graduate school in particular places a premium on "knowledge you can trade on" rather than wisdom.

During my junior year in Germany, the Yale faculty sagely let me do whatever I wanted. They assumed that just by being in an area teeming with culture, I would learn at least as much as in New Haven's competitive classrooms. Not trusting their permissiveness, I read through a trunkload of books. I also kept a 500-page journal in English, German, and French, traveled extensively, discussed politics, history, and philosophy in cafés, and learned a few things unavailable in six years of all-male education. When I returned to Yale, I was pleasantly surprised to receive "honors" for my work.

But by living in another country – especially one that had so recently been the enemy of my Jewish people – I gained profound insights into who I was as a Jew, an American, and a human being. I learned that of the three, the last had the profoundest claim on me. During the year I had seen a performance of the Czech play *The Good Soldier Shveik.* At one point the hero, a nebbishy private in World War I, is engaged by an enemy soldier. "Who goes there?" the enemy calls out. "A human being," replies Shveik. The two drop their rifles, share pictures of their families, wish each other luck, and go their separate ways. I returned to the States older and wiser, a private first class in life.

Write in your Wisdom Journal about an outstanding learning experience. What made this experience special?

THE WISDOM OF REVISING

It is a bad plan that admits of no modification.

–PUBLILIUS SYRUS (C. 42 B.C.E.), MAXIM 469

If you want to make God laugh, tell God your plans. The human being proposes, God disposes. Lots of proverbs make this point. As our situation and understanding of things change, we should stay flexible and be open to modifying our plans accordingly.

If most of us weren't realistic in this way, the landscape would be littered with would-be actors, firefighters, and the generically rich and famous. Of course, once we realize that talent and inclination play roles in career choice and not everyone in the professions we idealized in our childhood are happy, it becomes easier to revise our ambitions.

There are, naturally, individuals who show early signs of talent in a particular field. In cases of genius, it is a simple matter. From his toddler days as a child prodigy, Mozart remained a musician all his short life, and the world is fortunate that he did. Friendships, partnerships, and marriages sometimes have that "till death us do part" longevity also. People come together, they click, and the chemistry holds from then on. But that it is hard to predict this kind of marriage-made-in-heaven is underscored by the large and growing divorce rate in America and elsewhere. There is often wisdom in trying to improve relationships, with outside help if necessary. If all our best efforts come to naught, however, the most sensible solution may be to modify our plans.

The same principle holds true for commercial ventures and investments. The stock that made people fortunes yesterday can make them paupers today. Management changes, consumer-demand shifts, and competitors take away market share, and so on.

Thus, though there is wisdom in planning, good plans always include the possibility of midcourse correction and even dramatic revision, depending on new information received. We all remember that the best laid plans of mice and men can easily go awry. As an aeronautical engineer once told me, flexible wings help planes ride through turbulence, while inflexible ones snap off.

In your Wisdom Journal, discuss an instance where you modified your plans. What were the results?

PARENTAL WISDOM REVISITED

Children have more need of models than critics.

–A FRENCH PROVERB

Early March 1982. Chicago. Our older daughter, then fifteen, was about to drop out of school. She had been attending the private arts high school in the Loop. In the morning she had academic subjects, in the afternoon, drama, music, and art. She enjoyed the afternoon but had difficulty with the morning. Above all, she couldn't stand her biology class, which unfortunately started the day.

School attendance in Illinois is required until age sixteen. We considered our options. We decided to send M. to live with our former pastor and his wife in Honolulu. The pastor was a certified family therapist. Since M.'s birthday was September 1, all she had to do was complete tenth grade. Then she would be old enough to leave school legally before fall term. Three days later M. was in Honolulu. By summer's end she returned home, ready to complete high school. Her college career was spasmodic, but the years spent living, working, and studying in England proved to be richly educational. She eventually graduated from the University of Minnesota magna cum laude and was inducted into Phi Beta Kappa. The University of Saint Thomas gave her a full fellowship for her master's degree in English, which she completed on time and with excellent grades. Now age thirty-two and happily married, she is weighing career options.

I was not very patient with this daughter, and we were quite competitive. When the high school crisis hit, however, we were somehow able to do the right thing. In time, as a parent I became more able to let both children develop at their own pace. I found that the more space I gave them, the better our relationship.

Parenting is among the toughest assignments we human beings get. I don't know how my parents survived me. In the end, focusing on our own development while being supportive of other family members is probably the best bet. Patience, prayer, and a little luck probably complete the formula.

If you are a parent, discuss in your Wisdom Journal how it has gone for you. Otherwise, write about the parenting you have received. What lessons do you derive from these situations?

THE WISDOM OF SIMPLIFICATION

What is wisdom? Where can it be found? . . . It can be found only inside oneself. To be able to find it, one has first to liberate oneself from such masters as greed and envy. The stillness following liberation – even if only momentary – produces the insights of wisdom which are obtainable in no other way.

-E. F. SCHUMACHER, *SMALL IS BEAUTIFUL*, 1973

Wisdom may be available to each human being, but it does not come free. It must be mined and refined. The problem is that we are both miner and minefield, purifier and that which needs to be purified.

On March 20, 1977, E. F. Schumacher, an established hero among Western liberal intellectuals at the time, addressed the annual Conference on Higher Education in Chicago. He was the keynote speaker. I know the exact date because Professor Schumacher signed and dated my copy of *Small Is Beautiful* that day.

In the 1998 film *One True Thing,* William Hurt plays a narcissistic professor who likes to quote the Schumacherian slogan "less is more." The irony is that it was *more* comfortable for Hurt's character to show *less* concern for his wife and children than they were required to show for him. Greed, envy, and assorted self-serving behaviors were in evidence despite his popularity with the students as a with-it literature professor who had come of age in the 1960s.

I don't think Schumacher would have recognized much of himself in that film character. Wisdom, for Schumacher, is the fruit of work on ourselves. We "disarm" envy and greed, he argues, "by resisting the temptation of letting our luxuries become needs; and perhaps by even scrutinizing our needs to see if they cannot be simplified and reduced" (*Small Is Beautiful*). His is not the way of extreme asceticism but of ongoing self-monitoring and distinguishing our needs from our wants. "Buddhist economics" was the term coined to describe this form of vigilance.

Write in your Wisdom Journal about something you do now to keep your life simple. Then brainstorm three or four other things you might do to simplify it even more.

BIG-FAMILY WISDOM

"Is this one of our tribe or a stranger?" is the calculation of the narrow-minded; but to those of a noble disposition the world itself is but one family.

–FROM THE *HITOPADESA*, A CLASSICAL HINDU RELIGIOUS TEXT

"Are they Jewish?" was always a big question in my family. Especially from my Grandma Ida. The daughter of a scribe who meticulously copied Torah scrolls, she believed that true humanity began and ended with the descendants of Abraham, Isaac, and Jacob. To the extent possible, she socialized only with Jews. She did make a distinction between good Jews, who were observant in the same Orthodox way she was, and those who were Jewish in bloodline only. Still, she retained bragging rights about any nominally Jewish person who did good things in the world. Dr. Jonas Salk, who married a Parisian woman of Catholic background, would be an example.

Both my grandfathers took a different stance. My mother's father, a farmer, was known among his coreligionists as Goyischer (Gentile) Max because he hung around with a mixed crowd and seemed to have genuine affection for some of the non-Jews. My father's dad, Paul, was an endearing ne'er-do-well who not only socialized with Gentiles – after all, he was a cook on oceangoing freighters – but spoke with them in five languages. His fraternizing with the enemy drove Grandma Ida crazy.

I grew up in a much different world. An African American house-keeper who was in effect a surrogate mother, a Baptist boarding school, Yale, junior year and a year of work in Germany, a German Gentile wife, readings from many cultures, an Indonesian-Muslim spiritual guide, employment at the East-West Center, significant friendships with several Catholic nuns, years of living in Hawaii – for me Grandma Ida's path was out of the question. I had learned the concepts of *tiospaye* from the Lakota and *ohana* from the Hawaiians; both terms mean "extended kin group." I could write the Chinese characters for "big" and "family," which together form the standard Chinese for "everybody." Like it or not, the world's peoples had become my sisters and brothers. I had traded in my tribal passport for global citizenship.

In your Wisdom Journal, write down your "top ten" friends and role models. Then discuss your notion of family.

EQUAL-RIGHTS WISDOM

Our struggle today is not to have a female Einstein get appointed as an assistant professor. It is for a woman schlemiel to get as quickly promoted as a male schlemiel.

–Bella Abzug (1920–1998)

I was living in Chicago during the years when the Equal Rights Amendment failed to be ratified by the required two-thirds of the fifty states. Illinois was one of the holdouts. As a result more and more national conferences forsook Chicago, a big convention center because of its location and excellent facilities, and rebooked in pro-ERA states. The National Conference on Higher Education was a case in point. Every year I could attend it on the cheap by taking public transportation to the Conrad Hilton. Now I had to scramble for money to fly to D.C. or San Francisco and stay at the conference hotel.

Actually, when I moved from Germany to Chicago in 1973 to become director of program development at an innovative state university, I didn't find out till afterward that the internal finalist for the job was the coordinator of the women's studies program. Members of that program, and others, had protested the naming of an outsider and a male to the position. What made the situation especially tricky was that the women's studies program fell within my administrative responsibility. Fortunately I was genuinely interested in furthering women's studies, and my unsuccessful rival proved a good sport. So things worked out, and in the end we became supportive colleagues to each other.

Equal rights may be a long time in coming. With children of the same father and mother frequently unable to get along, how in the world will strangers who look, think, and talk differently ever be able to collaborate and regard one another as members of a single harmonious family? Moreover, we have so many areas of difference to overcome: gender, race, ethnicity, religion, age, sexual preference, appearance, socio-economic background, interest, talent, and genetic makeup, among others. When will all schlemiels be created equal? When will that amendment be passed? Nonetheless, progress has been made.

Discuss in your Wisdom Journal the extent to which life has improved for groups other than white Christian males.

SMALL-FAMILY WISDOM

"Home is the place where, when you have to go there,
They have to take you in."

-ROBERT FROST (1874–1963), "THE DEATH OF THE HIRED MAN"

In this well-known Frost poem, Silas, a seasonal worker at Mary and Warren's New England farm, arrives unannounced one day. Mary intuits that he has come home to die. "Home?" Everyone – even a vagabond – she believes, has to have some place to go, some safe haven, a home.

If you have read even a dozen of these daily meditations, you'll know that I am an internationalist, even a universalist. Just about everything I write argues for breaking the bonds of all narrow restrictiveness. So, if one of my main points is the wisdom of the broad view and inclusiveness, why am I talking about "small-family wisdom"?

Last night I ran into someone I hadn't seen for a year. A chef by trade but also a skilled photographer, he had given up chef work to start a freelance photography business. He had some flurries of intense activity, but low-paying jobs and deadbeat clients in Hawaii's poor economy kept him from success. He was, frankly, at his wit's end and depressed to boot. At this point his older sister in California, whom he hadn't spoken with for three years, researched his whereabouts and called up. She and her husband had just won a trip to Hawaii and wanted to see him. During their visit the couple, who are fairly well off, invited my friend to come live with them in California for as long as he wanted. Business there was booming.

I believe in the wisdom of both the small family and the big family, the smallest and largest concepts of home. First we have to work on being at home within ourselves and bringing peace to the sometimes squabbling family members that comprise us. Then we need to reclaim our small biological family, whether it's the one we came from, the one we helped to found, or the one, like that of Silas, that just came to be ours. Finally we should join and actively participate in the great family of creation. Here, as in so many things, it's not a matter of either/or but both/and.

Write in your Wisdom Journal about the "small family" you call home.

SURGICAL WISDOM

With the help of a surgeon, he might yet recover and prove an ass.

-WILLIAM SHAKESPEARE, *A MIDSUMMER NIGHT'S DREAM*, V, I, 318

My first surgery occurred in March 1945. The war in Europe was ending. But for me, at age five, the big news was, I was having my tonsils out. My parents promised ice cream when the operation was over, and for some reason I insisted that the surgeon bring me my tonsils in a bottle. (He did.) All I remember of the operation is the doctors putting a big, black plungerlike device over my nose and mouth and asking me to count backward from ten. I think I got to seven. My throat was very sore afterward, but I did get my ice cream, and my parents brought me my favorite book: *The Little Engine That Could* – the edition illustrated by Lois Lenski.

My next surgery did not occur till last summer, at age 58. My gum had developed an infection above two molars that had already had root canals. The only treatment was to make an incision in the gum, drill holes into the roots of the teeth, then drain, disinfect, and refill the area before sewing the incision shut. All this sounded perfectly awful. Because it would be accomplished with a local anesthetic, I asked for and received a sedative to keep me calm. The Valium worked, and the operation passed for me without incident – even when I got my first-ever stitches.

The next challenge occurred a few weeks ago. What I thought were dirty glasses turned out to be a fast-growing cataract in my right eye. Basically I was going blind. Fortunately the ophthalmologist could work me in quickly. This time I was worrying about an incision in my eye, another operation with a local and a sedative, and my first-ever intravenous needle. Maybe it was the army of folks praying for me, maybe the great operating room crew, but the whole experience was pleasant, I was calm enough to sleep during the pre-op period, and the light show during the surgery was incredible. Now I am delighted to have 20/20 vision in my right eye – and no cloudy glasses.

It is good to have recovered – time will tell what I will prove.

In your Wisdom Journal, describe a surgical experience you have had and how it has changed you.

ALIEN WISDOM

Your galactic brothers and sisters, known collectively as the Galactic Brotherhood, are here to help prepare you for the Shift. You haven't been able to detect them yet, for the most part, but they are already here.

–Fred Sterling, *Kirael – The Great Shift,* 1998

Don't get scared. I am not about to launch into an exposé of my encounters with extraterrestrials. If the Galactic Brotherhood is here, I for one haven't been introduced. Should they be around, I am happy to know they are my brothers and sisters. I am sick and tired of all the supremely powerful cosmic bozos our *fin de siècle* imagination has cooked up. I am ready for some nice space guys for a change.

What I have in mind is a matter closer to home: the wisdom from other, especially non-Western, cultures. I understood as a child that when someone asserted that their team or city or country or whatever was best, the judgment had more to do with the fact that it was theirs than with intrinsic worth. As a kid in New York City, I listened to the "Horn and Hardart Hour" on the radio. (Horn and Hardart owned a chain of restaurants called the Automat, a unique New York invention, long gone: You put coins into a slot next to a little window, then opened the window to take your meal – an automated cafeteria.) Anyway, every Saturday morning you could count on a feud between Miss Brooklyn and Miss Bronx. Each knew her borough was best and would not mince words to put the other down. It was verbal Punch and Judy.

Fortunately institutions like the East-West Center in Hawaii, the Oasis Center in Chicago, the Asian Institute in New York, and the Naropa Institute in Boulder, Colorado, make it easier for us Westerners to learn some "alien" wisdom. In addition, dozens of gurus impart their techniques for spiritual development. The dangers, of course, are that we might romanticize the exotic other, or get involved with an unscrupulous cult. As William James advised a hundred years ago, we need to balance the will to believe with the will to disbelieve. Come to think of it, balance is a chief characteristic of wisdom.

In your Wisdom Journal, write about a significant experience where you learned some wisdom from an "alien" source.

BACK-TO-BASICS WISDOM

May you have warmth in your igloo, oil in your lamp, and peace in your heart.

–AN ESKIMO PROVERB

We don't need very much really. Shelter, light, and peace – and another, or others, to share them with. The Eskimo proverb implies a second person, the one who is making the wish. "The same to you" is the obvious response.

Many of us have lost our regard for the simple but important things of life. Growing older fortunately builds in this appreciation. As our bodies begin to function less smoothly, we are grateful for each good night's sleep or well-digested meal. When you are over fifty, the doctor begins to ask you questions like, "How often do you get up at night?" It is taken for granted that you will.

Life can be cold and hard. Having a place of our own that is not only physically but psychologically comforting – a home, not just a house or an apartment – is a great blessing. Being able to return to this nest after work for rest and recovery makes going out the next day possible.

To be supplied with the necessary provisions – oil in our lamps – is a blessing too. Not to be in want and thus in the dark is very important for living. When a cataract developed in my right eye, turning everything into a white blur, I could no longer take light and vision for granted. Thank goodness for the new outpatient surgery that saves millions of people, myself included, from blindness.

Most important is peace in our hearts. Being a competitive person, I have always liked to win. As I get older, however, I am no longer so interested in moving heaven and Earth to be right. Serenity has come to replace the winner's circle in my scheme of things. Give-and-take, especially with my wife and children, now seems more important than winning. Letting go of that old imperative has made it easier for others to live with me and for me to live with myself – a basic of basics. Like much else, the source of peace is within.

What basics would you like to get back to in your life? Write briefly on this topic in your Wisdom Journal.

THE WISDOM TO FACE MISFORTUNES

Yield not to misfortunes but press forward the more boldly in their face.

–VIRGIL (70–19 B.C.E.), *AENEID*, VI, 95

Commercial airline pilots have always impressed me. Not only do they know how to make those big, heavy machines of theirs take off and land, but they keep them moving toward their destination whether they experience bumps along the way or not. In my periods of fearful flying, I would think, "Why don't the pilots do whatever it takes to find smoother air?" They most likely do try, within limits. In any case a more reasonable voice inside my head would usually respond, "There is only so much fuel on board, not enough for taking long detours just because you are afraid of turbulence."

Clearly pilots know the tolerance of their planes to the "bumps in the road," as a fearful-flier handbook I once read put it. Given their knowledge, the best way around – with the exception of thunderstorms – is almost always straight through. Sit back, relax, and don't worry about those periodic yaws and dips. In pilot talk, "it's just a little light chop."

I do distinguish between *misfortunes*, or episodes of turbulence in our lives, and *catastrophe*. It's hard to keep going if something really major occurs. But even then we do well to follow the encouraging commonplace that "where there's life, there's hope." Yielding ground is one thing. Running away or giving up altogether is something else.

Life is filled with turbulence, from mild to severe. A frequent flier, I am still around – a fact that shows turbulence to be a natural occurrence to be faced and gotten through, not a catastrophic danger. (There are also plenty of flights that are smooth from start to finish.)

Wisdom indicates that we should face the obstacles in our lives and keep going. Virgil's Trojan hero, Aeneas, overcame his and, according to legend, founded Rome. Courage and perseverance will help us to achieve our life's mission as well.

Give an example in your Wisdom Journal of a time you faced and successfully negotiated misfortune, or when it defeated and derailed you. Either way, what lessons do you derive?

THE WISDOM OF WATCHFULNESS

Watchful amongst the unwatchful, awake amongst those who sleep, the wise man like a swift horse runs his race, outrunning those who are slow.

–THE DHAMMAPADA

The journey from darkness to light, known as the process of enlightenment, is often described as an awakening. The Sufis, mystics of Islam, speak about the three states of being asleep, aware, and awake. From a spiritual perspective, most of us are fast asleep. Some few are aware of another, more conscious state toward which they are striving. Finally, a very small number are awake.

Being asleep, per se, is not a bad thing. Unfortunately we are given to sleepwalking, a practice that endangers both ourselves and others. Knowing where we are, where we are going, and where the obstacles lie is essential for reaching our goal as human beings. We have to be attentive and fully conscious to be able to discern what is really important from that which only appears so.

"Sleepers awake!" comes the call in the Kol Nidre service for the Jewish Day of Atonement, Yom Kippur. Jesus rebukes his disciples on the evening of his arrest for having fallen asleep during the time they should have remained awake to join in his vigil.

G. I. Gurdjieff, a Russian mystic, thought the bulk of humanity were automatons preprogrammed by their culture, religion, nationality, age, gender, and profession. Living in their personality and not their essence, sleepwalking humanity needed a kind of shock therapy, he believed, to wake them up to their real identities and missions in life. Using a variety of techniques, like having people walk at speeds different from their usual pace or perform complex movements, Gurdjieff tried to get people to self-remember. My personal favorite was his assigning aristocratic British ladies to dig up a dead tree trunk using fine silver teaspoons.

Chuang-tze, the Taoist philosopher, once posed the question: "Am I Chuang-tze dreaming he is a butterfly, or a butterfly dreaming he is Chuang-tze?" The only way to find out, presumably, is to wake up.

Change your route home, begin to shave on the other side of your face, or write with your "wrong" hand. Comment in your Wisdom Journal on what you learned from the experience.

THE WISDOM OF USING YOUR GIFTS

The glorious gifts of the gods may not be cast aside.

-Homer (9th–8th? century B.C.E.), *Iliad*, III, 65

Anyone reading these words has received at least two glorious gifts: life and talent. The more important one is life. Yet because it is so much of a given, life frequently gets taken for granted. Suicide is only the most obvious way of casting life aside. By rushing around, getting bogged down in trivia, frequently losing our temper, neglecting our health, starving our relationships, and avoiding the basic questions of living, we also misspend our limited time on the planet. The results, while less dramatic, are almost as deadly.

Identifying, then using our talent challenges us in another way. The main problem is discovering who we uniquely are. Everyone, I am convinced, has talent. Sometimes parents or teachers will recognize and foster it in us while we are young. Sometimes others decide, because of outside factors like family tradition, race, gender, or socioeconomic status, that we should do work for which we have limited or no talent. Sometimes in our desire for wealth or financial security, we ourselves choose a line of work that lies far from our interests or abilities. We go in for computer studies or get an MBA just because everyone says there are lots of well-paying jobs for people with these backgrounds.

How to know what our true talents are? The late anthropologist Joseph Campbell's advice to "follow our bliss" is still pertinent. When we do something that is easy and fun for us and people say we have a flare for it, this is generally a sign of talent. Talent, to be sure, needs to be cultivated, directed, and refined. Having a nice voice doesn't mean we are ready for the Met. And failing to strengthen our abilities, once identified, is also a minor form of casting them aside. Clearly, though, respecting the gifts of life and talent is a good way, in the words of Star Trek's Mr. Spock, to "live long and prosper."

What do you consider to be your main talent or talents? In your Wisdom Journal, explain why you think so and how you have applied it or them thus far in your life.

THE WISDOM OF LISTENING UP

Best is the man who can himself advise;
He too is good who hearkens to the wise;
But who, himself being witless, will not heed
Another's wisdom, is worthless indeed.

–HESIOD, AROUND 720 B.C.E.

Danny Kaye, comic extraordinaire, had some great lines. Most of them someone once told me were penned by his wife, Sylvia Fein. One of my favorites goes: "He was beside himself. His favorite position!"

Being beside yourself was not good. It meant you were very, very angry. Better hold your breath, count to ten, and start over. According to a Dutch proverb, anger is a short madness. I remember, as a child, having occasional bouts of this madness. I felt like a volcano about to explode. My parents would become concerned and, it seemed to me, even a little scared. In the midst of everything, I felt the taste of power. His majesty the child had arrived.

Talking to yourself was also not good. Some comics like Lou Costello would do it in the Saturday afternoon movies. It meant you were crazy. But even worse was hearing voices–and answering them. Then you were really nuts. They would toss you into the loony bin and throw away the key. Of course Joan of Arc, who was really Ingrid Bergman and very beautiful with her pageboy haircut, heard voices and even followed their direction. And she became a saint. But look at the cost. She was burnt at the stake. Forget voices!

But whoa! There are voices and there are voices. There is the still, small voice of conscience. There is our own inner voice, like the one Socrates had, which warned him against saying or doing something that would be wrong. There is my mother's voice telling me to wear rubbers when it rains. There is the voice of reason. There is the voice of intuition. There is even my wife's voice, which has been wrong far fewer times than I care to admit. "Listen up" is the vaguely military phrase invoked these days. Not bad advice.

Think about the voices you hear inside your head. What do they tell you? Do you accept or reject them? To what effect? Respond to these questions in your Wisdom Journal.

THE WISDOM OF UPOD

Our chief defect is that we are more given to talking about things than to doing them.

–Jawaharlal Nehru (1889–1964)

UPOD is not a federal agency, a creature with unusual feet, nor a phenomenon that might be featured on the Science Fiction Network. Rather, it's an acronym for something I don't do often enough and would like to do more: Under-Promise and Over-Deliver.

In my one-man campaign to save the universe, I fall victim again and again to OPUD, the mirror-image of UPOD. I Over-Promise and Under-Deliver. Trying to cram too many activities into my life, I invariably leave late for appointments and arrive full of apologetic chagrin. By taking on too much, I sacrifice quality of work or quality of life. In this context I have finally concluded why I resent my wife's daily ritual of watching one particular soap opera. (I work at home, so I know when those grains of sand start falling through the hourglass of time.) It's not that the show is a waste of time or even that it is riddled with clichés of language and behavior. No. It is because she has the leisure to do something for no other reason than that she enjoys it, while I am working night and day.

Taking on too much, even for good reasons, is bound to backfire sooner or later. Bills don't get paid on time. Pets don't get their shots when they should. The computer's electronic desktop doesn't get rebuilt monthly, as the manual recommends, and the Mac starts doing weird things. Worst of all, when you are in overload, someone – generally a family member – reminds you with the best intentions to take those negatives in for reprints so you can mail out duplicates to all your friends. That's when you lose it. Forget about years of meditation. Forget about your promise not to get angry during Lent. Forget everything. "How in the world can I take those blankety-blank negatives in when I haven't even begun our income taxes, which are due next week?!" But don't worry. From now on things will be different. I'll refuse to get sucked in. I promise.

Should you be joining me in Over-Promisers Anonymous (OPA)? Consider this question in your Wisdom Journal.

THE WISDOM OF BEING QUIETLY ACTIVE AND ACTIVELY QUIET

We must learn to be still in the midst of activity and to be vibrantly alive in repose.

–INDIRA GANDHI (1917–1984)

This paradox strikes me as particularly "Eastern." For us in the West, you are either active or passive. Maybe being "vibrantly active in repose" is conceivable. Anyone who can't fall asleep would understand this concept, though they might not use the adverb *vibrantly*. But to be "still in the midst of activity" – that takes some getting used to.

I finally understood this idea one day while playing tennis. My best shots always seemed to come when I stopped thinking about what I would do next and just freed my body to respond. The worst shots came when I tried to apply something new, some pointer from a lesson, say. The mind would get in the way of the body, with bad language often the result. On the other hand, through practice and visualization, the body eventually makes the new stroke its own. Then you find yourself applying backspin, for example, at just the right time.

I don't mean to denigrate thinking. However, the Zen concept of one-pointedness suggests that it is better to think, then act, rather than trying to act while thinking. Do the latter, and both thought and action suffer. The worst is to act while worrying. Worrying is a nonproductive activity that corrodes heart and mind alike while robbing us of the energy to function. Worrying is comparable to spinning the wheels of a car on ice. The friction wears down the tire tread while the car refuses to budge.

In the "To Be or Not to Be" soliloquy, Hamlet describes how when we are puzzled among contradictory options, "resolution / Is sicklied o'er with the pale cast of thought, / And enterprises of great pith and moment / lose the name of action" (III, i, 56). Think, decide, then act seems to be the way of wisdom. In this context Indira Gandhi's advice makes total sense.

Practice one-pointedness by doing some manual activity like sewing or weeding. Do not think about anything except what you are doing. Describe the experience in your Wisdom Journal.

WISDOM AND THE MIDDLE WAY

To those who choose the path that leads to Enlightenment, there are two extremes that should be carefully avoided. First, there is the extreme of indulgence in the desires of the body. Second, there is the opposite extreme of ascetic discipline, torturing one's body and mind unreasonably.

–*THE TEACHING OF BUDDHA*, BUKKYO DENDO KYOKAI EDITION

My late mother, who lived to be ninety-five, must have been a secret Buddhist. She always counseled me, with only moderate success, to take it easy. During my year in Germany, I remember reading a history of Greece. The one thing I recall is that the Greeks made the Golden Mean their ideal precisely because of their tendency to be immoderate. Their desire to run with Dionysus, the Profligate, was balanced by the presence of Apollo, the Lawgiver.

Chinese medicine is based on a similar concept. Yin and yang, the complementary forces in the universe, must remain in dynamic balance. If one becomes too yin or too yang, illness results. All foods are arrayed on the yin-yang spectrum. Practitioners of Chinese traditional medicine prescribe diets according to which force in you has gotten out of line.

Aristotle's ethics are also based on the middle way. The classic example is courage. For Aristotle, courage falls midway between its own excess and deficiency. If you have too much, you'll be foolhardy; too little, a coward.

Come to think of it, the wisdom of the middle way is instilled into us as children by the story of Goldilocks and the Three Bears. Remember when Goldilocks tries to sit down in the Bear family's sitting room, she finds one chair too hard (Papa Bear's), one chair too soft (Mama Bear's), and one chair "just right" (Baby Bear's). So it goes also with their food portions and beds. We learn from childhood on to look for situations, clothing, friends, partners, houses, and work lives that are "just right," which is usually somewhere between the extremes.

Much of the world's religious history is based on spiritual development through extreme ascetic practices. Fortunately the Buddha brought a measure of moderation to spiritual training.

How balanced is your life? Write briefly in your Wisdom Journal of how well you adhere to the middle way.

THE WISDOM OF LEARNING BY DOING

One must learn
By doing the thing; for though you
think you know it
You have no certainty, until you try.

–SOPHOCLES (496?–406 B.C.E.), *TRACHINIAE*

Most college professors never learn to teach until they have jobs. Future school teachers are required to take a practicum course and do a year of student teaching, but those preparing for the professoriate simply learn the subject matter. If they know and love it, the prevailing logic holds, they will be able to teach it. So, aside from an experience of correcting some senior professor's undergraduate papers, graduate students learn to teach on the job.

Come to think of it, many of life's important functions are learned, if at all, by doing them. Living with others, raising children, and managing time and money come to mind. No school I am aware of teaches relating or parenting or time and money management. We are left to learn from the good and bad examples in our lives. So, children of divorce tend to divorce. Abused kids tend to abuse kids. My father would max out all his many credit cards, and I have to watch myself like a hawk not to do the same. But we can also find and follow good examples, join parent-effectiveness training groups, read self-help books, and consult financial planners.

For better or worse, life is like that. Our second daughter certainly profited from the mistakes we made in raising her older sister. Too bad we couldn't have had a parent-training simulator, much like the flight simulators pilots and astronauts use, to learn parenting skills before we had to apply them to real children. The Hindu and Buddhist religions are both based on the concept of sequential rebirth–to give each soul the time it needs to learn all the lessons of human existence. Later relationships are in many instances (though not always) better than earlier ones, as are business ventures. The wisdom here is to realize that while to err is human, to forgive ourselves, learn our lessons, and do better next time is divine.

In your Wisdom Journal, describe an example from your life in which you learned something important by doing it.

THE WISDOM OF FRUGALITY

RULE 1 for becoming wealthy: Live well below your means.

–Thomas J. Stanley and William D. Danko,
The Millionaire Next Door, 1999 Calendar

At this stage of my life, I have few regrets. I do have one, though. I have not learned to live well below my means. As a matter of fact, I have tended to live at the extremes of my means and sometimes just beyond. In this I am like my father, except with fewer credit cards. He in turn was like his father, Grandpa Paul, a wonderful Zorba-like character who, in a time before credit cards, found other ways to spend money he didn't have.

Grandpa Paul arrived in this country in the 1890s from Rumania. He worked at a variety of jobs. At one point he recruited an African American female singer in Chicago, taught her to sing Yiddish songs, and made her the headliner in his traveling Yiddish vaudeville company. While the company was reasonably successful, Grandpa Paul had wanted more. In Scranton, unfortunately, he passed a few bad checks, and my father and uncle had to make good on them, then bail him out of jail. This episode ended Grandpa's career as an impresario.

My father never had any run-ins with the law. But his desire to live the life of a successful American caused him to max out a whole collection of credit cards. Calls from bill collectors became a regular event in our house. I vowed to avoid that plague, and I have. Where I have been less successful is at living consistently below my means and salting away ten or fifteen percent a month in a family endowment fund. My share of the kids' education is paid for, I rationalize. I even "pay myself first." Then when all the bills can't be covered, I have to take that money back from myself. So we face the years leading to retirement and beyond without a whole lot in the financial cupboard, and I regret not having made different commitments starting thirty-five years ago.

Reflect on your financial stewardship. Do you live well within your means? What might you do differently to improve your future finances? Respond briefly in your Wisdom Journal.

THE WISDOM OF MANNA FROM HEAVEN

The LORD said to Moses, "I will rain down bread from heaven for you. Each day the people shall go out and gather a day's supply, so that I can put them to the test and see whether they will follow my instructions or not."

-Exodus 16:4-5

A main theme of the Bible is, God will take care of you. A related theme is, you will be tested. I have experienced both.

After getting fired from a university vice presidency in 1990, I had a little more than a year to find another job. Actually, I felt certain I would find another job within the allotted time. After all, I had been an academic dean for nine years, an academic vice president for nearly three, and now was serving as assistant to the chancellor for international programs. I had published articles, presented widely, consulted, and had academic colleagues all over the country.

There is not much room at the top, though. A typical search would attract 150 or more candidates. I generally made the semifinals and was a finalist three or four times. In one case, for a small-college presidency, it came down to one other person and me. After two weeks I got the bad news. "You should be proud," the man said. "There were 250 candidates, and you came in second!" "Right!" I thought. "I would have done as well by finishing 249th."

After a year or so, I still had no job. My wife had spent years caring for her invalid mother. The earning side was up to me. So I became a consultant, writing grants and raising funds for nonprofits. I also taught courses, wrote a book, took out and repaid loans, did whatever was necessary. Somehow we survived. It was scary, though. Periodically I would ask God, "Will we still be in our house for Christmas?" One day God said to me, "Reynold, when was the last time I let you down?" I was stopped. "Never," I said. "Okay then. Quit worrying and just get on with it." I still worry, of course, but I am better about it. Experience is a stern master but a good teacher.

Write in your Wisdom Journal what you have learned from your hard times.

WEEDY WISDOM

What is a weed? A plant whose virtues have not yet been discovered.

–Ralph Waldo Emerson (1803–1882), "Fortune of the Republic"

In recent years the West has rediscovered the benefits of herbal medicine. "Rediscovered," because our grandparents and their ancestors used all kinds of household nostrums harvested from humble weeds. Nowadays these medicines come from the Orient or the world's indigenous peoples. Let's hope those folks are harvesting some hard currency for themselves from "our" latest breakthroughs.

To name, of course, is to pre-judge. To call something a weed is to pronounce it worthless, disposable, perhaps even malignant. "Why, that's just a weed" gives us permission to cast something aside. This is far from a harmless tendency: Names like *Jude, Zigeuner,* and *Behinderte*–Jew, Gypsy, Handicapped Person–gave similar "permission to dispose" to the weeders of Hitler's Germany.

The opening lines of the Tao Te Ching counsel, "The Tao you can name isn't the real Tao." Similarly, Jewish seers in biblical times understood that God was ultimately unnamable, and writing out the name we use for the Ultimate Reality was a way of taking it in vain.

Creativity seminars often use the puzzle of connecting nine dots, arrayed in three parallel rows, with four connected straight lines. The trick is to go outside the box created by the array of dots. Consequently, the phrase *going outside the box* has become familiar in problem-solving circles.

The cultures of family, ethnicity, profession, religion, and generation create boxes. A culture is a self-contained shelter and, as such, useful. As linguistic philosopher Benjamin Lee Whorf pointed out, language is the ultimate box. It delimits the very thoughts we can have. Consequently, learning another language–or at least learning to use our own language better–is an excellent way to get outside the box. Meanwhile we may widen our understanding if we refrain from calling anything "just a . . ." For, to paraphrase Emerson, "a weed may be a plant whose virtues *we* have not yet discovered."

In your Wisdom Journal, discuss some good, service, place, or person you once held in low regard but now consider worthwhile.

THE WISDOM OF CARING

We won't always know whose lives we touched and made better for our having cared, because actions can sometimes have unforeseen ramifications. What's important is that you do care and you act.

–CHARLOTTE LUNSFORD (B. 1931)

Not all popular movements are to be disdained. A recent one, spread by bumper stickers it seems, urges us to "do random acts of kindness." The phrasing no doubt stems from the random acts of violence that have become the staple shock-fare of the nightly news. The advice is meant to counterbalance such negative deeds.

Recently I have begun doing some fundraising for the Visitor Aloha Society of Hawaii, or VASH. VASH is a new nonprofit organization, barely two years old, that does nice things for tourists to Hawaii who have become victims of crime. (Given the six million visitors to Hawaii each year, the 4,000 reported crimes against them is minuscule, a mere .07 percent, or one crime for every 1,500 visitors.) In coordination with the agency, which itself receives referrals from the police department, hotels offer free accommodations, restaurants provide free meals, nightclubs give free tickets to shows, and so on, to victims of crime. The idea in our tourist-dependent state is to make sure crime victims leave Hawaii with the best possible impression.

In a less purposeful way, acts of caring are like seeds that can take root and become fruitful in others. Ultimately people – especially those younger or in lower authority positions than ourselves – need good examples. What we do or say can have a powerful effect on our children, spouses, partners, students, customers, even strangers encountered once. Many of us who teach have experienced alumni who comment on something we said or did in class that had a profound impact on them. Often we cannot remember the thing they tell us. One former student said to me, for example, "When I saw how much fun you were having in class, I decided to become a teacher." Of course, a hurtful word or a kindness withheld can traumatize people for life. Because it takes so little to care, or to be careful, it behooves us all to assimilate this wisdom in our daily living.

In your Wisdom Journal, describe the impact someone else's kindness has had on your life.

THE WISDOM OF THE NEW DAY

Tomorrow we again embark upon the boundless sea.

–HORACE (65–8 B.C.E.), *ODES*, I, VII, 32

Though "boundless," the sea is full of places to land if you can find them. Harbors abound in the boundless sea. Land ho!

Viewed from the moon, Earth is covered with a continuous splotch of blue. From that perspective, a person sees only one uninterrupted body of water. The only difference between the Atlantic and the Pacific is, literally, nominal. An invisible line runs from Tierra del Fuego, at the bottom of South America, to Antarctica. On one side is the Atlantic, on the other, the Pacific. Waves keep trying to erase this arbitrary boundary. But our mapmakers, representing civilization, keep drawing them right back in.

Sailors all, we awaken each day and embark on our renewed journey through life. I love the fact that in the first Old Testament Creation story, God created the world in stages, one day at a time. A night's sleep behind us, we arise refreshed, ready for the voyage ahead. Rise and shine! Up and at 'em!–which, as a child, I always took to mean, "Up and *Adam!*" In nautical lingo, we are all day sailors.

Horace's line can of course be understood negatively. In effect, life is futile. We have no destination. The sea is boundless, and, like Sisyphus with his boulder, we are required each day to sail out and return, regardless of wind and weather, with no mission, no cargo, no place else to go.

As a sailor, however, I can tell you that no two trips are ever alike. Wind, weather, current, and weight in the boat all change. New experiences foster new skills. Remembering similar situations, we respond with increased competence and confidence. Who knows? One day we may sail beyond the horizon and, like Columbus, discover brave new worlds.

When you wake up tomorrow, go outside, greet the morning, and ask for a blessing on the day trip on which you are about to embark. Before going to sleep at night, write briefly in your Wisdom Journal about the significant experiences of the "sail" just completed.

AFTERLIFE WISDOM

True philosophers make dying their profession, and . . . to them of all men death is least alarming. . . . Would they not naturally be glad to set out for the place where there is a prospect of attaining the object of their lifelong desire, which is Wisdom?

–Socrates, in Plato's *Phaedo*, early 4th century B.C.E.

Shortly before his death, Benjamin Franklin responded to the famous New England theologian Jonathan Edwards that he, Franklin, was unconcerned whether or not Jesus was truly the Son of God. After all, the sage of Philadelphia continued, he would soon have the opportunity to find out for himself.

We human beings have long consoled ourselves that if death was the great kidnapper, taking us away from everything familiar, it was also the great clarifier. For in the afterlife we would come to know reality not through a glass darkly but face-to-face. We would find answers to all the basic questions: Is there a God? Is Christianity (or any other belief system) the true religion? Do we meet up again with departed friends and relatives? Do we really go on trial, as it were, for the life just concluded? Are we rewarded or punished with heaven or hell? Is there a halfway house along the lines of purgatory? Does reincarnation exist, and will we have to be born again? Do we learn the truth about life in other worlds and dimensions? Are we put to work in the afterlife, or is it one long holiday?

In the epilogue to the *Republic*, Plato speculates that when we die, we do get the desired answers, we will be reborn, and – in crossing the River Lethe to re-enter the land of the living – we forget virtually all that we knew prior to rebirth. Nonetheless, he and his fictionalized spokesperson, Socrates, advocate neither suicide nor a life of thoughtlessness. We should seek wisdom here and now even if the final answers are contained in the sealed envelope of death. There is still plenty of wisdom on Earth for those willing to look.

Discuss your view of the afterlife in your Wisdom Journal.

SINGLE-POINTED WISDOM

Put all your eggs in the one basket and – WATCH THAT BASKET.

–MARK TWAIN, *PUDD'NHEAD WILSON*, 1894

Single-pointedness" is a Zen technique. It means to focus all your attention on what you are doing at the moment. If I am writing these words, I shouldn't be thinking about paying the bills or what I plan to wear tonight. I should simply be writing. Hypnotists use the same technique when they intone: "Concentrate on my voice. Listen only to what I am saying. . . ."

Back in the late sixties, when Zen was big on university campuses, I remember a visit by a Zen master to the experimental college where I was teaching. During the question period, someone asked, "What guidance does Zen have to help a person stop smoking?" "Easy," our speaker responded. "When you smoke, all you should do is smoke. Don't talk, think, read a book, or watch TV. Only smoke. If you follow this regimen for a week, you'll find it harder and harder to keep smoking and will eventually stop. Or else you will have a *satori* [spiritual breakthrough]." When asked why this technique might work, he explained that single-pointedness helps one determine which activities are valuable for an individual. Smoking, he allowed, was too weak a vehicle to hold our attention for such a span of time. Yet if it somehow could, it would bring us to a point where we would no longer need to smoke.

Zen single-pointedness goes against the Western value that suggests that the more things we can do at a time, the more accomplished we are. A paragon in this regard is the old-fashioned one-man band or, more recently, the working single mom, forced to make the most of her twenty-four hours. On the other hand, we consider people oafs who cannot "walk and chew gum at the same time." In this regard, the story goes that when Henry David Thoreau was in the final stages of dying, someone asked if he had glimpsed the other world yet. He responded, "One world at a time."

Try washing the dishes or doing another mechanical activity without thinking about anything else. Comment on the experience in your Wisdom Journal.

SELF-LOVE WISDOM

One who is in love with himself has at least this advantage – he won't encounter many rivals.

–GEORG C. LICHTENBERG, FROM THE INTERNET

Self-love is an official no-no in our culture. The Judeo-Christian position is epitomized in the ultimate self-sacrifice preached by Jesus in one of the farewell discourses to his disciples: "There is no greater love than this, that a man should lay down his life for his friends" (John 15:13). We all struggle against our innate selfishness by little bits of behavior, like filling another's glass, allowing someone else to go first, and so on. Similarly, we scold children for jockeying for parental favors, starting to eat before everyone has been served, or snatching a toy from a playmate.

A good deal of the political criticism of the free-market economy is based on a particular understanding of the Judeo-Christian ethic. To critics, business seems dedicated to mammon, the god of the bottom line and the almighty dollar. The socialist slogan, "From each according to their ability; to each according to their needs" sounds much less selfish and more "Christian."

Market economics assumes the basic acquisitiveness of human nature and attempts to refine it by requiring my gain to be achieved by giving you goods or services you want. I don't rob you; I trade with you. In this way, both our self-interests are met. Ideally the market economy is set up as a win-win mechanism to reconcile self-interests.

For the purpose of this essay, I am assuming that we all should be selfish in the best sense of the word. We have a self – planted in us by God – and it is our job to cultivate it and make it fruitful. This kind of self-cultivation is the true and most basic act of loving ourselves. Indeed, until we begin seeing the evidence of our gardening, we are hard to love by anyone but God. The fruitful tree has many visitors. The barren one gets the ax. Most significantly, if we are called on to love our neighbors as ourselves, what happens if we hate ourselves? Loving our true self by cultivating it may just be the ultimate act of charity.

How well do you get along with yourself? Write on this topic in your Wisdom Journal.

THE WISE TEACHER

The teacher who walks in the shadow of the temple, among his followers, gives not of his wisdom but rather of his faith and his lovingness.

If he is indeed wise he does not bid you enter the house of his wisdom, but rather leads you to the threshold of your own mind.

–Kahlil Gibran, *The Prophet,* 1923

Wisdom, like the Kingdom of heaven, lies within each of us. In many cases it is an undiscovered country, not yet on our maps. We may be afraid to set forth on our voyage of discovery, discontented with our old life but not yet ready for something else. The world may just be flat after all, with no new continent at the other end of the sea.

Obstetricians and midwives wisely wait for women to go into labor before setting to work. Taking a baby out before it is ready may put both mother and child at risk. Alas, we educators – and parents – induce labor all the time, forcing children to learn this or do that before their time. Then, if we have a family tradition of attending a particular college or entering a specific profession, our children better get ready to go there and become that. Family businesses often fail because the founder's only child, with little talent and less inclination, is forced to take over.

The wise teacher understands that each human being is his or her own school, his or her own temple. Gibran's mention of *temple* is important, because the teaching function is sacred and must be undertaken with due regard that wherever learning takes place is holy ground. It is not accidental that the Hebrew *rabbi* and Sanskrit *guru* both mean "teacher." Whether, when, and how we learn are mysteries. As teachers we can share knowledge and techniques with our students. At our best, though, we share ourselves by being who we are and doing what we do. Example along with experience is the best teacher. When we show kindness, love, and respect, our students are encouraged to learn from themselves. Learning, said Jean Piaget, is discovery. Land ho!

In your Wisdom Journal, recount an instance when you learned something significant "from yourself."

THE WISDOM OF VISUALIZATION

You have been endowed with the capacity and power to create desirable pictures within and to find them automatically printed in the outer world of your environment.

Picture yourself as winning, and that alone will contribute immeasurably to your success. . . . Your imagination allows you to create your future.

—Will Sherwood's "Your Daily Motivation" listserv, August 20, 1998

Was it Super Bowl XX that the Chicago Bears finally won? We were invited to a doctor's house to share the experience. They had televisions in every room, even the bathrooms. No need to miss a play.

As a long-time Chicago resident who had struggled through many a lackluster season with the Bears, I was ready for the killer defense keynoted by the Fridge, together with the offense led by Jim McMahon and Walter Payton, to finally do the Second City proud. I was not disappointed. Nor were the citizens of Chicago.

In the hype leading up to the game, we learned that Jim McMahon, a brilliant quarterback when he was on, had been undergoing extensive training in visualization. He would see himself having plenty of time in the pocket, he would visualize the receivers being just where they should be, he would find at least one of them open, he would throw the perfect spiral pass into waiting hands, he would see his teammate enter the end zone standing, the ball securely tucked away. Whatever he did worked. That Super Bowl was a great day for McMahon, the Bears, and Chicagoans everywhere.

Shakti Gawain, the late José Silva, and others have written and sold many books proclaiming the power of visualization. I myself have not tested or availed myself of its potential but know a number of people who have. At the very least, if seeing things go badly and being routinely pessimistic about outcomes can poison possibilities, it is logical that creating positive images of something one is about to do can inspire positive results. Checking out the power of prior visualization is on my to-do list. What do you think?

If you have experience with visualizing results as a way to attain them, write about it in your Wisdom Journal.

SAINTLY WISDOM

Stimmen, stimmen. Höre, mein Herz, wie sonst nur
Heilige hörten: daß sie der riesige Ruf
aufhob vom Boden; sie aber knieten,
Unmögliche, weiter und achtetens nicht:
So waren sie hörend. . . .
Voices, voices. Listen, my heart, as only
Saints once listened. When the gigantic Call
Raised them off the floor, they, the Impossible Ones,
Kept right on kneeling and didn't even notice.
That's how much they were listening.

–RAINER MARIA RILKE (1875–1926), "FIRST DUINO ELEGY"
(AUTHOR'S TRANSLATION)

The German verb *hören* means "to hear" or "to listen." It also means "to obey." The latter intent is found primarily in the adjective *hörig*. A *höriger Mensch* is an obedient person.

The story of Satan and his rebellious angels highlights, by way of contrast, a chief characteristic of angels (and saints): obedience. To hear is to obey. They listen to God's voice and follow orders. Guardian angels whisper in our ear when we are about to go off track. They may just be that "still, small voice" usually ascribed to our conscience or inner self.

Saintly wisdom is not about knowledge but behavior. Saints know enough to listen to God's voice and follow what they hear. For most of us, of course, it's not so easy. We hear lots of voices. How to discriminate among them and do the right thing? History is full of false messiahs who led themselves and their people astray. State institutions likewise have their quota of people who regularly hear God's voice. Jesus as Emmanuel, God-with-us, showed us the way. In the Garden of Gethsemane, just before his arrest, he prayed for guidance. As our human brother, he said, in effect, "Look, I would just as soon not die, especially in the way I am likely to." Then he added what I call the Great Nevertheless: "If it be possible, let this cup pass from me; nevertheless not as I will, but as thou wilt" (Matthew 26:39, KJV). Learning to listen to and follow not self-will, peer pressure, or the current fashion, but that still, small voice–that is the way of saintly wisdom.

How well can you hear and follow your still, small voice? Share an example or two with your Wisdom Journal.

TIGHTWAD WISDOM

The quickest way to double your money is to fold it over and put it back in your pocket.

–An old cowboy saying

You can increase your money in three ways: up your income, shrink your outflow, or do both at the same time. I come from a family that emphasized approach number one. My father really knew how to make money. As a commodities broker, he came out a winner no matter how his clients fared. He was paid a commission for every trade he completed. Whether his clients bought or sold, cleaned up or lost their shirts, Dad got his percentage. Over his many years on the Board of Trade and the Merc, he did very well. Most folks thought he was loaded.

In reality he only *seemed* loaded. He bought like a prince and spent like a king. An early aficionado of credit cards, he had them all and used them generously. He was not selfish. We all benefited from his largesse. Problem was, his expenditures outpaced his income, and his lifestyle remained on a high level regardless of cash flow. Credit cards bridged the gap, not always with happy results. Dad was no gambler, an occasional day at the races or a foray to Vegas notwithstanding. But he was also not a cowboy. He never doubled his money by folding it and returning it to his wallet.

A case can be made for the conservative approach to wealth creation. According to Drs. Stanley and Danko, authors of the 1996 best-seller *The Millionaire Next Door,* many U.S. millionaires are invisible because of habitual thriftiness learned early. Money doesn't get spent. It gets saved and conservatively invested. As a result more than a few Americans become millionaires despite relatively modest incomes. They simply never look like millionaires. The Bible, to be sure, is no friend of tightwads. In Matthew 25:14–30, the servant who buries the bag of gold his master entrusts to him rather than investing it like his colleagues is punished. Maybe the answer is to be a spendthrift tightwad – or an urban cowboy.

Discuss in your Wisdom Journal where you fall on the tightwad-spendthrift spectrum. Where would you like to be?

THE WISDOM OF ASSOCIATING WITH REMARKABLE PEOPLE

As a definition of who may be considered . . . remarkable, I will simply say . . . he can be called a remarkable man who stands out from those around him by the resourcefulness of his mind, and who knows how to be restrained in the manifestations which proceed from his nature, at the same time conducting himself justly and tolerantly towards the weaknesses of others.

–G. I. Gurdjieff (d. 1949), *Meetings with Remarkable Men*

I first encountered Gurdjieff and his program for harmonious human development in 1960. My friend Raymond, a philosophical taxi driver of German parentage, had long been involved in a local Gurdjieff group. We would meet at the Bon Ton Café on Chicago's Near North Side. Noting my interest, Raymond began feeding me Gurdjieff books – not books by the master himself but explications by some of his pupils. The first, whose title I forget, was by Kenneth Walker, a physician. The most exciting was P. D. Ouspensky's classic *In Search of the Miraculous.* According to Raymond, Gurdjieff's own books were so abstruse that they were best tackled in the company of more experienced followers. Because I never joined a group, this is a pleasure which I have thus far foregone.

I appreciated Gurdjieff's distinction between "personality" (one's outer, society-influenced self) and "essence" (one's true, inner self). The goal of self-development was identification with the latter. I also liked his Rule of Three: Because all forces evoked their opposites, pairs of opposing forces would balance each other out until a third force caused movement. Dynamics in short depended on catalytic intervention. When Gurdjieff's own *Meetings with Remarkable Men* appeared, I was impressed that someone would be considered remarkable only to the extent that they impacted us individually. His list included his father, the village priest, and a retired Russian general, among others.

Though I never became a Gurdjieff follower, his system served as bridge between intellectuality and the spiritual path. Thus he will always be remarkable for me.

In your Wisdom Journal, list five "remarkable" people in your life, then speculate on why you chose them.

TRANSFORMATIVE WISDOM

It was the next night, as I lay on my bed, I suddenly, with a start, became aware of a man sitting beside me in my chair. He had on a dark suit. . . . I could see him as plainly as anyone I look at. He wasn't black, and he wasn't white. He was light-brown-skinned, an Asiatic cast of countenance, and he had oily black hair. . . . I looked right into his face. . . . I didn't get frightened. I knew I wasn't dreaming. I couldn't move, I didn't speak, and he didn't. I couldn't place him racially – other than I knew he was a non-European. I had no idea whatsoever who he was. He just sat there. Then, suddenly as he had come, he was gone.

–MALCOLM X WITH ALEX HALEY, *THE AUTOBIOGRAPHY OF MALCOLM X*, 1964

The above scene occurred while the young Malcolm X was in jail. He had been working his way through the dictionary – painstakingly copying down every word and its definitions. He eventually gave himself a liberal education by reading widely. Still, it is surprising to find that one of the leading political activists of our time had a mystical encounter.

Malcolm came to associate the unidentified visitor with Elijah Muhammad, founder of the Nation of Islam, who later became his mentor. After the visitation Malcolm became stronger in his adherence to the virulently antiwhite Nation of Islam. During his 1964 pilgrimage to Mecca, however, he underwent another transformation. "In the Muslim world, I had seen that men with white complexions were more genuinely brotherly than anyone else had ever been. . . . That morning was the start of a radical alteration in my whole outlook about 'white' men." Had he lived, it is hard to know where his continuing transformation might have led.

Based on his description, I believe the person he saw was Muhammad Subuh, a light-skinned Indonesian who favored Western suits and offered a nonsectarian spiritual exercise now followed by people in eighty countries. Imagine if Malcolm had identified his visitor differently!

If you have had a dream or vision that began transforming your life, discuss it in your Wisdom Journal.

GLOBAL WISDOM

Socrates said he was not an Athenian or a Greek, but a citizen of the world.

-Plutarch (c. 46–120), "Of Banishment"

I have always had difficulty understanding why some of my fellow citizens use the term *One Worlder* as a pejorative. After all, what could be wrong with advocating the human family's coming together to form a single nation-state? I guess the sanitized version is, we Americans have worked hard to develop a prosperous country and a comfortable lifestyle. If we had a global government with democratic representation, we would be outvoted by the many countries that are less well off. They would end up taxing away our prosperity to improve their own lot.

Actually the United States is itself perhaps the most successful example of a multiregional state. Texas, New England, the Atlantic Seaboard, California, the Northwest, the Southwest, the Southeast, the Lower and Upper Midwest–each could be nations unto themselves. We are also a multiethnic country, where before long people of color will be more numerous than Caucasians, the race of our European founding fathers. Yet we live together in relative harmony. Despite occasional racial or religious incidents, ethnic cleansing such as has occurred in Yugoslavia, or the ongoing socioreligious violence in Northern Ireland or Israel is highly unlikely here. So why not a United States of the World?

The answer is, we need a critical mass of world citizens like Socrates before we can establish a viable global nation to put them in. As the Javanese proverb states, carpenters can't build tables better than themselves. Ethnicity and religion per se are not the problem. In Hawaii the population is two-thirds nonwhite, and there is a significant Buddhist minority. Nonetheless we manage to live together in peace, have one of the highest crossracial marriage rates in the world, and are famous for our trademark Aloha Spirit. Even issues of language and distance will fade once most of us have outgrown the adolescent chauvinism and provincialism dominating individuals all over the world. We will then exemplify the motto of the World Future Society by thinking–and feeling–globally, while living and acting locally.

Discuss your views of world citizenship in your Wisdom Journal.

THE WISDOM OF FOOLISHNESS

Traveler: "Say, Farmer, you lived here all your life?"
Farmer: "Not yet."

–From "The Arkansas Traveler"

We denizens of Western civilization love clear distinctions. Someone is either wise or foolish. So how can there be wisdom in foolishness?

Ask the Mulla Nasrudin. He is the wise fool par excellence of Anatolia, the Middle East, and North Africa. Once someone asked him, "Tell me, Mulla, which is better, the sun or the moon?" After a short pause, the Mulla answered, "Obviously the moon." "Why the moon?" his friend asked. "That's easy," replied the Mulla. "The sun shines during the daytime when it's light out anyway."

Or on another occasion, when the Mulla was working as a ferryman, he took a distinguished scholar across the river on his raft. Halfway across, the scholar asked, "Mulla, can you read and write?" "Why no, Your Excellency," Mulla replied. "Then you've wasted half your life," said the scholar. Said Mulla, "Excuse me, Your Worship, but can you swim?" "No," the scholar answered. "Well," said Mulla, "I am afraid you've wasted all your life. You see, we're sinking."

Perhaps my favorite anecdote is the Mulla as smuggler. Every month he would cross the border on his donkey as he returned from a foreign trip. The captain of the guards, convinced Mulla was smuggling, had his bags thoroughly searched each time but could never find any contraband. Years later, now old friends, the Mulla and the captain sat in a café, drinking tea. "Come now, Mulla," the captain began. "We are both retired. I simply must know whether or not you were smuggling back then." "Of course I was, my friend," the Mulla replied. "But what? My men searched everything," the captain exclaimed. Said the Mulla, "Why, donkeys!"

Wisdom sometimes comes camouflaged in seeming foolishness. Being smart – especially "certifiably smart" – doesn't guarantee wisdom, and this is true from Arkansas to the Mulla's Middle East.

Write briefly in your Wisdom Journal about any experience you've had with "foolish wisdom."

MAUNDY THURSDAY WISDOM

This is my commandment: love one another, as I have loved you.

-John 15:12

Every culture, be it national, professional, generational, or religious, has its special expressions. In graduate school I had to master the terms used by literature students: simile, slant rhyme, synecdoche, and so on. My generation replaced "swell" with "cool," only to see it replaced in turn by more recent superlatives like "awesome" and "sweet." So it is not surprising that, as I was exposed to Christian culture, I had to learn a new vocabulary. Of the terms I acquired, I think my favorite is still Maundy Thursday.

Not all Christian churches use this term. Both Catholics and Protestants in Germany, for example, speak of Green Thursday. And I believe American Catholics say Holy Thursday. Nonetheless, I first heard of Maundy Thursday during my undergraduate years, while attending an Episcopal church in New Haven. Later, as a Lutheran, I found it in common usage in that church as well. So what is Maundy Thursday? The named, or special, days during Lent, the forty-day fasting period that precedes Easter, begin with Ash Wednesday, the first day of the season. The next – in the last week of Lent (Holy Week) – is Palm Sunday, followed by Maundy Thursday, Good Friday, and Holy Saturday. Easter Sunday, which comes next, begins a new church season.

Maundy Thursday, which celebrates Christ's Last Supper, corresponds to the first Passover seder in Jewish tradition. In instituting Holy Communion, Jesus used the unleavened bread (matzoh) and special wine of Passover as the Communion elements of bread and wine. But that was not all. He gave his disciples, and all subsequent Christians, a great, new commandment: To love one another as he had loved them. *Maundy* comes from the older British verb form *commaund.* So, Maundy Thursday is the celebration, first, of Jesus' command that we share the bread and wine of Holy Communion to remind us of his ministry and ours and, second, of the Great Commandment. For as Saint Paul later instructs us, in 1 Corinthians 13:13, of the three things that endure – faith, hope, and love – love is the most important.

Reflect in your Wisdom Journal on how successful you are at loving your neighbor.

PASSOVER WISDOM

Smear some blood . . . on the lintel and the two door-posts. Nobody may go out . . . till morning. The LORD will go through Egypt and strike it, but when he sees the blood on the lintel and the two door-posts, he will pass over that door and will not let the destroyer enter your houses to strike you. You shall keep this as a rule for you and your children for all time. . . . It is the LORD's Passover, for he passed over the houses of the Israelites in Egypt when he struck the Egyptians.

-EXODUS 12:22-27

In some years a striking ecumenical event is caused by the calendar: the harmonious convergence of Passover and Maundy Thursday. Since some Christian churches like to put on a Passover seder to celebrate Christ's Last Supper, such timing is propitious. For me, a literal Judeo-Christian, I get a nice feeling when these two holidays coincide, a sense of solidarity with the very first Christians, who were all Jews.

This afternoon I had business with a Jewish associate. As I was leaving his office, I said, "Good Pesach." He said "Good Pesach" to me. As descendants of generations of ancestors fortunate enough to survive exiles, pogroms, and holocausts, we had lived to see another Passover. A Feldman and a Silverman in Honolulu, the most remote and least likely Jewish community in the world. "Good Pesach," indeed!

The angel of death has not always passed over Jewish houses. Ask Elie Wiesel. Ask the dwindling ranks of Holocaust survivors. We are the holy remnant, the piece of consecrated unleavened bread set aside at seder for the Prophet Elijah. Besides eating special matzoh and drinking special wine, we leave the door open just a crack and set an extra place. Who knows? This year the Prophet might visit our seder. An optimistic people despite everything, we make the ritual statement, "This year we are here but next year in Jerusalem." Our spiritual homing instinct is never far.

Have you ever experienced a Passover seder? If not, ask a Jewish friend or associate to invite you. Then write about your impressions in your Wisdom Journal. If you are Jewish, write about what Passover means to you.

GOOD FRIDAY WISDOM

It was about midday and a darkness fell over the whole land, which lasted until three in the afternoon. . . . Then Jesus gave a loud cry and said, "Father, into thy hands I commit my spirit"; and with these words he died.

–Luke 23:44–46

As a secular Jewish high school student, I could never understand why Christians referred to the occasion of Jesus' death as Good Friday. What could possibly be *good* about one's leader's execution? It wasn't until freshman English in college, when we were reading Milton's *Paradise Lost,* that I learned of the parallel Christian concept of *felix culpa,* the "happy fall" from the Garden of Eden. One term helped explain the other.

In the Genesis story, Adam and Eve are driven out of paradise as punishment for succumbing to Satan's wiles and eating the forbidden fruit. According to mainstream Christian theology, all humanity was subsequently burdened with Original Sin. Henceforth all human beings would start off at birth with a metaphysical black mark against them. The New England Primer, a children's ABC book from Colonial times, stated, "In Adam's Fall we sinnèd all." This fall from grace was nonetheless "happy," because it gave God the opportunity, through Christ's death, to make vicarious atonement for human sinfulness and give humankind, or at least believing Christians, a fresh start. Round one to Satan; the fight to God.

Similarly, Good Friday is good precisely because it is the completion of Christ's required self-sacrifice. No Crucifixion, no Resurrection. No Good Friday, no Easter Sunday. Jesus was faithful unto death so that all believing Christians might have a chance to live life relieved of the burden of Original Sin. Further, his faithfulness gave the rest of us an example of true obedience to God's will. Perhaps the main wisdom incorporated in the concept of Good Friday, though, is that an earlier setback can lead to a greater triumph later on, human suffering can yield positive results, and good will eventually win out over evil.

In your Wisdom Journal, write about something bad that happened to you that over time proved beneficial.

THE WISDOM TO KNOW GOD

I pray that the God of our Lord Jesus Christ, the all-glorious Father, may give you the spiritual powers of wisdom and vision, by which there comes the knowledge of him.

–Ephesians 1:17

Wisdom, like vision, is a charism, a divinely conferred gift. At least this is the Christian view. Interestingly, some etymologists argue that *wisdom* and *vision* both derive from the same source, the past participle of the Latin verb "to see": *visus*. Thus wisdom would depend on our ability to see and see clearly.

The Vietnamese Buddhist monk Thich Nhat Hanh talks about how one's consciousness resembles a pool. If stirred up by emotions like anger, envy, or worry, the surface cannot reflect things as they are. We then act – or react – based on distorted perceptions of reality. In the West people advise us in stressful situations to take a deep breath before making a decision. Or else to sleep on it. Wise words, because vision is a prerequisite of action. My driver's license, for example, indicates that I may not drive legally without glasses. To be honest, I have never been tempted to do so. But twenty-four hours after cataract surgery, my right eye, without glasses, had something close to 20-20 vision. Suddenly I could watch TV without glasses. What about driving? I sat in the car, took off my glasses, and could read the signs. But did I dare to drive without them? No. For if I get into an accident, my restricted license would make me liable for any losses. Better wait till my renewal.

As for knowing God, can a table know the carpenter who made it? Still, as creatures endowed with consciousness, we may be able to experience God, to know God within us. This has always been the premise of mystics, whose goal is union with the indwelling Divine. To the extent possible, let us pray that each of us may come to know God in this way.

Over the next five days, pray for wisdom each morning and evening. Reflect on any outcomes in your Wisdom Journal.

EASTER WISDOM

It was about daybreak on Sunday, when Mary of Magdala and the other Mary came to look at the grave. Suddenly . . . an angel of the Lord descended from heaven. . . . "You," he said, "have nothing to fear. I know you are looking for Jesus who was crucified. He is not here; he has been raised again, as he said he would be."

–Matthew 28:1–6

The origin of the word *Easter* is unclear. According to Saint Bede, an eighth-century English cleric and scholar, it was derived from the name of a Teutonic goddess of spring and fertility. Apparently such modern traditions as the Easter bunny, colored Easter eggs, and even egg-rolling contests are holdovers from rites for this goddess, called *Eastre* in Anglo-Saxon.

Easter, of course, as Christians and many non-Christians know, is the most important holiday in Christianity. Just as Jesus and even his disciples reportedly restored dead individuals to life, so he, too, was raised from the dead, just as he said he would be. The credibility of everything Jesus preached is anchored in the fact of the Resurrection. For Christianity is based on the belief that God will prevail over evil, that our spiritual self is our real self, and that, when it comes to our soul, death, in Dylan Thomas's famous line, will have no dominion.

The Easter event, Christ's triumph over physical death, is also the reason almost all Christians celebrate their Sabbath not on Saturday like the Jews or on Friday like the Muslims, but on Sunday. (Seventh-Day Adventists follow the Orthodox Jewish tradition of a sundown-Friday-to-sundown-Saturday Sabbath.) Sunday, for most Christians, really is the first day of the week, because spiritual survival of physical death puts our earthly life and death into perspective. Christianity is a Sunday, but also a Son-day, religion. Just as spring brings new life to seemingly dead trees, plants, and soil, so Easter symbolizes that our death, too, like Jesus', is only apparent. The angel here speaks Easter wisdom. Truly we have nothing to fear.

In your Wisdom Journal, write about your view of Easter and the Resurrection.

THE WISDOM OF PURIFICATION

Like sheaves of corn he gathers you unto himself.
He threshes you to make you naked.
He sifts you to free you from your husks.
He grinds you to whiteness.
He kneads you until you are pliant;
And then he assigns you to his sacred fire, that you may become sacred bread for God's sacred feast.

-Kahlil Gibran, *The Prophet,* 1923

Suffering is never pleasant, but pointless suffering is the most painful. If we know that what we are enduring, from final exams to labor pains, has a purpose, then the pain is bearable. It is contained within a context of meaning. It is the high but not unreasonable price of achievement. But if we seem to be the arbitrary victims of forces stronger than ourselves or, worse, the targets of sadistic, malevolent powers, human or otherwise, then we may pray for unconsciousness or even death as our only escape.

When it comes to suffering, believers are among the blessed. They generally understand pain as an indication that they are being purified or that they need to pay attention to something overlooked. If they are ill, God is giving them a chance to rest. If they lose their job, God has something more fitting in store. If a loved one dies, it was his or her time. If a child dies, there are mysteries only God understands.

Religious and spiritual traditions the world over use ascetic practices, in effect voluntary suffering, as a means to accelerate one's inner development. Fasting, vigils, and exposure to the elements are examples. Native peoples use sweat lodges and vision quests, some Shi'ite Moslems lacerate themselves, some African tribes have scarification rites. The Javanese refer to practices like these as *prihatin,* or making the feelings suffer. These techniques are intended to speed up inner growth. Some cultures even believe that such practices make later life-based suffering unnecessary and thus function like a spiritual flu shot. Whatever the case, little in life comes free. For people of faith, however, there is no crucifixion without a resurrection.

In your Wisdom Journal, describe some painful event that, in retrospect, helped purify you or enhanced your inner development.

ENLIGHTENMENT WISDOM

What is this light that shines through the chinks of my mind and pierces my heart, doing it no injury? I begin to shudder yet catch fire with longing: I shudder inasmuch as I am unlike him, yet I am afire with longing for him because some likeness there is. Wisdom it is, none other than Wisdom, that shines through my darkness, tearing apart the cloud that envelops me.

–Saint Augustine, *Confessions* (translated by Maria Boulding)

The term *wisdom,* when capitalized by Christian writers, usually refers to an attribute of Christ. It is the light of God's grace that seeks us out, shines through our darkness, and, as Augustine puts it, tears apart the cloud that surrounds us. We then become clear and can see things clearly.

Even in Hawaii the weather is not always as spectacular as in the promotional films. On our side of Oahu island, it is cloudy most of the time. Locals refer to our town, one of Honolulu's main suburbs, as Cloudy-ohe. (The real name is Kaneohe.) Actually I don't mind our weather that much because it is generally three or four degrees cooler than in Honolulu. Also, if you are sitting in front of a computer all day, you don't want to look out your window to see another beautiful day you can't take advantage of. So from my perspective, there is something to be said for clouds.

Hawaii is also famous for its microclimates. In Chicago people would comment, "If you don't like the weather, wait five minutes." Here we say, "If you don't like the weather, drive five minutes." We could be having a blinding downpour in our neighborhood while there's not a cloud in the sky over Waikiki. The relative wetness or dryness depends on factors like closeness to the shore versus the mountains or whether you are on your island's windward or leeward side.

Tonight as we were driving down Kaneohe's main street, the Ko'olau Range appeared draped in dark clouds. "Imagine how spooky a scene like that would have been for the Hawaiians," my wife said, "in the days before electric lights." Agreed. In a case like that, I would have prayed hard for Saint Augustine's light.

Write in your Wisdom Journal what enlightenment means to you.

THE WISDOM OF JUST-IN-TIME DELIVERY

Then he stretched out his hand and took the knife to kill his son; but the angel of the LORD called to him from heaven, "Abraham, Abraham." He answered, "Here I am." The angel . . . said, "Do not raise your hand against the boy; do not touch him. Now I know that you are a God-fearing man. You have not withheld from me your son, your only son." Abraham looked up, and there he saw a ram caught by its horns in a thicket. So he went and took the ram and offered it as a sacrifice instead of his son.

–GENESIS 22:10–14

This story of Abraham's near-sacrifice of Isaac is honored in Judaism, Christianity, and Islam. All three religions see it as an example of submission to God's will. Jews remember God's promise to reward Abraham's action by making of them a great nation. The Letter to the Hebrews (11:17–19) refers to Abraham's obedience as a pre-eminent illustration of faith. Islam has a special holiday, Id Adha, to recognize Abraham's obedience to Allah.

Three other things about this story strike me. First, our Higher Power seems to help us when we are in trouble, especially when we ask. Second, the timing is often impeccable. Third, the experience tends to increase our faith. I remember an instance from early in my career as a consultant. Money was not abundant, and as I was doing my bills, I came up $400 short. Punctilious about paying bills on time, I prayed for a solution. Later, as I was balancing my checkbook, I found an error in my favor of exactly $400. Apparently I had forgotten to log in a $400 deposit – something unusual for me, because I was punctilious with my checkbook too. That experience encouraged me to keep going as a newly self-employed person.

Dr. Demming, the economist, talks about "just-in-time delivery." My experience is that God, too, is a just-in-time Deliverer – a phenomenon that tends to increase one's faith. As a rabbi commented about Abraham and Isaac in Bill Moyers's television series on *Genesis,* what makes a miracle miraculous is the timing.

Write in your Wisdom Journal about a "just-in-time delivery" you've experienced.

THE WISDOM TO ENJOY LIFE

There are two things to aim at in life: first, to get what you want; and after that to enjoy it. Only the wisest of people achieve the second.

—Logan Pearsall Smith

The true scarlet letter in our puritanical culture is *E* for enjoyment. We are praised for working hard and honored for doing well. But we always feel a little guilty about relaxing and having fun. I know I do. The commandment we break most, I think, is the fourth. Interestingly, this injunction that we observe the Sabbath and keep it holy takes up more verses in Exodus, chapter 20 (four–verses 8–11) than any other commandment. Maybe we need the extra convincing. As I half-joke with our pastor, Christian ministers are the worst offenders. They routinely profane the Sabbath by working, with many of us doing likewise.

Yesterday was one of the first Sundays in a long time when I did no gainful work. I made a deliberate choice not to turn on the computer or look at my sagging e-mail inbox. "On six days thou shalt be glued to thy computer in the interest of earning thy daily bread, but on the seventh thou shalt lay back, have fun with thy friends, eat pizza, even go to the beach," said an inner voice sick and tired of my workaholic ways.

The real sages of our culture are those who not only know how to relax and have fun on the weekend but who marble their work week with timeouts, playful moments, and activities with no outward meaning or purpose. I refer to these minisabbaticals as putting holes into the Swiss cheese of life. One of my insights as a child was that *real* Swiss cheese had to have holes. Block Swiss might smell or even taste like the real thing, but it was unholey and therefore phony. Unfortunately, when it comes to personal time management, I tend to buy my Swiss in solid, holeless blocks.

Have you "lettered" yet on the Enjoyment team, or are you too busy rushing around to slow down and have fun? Discuss this question in your Wisdom Journal.

THE WISDOM OF CHANNELING YOURSELF

There is a vitality, a life force, a quickening that is translated through you into action, and because there is only one of you in all time, this expression is unique. If you block it, it will never exist through any other medium. It will be lost. . . . It is your business to keep it yours clearly and directly, to keep the channel open.

–Martha Graham (1893–1991)

Martha Graham is known for her highly individualized, expressive style as both choreographer and dancer. An American original, she was to modern dance what Picasso was to twentieth-century visual art· always changing, always recognizable, always unique.

Her statement is thus hardly surprising. Each of us is to recognize him- or herself as something unique throughout space-time. Nothing exactly like us has ever existed before nor will exist again. So we must resist imitating others or going with the flow of culture, art, or fashion. We are called to create our own unique culture, art, fashion. If we don't, the potential to do so will be lost forever.

What especially fascinates me, however, is Graham's statement that we must "keep the channel open" to our uniqueness. By implication we each contain a highly individualized cluster of gifts. However, just because they are there doesn't mean they are accessible. Polonius's advice to Laertes in *Hamlet,* "To thine own self be true," is really preceded by the Delphic Oracle's advice to Socrates, "Know thyself." We must come to know, embrace, and love who we are meant to be in order to become that unique person. Yet the channel between our ordinary self and our essence has a way of closing up like an artery blocked from the build up of plaque. Just as maintaining optimum health requires constant work and vigilance, so do discovering and maintaining who we truly are. For we cannot express our true self unless we have successfully struggled to know and become one with that self. Happy channeling!

In your Wisdom Journal, list three things you now do or might do to keep the channel to your true self open. How successful are you?

FAMILY WISDOM

The family you come from isn't as important as the family you're going to have.

–Ring Lardner (1885–1933)

At first glance I wasn't sure I agreed with Mr. Lardner. No self-respecting Chinese or Japanese would. After all, in Confucian cultures the larger unit, in this case the family, takes precedence over the smaller one, the individual. This priority is symbolized by placing the family name first, then adding the personal name. Family of origin, like one's elders and ancestors, is always more important than the nuclear family an individual and spouse create.

The saying "You can't choose your family; thank God you can choose your friends" places Lardner's thought in a different light. After all, your spouse is a friend you have chosen to live and have children with. People often talk about their significant other as their best friend. Furthermore you can't do anything about your biological family. They are a given. If we select our biological family prior to birth, as some New Age adherents believe we do, that fact has been erased from our memories.

I suppose Lardner means that if, say, we resent aspects of the parenting we have received, we have the chance in the family we "start" to do things differently and better. Our family of origin is analogous to fate; the family we create, to free will. Still, some aspects of the family we parent are beyond our control, for instance, the two gene pools that commingle in our children, or social prejudices based on our family's skin color, religion, or socioeconomic status. On the other hand, we have areas of freedom and flexibility in the families we come from. Human beings can and do change. Age does mellow some people. Circumstances and the shifting cultural climate can be transformative as well. I like one of James Redfield's "insights" in *The Celestine Prophecy* that each of us is required to confront and integrate those aspects of both our parents within us. Family wisdom may thus be our capacity to accept who we are in order to raise children capable of becoming who they are intended to be.

What wisdom have you gained from family life? Describe it in your Wisdom Journal.

THE WISDOM OF UNANSWERED PRAYER

He sendeth sun, he sendeth shower,
Alike they're needful to the flower;
And joys and tears alike are sent
To give the soul fit nourishment.
As comes to me or cloud or sun,
Father! thy will, not mine, be done.

–Sarah Flower Adams (1805–1848)

There is wisdom in the old saying, "Be careful what you pray for – you might just get it." King Midas found out the hard way. He discovered that Golden Delicious apples aren't necessarily delicious. The reality is, it may be better for us not to get everything we ask for. Jimmy Stewart's character in *It's a Wonderful Life* became so disillusioned that at one point he wished he had never been born. After being shown what life in his town would have been like without him, he changed his mind and was overjoyed to be able to live his previously unsatisfactory existence.

Whatever the case, prayers are not always answered. Our first child was a daughter, so I was hoping for a son to carry the illustrious Feldman name into the future. As child number two entered the world far enough for me to determine its gender, I said, "It's a girl!" in such an abject tone that Simone starting laughing. Christine was propelled out like a rocket, and the surprised doctor was just able to catch her.

On a less happy occasion, I had just left Munich to start teaching at a U.S. Air Force base in the Rhineland. Because the bachelor officers' quarters were full, I was billeted in the visiting general's apartment. The year was 1972. Back in Munich the Olympics had been thrown into disarray by the capture of Israeli athletes by Muslim extremists. Before going to bed, I prayed for the captives' safety. When my prayers seemed to bounce back from the ceiling, I knew things would not turn out well. They didn't. Wisdom here may lie in accepting the fact that my will won't always be done. There is related wisdom in the German proverb that we should pray as though no work could help and work as though no prayer could help.

In your Wisdom Journal, give an example of an unanswered prayer and the result.

THE WISDOM OF TAKING RISKS

Security is mostly a superstition. It does not exist in nature, nor do the children of men as a whole experience it. Avoiding danger is no safer in the long run than outright exposure. Life is either a daring adventure or nothing.

–Helen Keller (1880–1968)

The proverb that comes to mind is, "Nothing ventured, nothing gained." Still, most proverbs emphasize caution, prudence, and vigilance. For every "Go for it!" and "He who hesitates is lost," there are dozens of warnings like, "The crab that walks too far falls into the pot" (Haitian), "Sleeping people can't fall down" (Japanese), or "Fish don't get caught in deep water" (Malay).

The fact is, of course, that crabs have to walk just to find food. The concept of "too far" is relative. Besides, skilled crabbers wait by crab holes, so even going out for air can be life threatening. By the same token, sleeping people can't eat, relate to others, work, or make love. Sleeping all the time to avoid falling down will land one in the permanent sleep of death. And while deep-water fish may not get caught by shore-hugging anglers, they are hardly safe from mechanized commercial fishing boats or the predatory fish-eating monsters of the deep. Remember: No one gets out of life alive. That goes for even the cleverest of all.

Risk taking is our ticket to ride. Without a leap of courage, none of us would go to school, interview for a job, enter a committed relationship, buy a house, move to a new town, live in a foreign country, invest in the stock market, have an operation, board an airplane, or open a business. Some mornings just getting out of bed is a challenge, not to mention leaving for work. What unseen crabber might be awaiting us as we come out for air? Helen Keller, the most famous multihandicapped person in American history, surely knew that without taking risk after risk, she would have been doomed to the dark loneliness of her condition. Her courage has inspired generations of us to leave our caves of fear.

In your Wisdom Journal, write about an example of risk taking you are proud of.

THE WISDOM OF SELF-CONQUEST

If a man should conquer in battle a thousand and a thousand more, and another man should conquer himself, his would be the greater victory, because the greatest of victories is the victory over oneself; and neither the gods in heaven above nor the demons down below can turn into defeat the victory of such a man.

-THE DHAMMAPADA, TRANSLATED BY JUAN MASCARÓ

I know why I criticize others. It is much easier itemizing their faults than getting rid of even one of my own. We make progress when we learn to leave others in peace and start working on ourselves. Of course, the danger here is that we may substitute talking about our shortcomings for doing something about them. People in therapy often exemplify this syndrome. They can give you postgraduate descriptions of their problems, but they never seem to get any better. It's clearly harder to walk than talk.

Steps 4 through 7 in the Twelve Step programs offer a practical alternative. In step 4 we make "a searching and fearless moral inventory of ourselves." Then (step 5) we admit "to God, . . . ourselves, and . . . another human being the exact nature of our wrongs." In step 6 we become "entirely ready to have God remove all these defects of character." And in step 7 we humbly ask God to "remove our shortcomings." This is not an easy sequence of activities. Some people are in Twelve Step programs for years before they can do a moral inventory. The fear of self-criticism or even self-praise is too great. The universal salve of getting something off our chest by sharing it with others is well recognized. For many, though, the hardest thing is to ask God to remove these personal shortcomings (step 7). This is why there is an intermediate step just to get ready.

The Twelve Step programs comprise one of many ways up the mountain of self-conquest. The point is, each of us should be on one of them.

In your Wisdom Journal, list what you have been doing to overcome your lower nature and reclaim your highest self. Where are you now in this journey?

THE WISDOM OF PATIENCE

O Lord, now that I am a doctor, please send me patience.

–An original pun and only partially answered prayer

I got my doctorate in 1966. Patience has been a long time coming. Now it may be that this prayer has not yet been answered because I have never truly asked. Standing in front of God, even figuratively, and requesting something directly – not just longing for it – are horses of very different colors.

Patience comes from the Latin verb meaning "to bear, to undergo, to suffer." The past participle, *passus*, gives us the term "the Passion," or Christ's suffering on the cross. Jesus had to undergo Good Friday in order to reach the Resurrection of Easter Sunday. Faithful unto death, patient unto new life.

I have become more patient with age. Whereas I used to get frustrated by the smallest line or delay, I am now more willing to go with the flow. I help things along by having something interesting to read in my briefcase. Nowadays when I am stuck in traffic, I practice the breathing-in, breathing-out visualization technique prescribed in mindfulness meditation. More important, I use the mental ploy that the universe wants me to slow down and relax. The key perhaps is believing that if things don't work out, or at least not in the way I had imagined, perhaps they are not supposed to; perhaps God has something else in mind. God is the scheduler, not me.

To be honest, I am not there yet. A few weeks ago, for example, I wrote supporters of the World Wisdom Project. The project was short of cash, so I followed an earlier precedent of requesting loans. The response was heartening. Here, though, is the point. I had already received a few checks, but as yet nothing from the first person who pledged. So I e-mailed her to make sure she had my address and was clear about how the program worked. She e-mailed back that she had already mailed the check. No doubt it would arrive the next day, I thought, a little embarrassed by my impatience. Guess what? It did.

Discuss in your Wisdom Journal how patient you are and what you do to keep from becoming impatient.

THE WISDOM OF MORAL LEADERSHIP

Mohandas Gandhi is my choice for Person of the Century because he showed us a way out of the destructive side of our human nature. He demonstrated that we can force change and justice through moral acts of aggression instead of physical acts of aggression. Never has our species needed this wisdom more.

–STEVE JOBS, COFOUNDER OF APPLE COMPUTER INC., IN *TIME*, APRIL 12, 1999

Gandhi was killed when I was nine. But I distinctly remember having had a sense of him even when I was a child. He was a kind of Mother Teresa and Dalai Lama rolled into one. He was also my first hero from the East.

I must have read his autobiography, *The Story of My Experiments with Truth*, as a graduate student. Later I taught it in the Literature of Wisdom class. The younger generation rediscovered Gandhi when Sir Richard Attenborough's Academy Award–winning epic film came out. Prior to that he had been a kind of historical footnote to the life of Dr. Martin Luther King Jr. Students had heard the name somewhere but really didn't know who Gandhi was or what he had done.

In 1969 Arnold Toynbee, a distinguished British historian, honored the hundredth anniversary of Gandhi's birth by publishing an article on the significance of his life and work. What I remember from that article was Toynbee's assertion that Gandhi was a saint precisely because he wasn't afraid to tarnish his halo by working in the moral slums of politics. Gandhi's self-development, the strengthening of his character and resolve, his willingness to put his life on the line – all coupled with his experience-forged understanding of *Realpolitik*, English common law, and where and how to provide pressure. All this made him uniquely effective in winning India's independence from England without extensive bloodshed. In his essay "The Yogi and the Kommissar," Arthur Koestler argues that there are two diametrically opposed approaches to improving society: personal transformation (the yogi) and political intervention (the kommissar). Gandhi stood out not least for his uncanny ability to combine both. The international stage begs for more Gandhi-style leaders.

Rent Gandhi *from your video store and comment in your Wisdom Journal on its implications for public wisdom.*

CONSERVATIVE WISDOM

'Tis the part of a wise man to keep himself today for tomorrow, and not venture all his eggs in one basket.

–Miguel de Cervantes (1547–1616), *Don Quixote*

Members of political parties on the right may be a little disappointed with me. Not that I think their political philosophy without merit. On the contrary. The problem is, I find strong arguments for positions clear across the political spectrum. For me it is always a matter of balance and context. What works in one situation may fail miserably in another. As a pragmatist I keep my distance from any self-contained ideology.

In this quotation, Cervantes – or a character in the novel – is emphasizing the cautious side of wisdom. Unlike the author's knight, who risks his life for an impossibly idealistic concept of gallantry, the kind of sage described here would be sure not to tilt against windmills. She or he would calculate the probable risks and benefits before beginning any initiative. As an investor this sort of person would have a diversified portfolio and a solid reserve fund set aside for a rainy day. Mark Twain counseled, by contrast, to put all your eggs in one basket and then to watch that basket. Vigilance like this is not necessary if you plan ahead and contain risk by being careful from the outset.

In *Don Quixote* Cervantes contrasts the wildly idealistic hero with his realistic but pedestrian squire. You'll find a similar twosome in Mozart's opera *The Magic Flute* in the high-minded, courageous Tamino and his womanizing, cowardly sidekick, Papageno. Cervantes's point, pretty clearly, is that in the human comedy, we don't often find a perfect balance of realism and idealism. People tend to be too much of one or the other. What is really needed, the author implies, is idealism tempered with realistic expectations and common sense, or realism freed from its fixation on short-term considerations and enlivened by vision. Idealists of the Don Quixote–Tamino type could also stand a dose of humor. Like many a high-minded person on a mission, they seem constitutionally unable to laugh at themselves.

Where do you place yourself in the idealist-realist spectrum? Share your answer with your Wisdom Journal.

THE WISDOM OF SECOND CHILDHOOD

It takes a long time to become young.

-Pablo Picasso (1881–1973)

Youth, the saying goes, is wasted on the young. A cynical saying, perhaps, but one that many in midlife and beyond can relate to. Picasso seems a bit more hopeful, though: If it takes a long time to become young, then certainly we have the possibility of youthfulness in later years. What might we reasonably expect in our "second childhood"?

Biologically, human life is a circle of sorts. We start off small, weak, and dependent and end up that way, too, though never quite as short as we were as infants. Our vocabulary and language skills start off small, too, then peak in our middle years, and trail off with approaching old age. To be sure, the progression from childhood to old age is rather Hegelian: thesis-antithesis-synthesis. As the riddle of the Sphinx asks, What goes on four legs, then two legs, then three legs? The answer is, a human being: crawling on all fours as a baby, walking upright in the years of vigor, then tapping along with a cane as an elder. In other words, second childhood is never quite like the first.

As preadolescent children we are still natural, spontaneous, unaffected by the views and requirements of adult civilization. Then, as our minds fill with the truths and half-truths of our culture, many of us lose contact with that inner child who, Jesus told us, was the prototype of the citizens of heaven. As the ambitions and pretenses of the earning years give way to the joys of grandparenthood, we have a second chance to become like little children. Pablo Picasso, who lived to his ninety-second year and was by all accounts a very complex adult, had reason to know how arduous it was to regain inner youth. Yet as an artist, to the end his work was always fresh, new, unique. Perhaps he did manage to become young after all those years.

Think of all the people over the age of seventy in your circle. In your Wisdom Journal, write about the one who impresses you most with her or his youthful demeanor and attitudes.

THE WISDOM OF REMEMBERING GOD

Lovers remember God, Glorified and Exalted is He, whatever their condition. During their remembrance their eyes are filled with tears, their hearts are radiant with the love of God, their innermost being is full and vibrant with the fear of God. The eyes of their hearts behold the divine mysteries. They reflect upon their origins and their ultimate destinations. Their hearts are ablaze with the love of God.

–Sheikh Muzaffer Ozak Al-Jerrahi, *The Unveiling of Love*, 1981

Sheikh Muzaffer Ozak Al-Jerrahi's book is subtitled *Sufism and the Remembrance of God*. The head of the Halveti-Jerrahi Order of Dervishes, he was born in 1916; whether he is still alive and leading his order, I do not know. What I do know is that one of the chief spiritual practices of the Sufis, as Muslim mystics are called, is *dhikr*, remembering [God].

Now you might ask, "How can we possibly forget God?" My response is, our God-given free will makes us absolutely able to do so. The state of the world, evidenced by many individuals, households, and not a few governments and businesses, is proof that we suffer, collectively, from a kind of spiritual Alzheimer's disease. We forget that we are creatures who did not create ourselves and that we do not inhabit the planet by ourselves. Our actions reflect this forgetfulness. To wake us up to reality, Sufis have a variety of practices – most famous, perhaps, the whirling of dervish orders – that serve to re-attune us to the Great Life Force animating the universe. The dervishes become like planets. Turning on their axes, planets rotate in fixed orbits around the sun, which provides their energy and guides their path. Planets are fully submissive to the laws governing their movements. If human beings were to follow suit, they would manifest *Islam*, Arabic for "submission," and the result would be *salam*, "peace."

By remembering our relationship to God each day, we can awaken the eyes of our heart, see our purpose for living, and become filled with the love that we Christians equate with God.

Try returning your thoughts to God for the rest of the day. Write about the experience in your Wisdom Journal this evening.

THE WISDOM OF PUZZLEMENT

If it is true that the ability to be puzzled is the beginning of wisdom, then this truth is a sad commentary on the wisdom of modern man. Whatever the merits of our high degree of literacy and universal education, we have lost the gift for being puzzled. Everything is supposed to be known – if not to ourselves then to some specialist whose business it is to know what we do not know. . . . Even children are rarely surprised. . . . To have the right answers seems all-important; to ask the right questions is considered insignificant by comparison.

–Erich Fromm, *The Forgotten Language*, 1957

Erich Fromm was one of my favorite authors in my late teens and twenties. I read many if not all of his books. This particular one, subtitled *An Introduction to the Understanding of Dreams, Fairy Tales and Myths,* I took with me on my junior-year exchange stay in Germany.

I had taken a course with Professor Pottle on the English Romantics the year before and had remembered Keats's concept of negative capability. The idea, in any case, is that one would get what we now think of as our left brain out of the way in order to receive creative inspiration. At night while we slept, our daytime logic was suspended so that we might be visited by dreams. The Romantics also thought that being close to nature – what my German painter friend Richard Engels used to refer to as a "nice valk in the voods" – could also get us out of our heads.

Jesus famously exhorted his adult followers to become like little children – open, trusting, full of wonder. Saint Paul, writing to the mainly Greek Christian congregation in Corinth, advised: "If there is anyone among you who fancies himself wise, . . . he must become a fool to gain true wisdom. For the wisdom of this world is folly in God's sight" (1 Corinthians 3:18–19). Knowing all the answers is the quality of a "wise guy," not a sage. As Fromm suggests, asking good questions may be the highway to enlightment.

In your Wisdom Journal, describe what you do when something puzzles you.

THE WISDOM OF OTHER-DIRECTEDNESS

I've learned that if you stay focused on yourself, you are guaranteed to be miserable.

—An anonymous contributor, age 71, to H. Jackson Brown,
Live and Learn and Pass It On, 1991

A classic book of the 1960s was David Riesman's and Ruel Denny's *The Lonely Crowd.* The authors criticized the twin American habits of rugged individualism (inner directedness), on the one hand, and dependence on others for approval (other-directedness), on the other. Instead they put forward the more balanced position of autonomy, which required one to develop an authentic selfhood able to live in mature interdependence with others.

In the above quotation, the 71-year-old anonymous speaker is simply criticizing the rut of self-centeredness. Clearly the United States has no monopoly on self-centered people. Anyone who has traveled abroad knows that weeds as well as flowers are found almost everywhere. This human failing, possibly exacerbated by our modern consumer culture, makes relating to others difficult if not impossible. Paradoxically it doesn't do much for relating to oneself either.

At one point in his *Life of Samuel Johnson* (1791), James Boswell faithfully reports an instance when his beloved Dr. Johnson turned on him and stated in his rich eighteenth-century cadences: "Sir, you have but two topics, yourself and me. I am sick of both." As interesting as we may be, we are not universally so. Genesis explains that God created Eve because it was not good for Adam to be alone. It is when we stop being there just for ourselves that we make a space in which our individualities can grow. Some say this is the reason God created the universe. Even the All-Present needed to articulate some space in which to grow. This is also why one of the best ways to overcome depression without drugs is to do something positive for someone less fortunate. Some psychiatrists routinely send their less seriously ill patients to do volunteer work for just this reason.

In your Wisdom Journal, list three things you might do to take your attention away from yourself.

THE WISDOM OF PREPAREDNESS

There's a special providence in the fall of a sparrow. If it be now, 'tis not to come; if it be not to come, it will be now; if it be not now, yet it will come: the readiness is all.

-WILLIAM SHAKESPEARE, *HAMLET*, V, II, 232

When I was involved, as dean, in the general-education reform movement, I remember one consultant in particular: Professor Milton Mayer from the University of Chicago. In a world characterized by change, he said that a well-educated undergraduate needed to be prepared for anything. "Prepared for anything" also means being sensitive to context. As our parents and teachers used to say, "There is a time and a place for everything." In Jane Austen's novels, for example, the suitor would plot and scheme to set up just the right occasion to propose.

I remember assaulting my parents for things I wanted at the first possible moment, which was generally the worst possible moment. Patience is an acquired virtue for most of us. My own kids did the same, usually just as I was coming home, dog tired, from work.

Cats, on the other hand, though notably impatient about some things, seem to have patience hardwired into them when it comes to hunting. As a rule they will conceal themselves and wait for prey to move past them. Even then they wait and wait . . . and wait. Then they spring. They are apparently programmed to defer gratification till just the right moment. Professional athletes have that same patience and economy of motion. A baseball player, for example, who is a "patient hitter" with a "compact swing" will likely experience success. Surfers will wait for ten minutes, letting wave after wave pass, till the perfect one comes along. Then they must catch it just right. Too early, and the wave rolls over them. Too late, and they miss it. The readiness really is all.

How can one gauge the right (or wrong) time to do something? Think of an instance when your timing was perfect (or perfectly off) and write about it in your Wisdom Journal. What three pieces of advice would you give yourself for the future?

THE WISDOM OF MINDING YOUR P'S AND Q'S

The heart has its reasons which reason knows nothing of.

-Blaise Pascal (1623-1662), Pensées, IV, 277

In 1995 the *New York Times* science writer Dr. Daniel Goleman caused a stir with the publication of his book *Emotional Intelligence.* His basic point was something all of us have always known intuitively: cognitive intelligence isn't everything. In fact, Goleman argues, emotional intelligence, or E.Q., often matters more than I.Q. Because most of us have experienced-or at times been-pretty dumb smart people, his conclusion should not come as a shock.

I once wrote an article entitled "The Educated Person-What Does That Mean?" I argued, somewhat melodramatically, that unless education took account of humanity's complex learning needs, we might have neither education nor humanity nor a future. I examined four distinct ideals of the educated person: from the Western world, classical India, Confucian China, and communist China. I then added a fifth ideal, "the holistically educated person," who "will not be measured by I.Q. alone but by B.Q. (Body Quotient), E.Q. (Emotion Quotient), and S.Q. (Spirit Quotient) as well."

The idea of a multiply developed human being is not new. Horace talked of a sound mind in a sound body. In the late nineteenth century, Rudolf Steiner emphasized educating the imagination, voice, and body as much as the intellect. In the 1920s G. I. Gurdjieff established a school in France for the "harmonious development of man." Gurdjieff's idea was that one's body, emotions, and intellect needed to be integrated to produce a fully mature human being. More recently Howard Gardner of Harvard has researched and written on "multiple intelligences."

Clearly, to reach our full human potential, we need to mind all our P's and Q's, not just our I.Q. What's the use of being an intellectual giant and a moral or emotional dwarf? I would add another Q-our Wisdom Quotient. For if all our other indicators are high but our W.Q. remains low, we may prove a danger to both ourselves and society.

Brainstorm three to five criteria in your Wisdom Journal against which to measure someone's wisdom.

THE WISDOM OF LEAVING HOME

One doesn't discover new lands without consenting to lose sight of the shore for a very long time.

–André Gide (1869–1951)

Leaving home is a biblical imperative. If you don't believe me, review Genesis 2:24. Now you might rebut that even the modern translations talk about "a man" having to leave father and mother. Nothing is said about a woman. Recently I was discussing with my wife and a young woman friend of ours about how it seems easier for female adult children to return to their parents than for their male siblings to. It is almost as if young men, once out on their own, read an invisible sign warning that their tires will be wrecked if they reverse direction. Once you're out, you're out, seems to be the feeling. Then, too, men still earn more than women, and mothers are generally the ones left with any children when a relationship breaks up. No wonder women go home. It is the place, as Robert Frost wrote, where they have to take you in; and sometimes that is what we need more than anything else.

Home has all the plusses and minuses of the womb. It's nice and cozy, but it's also restrictive. You don't have to do anything, but then you can't do anything. You don't have to pay, but you don't have a say either. And sooner or later, you get forced out. Ultimately there is no free lunch.

The greatest limitation of home – be it nuclear family, hometown, native country, church, generational cohort, or profession – is that it posits only one officially sanctioned way of being in the world. Now that way may in fact be best for most of us or at least for me. But we'll never really know until we get out on our own and compare it with other modes of living. Doing this, alas, means casting off for a far country, risking seasickness and sea monsters, and perhaps never coming home at all. Yet here lies a paradox. For, like the prodigal son, in losing ourselves we may just find ourselves.

Write about your experience of leaving home in your Wisdom Journal.

THE WISDOM OF KINDNESS

What wisdom can you find that is greater than kindness?

–Jean-Jacques Rousseau (1712–1778)

Those who have studied philosophy may recall that of the two great eighteenth-century French philosophers, Voltaire (1694–1778) epitomized the classical view while Rousseau, his younger contemporary, stood for the romantic. We might sum up the difference in this way: Voltaire – head, Rousseau – heart. It is thus not surprising to find Rousseau preferring kindness, a virtue of the heart, to wisdom, which seems more related to intellect. Indeed there is some basis for this distinction. Consider King Solomon, the Hebrew paragon of wisdom. From what one can gather in the Bible, he was not a very nice guy. If you were a man with a beautiful wife, for example, you would not have wanted to live in his vicinity.

Buddhism, a sensible and balanced religion in many ways, holds *prajna* (wisdom) and *karuna* (compassion) as the two chief virtues of fully realized human beings. Buddhist life cultivates both wisdom and compassion, for without wisdom our compassion may be poorly directed. Although some Buddhist traditions give pride of place to one or the other, they are generally viewed as insufficient unless conjoined.

In some forms of Christianity, a similar tension exists between law and faith or works and grace. In the New Testament, Saint Paul was the great champion of faith. Saint James by contrast emphasized works, as in this famous passage from his epistle: "For as the body without the spirit is dead, so faith without works is dead also" (James 2:26, KJV).

Choosing between a cold, distant wise person and someone foolish but kindly is an impossible task. Rousseau, Buddhism, and Saint James can help us see that true wisdom is accompanied by compassion.

In your Wisdom Journal, discuss whether the wisest person you know is also kind.

THE WISDOM OF INCLUSIVITY

Some Christians speak not only of the "uniqueness" of Christ but of the "exclusiveness" of Christ. It cannot be said too plainly, however, that exclusivity is utterly contrary to the Jesus we meet in the synoptic Gospels. . . . Jesus kept company with everyone in the world of his day. . . . In fact, many who are exemplars of faith and recipients of loving mercy in the Gospel narratives are those we might call "people of other faiths." . . . Jesus did not see "Christianity" and "Judaism." . . . He saw faith. There is no question but that he would have kept company with Patwardhan and Krishnamurti, with Gandhi and Tagore.

–Diana L. Eck, *Encountering God*, 1993

Encountering God is one of the best books on religion I have ever read. Diana Eck, professor of comparative religion and Indian studies at Harvard, writes about her initial encounter with Hinduism. A Methodist from Bozeman, Montana, she had never met a non-Christian until her freshman year at Smith College. When she went to Banaras, India, in 1965, she encountered the first challenge to her beliefs. It came not through books or ideas but in the form of "Hindus whose lives were a powerful witness to their faith."

The major Near Eastern religions all tend to exclusiveness. You are either a Jew or a Christian, a Christian or a Muslim. You can't be both or all three. That would be religious bigamy. Christianity and Islam, moreover, are religions that proselytize: both claim to have the Truth, and both go about seeking converts. Hindus, Buddhists, and Taoists, on the other hand, are unlikely to press others to convert, or to condemn people to hell for not joining their religion.

I agree with Diana Eck that a God of love, as manifested in Jesus' life and sacrifice, cannot be exclusivistic. When Jesus asked God from the cross to pardon the Jewish religious officials who had condemned him, he might also have been speaking for us latter-day owners of God's truth. "Forgive us, God. We really don't know what we are doing."

Write in your Wisdom Journal how you regard people of other faiths.

THE WISDOM OF GRACE

Grace happens!

–From a bumper sticker

Many Americans will know that this bumper sticker is a variation of–really a response to–a saying hugely popular in the 1980s. The noun that graces the far more common observation is now frequently seen in print and heard from the lips of well-dressed elementary-school children. There is no need to repeat it here.

We live in a society of believers–believers in Murphy's Law, that is. If something can go wrong, says Murphy, it will. In fact some people may have already undergone conversion to the more rigorous sect characterized by Sullivan's Law. According to this belief, the Murphy of Murphy's Law was an optimist. And of course, plenty of evidence can be found to bolster the argument that entropy and the Second Law of Thermodynamics exist in human affairs as much as in physics. One war is hardly over before two more start up. Irrational hatreds fuel racial and ethnic feuds lasting centuries. Innocent children are constantly victimized by irresponsible adults. Things don't get better, they get worse. You don't grow younger, you grow older. The good old days seem gone forever. And no one escapes death.

Yet grace does happen. The gifts originating in powers greater and wiser than ourselves are ubiquitous. They are present twenty-four hours a day, seven days a week, wherever we happen to be. But like radio or TV waves, we'll never hear or see them unless we have the equipment to make them manifest. This, I am sure, is why Jesus constantly harped on "ears to hear" and "eyes to see" and performed so many miracles curing deaf and blind people. We consider something absent if we are unable to perceive it. Isn't it at least as sensible to doubt our capacities? After all, as the old saying goes, absence of proof is not proof of absence. When we begin seeing with eyes of thanksgiving rather than eyes of blame, Murphy and Sullivan will begin to lose their following. Then grace will visibly abound on the earth, and we may even change our major from war to peace.

In your Wisdom Journal, describe an example of grace you have experienced.

FELINE WISDOM

Cats are angels with fur.

-Sark, *Inspiration Sandwich*, 1992

My mother hated cats. Apparently one had scared her half to death when she was small. So whenever she visited us, she had a problem. The problem's name was Winston.

Winston is our black cat. He is quite friendly. He is big, though – really a small panther. Mother's problem was that, despite her negative feelings toward cats in general, she liked Winston. In the early stages of Alzheimer's disease, she hit upon a solution. She would refer to Winston as "the dog." On coming downstairs her first question would be, "Where's the dog?"

My wife and I are convinced that Winston is our guardian angel, undercover as a household pet. I mean, how could he ever blow a cover like that? But he would almost betray himself sometimes. For example, he was not a lap cat. However, if you were sad or had a bellyache, up he would jump and provide cat therapy until you were feeling better. "Dr. Winston," we called him.

He entertained us too. For example, he would play this game with my mother-in-law, who lived with us and who had been partially crippled from a stroke some years before. Toward dinnertime he would array himself on her chair. As she approached he would cock his ears but otherwise feign indifference. As Oma – German for Granny – got close, she would raise her cane to chase him away. "That's Oma's chair!" she would say. Waiting till the last possible moment, Winston would finally jump down. From the day she died, he refused to use her chair.

Once, a few months before Oma's death, Winston became uncharacteristically agitated. He kept running back and forth between my wife and the stairs. Then my wife heard a thud. Oma had taken a fall. Somehow Winston had sensed that something was not right and did his best to warn the one person able to do something about it.

Write in your Wisdom Journal about your experience with or opinions about feline or other "animal wisdom."

THE WISDOM OF OTHER VOICES

As liberal or progressive educators, we think we have moved beyond the old simplistic idea that western culture represents the pinnacle of civilization not only technologically but cognitively. This form of self-congratulation in turn makes it all the more difficult to see the possibility of other routes to wisdom, other intelligent ideas of evidence, other valid ways of exploring the limits of human potential, other methods of learning and teaching.

–Helen Fox, *Listening to the World*, 1994

My older daughter did her master's thesis on voice in expository writing. The idea she countered was that, when it came to prose, "voice" was restricted to creative writers. In the natural and social sciences, one was required to write as objectively as possible. The reader was to have no sense that a living, breathing human being stood behind the words on the page. Even in the humanities, one was instructed to keep personal references and style to a minimum. It took the women's movement to give the lie to this objectivist myth and the depersonalized style that went with it. In literature, thanks to Stanley Fish and others, a reader's response to a text came to be seen as having as much importance as the text itself.

As a teacher of English to nonnative speakers, Helen Fox began finding students highly literate in their own cultures unable to write American academic English. In some cases their reaction was quite emotional, as if learning to write in this new way would rob them of their cultural birthright. Early in her career, Fox was surprised to discover our unwitting cultural imperialism – we assumed that we had the one right way of doing things and that everyone else was wrong.

Certainly there are many ways to wisdom. Coming from the culture currently dominating the world, we would do well to turn off our "send" function from time to time and begin listening to the different ways of thinking, knowing, and expressing that have developed around the world. We may learn something.

View a film from a non-Western country; then comment in your Wisdom Journal about how it differs from typical American movies.

CRONE WISDOM

When I am old I shall wear purple
With a red hat that doesn't go . . .
I shall gobble up samples in shops and press alarm bells
And run my stick along the public railings
And make up for the sobriety of my youth,
. . . And learn to spit.

–JENNY JOSEPH, "WARNING"

Diana, the triple goddess, appears as virgin, mother, and crone. Many of us recognize the third term only as a synonym for "old lady" or "witch." The usual phrase is "old crone," with *old* for emphasis. When I was a child, I thought people were saying "old crow." To be sure, my unabridged dictionary defines *crone* as "an ugly, withered, witch-like, old woman" and derives it from the Middle English for "old ewe."

The women's movement has reclaimed the term to mean, first, a postmenopausal woman, one who can no longer conceive or bear children. But, as in Ms. Joseph's poem, it connotes much more than that. Crones are less likely to feel compelled to base their standing on appearance, behavior, or type of marriage they were able to make. Good looks along with the wealth of one's father, or family, have been the universal ways for women to get ahead. Brains, skill, and hard work have mattered less. Crones, however, can spite conventions. They can wear colors that don't match. They can spit. They can be free of the rules imposed on them by male-dominated societies that determine their market value. There is no market for crones.

Most important, by being free of the burdens of childbearing and, often, work outside the home, crones have the time and experience to mentor younger women. They have survived the heights and depths of female life. They have been through relationships and jobs, had and lost children, cared for grandchildren. They have mellowed in some regards, but are less willing to back down from principles just to get along and not make waves. "Old wives' tales" unfortunately is what we men often call the harvested and shared wisdom of crones. This is not something for us to be proud of.

In your Wisdom Journal, describe an old woman you consider wise.

THE WISDOM OF HOSPITALITY

Sometimes give your services for nothing, calling to mind a previous benefaction or present satisfaction. And if there be an opportunity of serving one who is a stranger in financial straits, give full assistance to all such.

–Hippocrates (c. 460–377 b.c.e.), *Precepts*

As we know from signs at garage sales, not everything is to be sold. Often you will find boxes with items you can take for free. Generosity, hospitality, and charity are among the most commendable human characteristics. Sometimes it is best just to give things away.

Nearly five centuries before Christ, Hippocrates advised physicians to serve those who could not pay, even if they were strangers. The reason: The physicians themselves may have been in need and a generous person helped them out. Or, through no doing of their own but thanks to an excellent mind, supportive parents, powerful friends, and outstanding teachers, they were enabled to become physicians. Finally, they themselves may now be enjoying good fortune. In gratitude for any or all of these "benefactions," generosity and hospitality are prescribed.

When I was a student in Germany, people were kind to me on a number of occasions. I recall a taxi driver in Heidelberg who refused my fare because I, as an American, had taken the trouble to learn his language. Or my landlady, Frau Laupp, who did a superb job of washing and ironing my laundry, well beyond what was required by what I paid her. Or my friend Hans's parents in a suburb of Essen, who took me in and treated me as part of the family during several long vacations.

My wife and I have continued to welcome young people and others in our home as a way of passing on the hospitality we ourselves have received and continue to receive in our lives. By returning the kindness we have experienced, we participate in a process of receiving and giving not unlike the rain cycle, whereby water absorbed from the earth is stored in clouds, then returned to the earth as life-giving rain.

Note in your Wisdom Journal examples of hospitality you have given and received. How do you feel when you participate in them?

WISDOM OF A WOMAN OF VALOR

Who can find a capable wife?
Her worth is far beyond coral.
Her husband's whole trust is in her,
and children are not lacking. . . .
Like a ship laden with merchandise,
she brings home food from far off.
She rises while it is still night
and sets meat before her household.
After careful thought she buys a field
and plants a vineyard out of her earnings. . . .
Charm is a delusion and beauty fleeting;
it is the God-fearing woman who is honoured.
Extol her for the fruit of all her toil,
and let her labours bring her honour in the city gate.

–Proverbs 31:10–15,30–31

In the King James Version, the heroine of Proverbs, chapter 31, is known as "the virtuous woman." The New English Bible prefers the term "capable wife." In English-speaking Jewish communities, however, this role model is familiar to us as "the woman of valor."

Growing up in Jewish society, you are bound to come across a few examples. As the above lines suggest, women of valor are hardworking, self-sacrificing, thrifty, good at business, devout, and held in high regard in both their families and the broader community. An unmentioned trait is that these women are also tough and not to be trifled with. Two examples in the Old Testament are Esther and Judith. Esther successfully risked her life to save the Jews of the Persian Empire. Judith, whose story is told in the Apocrypha, seduced and personally beheaded the enemy king, Holofernes.

My Aunt Eva would also qualify. She married and cared for my father's brother, Murray, who was ill throughout most of their marriage. She raised their only son while running the family shoe store alone in a tough New York City neighborhood. Robbed several times, she kept going, paid the bills, retained her sense of humor, married and cared for another failing husband after Murray's death, and lived to be ninety-three. I am blessed to have had this woman of valor in my life.

Write in your Wisdom Journal about a strong woman you know.

WOMAN'S WISDOM

Woman is the creator of the universe,
the universe is her form;
woman is the foundation of the world,
she is the true form of the body. . . .
There is no prayer to equal a woman.
There is not, nor has been, nor will be
any yoga to compare with a woman,
no mystical formula nor asceticism to match a woman.
There are not, nor have been, nor will be
any riches more valuable than woman.

–From the *Saktisangama Tantra*, quoted in Manuela Dunn Mascetti, *The Song of Eve*, 1990

To some this may sound like reverse-gender chauvinism. Men have always been put, or have put themselves, on a pedestal. Now it's women's turn. One extreme begets another. To others this may sound like a classier, more poetic version of that song from *South Pacific:* "There Is Nothing Like a Dame." Whatever it is, it is a long way from Rex Harrison's plaint in *My Fair Lady*, "Why Can't a Woman Be More Like a Man?" Why, after all, should she be?

I like the way the poem's words sound but disagree with the sentiment. I would still feel the same if "man" were substituted for "woman." Or "American." Or "Caucasian." Or any other designation. When Muhammad Ali boasted before a fight that he was the greatest, so long as he remained the world heavyweight champion that claim was literally true. He was the best in his class. But Orthodox Muslims hearing his vaunt might shudder, because all such superlatives, in their belief, belong to God alone. This is especially true of *greatest,* as in the common Arabic formula, Allahu Akbar, "God is the greatest."

Yet, just as Ali was right in one sense to claim himself as the greatest, so there are grounds for asserting the matchlessness of woman. Only woman can bear human life. As Sojourner Truth said of Jesus, he had a human mother but no human father. No man can shelter another human life within his body. Earth, who bears all of us – and bears with us all – is also a mother. Human life is unthinkable without woman.

What constitutes "woman's wisdom"? Respond to this question in your Wisdom Journal.

THE WISDOM OF GOD'S TIME

Nam homo proponit, sed Deus disponit.
For man proposes, but God disposes.

–THOMAS À KEMPIS (1379–1471), *THE IMITATION OF CHRIST*

The Germans have a similar saying that also rhymes: *Der Mensch denkt; Gott lenkt.* The literal translation is, "The human being thinks; God steers." If you attend to the words, you realize that steering a person in a particular way is tantamount to directing, or managing, that person. According to a knowledgeable friend, Sufi teachers advise their disciples to give up planning. Or if that is impossible, disciples are urged to plan not to plan.

I remember planning my father's eightieth birthday party. I booked nonrefundable flights for my younger daughter and myself. My sister and I would host family and a few friends at a restaurant near my parents' Fort Lauderdale apartment. Then, a few days before we were to leave Chicago, my sister called to say Dad had fallen and broken his hip. He was in the hospital· New plan: We would put together a little bedside party. What I didn't know till arrival was that Dad had fatal bone marrow cancer as well. So his eightieth birthday celebration became a very small affair indeed.

In the spring of 1990, my wife planned to take her invalid mother to Munich to attend a great-grandson's wedding. The occasion was important for my mother-in-law because she had partly raised this great-grandson while his parents were divorcing. Tickets had been purchased, arrangements made. Who could know that Grandma would die on the planned day of departure?

Just last week a retired dentist we know here in Honolulu slipped away. He had been suffering from multiple cancers and had lived the past two years in a kind of informal hospice at our pastor's house. The doctors had Joe dead thirteen months ago. He rallied, though, and fooled them. This time things truly looked bad. His children were notified. Tickets were booked. Joe was especially looking forward to seeing his new and only grandchild. His doctors and others thought he would just make it. He died four days too early.

In your Wisdom Journal, write about an experience where God's plans and yours diverged.

BECOMING WISER

A person who was unwise in younger years but later finds wisdom, illuminates the world like the moon after becoming free of clouds.

–THE DHAMMAPADA

We tend to assume that older is wiser, but we all know people who are grown up in body but immature in their judgments and actions. And we have certainly all experienced the Sisyphean torture of moving vigorously toward a goal only to fall back to square one – whether by our own fault or owing to an outside cause. Then there is the matter of nature and nurture. While the debate about the relative importance of these factors goes on, both can at times seem stacked against us just as much as they can seem to be in our favor. Getting older, by itself, clearly does not mean getting wiser, nor does wisdom come easy.

Yet in the saying from the Buddha quoted above, the clear implication is that one *can* become wiser. In fact the lines suggest that in our essence we are always potentially wise. Take the moon. It is always round and "shining." Yet sometimes it *appears* to us on Earth to be less than round or whole. Moreover, when blocked by clouds, it does not seem to shine at all. A person living in a permanently cloudy area, assuming there were such a place, could be forgiven for thinking that the moon was a mythological body that didn't really exist. Seeing, for most of us, is believing.

The Dhammapada, some 423 sayings attributed to the Buddha, helps us understand that we can become wiser, even enlightened, and guides us along the path. "Recovery," "conversion," "salvation," "enlightenment" – the world's religious and spiritual traditions are full of good news. Perhaps we need only listen and follow.

Reflect on your life. Think of some positive changes you have made. How have you been able to keep them intact? In what way are you a wiser person today than ten years ago? Write your answers in your Wisdom Journal.

THE WISDOM OF INNER HEARING

Wonders are many, and none is more wonderful than man.

–Sophocles (c. 496–406 B.C.E.), *Antigone*

Today, May 7th, is the anniversary of the first performance, in 1824 in Vienna, of Ludwig van Beethoven's Ninth Symphony. Known as "The Choral" because of the scoring for solo voices and choir, the Ninth sets to music Friederich Schiller's "Ode to Joy." Churchgoers are familiar with the melody, too, because it serves as the basis for that most popular and uplifting English hymn, "Joyful, Joyful, We Adore Thee." But one fact makes Beethoven's accomplishment all the more amazing. When he wrote the Ninth Symphony, the composer from Bonn was completely deaf.

How in the world, you might ask, can a deaf person compose melodies that please and impress the hearing? How indeed! Or how could Helen Keller, who was blind as well as deaf, learn to read, then write in rich, graceful prose?

Given the myriad stimuli of the outer world, we can easily forget something important: In addition to the outer world, or environment, there is also an inner world. We *can* see with our eyes closed, as anyone who has ever dreamed knows. Infants cry when they are wet or hungry. But have you ever noticed how they occasionally smile to themselves? Maybe they are remembering or experiencing something within.

Beethoven, to be sure, was not born deaf. Perhaps he simply remembered what a beautiful melody looked like on paper. Perhaps the visual architecture of the music translated into something equally pleasing to the ear. I have not studied the topic nor read Beethoven biographies to see what the experts say. The concept, though, is fascinating – the possibility that we have inner as well as outer hearing – that we can "hear" even if we are deaf, "see" even if we are blind. In esoteric circles it is held that inventions are readied in the spirit world before human beings "invent" them. Maybe this is the true meaning of an idea whose time has come. Whatever the case, the extent of our human capacities truly inspires wonder.

In your Wisdom Journal, describe an experience of having had an inspiration.

THE WISDOM OF SOUND PRIORITIES

Beloved Pan, and all ye other gods who haunt this place, give me beauty in the inward soul; and may the outward and inward man be at one. May I reckon the wise to be the wealthy, and may I have such a quantity of gold as none but the temperate can carry.

–PLATO (428–347 B.C.E.), *PHAEDRUS*

The first sound priority is knowing that by ourselves we are limited beings who may get life wrong and not realize this fact until it's too late – at least this time around. Faith in powers higher and wiser than ourselves is thus an immense gift.

Next is understanding and really living from an acceptance that the inner self, or essence, is more important than the outer, or personality. The former pertains to that part of us that will continue after our mission on this planet is done. The latter pertains to our spacesuit. Being overly concerned with the outer aspects of life distracts us from the need for spiritual development – from those activities that, in Emily Dickinson's great line, make "internal difference, / Where the Meanings, are."

The next priority is integrating the inner and the outer self. Integration leads to integrity. Wearing a mask that belies who and what we are causes us, literally, to be hypocrites, from the Greek word for actors, people who wear masks and pretend to be someone or something they are not. Working on ourselves has the goal of bringing the inner and outer person, the essence and personality, together. According to the Javanese, superior batik makers take special care, as they wax each side of the cloth, to match up the dots and lines of the design. Such is the nature of integration.

Finally, one must understand that true riches, like the Kingdom of heaven, lie within. We must be careful to have only as much material wealth as we can carry without letting it go to our heads. Instead, as Plato advises, we should consider wisdom the true coin of the realm. May we have the eyes to see and the ears to hear what Plato is telling us.

What are your priorities in life? Where do inner life and integration fall on your list? Discuss this in your Wisdom Journal.

THE WISDOM OF POSITIVE THINKING

There is nothing either good or bad, but thinking makes it so.

—William Shakespeare, *Hamlet,* II, ii, 259

The Power of Positive Thinking and *How to Win Friends and Influence People* influenced me greatly in high school. Both made sense and, to the extent that I followed them, seemed to work. But it wasn't until I was a college dean in Chicago many years later that someone introduced me to Napoleon Hill's extraordinary *Think and Grow Rich,* published in 1937.

I remember highlighting half the words in the book, then spending most of a Saturday entering whole sentences and paragraphs into my old Apple IIe. We took an hour at the next staff meeting discussing Dr. Hill's wisdom and figuring how we could apply it to our programs of adult, continuing, and nontraditional education.

As administrators at an urban university with lots of older, minority, and first-generation college students, how could we not be inspired by the all-American exhortation of the dust jacket: "If you learn and apply the simple basic techniques revealed here, you will have mastered the secret of true and lasting success, and you may have whatever you want in life"? It was heady stuff. For example, *"All achievement, all earned riches, have their beginning in an idea!"* Or, "Whatever the mind of man can conceive and believe it can achieve."

Hill's hero and primary role model was Andrew Carnegie, who originally imparted the "secret of life" to him. Though never stated explicitly, it amounts to something like "inspiration plus perspiration catalyzed with a positive mental attitude over time can only lead to success." Canfield and Hansen, in their *Aladdin Principle,* say approximately the same thing. We each have a genie within, and that genie can do magic. We just have to learn how to call the genie forth. I am American enough to love this idea, puritanical enough to fear its success, and religious enough to believe that by taking thought, I can do only so much. The rest is up to God.

What are the possibilities and limitations of what Hill and Chicago tycoon E. Clement Stone named Positive Mental Attitude (PMA)? Discuss in your Wisdom Journal.

WISDOM THROUGH SUFFERING

By suffering comes wisdom.

–Aeschylus (525–456 B.C.E.), *Agamemnon*

This is a hard lesson to learn – or accept. So much suffering seems unwarranted and pointless. The shock and pain of someone whose spouse walks out after thirty years of marriage. The devastation of parents whose child is killed by a drunken driver. The grief of survivors for loved ones lost in a war. The anguish for her young children of a forty-year-old mother dying of breast cancer. Our stunned disbelief in the face of Auschwitz.

We may not like going to the dentist for a filling, but at least the discomfort makes sense. It prevents greater discomfort and pain later on. The cramps and aches of the long-distance runner come about through his or her own choice. No one forces people to do marathons. The pangs of launching a project or having a baby are the accepted and well-understood price of bringing something new into the world. As athletes say, "No pain, no gain."

But suffering? Aeschylus is the first, chronologically, among the writers of classic Greek tragedy. If I am not mistaken, Kenneth Burke, the literary critic, came up with the concept of tragedy's three P's: purpose, passion, and perception. Take Oedipus the King. His *purpose* was to avoid the fate prophesied for him that he would murder his father and marry his mother. To assure his success, he leaves his home city-state. But he is unaware that he has been raised by foster parents who had rescued him when his birth parents, also attempting to avoid the prophecy, arranged for his death as an infant. Along the way Oedipus kills a stranger who turns out to be his father and marries another stranger who is his mother. When he discovers what he has done, his suffering, or *passion,* in the sense of Christ's Passion on the cross, is so great that he blinds himself. His *perception?* As a blind man, he now *sees* that despite our best efforts, we cannot avoid our fate. Certainly his suffering has brought him wisdom. But at a tragic cost.

Do you agree that wisdom can come through suffering? Write freely for ten minutes on this subject in your Wisdom Journal.

THE WISDOM OF · LEARNING FROM OUR CRITICS

The wise may learn many things from their foes.

–Aristophanes (440–380 B.C.E.), *The Birds*

It is hard to be criticized, whether by friend or foe. After all, our intentions are noble. We are doing the best we can. We are nice people. No matter. We may have bombed, and the sooner we know, the better. We can't improve what we incorrectly believe to be flawless.

As a good student, I routinely got A's. Each A paper reinforced in my mind that I was a good student. Yet the real learning came from the exceptions – the papers on which I got a B+ or lower. Being a really good student means internalizing criticisms and next time around, correcting likely mistakes before submitting a final draft.

One of my friends is a retired speech professor who talks for a living and helps other people do so too. He refers to himself professionally these days as "The Talk Doctor." His "pro-tirement" business card pictures him all dressed up as a physician with stethoscope in hand.

As someone with more to do than the time to do it, I become impatient with long-seeming speeches, unless, of course, I am the one giving them. So when the Talk Doctor pauses in a detailed account of something, I tend to complete his thoughts in an effort to speed things up. While now and then I guess right, often I get it wrong. Meanwhile I only extend the conversation as the Talk Doctor prescribes more listening and less interrupting on my part.

I am more attentive now, I think, and if things go on for too long for me, I'll mention an appointment I need to leave for. Come to think of it, the Talk Doctor does the same. I am working on interrupting less and banishing my practice of finishing other people's sentences for them. It's hard to be told what one does wrong. But in listening and trying to improve, there is often a blessing.

In your Wisdom Journal, describe an instance where you improved something you do by heeding a criticism.

MOTHER'S DAY WISDOM

God could not be everywhere, therefore he made mothers.

–A Hebrew proverb

Wait a minute! Of course God can be everywhere. Have my ancestors forgotten the "omnis"? You know: omniscient, omnipotent, and omnipresent. But just because God *can* be everywhere at the same time doesn't mean God *has* to be. After all, God has free will too. Just think about it for a minute. If God were everyplace at once, there would have been no need for Jesus Christ to incarnate. For each of us would already have been incarnations – beings full of the omnipresent God. As separate beings with our own will, though, we are free to accept or reject the divine will, assuming we can determine what that is for us from situation to situation. With each correct choice, we move closer to welcoming God into our life. But God will not force us. For if we fallible human parents respect the closed doors of our teenaged children, can we expect less from the Creator of the Universe?

Enough theology. This really is about the wisdom of mothers and mothering. My sense of the Hebrew saying is that, out of respect for the Creation, God delegated the maternal function to mothers. Just as the birthing process kicks in automatically when the time has come, so, I believe, does a mother's desire to feed, protect, and care for her child. Men can be nurturing. Teenagers can be effective, responsible babysitters. But the maternal instinct is the primary property of mothers.

Not that every biological mother is a good one. Immaturity or mental illness can compromise even a strong desire to mother well. And some mothers are overprotective, and instead of mothering, they smother. Hence all the jokes about Jewish – or Italian – mothers. Moreover, some individuals, such as adoptive mothers, are not biological mothers but are incredibly nurturing. In my childhood, Florine, our African American housekeeper, a woman who had never had children, was my primary caregiver. Despite the presence of my mother, when we had air-raid drills during World War II, I always ran to Florine's bed. I knew where I would be safe.

Write in your Wisdom Journal about those characteristics of your mother for which you are most grateful.

THE WISDOM OF THRIFT

Use it up, wear it out;
Make it do, or do without.

–A NEW ENGLAND MAXIM

I come from a family of spendthrifts. I profited from this profligacy, receiving four years and two summers of boarding school, several years of summer camp, a Yale undergraduate education, and junior year abroad. After my BA degree, I was on my own. Fortunately, generous fellowships coupled with part-time jobs, my wife's work, and a National Defense Act loan helped me complete my PhD with little indebtedness.

My father's deal with me for my junior year was to transfer $200 to my Heidelberg account every month for twelve months. At that time (1958), $2,400 would have exactly covered tuition, room, and board at Yale. In exchange for German currency, $200 bought roughly the amount of my future father-in-law's monthly salary as an elementary school principal. The only difference was, he had a family to support. All I had was myself.

Despite my relative affluence, however, I tried to see how far I could stretch my money. I was responding, in part, to the wasteful ways in my parents home – we never ate leftovers, for example, tossing out perfectly good food the night it was served. So I traveled thriftily around Europe. At one point my German friend Hans and I spent ten days in Paris on $25 apiece. If you think freeloading might have been a factor in this achievement, you would not be wrong. But it was a marvelous trip.

In the 1960s, environmental concerns motivated me to recycle the clean sides of typed pages for notes. I also went around the house turning off lights. Here again, my parents figured electricity was there for the asking, so why not keep everything lit up all the time? I also learned to wear hand-me-down clothes. We may have subsidized half our kids' college through clothing ourselves and furnishing our home from thrift shops. Careful in small things, I nevertheless still tend to live beyond my means. I hope to break this habit before being transferred off the planet.

How thrifty are you? Do a brief self-assessment in your Wisdom Journal.

THE WISDOM OF HARD WORK

So long as there is anything the superior person has not studied or cannot understand, he or she will never stop working.

–Confucius (551–478 B.C.E.)

When I embarked on learning Chinese fifteen years ago, one of the first Mandarin words I learned was *nu-li* (pronounced noo-lee), which means "hard-work(ing)." This contrasts with lesson one in my Japanese primer, where the initial vocabulary was all about introducing oneself. A Chinese proverb advises, "Be the first to the field, the last to the couch."

Mr. and Mrs. Li, my Chinese teacher and his wife, were visiting scholars from Shanghai. When we met, Huang-lei, the wife, had just arrived. They were poor as church mice. In fact they were able to live gratis for several years at our church in exchange for custodial work. While studying for their PhDs in linguistics, the Lis worked at least three jobs at a time. Besides teaching Chinese privately and doing some things at church, they worked in stores in Chicago's Chinatown and also conducted a low-level import business. They seemed to live on nothing, but every once in a while they threw a nine-course party that would knock your socks off. In a few years, they were able to bring their twelve-year-old daughter, Linda, from China to live with them. After the Tiananmen uprising, they were granted permanent residency. Around that time Li told me they had managed to amass a nest egg of $50,000.

Jawaharlal Nehru once said: "Life is like a game of cards. The hand that is dealt you represents determinism; the way you play it is free will." The Lis had been dealt a tough hand. Li's father, a factory owner, had died in a Communist prison. Li's parentage would keep him from ever becoming more than assistant professor in China. Yet he knew the wisdom and power of *nu-li*. Once in the States, he and his wife worked hard, soon reaping material benefits beyond what most native-born citizens would ever achieve.

What kind of worker are you? Are you willing to work hard over an extended period – to do whatever it takes to reach your objectives? Write in your Wisdom Journal about your work style.

THE WISDOM OF CHILDREN

Dear God
What does it mean you are a jealous God. I thought you had everything
Jane

–From Stuart Hample and Eric Marshall, *Children's Letters to God*

If the world's classical traditions attribute wisdom to age, the romantics saw it in children. It took the boy hero in Hans Christian Andersen's "The Emperor's New Clothes" to see–and to say–the emperor was naked. And in Wordsworth's "Intimations Ode," it was again the boy, not yet jaded by this world, who was still close to nature, his own soul, and a sense of spiritual presence.

Yet the innocent eye of youth does not merely fade with the passing of years. It is educated out of us. Some of us will remember Lieutenant Cable's song in *South Pacific*. In love with a young Polynesian woman on the island where he is stationed, Cable knows he will never be able to marry her and bring her back to the States. He sings: "You've got to be taught before it's too late / Before you are six, or seven, or eight / To hate all the people your relatives hate– / You've got to be carefully taught!"

So Jane writes to God and confronts the second commandment (Exodus 20:5). The four English Bibles we own all use the adjective *jealous*. The King James Version reads, "For I the Lord thy God am a jealous God." To Jane, *jealous* means *envious*. She remembers her friend Sally taunting her, "Janie, you're just jealous because my doll is prettier." So Jane reasons, "Why in the world should God be jealous, when God has everything?"

Jane is right–up to a point. Because if we follow other gods, God clearly doesn't have us. Still, it often takes the fresh mind of a child to see through the contradictions of society. Jealousy is no virtue. Why indeed should God be jealous?

Can you remember something you knew or said as a child that was "beyond your years"? Write in your Wisdom Journal about this experience of childhood wisdom.

THE WISDOM OF LOOKING BEYOND APPEARANCES

Beware, as long as you live, of judging people by appearances.

—Jean de La Fontaine (1621–1695)

According to tradition, Socrates was homely, even ugly. Ironically it was his student Alcibiades, regarded by his associates as a hypocrite, who recognized the great man's inner beauty. Socrates, he claimed, was like the doll of the god Silenus. The outer doll, hollowed out like the Russian *matrioshka* to contain a figurine, was unsightly. The inner doll was beautiful.

My favorite professor at Yale, Alec Witherspoon, looked like a cross between a bullfrog and Scrooge McDuck. Not only that, he had strange mannerisms when he spoke. I remember thinking to myself the first day of class, "Oh, no. Is this who I am going to have for English the rest of the year?" Later in Dick Cavett's autobiography, I read how as a Yale undergraduate, Cavett had accompanied his roommate to one of Withy's classes, just to see and laugh at this strange fish. How wrong Dick and his roommate were! How unfounded my concern turned out to be!

From that experience I have learned to withhold judgment based on how an individual at first appears. (It can, of course, work the other way too. Someone handsome or beautiful at first sight can turn out to be uninteresting, superficial, or even mean.) Either way, one soon comes to see the outer person differently, as modified by getting to know something of the inner person.

Recently I became aware that I sometimes get frustrated by the car directly in front of me. "Why are they driving so slow?" I think. Then I realize that they are being slowed up themselves by the traffic in front of them. Maybe someone is turning. Maybe there has been an accident. In any case their driving under the speed limit was not their fault. At this point I regret the hair trigger on my willingness to think ungenerous thoughts about others. Had I only taken the longer view!

Write in your Wisdom Journal about an incident in which you either judged too quickly or withheld judgment until more evidence was in. Give yourself some good advice for the future.

THE WISDOM OF TRUST

In God we trust, all others pay cash.

–A SIGN NEAR A CASH REGISTER

Here's a formula for relationships that will fail: Don't trust your partner. One reason so many relationships founder is that trust comes hard. Every time we have been let down seems to get between us and our ability to give others the benefit of the doubt. What to do?

Well, first off, you can practice trust. For example, volunteer to lend your teenage son or daughter your car. Dispense with the usual sermon that, though delivered in the most measured tones and with impeccable logic, will be perceived as "yelling at me." Then go pray – for your child's safety and your own peace of mind.

I've been a fairly frequent flier since my boarding school days. Nevertheless I go through periods of relative calm and considerable angst when it comes to being in an airplane. I am currently in a calm phase. On my last flight, I tried an experiment. I put my sleep blinders on as we entered the final approach. My goal: To let the pilot land without my assistance. Usually I get concerned if there are low-lying clouds impairing the view of the ground. I look out the window and am relieved when land appears. But this time I was good. I paid attention to my breathing and tried not to notice the yawing from side to side or the change in motor pitch. I managed to remain calm until we were on the ground.

I believe you can build trust like a muscle. In personal relationships, the positive feedback you get from the person you trusted – for example, your daughter with the Honda – will make encore performances less challenging. Even during my nervous flying periods, I tend to relax, or stop caring, on night flights or toward the end of long ones. Then there is the practical approach incorporated in these words of Rudyard Kipling: "I always prefer to believe the best of everybody – it saves so much time."

In your Wisdom Journal, do a trust inventory of yourself. How trusting are you? Do you tend to get taken advantage of, or does your trust invite the trust of others?

HYMN WISDOM

Let the pealing organ blow,
To the full-voiced quire below,
In service high, and anthems clear
As may, with sweetness, through mine ear
Dissolve me into ecstasies,
And bring all Heaven before mine eyes.

-John Milton (1608–1674), "Il Penseroso"

I first encountered Protestant hymns as a toddler. Like many other suburban Jewish families in those days, we had a live-in African American housekeeper. Florine often hummed while she worked, and I later came to recognize her tunes as hymns.

At age eleven I was sent to Peddie, an all-boys American Baptist boarding school in New Jersey. There, in addition to mandatory Bible class, we had compulsory daily chapel, monthly Sunday morning convocation, and a vespers hymn-sing every Sunday night. By sophomore year I had joined the choir, and soon I landed a place behind the organ where I could sleep with impunity during the boring chapel sermons. My favorite service was vespers, which an earlier Peddie wit had dubbed the Holy Hit Parade. Here we could pick our favorite hymns. The time of day notwithstanding, someone would inevitably select "Holy, holy, holy, Lord God Almighty! / Early in the morning our song shall rise to thee." Before we were dismissed, however, justice would be restored when someone picked "Day is dying in the west, / Heaven is touching earth with rest; / Wait and worship while the night / Sets her evening lamps alight."

Since prep-school days, I'll find myself intoning snatches of hymns at odd moments. When I become aware of the words, they are usually appropriate. For instance, if I am puzzled by a situation, I may find myself humming "Once to Every Man and Nation Comes the Moment to Decide." Hymns were probably a factor in my conversion to Christianity at age twenty-seven. Visiting the Peddie campus twenty-five years after graduating, I entered the vacant chapel, picked up a hymnal, and burst into tears. Beneath the cross of Jesus I fain had taken my stand.

If you have a favorite hymn, think about the text, then write in your Wisdom Journal what meaning this hymn holds for your life.

UNSEEKABLE WISDOM

I am not sure one can actually "cultivate" wisdom. I do not see it as something one can seek directly, for itself, but more something that comes as a byproduct of everything else we are doing in our lives. In this sense it is very much like compassion, another byproduct of skillful living.

–From Roy Wood's posting to the W-isdom listserv, May 4, 1998

I am reminded of the Sufi advice that although you cannot seek God, you must never not seek God. Normally we seek things that we have some chance of gaining: an education, a fulfilling relationship with another human being, a satisfying profession, an acceptable lifestyle. Yet seeking God, or wisdom for that matter, may be like an ant trying to make off with a boulder. Ants have the capacity to carry objects considerably bigger than themselves. But even a pebble would be beyond their capacity, let alone a boulder.

Still, Jesus does give us the A.S.K. formula in Matthew 7:7 and Luke 11:9: Ask and you shall receive; Seek and you shall find; Knock and the door shall be opened. As for wisdom, Proverbs 4:7 provides clear marching orders: "Wisdom is the principal thing; therefore get wisdom." If wisdom were beyond human reach, why would the Bible give us this imperative?

Actually I think Roy Wood does have a point. Although there are many things one can do to attain wisdom or to become wiser – some of them contained in this book – wisdom is finally a gift, an act of grace. We may do the studying, but it is the college or university that grants the degree.

We started with the Sufis, so let's give them the last word. According to Islamic mystical practice, for a wish to become true, for a prayer to be valid, it must be stated as an intention and offered to God. In this context it is my intention that each of you reading these words will be granted a full measure of wisdom. *Insha'llah!* May God say Amen!

In your Wisdom Journal, write about three or four things you are currently doing to become a wiser person.

WHOLE-VILLAGE WISDOM

My father explained the importance of our example. . . . We know that not just one pair of eyes is watching us, but the eyes of the whole community are on us. It's not a case of giving things up. We have a lot of freedom, but, at the same time, within that freedom we must respect ourselves. . . .

Suddenly they treated me like an adult. My father said . . . "From now on you must contribute to the common good."

-Rigoberta Menchú, 1984

Rigoberta Menchú comes from a traditional Central American indigenous society. If you've seen the film *El Norte,* you'll have a good sense that this is a dangerous background, given the prejudices of the surrounding nonnative community. In 1978 Rigoberta's father, mother, and brother were all brutally killed in separate acts of violence by the national army. Despite her youth Rigoberta became the leading spokesperson for her people and won the Nobel Peace Prize for her efforts.

The sort of upbringing described here, with the entire community acting like parents for every child, is typical of tribal societies. Many of us are familiar with the African proverb, "It takes a whole village to raise a child." Though perhaps this proverb has been overused in recent years, it carries a great deal of truth. In present-day America, too many children are being raised by overtaxed single parents.

In his book *The Truly Disadvantaged,* University of Chicago sociologist William J. Wilson states that, whatever good integration did for African Americans, it had one unfortunate side effect. It took professionals out of the ghetto. Where before the neighborhood doctor or lawyer might tell a young person to take that cigarette out of his mouth, there were now no successful role models to serve as collective parent. Educated African Americans had moved to the suburbs. Only the poor were left behind. Based on its multiyear study of a half-million American youth, the Search Institute has also concluded that children raised without three trustworthy adults in their life are at significant risk for the future. Isn't it time for us to rejoin the village and contribute to the common good?

Write in your Wisdom Journal about the significant adults you knew in your youth.

WISDOM IS YOU

Wisdom is the experience of your own nature, it is the expression of your self-being. It is the flowering of your own consciousness. It is not information, it is transformation.

And that is the whole effort here: not to make you more informed – about god [sic], about truth, about love – but to make you more informed about your own potential.

–Rajneesh, as quoted in an Institute of Noetic Sciences brochure

Some years ago when I first heard about Baghwan Shri Rajneesh, sometimes referred to as Osho, he was being deported from his ashram in Oregon on federal tax-evasion charges. There were rumors that he was a polygamist, but avoided breaking the law by not actually marrying his consorts. A typical East Indian cult leader, the media assured us, he played on the needs of innocent young Americans, took their youth and money and, by implication, rendered them unable to participate in the American way of life.

But come to think of it, two of my colleagues, both with doctorates from prestigious universities and enviable careers, were for a while "Rajneeshis." One, to be sure, lived for several years in a group-marriage situation and made recreational use of marijuana. The other apparently followed the master to India and lived as a celibate for a time. This individual is one of the most dependable people I know. Naturally I was delighted when yet a third colleague forwarded the above quotation to me. Who or what to believe about Rajneesh? For our purposes I'll accept the wisdom of the quotation.

Like other spiritual leaders from the Hindu tradition – Deepak Chopra comes to mind – Rajneesh emphasizes the immanence of wisdom. We each carry our own supply. We have only to access and use it. But maybe we should think of wisdom as being latent and usable only if reconstituted like powdered milk. Work on ourselves thus becomes comparable to adding water and stirring. So while wisdom is available to each of us, it may not be readily available. In spiritual matters as in other things, there is no free lunch.

Discuss in your Wisdom Journal how you access your own nature in order to experience personal transformation.

THE WISDOM OF TITHING

Every tithe on land, whether from grain or from the fruit of a tree, belongs to the LORD; it is holy to the LORD. . . . Every tenth creature that passes under the counting rod shall be holy to the LORD; this applies to all tithes of cattle and sheep.

-LEVITICUS 27:30–32

I wonder what percentage of Christians or Jews tithe. A tithe (tenth) or less, I am sure. In case you are curious, I don't–yet. The best I have done is around seven percent of my gross income, and that included all gifts to charity, not just to my church.

Now you may argue, as I have, that the ruling in Leviticus came at a time before public taxation. Each of us in America–and virtually every other country in the world–is taxed on both income and purchases. These are not free-will offerings. I leave it up to you to form an opinion as to whether and to what extent our taxes eventually do God's work. Taken together, the taxes we pay work out to much more than ten percent. In some countries, Germany for example, a required church tax pays the upkeep on houses of worship as well as the salaries of parish employees. In America with its separation of church and state, ministers have to preach a good deal on stewardship. After all, if too little money comes in, the parish staff become volunteers.

Still, in the interest of sound living, it is good to simplify our lives and live within our income. Stewardship in this instance begins at home. Our pastor in fact suggests that everyone do a double tithe: one to the church and the other to themselves. The tithe to ourselves is roughly the ten to fifteen percent of gross income financial planners like us to invest in a wisely diversified portfolio. If we give to God and ourselves first, we are forced to live within the balance. Meanwhile the church is strengthened, and before long we have income-producing assets that can enrich our lifestyle while guaranteeing a financially acceptable retirement. Now the only question is, why didn't I acquire this wisdom when I was twenty?

Write in your Wisdom Journal about your habits of personal and charitable stewardship.

THE WISDOM OF DECISIVENESS

Once you make a decision, the universe conspires to make it happen.

-Ralph Waldo Emerson (1803–1882)

We all know the limitations of this wisdom. The universe will not conspire to help me fly if I dive, arms flapping, off the Empire State Building. But we also know instinctively what Emerson is talking about. If we really go for something, put all our energy and heart into it, we do start to see things breaking our way. It is almost as if the universe respects our spunk and decides to help us out.

Even failure becomes grist for our mill. A friend of mine in Chicago, an English major and a poet, started his career teaching difficult children in a public home for boys. An acquaintance of his knew of the availability of some high-speed cassette-duplicating equipment and suggested that my friend might like to join him in buying it and setting up a tape-duplicating business. My friend took the plunge, and a long, hard fall it was. After a short time, his partner left for California. Even when the business began to expand, cash flow was always critical. To obtain contracts they had to work with very narrow margins. After years of heroic effort, my friend threw in the towel and declared bankruptcy.

Meanwhile he had learned many new skills and had become adept at raising capital. This time he went into the computer software business by buying an existing company that featured a checkers and chess program. Again the way forward was challenging, but before long my friend produced a successful data-management program, and his picture appeared on the cover of a software magazine. A few years ago, his company was bought out by a large software firm. He must have done very well, because he was able to give a seven-figure donation to charity.

I have noticed in my own life that when I make a major decision and persevere, things do seem to fall into place. It is not easy to be decisive, but the universe seems clearly to reward this kind of heroism.

In your Wisdom Journal, comment on whether Emerson's claim has been manifest in your life.

THE WISDOM OF FAITH

God our Father has made all things depend on faith so that whoever has faith will have everything, and whoever does not have faith will have nothing.

–MARTIN LUTHER, "FREEDOM OF A CHRISTIAN," 1520

Faith is our direct link to universal wisdom, reminding us that we know more than we have heard or read or studied – that we have only to look, listen, and trust the love and wisdom of the Universal Spirit working through us all.

–DAN MILLMAN, *THE LAWS OF SPIRIT,* 1995

My rule has been one quotation per day. I've included two today because of the breadth and importance of the subject and because I couldn't make up my mind. Both illuminate aspects of faith. Both also say something to me.

Luther was a lover of all-or-nothing statements. It is ironic that this particular one found its way into one of his last attempts to reconcile with Rome. Personal faith was at the core of Luther's reform, which came onto the world scene at roughly the same time as individualism and nationalism. A serious biblical scholar and translator as well as an Augustinian monk and Catholic priest, Luther knew that when Jesus healed people in the Gospel stories, he assigned credit either to the Father or to the individual's faith. Even today the scientifically inclined will credit indisputable "miracle cures" to the strength of the patient's belief in doctor or treatment. The technical term is "placebo effect."

If Luther's statement on faith is as stern as the portrait of him by Lucas Cranach, Dan Millman's statement reminds us of the tolerance and optimism that characterize much human-development literature 480 years later. Faith, per Millman, is recognizing that each of us contains the wisdom of the universe, or at least the ability to get whatever we need from Universal Spirit. It seems as though every person has the potential for linkage to a kind of cosmic Internet. Faith activates that potential and makes sure we use it.

Luther and Millman do seem to agree on one thing: Faith is the key. Without it the most important doors of living will not be opened.

How do you describe faith? Write about it in your Wisdom Journal.

THE WISDOM OF GOD'S GUIDANCE

When looking back on the lives of men and women of God the tendency is to say – "What wonderfully astute wisdom they had! How perfectly they understood all God wanted!" The astute mind behind is the Mind of God, not human wisdom at all. We give credit to human wisdom when we should give credit to the Divine guidance of God through childlike people who were foolish enough to trust God's wisdom and the supernatural equipment of God.

–Oswald Chambers, *My Utmost for His Highest,* 1935

Here is the theocentric, or God-centered, notion of wisdom. True wisdom, according to this view, is an attribute of God. Human wisdom by itself is insufficient to stand up to the changes and chances of life. The saintly aren't the sophisticated, as Oswald Chambers implies, but the childlike: individuals smart enough to get out of the way and allow the wisdom of God to prevail on all occasions. Those of us who assume that human wisdom is the pinnacle of achievement will therefore misconstrue the "men and women of God" as those who have merely mastered the art of living.

The human-centered idea of wisdom begins with human free will and a kind of tacit agreement from the Deity, if Deity there be, to leave humanity to struggle its way to right living. This view, not surprisingly, is the mirror image of the theocentric conception. Here, human wisdom *is* sufficient to handle whatever situation life may deal us. It is merely a question of being innately wise or learning from experience how to deal with life's challenges. To strict humanists the theocentric approach comes across as a kind of *deus ex machina* – like James Bond arriving just in time to save the imperiled heroine.

As a believer with a strong humanistic education, I think we should use our mind and will to deal with whatever confronts us. We shouldn't presume on God to do our work for us. But we should also be gingerly in applying ourselves, always willing to "let go and let God." True wisdom, as the Serenity Prayer suggests, is knowing when to do which.

Write in your Wisdom Journal how you sort out the conundrum of human wisdom and God's wisdom.

CRYING WISDOM

Keep me from the wisdom which does not cry, the philosophy which does not laugh, and the greatness which does not bow before children.

–Kahlil Gibran (1883–1931)

As a child I cried easily. As an adolescent at a boys' boarding school, however, I learned to grow up, be a man, and suppress my tears. By the time I was a Yale sophisticate, crying was something only girls did. I had banned it from my repertoire of behaviors.

Recently, at the memorial service for an 83-year-old friend, the master of ceremonies, himself 64, started crying. So moved was he by describing how the person we were honoring had saved the life of his infant son many years before that he had to pause for several minutes to regain his composure before completing the eulogy. (Interestingly, his ex-wife, who read her own testimonial twenty minutes later, touched on the same incident but got through the whole piece dry-eyed. So much for gender stereotypes!)

Maybe it is age, maybe my spiritual practice, but I have relearned crying. Not just at home or when I am alone somewhere or in the dark semiprivacy of a movie house. The tears now come when and where they will. On Good Friday in church, for example, I am always moved by the "good" thief's request to Jesus for salvation, and Jesus' response. Sometimes when I am talking about a person who went out of his or her way to perform a kindness, my voice will also begin to quiver.

I have shed the high seriousness of my earlier days, and now I laugh a lot. It is amazing how good you feel after a good laugh or cry. My chest always seems less constricted, and thoughts or concerns that had been oppressing me evaporate. Best of all, though, is playing with young children. Last night at a party, I spent twenty minutes making up and participating in games with a six-year-old. Afterward I felt fully awake and totally free.

Share in your Wisdom Journal how you are with crying, laughing, and hanging out with little kids.

NOSE-ON-YOUR-FACE WISDOM

The more you look through your drawers, under the bed and bureau, in the closet and on the bathroom shelf for the spectacles you are already wearing, the further you will be from finding them. According to Zen, the point . . . is as self-evident as it can be, just as there is nothing more totally obvious and fundamentally self-evident than the infinite Reality in whose consciousness and being we live and move. Our trouble is that the egoistic viewpoint is so thoroughly complex that it has extreme difficulty in recognizing the essentially simple.

–ALAN WATTS (1915–1973), *THE SUPREME IDENTITY*

Back in the 1940s, adults would play a game with us kids called Got Your Nose. Basically, an adult, generally a male, would tweak your nose with his index and middle fingers. Then he would stick his thumb between those two fingers and say, "Got your nose!" I would chase the adult and whine, "Give me back my nose." I never thought to go to the closest mirror, inspect the alleged damage, and call the adult's bluff.

Life plays a similar game with us called Got Your Glasses. As in Watts's extended metaphor, we chase life and whine, "Give me back my glasses." We never stop to check if we might still be wearing them. The rule is, we never find things by looking in the wrong place. The corollary is, we can't find something that isn't lost.

Watts's related point is that our complexity does us in. If the solution to a problem is simple, we will never arrive at it by looking for something complex. We must in effect become as simple as the problem. When it comes to the inner life, we must be like a river and flow. A frozen river will never reach the sea. Nor will a frozen inner life achieve self-realization. Dead people, Lao Tzu said, are stiff. Babies, by contrast, are flexible. The old Chinese master would have understood Jesus' advice that unless we become like little children, we will never enter the Kingdom of heaven.

Breathe in and think "river"; breathe out and think "flow." Do this five times. Write about the experience in your Wisdom Journal.

OPPORTUNITY-MAKING WISDOM

A wise man will make more opportunities than he finds.

–Francis Bacon (1561–1626)

Gioacchino Rossini supposedly once said, "You can give me a laundry list, and I will write you a beautiful opera." The composer of the "William Tell Overture" and many other entertaining pieces of music probably never uttered any such words. Did they even have laundry lists back in the early nineteenth century? Still, the idea is a good one. It highlights the alchemistic human ability of taking the base metals of everyday life and turning them into golden opportunities for learning, loving, and achieving.

We are such an input-driven society. Before we go into business, we buy all kinds of equipment and supplies. We must be prepared for any business coming our way. But the real art is finding a niche, attracting customers, and providing the goods or services they need. We must create a business, not an office. Similarly, there are people with state-of-the-art kitchens and everything in their fridge. Yet they can't cook, and their meals are hardly edible. On the other hand, some people with very little by way of equipment and supplies can serve up a feast.

Obviously this is not an either-or situation. You do need some food to prepare a meal. Even Jesus, when he fed the five thousand, started with a few loaves and fishes. Nor do I wish to suggest that low-quality meats and produce are better than their fresh, high-quality equivalents. If you can afford it, buy the best. The same goes for equipment. But not even the highest-quality supplies and equipment can replace a skillful, inventive cook.

Life situations are similar. Viktor Frankl turned his years in a concentration camp into a learning lab and a place to continue his development. On a small scale, each of us can keep a paperback in our pocket to while away our waiting time on lines, or learn to do mindfulness meditation exercises while stuck in traffic. To the wise there are no bad times, only different kinds of opportunities.

In your Wisdom Journal, write about an occasion when you made the most of an unpromising situation.

THE WISDOM OF PROGRESS, NOT PERFECTION

Most of our failings are habits we have allowed ourselves to form and keep. We will probably never be perfect, but we can be less imperfect.

–The Twelve Steps and Twelve Traditions of the Al-Anon Groups, 1980

I joined Al-Anon in 1992 so that I could help a recovering alcoholic in my family. It soon became clear to me that I had played a role in the alcoholic's disease and that, by working on myself, I could assist in the recovery process. Before long I also discovered that I had areas in my life that had not yet been reached by my other self-development regimens. By using the tools of the program, I was slowly but surely helping to craft a better me.

One of the great psychological insights of Twelve Step programs is that the call to personal perfection can be deadly. As children our parents require us to toe various lines–to be like this, dress like that, think this way, have these values, play with those kids, prepare for this profession. When we become parents ourselves, we try to screen out what we consider to be the most negative parenting behavior we have experienced. Still, we tend to overlook the insidious ways in which we try to perfect our own kids.

The real bugaboo, of course, is our drive to self-perfection. No one is quite as heavy as we are when we get on our own case. Perfection sets the bar so high that we can never clear it. In this regard, I am afraid, a well-known New Testament verse may have an unfortunate effect. In the King James Version of Matthew 5:48, Jesus counsels: "Be ye therefore perfect, even as your Father which is in heaven is perfect." This is a pretty Olympic standard for us Sunday duffers. The Al-Anon insight is that the drive to perfection only sets us up for failure. The phrase you hear at meetings is "progress, not perfection." This garden-variety piece of wisdom is one of the reasons Twelve Step programs have helped so many people.

Write in your Wisdom Journal how you deal with your perfectionist tendencies.

THE WISDOM OF ASKING FOR GUIDANCE

I am Yours and born for You,
What do You want of me?
Majestic Sovereign,
Unending wisdom,
Kindness pleasing to my soul;
God sublime, one Being Good, . . .
What do You want of me?

–Saint Teresa of Ávila (1515–1582)

Asking questions is fifty percent of finding answers. Maybe more. Science is built on asking good questions. Learning how to construct them is one of the main tasks, I would say, of an excellent liberal education.

My dear friend the late Sister Eileen Rice, who died at age forty-nine from cancer of the everything, gave my daughter Christine and me a special present. She invited us to produce a one-hour video documentary about her life. Sister Eileen *was* the teacher education department at Siena Heights College in Adrian, Michigan. And what a teacher she was! Christine and I spent two days at the college interviewing Eileen and her colleagues, friends, and present and former students. Eileen, of course, was the main interviewee. At one point we asked about influences on her own formation as a teacher. She mentioned, among other things, the askers of "stunning" questions. She referred to those people, a kind of "anonymous Greek chorus," as she put it, who after a lecture would come up with pointed, useful questions that would bring the discussion to a new level of clarity.

We self-sufficient moderns tend to answer more than we ask. Like so many radio talk show listeners, we prefer to call in and speak our minds rather than let others have their say. We have neither the time nor the inclination to "receive." Saint Teresa here helps us to understand that God is the source of our wisdom. The best bet, therefore, is to ask God for guidance as often as possible, to learn to discern the answers, then to have the courage to follow.

Do you ask your Higher Power for guidance? Discuss this question in your Wisdom Journal.

THE WISDOM OF FEELING ALIVE

People say that what we're all seeking is a meaning for life. . . . I think that what we're seeking is an experience of being alive, so that our life experiences on the purely physical plane will have resonances within our innermost being and reality, so that we actually feel the rapture of being alive.

–JOSEPH CAMPBELL (1904–1987), *THE POWER OF MYTH*

In the materialistic civilization that is spreading throughout the world, much of what we learn is motivated by our desire to take actions that will help us acquire things. To put that another way, we know so we can do so we can have. An ironic bumper sticker in vogue twenty years ago tried to call these false values to our attention: "Whoever dies with the most toys wins." Matthew framed a similar thought in Jesus' question, "For what is a man profited, if he shall gain the whole world, and lose his own soul?" (Matthew 16:26, KJV).

Fortunately we are so made that most of us are never satisfied with material things alone. Sometimes, though, we mistake quality for quantity, and think, "If one million won't make me happy, maybe two will." Thus ensues our personal spiral of rising expectations. We chase the pot of gold at the end of the rainbow, but the rainbow keeps eluding us until it disappears altogether. Thus we are truly fortunate when we come to understand that material possessions are not the way to happiness.

But if not possessions, what? We now begin chasing another rainbow: the meaning of life. We wait for Godot or ask Alfie what it's all about. We look for Mr. or Ms. Goodbar, or we join Peggy Lee and just keep dancing. Here, actually, we are getting close to Joseph Campbell's meaning. He counsels us, in finding our partner or our true work, to follow our bliss. Happiness will indicate when we have struck gold–in a relationship, our profession, or living. The proper progression, Campbell implies, is to know in order to become in order to be. Much wisdom, East and West, advises that we simplify our lives, lighten our loads, and just live. Campbell would agree.

In your Wisdom Journal, describe an experience when you felt "the rapture of being alive."

THE WISDOM OF SIGNS AND PORTENTS

A child said What is the grass? *fetching it to me with full hands;*
How could I answer the child? I do not know what it is any more than he.
I guess it must be the flag of my disposition, out of hopeful green stuff woven.
Or I guess it is the handkerchief of the Lord,
A scented gift and remembrancer designedly dropt,
Bearing the owner's name someway in the corners, that we may see and remark, and say Whose?

–WALT WHITMAN (1819–1892), FROM "SONG OF MYSELF"

As the year 2000 approached, many scanned the horizon for portents. For some the Y2K scare was a high-tech fulfillment of biblical prophecy. People stored up water and canned goods and bought generators. Not a few prayed to be among the Elect when the Rapture comes.

Looking for signs can become an obsession. Seeing them, however, can be surprising. Several years ago I drove a young Ukrainian friend to his immigration hearing at the U.S. Federal Building in downtown Honolulu. The brothers in our meditation group had joined in prayer for Sasha the night before. Frankly, though, I didn't think he had much of a chance. His visa had long since lapsed, and his case for political asylum rested entirely on his account of mistreatment by Ukrainian officials because of his adherence to Buddhism. As we came through the Pali tunnel, 3,000 feet above sea level, I noticed a rare occurrence. Looking toward Honolulu and the ocean beyond, I saw a rainbow. (Generally one sees rainbows here when looking toward the mountains.) Moreover, this particular rainbow ended just over the Federal Building. Maybe I had been too hasty in my assessment, I thought. Later, after Sasha had been given asylum, his attorney commented: "It must have been your prayers. I've seen that judge deny much stronger cases."

Whitman pictures the grass as God's dropped handkerchief. It may be that signs of comfort and confirmation abound like grass if we have the eyes to see them.

Write in your Wisdom Journal about your experience with prophetic indications.

RECEPTIVE WISDOM

It is easy to advise the wise.

–A Serbian proverb

As I write this meditation, NATO is celebrating its fiftieth anniversary and the bombing of Yugoslavia is entering its second month. Since the Serbians are the "bad guys" for us in the present war, it is hard to accept them as a source of wisdom. I mean, aren't they the people responsible for ethnic cleansing? Don't they have that neo-Hitler of a leader with a name no two newscasters pronounce alike?

As a kid growing up during World War II, I remember how bad we all thought the Germans and the Japanese were. My father never had a good word to say about them. I remember when he asked me one summer to entertain some Japanese clients of his. It was 1955, ten years after the War. I was fifteen. My job was to take them out to a Japanese restaurant in Chicago. I was delighted to be entrusted with the hundred-dollar bill and the responsibility that went with it, as well as to have the chance to learn a few Japanese words and to practice eating with chopsticks. (I also got to practice smoking, an important part of Japanese meals, I learned.) My father's rationale: "I just can't stand those damn Japs!"

The reality, of course, is that wisdom is wisdom. The Germans, the Japanese, the Russians, the Serbians have it. Unfortunately a culture's wisdom resources don't guarantee that its government or its citizens will act wisely. But isn't that the point? If the rich get richer, the wise get wiser. Why? Because part of wisdom is the ability to recognize good advice regardless of its source, and to be willing to accept it and act on it. It's hard enough to say "I'm sorry." It is even harder to make amends that go beyond mere words. Hardest of all, though, is to change one's actions and attitudes so as to avoid making one's same old mistakes in the future.

How well do you listen to advice? How easily do you take it? Respond to these questions in your Wisdom Journal.

THE WISDOM OF THE SEER

The eye with which I see God is the same eye with which God sees me.

–Meister Eckhart (1260?–?1327)

I have always been fascinated by words. During my junior year in Germany, I had a major verbal breakthrough. I had known, of course, that *Netherlands* meant the same thing as *Holland*. The reason had just never occurred to me. I took this equivalency on faith.

At some point, as my German improved, I learned the adverb *nieder*, meaning "down" or "below." For example, *Leg' Dich nieder* is an old-fashioned way to say "lie down." On German radio newscasts, I also heard about *die Niederlande*. Then it hit me. The Netherlands didn't simply mean Holland; it was also a descriptive name meaning "the low lands." Then, of course, I remembered a related term in English that figured especially in older literature such as Milton's *Paradise Lost*, in which Satan's domain is sometimes referred to as "the nether kingdom."

What's the big deal? For me the big deal is getting to know something from the inside, really to understand why something is so, not just to take it on faith. Once I *get* it, the feeling is like learning to ride a bike. You never forget.

So imagine my delight when I *got*, from reading one of Ralph Waldo Emerson's essays, that a *seer* is really a *see-er*. Elsewhere I learned, with similar joy, that *atonement* derives from *at onement;* that *enthusiasm* comes from God (Greek *theos*) being *in* us; that *inspiration* means having the *spirit* with*in*; and that *insight* implies *seeing in*to something, not taking it at face value.

I think when we suddenly *get* something, God is in us. We are at one with what we get, inspired, enthused. We were blind and now suddenly, after years perhaps, we see. And the eye with which we have seen this (for us) new reality is, at that moment, God's eye. For when we *understand*, we are really *standing under* the aegis of God. We are *en-lightened*.

Can you recall a breakthrough you had in understanding something? Write about it in your Wisdom Journal.

THE WISDOM OF GETTING IT

A word to the wise is sufficient.

-An English proverb

It took me a while to get what these seven words meant. Finally one day I got it. I don't remember doing anything different or even working on the problem. In some mysterious way, between one hearing and the next, what had always before been opaque became transparent. I was blind but now I saw.

Crossword puzzle aficionados know the experience. You think and think and think. But certain clues just don't lead you anywhere. Finally you give up and put the puzzle aside. Then, when you return, the right word jumps to mind. You ask yourself, "How could I have been so blind?" It's so easy once you get it.

"Getting it" happens in all kinds of endeavors, not just with words. We remember the miracles of learning to float, then to swim. Or of ice skating or riding a bicycle for the first time. We fail and fail and fail. Then, miraculously, we get it. And the nicest part is, once we get it, our body remembers forever. After years of not being on a bike, I recall my confidence as I rented one in Door County, Wisconsin, and headed down a woody trail. I just got on and rode as if I had never stopped biking.

As the proverb suggests, a wise person is someone who "gets" things easily. Confucius had the same idea in mind when asking one of his disciples whether he or another disciple called Hui was brighter. The disciple in question responded, "How dare I compare myself with Hui? Hui hears one point and knows all about a subject; I hear one point, and know a second." The same holds not just for knowledge but for correction and judgment. You don't need to say much to a wise person who makes a mistake. He or she usually acknowledges the error right away and is capable of avoiding the same mistake next time.

Anyway, I'm sure you get what I mean. Enough said!

Write in your Wisdom Journal about an experience of an intellectual or spiritual breakthrough. What conclusions do you draw about your way of processing reality?

"RICH MAN" WISDOM

If I were a rich man . . .

–TEVYE'S SONG IN STEIN AND BOCK'S *FIDDLER ON THE ROOF*

I've seen *Fiddler on the Roof* six times: on stage in Chicago and Honolulu, in the movies twice (once on a U.S. military base in Germany), on TV once, and in an outdoor community theater rendition in Saint Paul. Oh, yes, and I saw the play *Anatevka,* on which the musical is based, years ago in New Haven. I also own the movie sound track, bought in Germany, where both show and film were big hits. You might say I'm a *Fiddler* nut. It's the story of my ancestors, after all.

Tevye, the milkman, carts his products each day to his friends and coreligionists in the little *shetl* community of Anatevka, lodged like a Jewish island in a hostile Russian sea. At one point someone asks the rabbi if there is a prayer for the czar. After reflecting, the old man says, "May God bless the czar . . . and keep him far away from us." Unfortunately God doesn't answer either half of the prayer, and before long the Jews of Anatevka are leaving for America.

A philosophical milkman, just as Kazantzakis's Zorba is a philosophical ne'er-do-well, Tevye asks God what would be so bad if he, Tevye, suddenly found himself with a cool million. Then Golda, his wife, could have servants, dress up like a countess, and boss people around to her heart's content. He, meanwhile, could study the Torah each day in the synagogue and become learned in the words and ways of the Almighty, blessed be He. Many a Jewish immigrant family to America later realized this dream, with children going to Harvard, Yale, and M.I.T. rather than a *yeshiva,* and parents retiring to Florida. I am less well off financially than my parents. But I do wonder about the "cool million" sometimes. What *would* I do if I had that much money? How would I spend it–and my days? What would become of me as a person? Would wealth spoil me?

Pretend you've just come into one million dollars tax-free. In your Wisdom Journal, write a budget of at least ten items showing how you would allocate the money. Think about what your choices say about your values.

THE WISDOM OF PERSEVERING

Heroism consists of hanging on one minute longer.

–A Norwegian proverb

Perseverance is perhaps the most modest of the commonly accepted virtues. When I think of heroism, I picture something much more dynamic, like a lone soldier with a rifle and a few grenades rushing a well-defended enemy pillbox. Fortunately most of us are not called on to put our life on the line in quite that way. We can leave the derring-do to the likes of Luke Skywalker, Jean-Luc Picard, or the latest Agent 007. Whatever foes they face, the Force (or the scriptwriter) will be with them, and they will live to venture forth another day in the relative safety of a Hollywood back lot, as long as their pictures keep selling.

Real life calls for another kind of heroism; call it minute-by-minute heroism. Living through night after night of limited sleep with a colicky baby. Returning to school term after term, seemingly forever, as a part-time working student and parent. Searching for a decent job with real responsibility, intellectual challenge, and a living wage.

Most projects of value seem to take time and effort. An up side to the heroic-rush-into-the-enemy-lines type of courage is that in a matter of seconds, you are either dead or about to be nominated for a congressional medal. Life, on the other hand, offers us the slow life or death of a marriage or of relating to parents. Or of battling a life-threatening disease. Or of earning a living and, as my late father used to put it, keeping a few steps ahead of the sheriff.

Of course, if you hang in there long enough, you may eventually be blessed with light at the end of the tunnel. No guarantees. But it seems to be the nature of things that situations change. In any case there is event heroism and process heroism. We may be called on to show the first, but there is no doubt that life will test all of us again and again for the second.

In your Wisdom Journal, describe a heroic person you know well. Why do you think the individual qualifies?

THE WISDOM OF BEGINNING

The beginning is the most important part of the work.

-PLATO (C. 427–347 B.C.E.), *THE REPUBLIC*

Lots of proverbs and quotations underscore the importance, and the difficulty, of beginnings: "A work well begun is half done." "If you can conceive it and believe it, you can achieve it" (Napoleon Hill). "Every beginning is difficult" – a saying that appears almost word for word in many languages. *Jeder Anfang ist schwer* (German) and *ogni principio è dificile* (Italian) are just two examples.

The importance of beginnings, I suppose, is obvious. The Torah opens with the Hebrew words *Bereshish Adonai,* meaning "In the beginning, God." When telling a story or filling out a police report, you are advised to "begin at the beginning." The journey of a thousand *li,* the proverb assures us, begins with a single step. No first step, no journey. And if the place where we begin strikes another as odd, we shrug our shoulders and explain, "You have to start somewhere."

Without an original vision, the new structure will never get built. Without a fertilized egg, the baby will never be born. Without keying in the first sentence, the book will never be written. In the spiritual training I follow, the person in charge signals us to start our thirty-minute active meditation by saying, "Begin!"

Yet for anyone about to embark on some new project – school, diet, running program, marriage – there is a hesitation, a fear. Procrastination raises its ugly but familiar head, and we put off till tomorrow that which should be started today. In consequence, *mañana,* per the Spanish proverb, is the busiest day of the week. On the other hand, once we take that first step, the new undertaking seems only half as daunting as our fears. Soon routine helps us continue, and before we know it, we are halfway to our goal. Given gravity, it takes a great deal of fuel for a rocket just to lift off. However, thanks to momentum, it takes less and less to reach escape velocity. So today's words of wisdom are, "Just begin!"

In your Wisdom Journal, write briefly about a technique you use to get yourself started on an activity you tend to put off.

MEN'S WISDOM

The Wild Man is part of a company or a community in a man's psyche, and it would be just as foolish to concentrate on him exclusively as to concentrate on the Warrior exclusively. Just as the man in our story exists as a companion to feminine energy, sometimes following its lead, sometimes not, so the Wild Man lives in complicated interchanges with the other interior beings. A whole community of beings is what is called a grown man.

–Robert Bly, *Iron John*, 1990

Our Creator has put into us the seeds of our own development, both individually and as a species. Life itself contains this force, called evolution. Dr. Jonas Salk, who didn't talk a great deal about God, capitalized the term *evolution* in his writings, indicating the importance of this force in his thinking.

The last few hundred years have seen a number of major movements. The industrial, atomic, technological, and genetic revolutions, among others. The antislavery, pro-labor, civil and human rights, and pro-democracy movements. The franchise has been extended to the non-landed, women, the nonnative-born, and to those as young as eighteen. The rights of children have been strengthened. Most recently the women's movement has been midwife to a men's movement. Both have spiritual as well as political ramifications.

I am a father of daughters, I am widely read in women's studies, and I am a member of an Al-Anon group comprising mainly women, and I believe there are important differences between men and women. Pathology enters only when we use those differences to demean others. To become whole, men need to recognize and draw on their feminine side, while women need to do the same with their masculine side. But as Bly points out, men also need to come to terms with what makes them men, including their Warrior and Wild Man. I find this balance via membership in Christian men's groups and a male-only meditation group. Men's wisdom, for me, means identifying and nurturing the masculine within me while giving due consideration to the other parts of myself.

If you are a man, discuss in your Wisdom Journal what your masculinity means to you. If you are a woman, speculate on what "positive manhood" might consist of.

TOOLBOX WISDOM

If the only tool you have is a hammer, you tend to see every problem as a nail.

–Abraham Maslow (1908–1970)

As a young academic administrator, I was too permissive. At least that was what other administrators said. I remember trying once to get tough. As a result I went too far in the other direction. If the only instrument you have is a cotton swab, you tend to see all problems as ears. When I tried switching to a hammer, the results were not encouraging.

Freshman-composition teachers comment on how many of their students make extreme judgments. For these students, movies are either "awesome," or "they suck." Nothing about good characterization and excellent photography being compromised by a poor script. The average freshman's critical toolbox contains only two or three instruments. One of our major jobs as comp teachers is to equip students with an array of critical tools and to give instruction on how to use them.

When it comes to living wisely, it makes sense to have a well-stocked toolbox. You never know when a particular tool may come in handy. Years ago, not long after the Iran hostage crisis, I represented our congregation at a Lutheran church convention in Springfield, Illinois. Wartburg College was having an alumni gathering in the adjoining rooms. Their keynote speaker was Kathryn Kolb–I believe that was her name–one of only two women held hostage by the Ayatollah Khomeini's government. Our bishop, with the endorsement of the conferees, prevailed on her to address our group also. She told us how, thanks to her early enforced memorization of biblical passages, she was able to comfort herself and the rest of the hostages. They were denied any reading material except propaganda about Iran's Islamic revolution, so Ms. Kolb was the only one able to lead worship services. Maybe the time had come, she speculated, for Christian schools to reclaim memorization, a tool that came to have unexpected significance in her life.

In your Wisdom Journal, discuss two or three of your most important tools for dealing with setbacks in your life.

THE WISDOM OF SEEING WITH FRESH EYES

You cannot step twice in the same river; for other and ever other rivers flow on.

–HERACLITUS (540–480 B.C.E.), *COSMIC FRAGMENTS*

Yesterday I experienced the danger of seeing things as if they had not changed. Arriving at Miami International Airport, I followed the instructions of my niece, Leslie, to take a taxi to her marine electronics shop, Aquatronics, about five minutes away. After a few hours there, I would go on to my sister's place. From the moment I entered that taxi until I left Aquatronics to go to my sister's place, I might as well have been in Havana. Everything was in Spanish.

Fortunately I speak passable Spanish, so I was delighted to have the chance to use it. Let me explain. My sister had been married to an Argentine businessman and lived in Buenos Aires for twenty-five years, until he died. She then moved to south Florida with her three kids. Leslie, the oldest, was fifteen at the time. Now forty-one, she is married to an Argentine electronics engineer. Together they own a business selling electronic equipment to wealthy Latin Americans for their pleasure boats. Most of Leslie and her husband's business and private life takes place in Spanish. Though not literally her mother tongue, it is the language she speaks like a native, in this case a *porteña,* or someone born in Buenos Aires.

I arrived at my sister's apartment after several hours of speaking exclusively Spanish. A bit later the handyman came to replace some fluorescent lightbulbs. I was asked to hold the new bulbs. The man was tall, with black hair and a mustache. Perhaps in his late forties, he spoke with a distinct accent. I said something to him in Spanish. Before he could reply, my sister turned to me and said: "Not Marcel. He won't understand. He's from Rumania."

An African proverb makes the point: "When the music changes, so does the dance." I had not had the ears to hear, nor the eyes to recognize, the change. Wisdom surely includes both.

Have you ever gotten stuck in the past and failed to recognize or adjust to a new situation? If so, describe the event in your Wisdom Journal. If not, comment on my faux-pas.

PIPE TOBACCO WISDOM

Mix a little folly with your wisdom; a little nonsense is pleasant now and then.

–HORACE (65–8 B.C.E.), *ODES*

Al Watson, my boarding-school mentor, smoked a pipe. As we sat in his apartment and listened to Mozart, he would puff reflectively. Clouds of fragrant smoke filled the room like incense. I wasn't old enough to smoke yet – at my school you had to be sixteen and have parents' permission – but I definitely planned to do so as soon as I got to college.

One thing I remember about Al is that he mixed his own tobacco. A shop in New Haven made it up for him. Part of our eleventh-grade magical mystery tour of Yale included a stop by the pipe and tobacco store across from the Shubert Theatre. Al and the owner knew each other by name. They talked about this and that while a new supply of his special blend was prepared. We were introduced as "future Yale men" who would doubtless become loyal customers once we moved into the Old Campus, a block away. During that visit I bought my first briar, and later that day discovered that the special blend didn't taste nearly as good as it smelled.

Although I eventually owned a pipe rack and maybe eight pipes, I never became much of a smoker. For one thing, I couldn't keep my pipes lit. For another, the smoke never really tasted good to me. At the time I was disappointed with my lack of competence. Now I am grateful. But I did like the idea of being able to mix my own blend of tobacco, and still do. In our diverse global culture, we are subjected daily to different impressions, ideas, ways of living. It is a blessing to be able to take the ones fragrant to us and mix them into our lives. On this general topic, Horace has a point too. To strive for perfect wisdom is in itself a folly. It leads to arrogance and frustration. Mixing in a little nonsense is definitely good for the soul.

In your Wisdom Journal, discuss how you assimilate and use ideas or practices from other cultures.

MIDLIFE-CRISIS WISDOM

Nel mezzo del cammin di nostra vita
mi ritrovai per una selva oscura
ché la diritta via era smarrita.
Midway through this life of ours
I found myself in a dark wood
Where the right path was unclear.

-Dante, *The Divine Comedy* (author's translation)

We create these benchmarks for ourselves – 18, 21, 35, and the big four-oh – or, at my stage of life, 60 followed (if we are lucky) by three score and ten. Our thirty-fifth and fortieth birthdays are especially significant because they signal the halfway point in our life expectancy. We are now definitely no longer children. According to tradition we should already have children of our own. If not and we are women, the ticking of the biological clock becomes loud indeed. Or if we are still uncertain about our career, how much longer do we have to study and practice "what we were meant to do"? Time is starting to run out for everything.

Simone and I have a friend who just threw an incredible fortieth birthday party for herself. She's a bright, attractive woman – friendly, articulate, a gifted salesperson. In her twenties she had already worked things out so that she could make a good living by selling jewelry on weekends at swap meets in her native Southern California. During the week she would occasionally fly to Mazatlan, Mexico, for a mini-vacation. But forty hit hard. Here she had everything. A good job, a nice apartment, a pleasant lifestyle, a loving family of origin. But she also had nothing. No life partner, no kids, and no assurance that she was really applying her God-given gifts. She prayed for guidance. A few months later, within two days of each other, she was diagnosed with fibroid growths in her uterus and she lost her job.

Dante's masterwork is entitled *The Divine Comedy* because, though it begins in darkness, it ends in light. Sometimes we have to lose our way to find it or, like Saint Paul, become blind so that we can see. For those with faith, a midlife crisis can also be a midcourse correction.

Write in your Wisdom Journal how a dark time in your life has led you to greater enlightenment.

PLANT WISDOM

Evidence now supports the vision of the poet and the philosopher that plants are living, breathing, communicating creatures, endowed with personality and the attributes of soul. It is only we, in our blindness, who have insisted on considering them automata.

–PETER TOMPKINS AND CHRISTOPHER BIRD, *THE SECRET LIFE OF PLANTS,* 1973

I remember seeing the special on TV. It predated, but resembled in spirit, the *Unsolved Mysteries* show in popular syndication today. One experiment sticks in my mind. Two saplings taken from the same tree were planted in identical soil, fed the same amount and type of food automatically at the same time each day, housed in identical climate-controlled environments, and given the same amount and type of artificial light. The only difference was, while one was exposed to heavy-metal rock music, the other had Mozart piped in for the same number of hours. Videos documented the progress. After a few days, the Mozart plant had grown more than the heavy-metal one. After a week, if memory serves, the size difference was noticeable, and the Mozart plant appeared healthier and more vibrant. By the third week, the Mozart plant was flourishing while its heavy-metal sister had died.

Now I have to be careful here. My younger daughter is a rock-and-roll musician. And Mozart is my favorite composer. My point, however, is generic. Plants really do seem more fully alive than we tend to think. *The Secret Life of Plants* sold over 100,000 hardcover copies before coming out in paperback. An instant classic among New Agers, it is actually a well-researched, rather thick collection of clinical studies, replete with bibliography and index. The experiments are sometimes bizarre, such as the one in which a plant, attached to a lie detector, reacted violently when the researcher thought about burning its leaves. (Apparently the plant was unable to tell that the researcher was lying for the sake of the experiment.) Now, what plants can or can't do remains a matter of speculation. Still, as our species becomes more humble, we may learn a thing or two from the lowly world of vegetation.

In your Wisdom Journal, write briefly about your relationship to plants.

PRIMAL WISDOM

It used to be commonly thought that man's preoccupation with superstition was but the previous stage to a concern for religion, which in its turn was only the forerunner of science. . . . Today, as technocratic society falters on the brink of the cliff of its own making, many members of our society – and not only its younger ones – are reshuffling the Tarot pack, consulting the astrologers and searching their souls for spiritual and mystical guidance in the wasteland of materialism.

–ROBIN CLARKE AND GEOFFREY HINDLEY, *THE CHALLENGE OF THE PRIMITIVES*, 1975

Rousseau introduced Western civilization to the Noble Savage just as the Industrial Revolution was picking up steam. Former peasants were crowding into Manchester and London to work long hours in the polluted, unsafe factories of the late-eighteenth and early-nineteenth centuries. Although there was still enough countryside to inspire Wordsworth, Coleridge, and the Lake poets, the brick, stone, and iron of the cities would bode ever larger in the consciousness of the people. Before long Dickens's novels of urban blight and exploitation would be eagerly read in the nation's periodicals.

There is, of course, a temptation to romanticize country living in general and primal societies in particular. Thoreau is right to note rural as well as urban despair. Today middle-aged farmers have one of America's highest suicide rates. Meanwhile huge urban areas are springing up like mushrooms in less developed countries as peasants are deserting their *kampongs* for the lure of the city.

The British anthropologists quoted above do have a point. People linked through commonly understood traditions and the belief that all things, animate and inanimate, are endued with spirit, tend to live with respect for one another and their environment. Knowing they are dependent on scarce food, they will kill sparingly, for sustenance or sacrifice but not sport. They will use fuel carefully and assist one another in the knowledge that without community they cannot survive. Wisdom seems to be calling us to adapt a communitarian, environmentally sensitive, spirit-filled ethic of primal peoples to meet the needs of our overly individualistic postindustrial society.

Discuss in your Wisdom Journal several lessons you think primal cultures have for us today.

MARITAL WISDOM

A good marriage is the union of two forgivers.

-Ruth Bell Graham

The true amount of sleep, according to psychologist Viktor Frankl, comprises the hours slept times the quality. I suppose one can arrive at a similar formula for marriage. In the words of an old cigarette commercial, "It's not how long you make it, but how you make it long."

I don't intend to set myself up as a marriage expert. I have been married only once, for over thirty-five years. Before marriage I had several serious girlfriends, but in those benighted days, few unmarried couples lived together. I was not among them. I can say this, though. The willingness to forgive has to be a key to staying together for more than a few years.

In this regard Simone and I made a lucky choice of marital policy early on. We agreed never to let the sun set on a quarrel. So if we had a disagreement about anything, we *had* to apologize to each other by nightfall. Usually by that time, the life-and-death issue of only a few hours before had shrunk to its true size, and we ended up laughing, crying, or both, about having gotten so hot under the collar over nothing.

A few years after we got married, someone gave us a little sign that counseled us not to yell at each other unless the house was burning. We have not done as well with this practice as with the sunset rule. Still, it is there in our consciousness, and these days I am working on anger management as a primary area of personal development. We practice above all during the annual Ramadan fast, which we have done for thirty years. Besides having to control our tempers during the fasting month itself, we follow the Muslim tradition at month's end of asking each other's forgiveness for any wrongs we consciously or unconsciously perpetrated toward each other in the past year. This is a good crosscultural wisdom technique, one Simone and I heartily recommend to fellow non-Muslims reading this book.

Discuss in your Wisdom Journal the role forgiveness plays in your marital or other relationships.

EATING WISDOM

Der Mensch ist, was der Mensch ißt.
We are what we eat.

–A common saying, given here in German and English

When it comes to eating, the basic wisdom is – you have to eat to live. When people with debilitating diseases are close to death, a key sign is their refusal to eat. My father waved away all meals during his last few weeks. I remember him small, fragile, but alert in his hospital bed, his only sustenance coming from IVs in either arm.

The next level of wisdom has to do with quantity. The keynote is: We eat to live but shouldn't live to eat. If we are able, we should keep how much we consume to a reasonable minimum. Too much of a good thing is no longer good. What the body can't use and is unable to eliminate gets stored as fat. And the more fat we carry around, the worse for our cardiovascular system. Some people, of course, require more fuel than the majority just to keep going: the slender individuals who pack away second and third helpings at potlucks but never seem to gain weight.

Wisdom also has to do with the quality of what we eat. Here there is a whole variety of issues, some controversial. The American Heart Association and common sense recommend a balanced diet, with foods from all the major food groups. The current model, called the food pyramid, suggests how many servings from each group an individual should consume per day. Quality also concerns the healthiness of what we eat. Then things get murky: organic versus inorganic, privileging certain food combinations, avoiding specific components (fats, sugars, caffeine, etc.), vegetarianism versus meat eating, and so on. Concerns also surround when we eat, how much we chew, and our emotional state while eating. Because people are different, we need to examine what works for us.

At its most esoteric, "we are what we eat" implies that different foods have different properties. For example, because salmon swim upstream to spawn, eating salmon may help us resist conventionality. Whatever the case, wise eating clearly requires serious consideration, discipline, and persistence.

Discuss your eating issues in your Wisdom Journal.

GAMELAN WISDOM

Music hath charms to soothe the savage breast
To soften rocks, or bend a knotted oak.

-WILLIAM CONGREVE (1670–1729), *THE MOURNING BRIDE*

I remember my first encounter with East Indian music. It was in 1961 in Chicago. My Indian friend Kasi told me to listen to it as if it welled up from within me. The mental trick worked. Rather than hearing this music as an exotic cacophony of wobbly voices, it came to me as something friendly, almost familiar. Since then I have applied this listening technique to Native American drumming and Chinese opera music, among others, with similar results. If we can short circuit the superficial strangeness, whole new worlds of listening await.

I don't remember when I first heard Indonesian music. It may have been 1963, from a German recording my wife brought when she emigrated from Europe. This record contained a variety of Indonesian songs and dances from the different major cultures in the Archipelago. Some, influenced by the Portuguese, sounded like familiar Hawaiian songs. Javanese gamelan music, however, was unlike anything I had ever heard before.

The gamelan is an ensemble made up primarily of bronze percussion instruments plus drum, wooden flute, and an unusual bowed instrument with one or two strings. A large gong, which I later learned symbolizes the voice of God, starts and finishes every piece. Unlike the frenetic Balinese gamelan, the Javanese version is quiet, almost sedate. Yet there is a kind of organized chaos to it, too, like life itself, with different instruments pursuing different rhythms and vaguely related melodies at the same time. Then everything speeds up just before slowing down and ending.

The overall effect is one of mystery. Here is music that one can truly call "interior." Attending a concert of gamelan music, I didn't have to use Kasi's mind trick at all. The music really did come from within and only *seemed* to originate on a stage twenty yards away. As I listened I became calm – better able to tap whatever wisdom lay within me. I had heard the music, and somehow I had changed.

In your Wisdom Journal, describe an experience of listening to "exotic" music.

THE WISDOM OF POPE JOHN XXIII

They found him [the boy Jesus] then, sitting in the midst of the doctors "listening to them and asking them questions." In those days an encounter with the doctors was very important and meant everything: learning, wisdom, and the direction of the practical life by the light of the Old Testament.

Such, in every age, is the task of the human intelligence: to garner the wisdom of the ages, to hand down the good doctrine and firmly and humbly to press ahead with scientific investigation. We die, one after the other, we go to God, but mankind moves towards the future.

-Pope John XXIII (1895–1962)

As a non-Catholic, I love Pope John XXIII. First, he was a hero of the Jewish people. As papal representative to Greece and Turkey during World War II, he saved thousands of Jews from Nazi death camps by authorizing baptismal certificates for them. Later, as pope, he apologized for centuries of Jewish persecution by the church and its members. Third, he liberalized Catholic teachings through the Second Vatican Council, which he convened. Finally, and appropriately for Father's Day, he was a true *mensch:* a warm, approachable human being and real Papa. For our twentieth anniversary, my wife, a fellow Lutheran, bought me a medal embossed with his image. I have worn it proudly over the years.

John's vision was truly catholic. In his discussion of Luke 2:26–49, he emphasizes the two-way nature of the twelve-year-old Jesus' conversation with the Temple rabbis. As God's Son he might have simply lectured them. Rather, he respected them as stewards of his people's traditions and so listened as well as questioned. Throughout his ministry Jesus received spiritual pearls from the past, but also cleansed them of false doctrines and practices and placed them in new settings. Wisdom requires that in every generation we recover the essence of religious truth for ourselves so that after we "go to God," humankind can continue moving smartly toward the future. Thank you, Papa Giovanni, for the reminder.

In your Wisdom Journal, write about a religious leader who impresses you, and explain why.

THE WISDOM OF WALKING YOUR PROBLEM OUT

Solvitur ambulando.
The problem will walk itself out.

–A Latin saying

The crisis occurred during sophomore year. I had been acing my way through college. Then came Professor Donaldson's Chaucer course. No matter how much time and effort I spent on the weekly papers, I couldn't do better than C+. Me, getting a high grade of C+! Unthinkable. Yet there it was, happening every week.

I went to see my advisor, Professor Alexander McClaren Witherspoon. Withy, as he was known, was also an English teacher. Unlike E. Talbott Donaldson, Maynard Mack, Cleanth Brooks, or William K. Wimsatt, he did not enjoy an international reputation. He remained an associate professor, even though he had been in the department for decades. Literature, not publishing, had been his calling. And helping generations of Yale men become well-read Christian gentlemen.

Telling him about my predicament, I burst into tears. "Now, now, boy." He said. "*Solvitur ambulando.* It will work itself out step by step. Why don't you go talk with Professor Donaldson during his office hours? He is a reasonable man. I'm sure the two of you will find a workable solution."

I followed Withy's advice. Professor Donaldson proved more than reasonable. He had had other complaints about his graduate assistant's penchant for low grades. "Giamatti was just in to see me about the same thing." (A. Bartlett Giamatti, my classmate, would go on to become a noted Renaissance scholar, president of Yale, and commissioner of major league baseball.) Professor Donaldson changed my paper average to B+, and I made the dean's list for the fourth straight term.

Withy was the main influence on my career as a college teacher. I always put the formation of my students first, my advancement as a scholar second. I also continued to teach throughout my years as an administrator. Above all, I learned from Withy the importance of patience in facing the problems of daily life. Relax. Take one step at a time. Your life isn't ruined yet. "Now, now, boy. *Solvitur ambulando.*"

How do you react to personal problems? Write for ten minutes in your Wisdom Journal about it.

COMPENSATORY WISDOM

Remember when life's path is steep to keep your mind even.

–Horace (65–8 B.C.E.)

In the Twelve Step program, we talk about turning our will and our lives over to the care of God as we understand God (step 3). This doesn't mean that we abdicate responsibility for what we do or don't do. Rather, we come to realize that although we are entrusted with our life, we do not own it. We are more like a long-term tenant. We may live as if our life is fully our own; however, when the time comes to die, we must return who and what we are, or have become, to God, who in this analogy is like our landlord.

The Twelve Step program also makes clear that in life there is our part and God's part. Serenity lies in learning which is which and, if we think of life as a theatrical play, taking care to speak only those lines assigned us.

Sometimes, as Horace mentions, life's path is steep. As often as not, we have created the path and are responsible for where we are on it. Making mistakes is our human birthright, the necessary concomitant of free will. On the other hand, our past is our past. What has occurred cannot be changed. The most we can do is make amends, to ourselves and others we have harmed, for our errors of commission and omission. We can only apologize and move on, then try not to make the same mistake again. Tomorrow is another day.

By understanding that although we can't do everything, we can do something, we make it more possible for ourselves to keep an even mind. We are not called upon to be perfect, only good. Or, more accurately, we are called to a life of self-improvement and learning from experience. Wisdom counsels that there is always a choice – even when we face death. When life's path becomes steep, we can with God's help remain tranquil and focused.

Write in your Wisdom Journal how you manage in a crisis. Are you able to keep an even keel when the seas of life are rough?

VACATION WISDOM

A little work, a little play,
To keep us going – and so, good-day!

–George du Maurier (1834–1896)

I am sitting on a *lanai* (Hawaiian for verandah), looking through a half dozen palm trees to the glittering sea. This is the first day of our week's vacation on Kauai, the northernmost of the major Hawaiian islands. It is our first true holiday in twenty-seven months.

Yesterday, as we arrived at Lihue Airport, it was raining. "We've been having beautiful weather," the airport shuttle driver explained, "but I guess we'll get some rain now." If the weather cooperates, Simone and I plan to sun, swim, and take long walks along the beach. If not, we'll watch old movies and just take it easy. Either way we intend to have fun and recharge our batteries.

Nature instructs us in the wisdom of balance coupled with diversity. First this, then that. Never always the same. Even in Hawaii there are subtle shifts in the seasons. The weather gods supply enough rainy days for residents to rewelcome the sun with enthusiasm. Night succeeds day, sleep follows wakefulness. Yet out of our workaholism and fear of being unable to do it all, we overlook the need for down time and "non-productive" play.

Play may just be the most productive activity around: The breathing out that makes breathing in possible. As we must work for our vacations, so our vacations enable us to keep working. "All work and no play makes Jack a dull boy," Poor Richard counsels. And employers want a dull worker about as much as a dull knife.

"Okay," you respond. "I already know this. Our family does at least two weeks at the lake each year, with a third week sometimes over Christmas." Good for you. Skip to the next reading. But plenty of people out there, like me, intersperse work with other work. I exemplify the observation that we preach to others the very things we need to practice ourselves. Come to think of it, I am writing this essay during my vacation. However, I am about to throw on my swimsuit and go for a walk.

Do you have enough play in your life? Reflect in your Wisdom Journal on how well you balance work with leisure.

MARATHON WISDOM

The journey of a thousand li *begins with a single step.*

–A CHINESE SAYING

The very first person to run a marathon died for his efforts. In 490 B.C.E., an anonymous Athenian ran from the village of Marathon to Athens – approximately 26 miles – to carry the news that the Athenians had defeated the Persians. He completed his run, made his announcement, and dropped dead.

On December 13, 1998, at age 59, I participated in my first marathon. Honolulu. Five a.m. A fireworks display lights the sky, signaling the start. Twenty-seven thousand men and women, from preteens to octogenarians, are off.

I am part of a 70-person team raising money for homeless people. As development director for the organization, I feel the need to take part. There are people in front and behind for as far as the eye can see. It's an incredible spectacle. I feel part of some historical scene. At mile seven for us and mile twenty-five for them, the leaders, Kenyans who will soon cross the finish line in about two hours and fifteen minutes, pass us going in the opposite direction. They run like greyhounds. As for me, I will cross the finish line seven hours and forty-one minutes after starting. I walk virtually the whole way, talking story with my friend Ethel here, practicing my thirty Japanese phrases with participant native speakers there. The last hundred yards I sprint, with echoes of *Chariots of Fire* in my head. Collectively we raise $41,000 for homeless people. I have completed my first marathon.

Writing this book is also a marathon of sorts. A book of 366 entries gets written one entry at a time. A successful savings program works the same way. So does learning Chinese characters. So does life. You find a good direction, then put one foot in front of the other. Today I began training for the 1999 Honolulu Marathon. God willing, I'll complete it in under seven hours.

Have you ever done an extended project like painting or reroofing your house or getting your master's degree? Write about it in your Wisdom Journal. What wisdom did you glean?

PILGRIM WISDOM

Then I saw in my dream that the Shining Men bid them call at the gate . . . to whom it was said, These pilgrims are come from the City of Destruction for the love that they bear to the King of this place. . . .

And lo, as they entered, they were transfigured, and they had raiment put on that shone like gold.

–John Bunyan (1628–1688), *The Pilgrim's Progress*

For many of us in secular America, *pilgrim* denotes one of the English Puritans who landed at Plymouth Rock in 1620. The word reminds us of pumpkins, fall leaves, turkey, maybe even black cats and witch hunts. It may also bring to mind the struggle with our puritanical tendencies, regardless of when our ancestors arrived.

For Catholics, a pilgrim is likely a person traveling for spiritual renewal to Lourdes or Rome. Centuries before John Bunyan, Geoffrey Chaucer told how each April people of all social classes in England would walk to Canterbury to pray at the tomb of Saint Thomas à Becket. Becket, archbishop of Canterbury during the reign of Henry II, was murdered in his cathedral in 1190 for putting loyalty to church above loyalty to king. Soon news spread that persons who prayed to the martyred cleric in Canterbury Cathedral would receive miraculous cures. Not long after, pilgrims began to arrive.

The concept of pilgrimage is common in many religions. Chinese worshipers climb the many steps to Buddhist shrines. Hindus seek out the sacred city of Benares. Jews attempt to visit the Holy Land to pray at the Wailing Wall. Muslims are required to try to go on *hajj* to Mecca.

In his essay "Walking," Thoreau stated that the verb *saunter* could be derived from two French phrases: *sans terre* (without country, homeless) or *à la Sainte Terre* (to the Holy Land). Thoreau preferred the latter derivation. So do I. Fortunate are those whose life's walk seems meaningful to them – who have a clear sense of purpose. Blessed are the pilgrims, for they are spared the curse of just wandering around.

Do you have a sense of pilgrimage in your life? In your Wisdom Journal, spend ten minutes sketching out where you have been and where you think you're headed.

RETREAT WISDOM

The longest way round may be the shortest way home.

-An American proverb

It just occurred to me as I was taking my vitamins. Usually I put the six or seven pills into a cap from one of the containers. That way I know if I've gotten them all. This morning, as I was replacing the cap, I had trouble screwing it back on. The problem was, the cap was at a slight angle and would not mesh with the threads on the neck of the container. I spontaneously turned the cap in the wrong direction until it clinked into alignment. Then, a few turns later, the pills were tightly sealed.

When we talk about the normal progress of things, including our lives, we often say, "Two steps forward and one step back." As the example above suggests, however, the tactical reality may be just the opposite. In order to move forward, we have to first retreat. Continuing to bark up the wrong tree doesn't exactly attract birds or squirrels. It makes sense to move away from that tree and look for another. Ego, of course, can get in the way, and we bark even louder. Now the whole forest empties out, and we vent our frustration by biting the bark of the tree.

Our younger daughter's godfather, the late Uncle Ludwig, had been the German naval attaché in Rome during World War II. Like many Germans, he had a rather low regard for Italians as fighters. He once shared the joke going around among his colleagues in those days. Italian tanks, he said, had five gears. One forward and four in reverse. But if that old saying is right and we humans should make love not war, then tanks geared to move backward, not forward, ought to cause celebration, not derision. In our daily lives, too, we should learn the usefulness of going in reverse. On our globe the fastest way from one "side" to the other is not a straight line but the polar route. Similarly, the best way forward is sometimes to retreat.

In your Wisdom Journal, describe an occasion where you were finally able to achieve your goal by backing off. Do you consciously apply this life strategy now?

BLUE SKY WISDOM

Blue skies shining on me.
Nothing but blue skies do I see.

–THE OPENING LINES OF A POPULAR SHOW TUNE BY IRVING BERLIN

Blue Sky Associates is the name I dared give to the nonprofit organization I founded in 1991. I say "dared give," because at least a half dozen colleagues counseled me not to. "You know what 'blue skying' means in the world of finance, don't you?" asked these mainly humanistic professors, with concern and even a little panic in their voices. I did, but they went on anyway: "It means going off on a lark. Making foolish investments. Doing something really dumb!"

When people asked me where I had come up with this name, I told them the truth. Out of the blue sky. I don't have the foggiest idea where it came from. It just arrived. And that's the point. When spirit e-mails you, the message comes without sender address or prior correspondence. It just manifests within you and is self-evident, like something always there that you had never noticed.

It is striking how we take perfectly good turns of phrase and use them for something bad. "Blue skying" is only one example. Think of the insurance term "act of God." In case you are not familiar with it, it refers to a violent act of nature, like a tornado, typhoon, or earthquake. Why does God get pinned with responsibility for events like these? If you have to blame a religious figure, why not call them "acts of Satan"? We also construct negative phrases like "vicious cycle" without a parallel positive expression such as "virtuous cycle." Why do we downgrade the inherent positive possibilities of blue skies and the divinity? Why do we fail, in language, to name both positive and negative cycles?

Blue, of course, can have many connotations. In colloquial English it means "sad." In German, *blau* is slang for "drunk." Blue Sky Associates, however, stands for a group of individuals wishing to share their creativity to transform human development. The World Wisdom Project is currently their major undertaking. You can do worse than get an idea from God's blue sky.

In your Wisdom Journal, write about where you get the ideas for your creative projects.

CHRISTIAN WISDOM

Rejoice evermore.
Pray without ceasing.
In every thing give thanks: for this is the will of God in Christ Jesus concerning you.

–1 Thessalonians 5:16–18, KJV

It takes a convert like me to dare talk about Christian wisdom in 350 words or less. But then, if our born-again siblings in the faith are right, we are all converts. Even children of Christian parents are only nominal Christians until the day they first believe. So here I go.

Saint Paul, one of my ancient Jewish-Christian predecessors, is not known for brevity. To be sure, he had a lot of ground to cover in his epistles to help the new churches understand and follow their recently adopted religion. Distance and sometimes imprisonment made it impossible for him to spend as much time with them as he wished. Still, for all his novella-length letters, he got off some stunning one-liners. In fact, when I was considering possible lead quotations for this essay, including the Great Commandment and other key statements by Jesus, I still came back to Paul's summary advice to the Thessalonians.

First, rejoice evermore. Sounds impossible. What about when we don't feel well, we get an unexpected $4,000 bill, or a favorite relative dies? It doesn't matter. The primary matters in our lives have been taken care of. As long as there is no chemical imbalance causing depression, quiet joy should simmer in us at all times. Second, pray without ceasing. I think of J. D. Salinger's Franny and Zooey, trying their hardest to pray unceasingly. Such prayer isn't about *trying.* It's about knowing our limitations and asking God in all we do to assist us so that God's will, not ours, gets done. Third, give thanks in every thing. Even the Crucifixion? Even the Holocaust? Even tragic things that befall our neighbors or ourselves? People of faith, Christians and others, understand that although we propose, God disposes. Besides, it takes a while to judge whether something is a factor for good or not. As Christians we believe that all things ultimately are. We pray, but God says Amen.

In your Wisdom Journal, describe the best Christian you know. What makes that person stand out?

STORYTELLING WISDOM

Hidden in all stories is the One story. . . .

In telling them, we are telling each other the human story. Stories that touch us in this place of common humanness awaken us and weave us together as a family once again. . . .

Facts bring us to knowledge, but stories lead to wisdom.

–RACHEL NAOMI REMEN, MD, *KITCHEN TABLE WISDOM*, 1996

Since I've begun writing this book, people have been sending me quotations, proverbs, ideas, even stories. Some appear in these pages. Still, I was surprised when Dr. Remen's book, with which I instantly fell in love, arrived in the mail. Although it came from the Institute of Noetic Sciences, of which I am a member, I don't remember having ordered it. It just showed up. No bill, no gift card. Strange!

When I was five or six, we lived in Great Neck, Long Island, a New York City suburb. Every Saturday morning my parents would drive me to the local public library, where an adult would read us stories. My favorite was *Winnie the Pooh.* I remember hearing these stories being read and being intrigued by the quirky animals and their quaint way of speaking. (When I was older, I learned that they were *English* animals speaking with a British accent.) Those and other stories touched me in a particular place and opened something inside me. Still, I had an unusual side effect from those Saturday morning sessions. I was slow to learn to read–I preferred being read to. There was something about the voice, the presence of another person.

In Hawaii a common pidgin expression is, "No talk stink, talk story." There was even a "Talk Story" conference some years ago organized by the writer Maxine Hong Kingston. Our all-too-human tendencies to gossip or criticize (talk stink) should be put on hold. Instead, we need to share ourselves, our experiences, with others through story. For while analysis excludes, stories include. Stories, by making available the lives and cultures of humankind, really can lead to wisdom.

In your Wisdom Journal, write about your favorite childhood story. Why do you think this story appealed to you?

MANTRIC WISDOM

O Attic Shape! Fair attitude! with brede
Of marble men and maidens overwrought
With forest branches and the trodden weed;
Thou, silent form, dost tease us out of thought
As doth eternity.

-John Keats (1795–1821), "Ode on a Grecian Urn"

Even my *Webster's Desk Dictionary* includes *mantra*. The definition: "a word or formula to be recited or sung." The unabridged *Random House Dictionary* adds only that this Hindu term derives from a Sanskrit noun meaning "speech" and that the correct adjectival form is "mantric." We graduates of the 1960s know, of course, what a mantra really is: a word or words used to attain an altered state of consciousness. Nowadays practitioners of centering prayer or Christian meditation use "sacred word" or "sacred syllable" to describe the same thing.

The best practical definition of *mantra* I've found appears in the lines quoted above from Keats's ode. Mantras work in the same way the poet says the sculpted surface of the ancient Grecian urn does: They "tease us out of thought." Discursive thinking is the enemy of meditation because it locks us into the logical left-brain mode and keeps us from the receptive state required.

Music, paintings, architecture, stained-glass windows, sculpture, dancing, flowers, and incense – items that can "get us out of our heads" – are used by organized religions as well as mystics. For the former, these elements establish the appropriate atmosphere for worship. For the latter, they help aspirants achieve thought-free meditation. Even the telling of beads, a practice shared by Hindus, Christians, and Muslims, can assist one to become quiet and empty.

For those of us from the Western world, the intellect is regarded as our highest instrument. We use it incessantly. Challenged to sit and do nothing, we can't turn off our minds. Yet, because much of the world's wisdom seems to have been received by those able to quiet their minds, it might not hurt us to learn how.

Sit quietly. Repeat your first name slowly thirty times. Continue sitting for five minutes. Report your experience in your Wisdom Journal.

SHAKER WISDOM

Shaker your table!

–A sign in the restaurant at the Pleasant Hill Shaker Village, Kentucky

The first time I heard the word *Shaker* was when my mother talked about Shaker Heights, Ohio. The Cleveland suburb, built in the area of a former Shaker settlement, was where Mother had attended the last years of high school before going on to Ohio State.

In the mid-1970s, however, Shaker culture came to have a direct impact on my life. The university where I was working at the time was reviewing its general-education requirements, a process in which I was involved. So when I read about an event called the Shakertown Conversation on General Education, I called for information. Some months later I found myself in the restored Shaker community of Pleasant Hill, Kentucky. About twenty of us from all over the country, nearly all unforgettable characters, showed up for an intense weekend of good conversation, incredible food, fellowship, and the palpable presence of a now-disappeared community of nontraditional believers. We came back year after year.

A small group of dissident English Quakers, called Shaking Quakers or Shakers, left England in 1774 for America. Under the leadership of a 38-year-old Manchester woman called Mother Ann Lee, who was considered to be the Second Coming of Christ in female form, they founded their first settlement in Watervliet, New York. The year was 1776. Shakers believed in hard work, communitarian self-sufficiency, and celibacy. Their worship began as formal dance and ended in free-form movement led, they said, by the Spirit. They maintained their numbers by raising orphans and foundlings, some of whom stayed on, and by buying slaves into freedom to live and work in their communities as equals. By 1826 there were eighteen communities, including Shakertown, and about 6,000 members. They created the simple elegance of Shaker houses and furniture and invented the Shaker broom. No new members were admitted after 1964. Today the few remaining Shakers live in New England. But after a dozen or more annual pilgrimages to Shakertown, something of their spirit lives on in me.

Skim a book on Shaker art or culture in your library, then comment in your Wisdom Journal.

MAJORITY WISDOM

A man with God is always in the majority.

-John Knox (1505–1572)

The world is coming, slowly but surely, to majority rule. That said, we can't forget that China, the most populous nation on the planet, remains a "People's Republic" in name only. Still, more and more countries have adopted democratic systems in recent years. Meanwhile, near-universal access to basic education and television is slowly but surely developing a literate electorate with some sense of global issues.

Not that the majority is always right. If every American over eighteen were asked to vote on whether Shakespeare's *Hamlet* or the movie *Titanic* were the better work of art, *Titanic* would win by a considerable margin. Most people would be honest and vote on which they liked better or which had the bigger emotional impact. Issues of plot, character, theme, and language would not be raised. Accessibility, special effects, even sex appeal of the principal actors would be the main factors.

Critics of democracy, from Plato to the present, point out that the masses can generally be manipulated by demagogues and bought with bread and circuses. "I hate the profane masses and keep my distance," wrote the Roman poet Horace two thousand years ago. But in democracies at least, contending parties can each use techniques of persuasion to sway voters, whereas in authoritarian states, only the group in power can do so. To paraphrase Winston Churchill, democracy is the worst form of government, except for all the others.

There are also problems with the majority-of-one idea. Anyone can allege a special mission from God. Dictators seem especially prone to asserting their special place in history. Jesus specifically warned us to watch out for false messiahs. Fortunately just as good wine needs no bush, good leaders need not advertise their virtues. Those of us alive at the turn of the century are fortunate to have breathed the same air for a while with the likes of Nelson Mandela, Bishop Tutu, Mother Teresa, and the Dalai Lama. They don't have to toot their own horns. Their stature is evident to anyone with eyes to see.

Sketch out in your Wisdom Journal some characteristics of your ideal government.

THE WISDOM OF PERSPECTIVE

I went to Johnson in the morning, and talked of it [landlord problems] as a serious distress. He laughed, and said, "Consider, Sir, how insignificant this will appear a twelvemonth hence."

–Boswell's *Life of Johnson*, 6 July 1763

How easily we nickel and dime ourselves to death with daily catastrophes! My friend Varindra, early in his career, edited Sri Lanka's leading newspaper. Every morning there was some major crisis to report. His wife once asked him, "Varindra, if your stories are so significant, why don't you keep the same headline for three days?"

Of course, sometimes we really must deal with serious issues – mortal illness, war, the death of a major relationship. But dramatizing them hardly helps. I take the general semanticists' advice to de-escalate our vocabulary. For example, I never use the words *flu* or *ill* when *cold* or *under the weather* will do. Why make matters worse for a moment's stardom in some pseudocosmic drama of one's own creation?

Sometimes it is helpful to look back on other tough situations that we have overcome. In the ancient Anglo-Saxon poem "The Sea Farer," the poem's narrator, caught in rough seas, recalls other sea perils he has survived. The refrain counsels: "That passed over. So, I pray, will this."

But I am mainly talking about the small everyday inconveniences, such as disagreements with a landlord or getting delayed in traffic. "Road rage" is a recent social disease. Frustration-based anger can lead us to literally blow our top, resulting in a stroke or other cardiovascular incident. One of the Twelve Step slogans, "How important is it?" can be an effective antidote, to be used like a nitroglycerin tablet at the first sign of temper. Indonesians use the expression *Bagaimana nanti?*, which means, literally, "How later?" The expanded meaning is, "Let's check back on this situation in a few weeks or months to see how significant it is then." Dr. Johnson prescribes waiting a "twelvemonth." Try these techniques for yourself and see what works for you.

Consider some situation in your past that caused you to become angry or fearful. Write in your Wisdom Journal how you would deal with it if it were to recur today.

MOTIVATIONAL WISDOM

Stay optimistic and try to see an opportunity in every calamity;
not pessimistic and see a calamity in every opportunity.
The optimist sees the donut, the pessimist the hole.
There is always a good side to every situation. . . .
View every problem as an opportunity.
When it is dark enough, you can see the stars.

–"Your Daily Motivation," for July 9, 1998

Eight years, three months, and eleven days ago I was fired. It was actually the second time. The first time, in 1970, I was reorganized out of a federal position. Since I had been on leave from a university professorship, I didn't much care.

But eight years ago, I had no spare job to fall back on. It was a bad situation. I was a university vice president, and a new president–the third in my time as a v.p.–had inherited me. He wanted me to fire a particular dean, a man I considered to be an asset to the institution. I knew the drill: either I fire the dean or we both get fired. That Friday I had an all-night argument with God. At about four in the morning, a little voice inside me said, "If you truly understood the role of that man [the president] in your professional life, you'd thank him as an angel from God. It's time to do something new." I chose not to fire the dean.

At age fifty, with twelve years as dean or vice president, I found myself unable to get a new job. I kept coming in near the top–in one case, second out of 250 applicants. But no job. With my final payday looming closer, I brashly called the hiring agent where I had placed second. They were starting a capital campaign, I said, and I was a good fund-raiser. (Fact is, I had written a few successful grants in my academic career.) They needed me, I told them. Two weeks later I had a $30,000 fund-raising contract. A new consultant was born.

Today I am facing the loss of two major contracts and 60 percent of my income. Hawaii is an expensive place to live. But my worry-meter is low. Thank God for memory. I've been there before. This too, I know, will pass.

Think of a disappointing situation that has turned out well. Write about it in your Wisdom Journal.

THE WISDOM OF ALOHA

If you examine the history of the Hawaiian conversion to Christianity, what you see is the ability of Hawaiians to accommodate the ideas that came in.

. . . They kept hold of their own traditions and also changed as they went through the process of accepting other ways of life.

This was a necessity in Hawaiian family life, primarily because of intermarriage, but also because of a philosophical understanding that humans are the same psychically and psychologically no matter what the racial background. I think this is the major contribution that Hawaiian spirituality has to make to the world's future.

-RUBELLITE KAWENA JOHNSON, *LOCAL KNOWLEDGE, ANCIENT WISDOM,* 1991

For "visitors," as we call tourists to Hawaii, *aloha* (love, affection, compassion, mercy) may take on a plastic feel, like the imitation flower leis so common around the state. Periodically one of the Honolulu dailies calls for a revival of the Aloha Spirit. After all, Tahiti, Bali, and other tropical paradises are becoming more accessible, and our economy has been depressed while the U.S. mainland is booming. In the old days, we had tropical agricultural and military-related spending to fall back on. No more. Production costs priced us out of the sugar and pineapple markets, and military downsizing has made Hawaii a one-industry economy.

All this notwithstanding, aloha still impacts everyday life in the fiftieth state. On a mundane level, strangers smile freely at one another in stores, on the sidewalk, at the beach. (Try it in New York City, and prepare to run.) Drivers are also accommodating, using a variety of hand signals – and almost never the horn – to communicate intentions. Letting others into traffic is routine, an act acknowledged with a friendly wave. More significant, ethnic and racial intermarriage is the rule – more than 50 percent of our marriages are intermarriages. Is the Old Adam alive and well in Hawaii? Of course. It's a place filled with human beings. But when it comes to race relations and aloha, Hawaii still has a lot to teach the world.

In your Wisdom Journal, suggest three ways we might practice aloha more effectively in our daily lives.

LIBERATION WISDOM

When I walked out of prison, that was my mission, to liberate the oppressed and the oppressor both. Some say that has now been achieved. But I know that that is not the case. The truth is that we are not yet free; we have merely achieved the freedom to be free, the right not to be oppressed. We have not taken the final step of our journey, but the first step on a longer and even more difficult road. For to be free is not merely to cast off one's chains, but to live in a way that respects and enhances the freedom of others. The true test of our devotion to freedom is just beginning.

–NELSON MANDELA, *LONG WALK TO FREEDOM*, 1994

Back in the 1960s, Erich Fromm helped us distinguish between "freedom to" and "freedom from." "Freedom from" means we have escaped from a situation that had imprisoned us. Think of an individual who has just left a bad marriage. Unfortunately, leaving one bad situation does not guarantee that another will not arise. Often those factors within us that contributed to the old relationship will duplicate themselves with someone else. "Freedom to," on the other hand, means that we are now in the position – psychologically, socially, politically, or economically – to do things differently, to become "a new person."

The issue of substance abuse illustrates the point. That a person has stopped drinking isn't the same thing as being sober. The Twelve Step program refers to "dry drunks" to cover this syndrome: The abuse of a particular substance may have ceased, but the same addictive behaviors, abuse of self and others, continue. That is why the cessation of drinking is only the condition for *admission* to Alcoholics Anonymous. The program itself focuses on personal transformation. Freedom from drinking is thus prologue to becoming someone who no longer needs to drink.

Nelson Mandela, one of the great leaders of the twentieth century, knew this distinction. Further, he understood that both oppressed and oppressor must be transformed, because the same system imprisons both. Fortunately his spirit could never be shackled despite years on Robben Island. His wisdom can help free us all.

In your Wisdom Journal, discuss your idea of true freedom.

HEROIC WISDOM

The problem of mankind today . . . is precisely the opposite to that of men in the comparatively stable periods of those great co-ordinating mythologies which now are known as lies. Then all meaning was in the group, in the great anonymous forms, none in the self-expressive individual; today no meaning is in the group – none in the world: all is in the individual. . . .

The hero-deed to be wrought is not today what it was in the century of Galileo. Where then there was darkness, now there is light; but also, where light was, there now is darkness. The modern hero-deed must be that of questing to bring to light again the lost Atlantis of the co-ordinated soul.

–Joseph Campbell, *The Hero with a Thousand Faces,* 1968

The late Joseph Campbell was a phrase-maker. "The hero with a thousand faces," the title of his most popular work, is such a phrase. So is "the lost Atlantis of the co-ordinated soul."

The myth of Atlantis is premised on the ancient idea of a Golden Age succeeded by declining levels of social harmony and achievement until humankind destroys itself. Then a small remnant begins the long climb to a new Golden Age. People who subscribe to the existence of Atlantis, Lemuria, and other ancient utopias surmise that technology and spiritual development had reached the apex of development in tandem. Interstellar travel co-existed with ESP and the ability to converse with God. Then, somehow, things got out of whack. Spiritual maturity was unable to keep pace with technological progress; this imbalance caused civilization to destroy itself, and the island utopia sank to the bottom of the sea.

The "co-ordinated soul," like Jung's integrated one, is likewise based on balance. Body, emotions, intellect, and spirit are rightly ordered, with one's highest powers in control. Like sociologist Robert Bellah, Joseph Campbell decried the modern imbalance that favors the individual over society – the head over the soul. We, too, were flirting with self-destruction. The role of today's hero is thus to help rebalance our boat before we, too, tip turtle and sink.

In your Wisdom Journal, describe someone who exemplifies this kind of hero.

RESPONSIVE WISDOM

Freedom is what you do with what's been done to you.

–Jean-Paul Sartre (1905–1980)

How different this sentiment is from Sartre's famous line that "hell is other people" *(L'enfer est l'autrui)!* Of course, Sartre was a playwright as well as a philosopher, and this line about hell comes from his play *No Exit,* which takes place entirely in hell. As literature majors quickly learn, characters in books or novels don't necessarily reflect the viewpoints of their authors. They may in fact represent opinions contrary to those of their creators.

The "freedom" quotation sounds more like Sartre, founder of the philosophical movement called existentialism. The term, which Sartre coined, derives from the movement's principle that existence precedes essence. The meaning is that human beings are not determined by fate, genetics, or any other external factor (essence) but are free to make choices, the consequences of which they must bear (existence). But, you say, we do come burdened with all kinds of "external" conditions: our genes, our parents, the places where we grow up, the times we live in, the teachers we get, and so on. How can we discount traumatic experiences like having abusive or neglectful parents, being born into a war zone or ghetto, belonging to a maltreated minority, attending the worst school in the district?

Here Sartre would argue for "engagement." We need to face whatever life deals us and make responsible choices. Helen Keller is an obvious model of this kind of initiative. So is Viktor Frankl, who considered himself an existential psychotherapist. Frankl had no control over being captured by the Nazis and sent to a death camp. Once there, however, he turned it into a learning laboratory for himself, and by creating meaning out of absurdity, he was able to keep himself alive. Sartre was an atheist and a communist. We might wonder, What wisdom could he possibly have? To judge by his definition of freedom, quite a bit. For freedom begins not with what we can't do, but with what we can do, starting from wherever we are. And responsibility, as the word suggests, depends on our ability to respond.

Think about the best example of something you have done "with what's been done to you." Write about it in your Wisdom Journal.

SINGING-BIRD WISDOM

Mrs. Bertha Flowers was the aristocrat of Black Stamps. She had the grace of control to appear warm in the coldest weather, and on the Arkansas summer days it seemed she had a private breeze which swirled around, cooling her. . . .

[She told me, still a girl,] "Words mean more than what is set down on paper. It takes the human voice to infuse them with the shades of deeper meaning. . . ."

She said that I must always be intolerant of ignorance but understanding of illiteracy. That some people, unable to go to school, were more educated and even more intelligent than college professors. She encouraged me to listen carefully to what country people called mother wit. That in those homely sayings was couched the collective wisdom of generations.

—Maya Angelou, *I Know Why the Caged Bird Sings,* 1969

I had long been aware of this book. It wasn't until meeting Maya Angelou in 1987, however, that I actually read it, followed by the rest of her autobiography. I had first seen her in 1960 or 1961 in Chicago as a warm-up act for the Clancy Brothers. She was a singer and dancer back then. But when she keynoted the inauguration of the new president of Northeastern Illinois University twenty-some years later, I really took notice.

She was on campus for several days, and as a dean, I got to be one of her escorts. During her evening performance, she interpreted two hours' worth of African, African American, European, and European American poetry and prose. I mean, she was something. Six feet tall and regal in her African outfit, she recited all her material by heart. My two African American student aides, sitting very straight in their chairs, were entranced. We all were.

Her mentor's advice had served Maya Angelou well. Her voice, now deep as the ocean, now soaring like an eagle, gave us much more than inspired words. During those few hours, she planted living seeds. Something in each of us shifted and changed. You could sense it. Somehow she had connected us with the "collective wisdom of generations."

In your Wisdom Journal, describe a "magical" experience with the spoken word.

AUDITORY WISDOM

I heard a fly buzz when I died –
The stillness in the room
Was like the stillness in the air
Between the heaves of storm.

–Emily Dickinson (1830–1886)

Hearing, they say, is the last sense to go. A few years ago, the popular press featured articles on how patients under anesthesia remembered things their surgeon had said while they were "unconscious." Apparently, based on subsequent research, patients who heard positive remarks tended to heal more quickly than those who heard things like, "George here really doesn't look good." The articles encouraged surgeons to refrain from negative comments during or just after operations and, instead, to say upbeat things.

Among Christians, the Pentecost story, recounted in Acts of the Apostles, chapter 2, is considered the mirror image of the Tower of Babel (Genesis, chapter 11). In the Old Testament tale, all the world once spoke a single language. A group of people settling "in the east" decided to build a city with a tower so tall it would reach the heavens. Their goal: to make a name for themselves. Jehovah, not pleased, threw a monkey wrench into their plans by giving them each a different language. Their Tower of "Babble" was never completed. In the New Testament story, a sound like a strong wind announced the descent of tongues of fire on Peter and the disciples. When they preached to the international Jewish community gathered in Jerusalem for the feast of Pentecost, "each heard his own language spoken" (Acts of the Apostles 2:7). Biblical scholars like to point out that this was a miracle of hearing as much as of speaking.

Becoming quiet and learning to listen to that still, small voice is a main feature in many spiritual practices. Perhaps our last sense to go should be the first one we cultivate.

Find a place where you can hear birds. Sit quietly for twenty minutes, then write about the experience in your Wisdom Journal.

THE WISDOM OF AVOIDING MISTAKES

Cato used to assert that wise men profited more by fools, than fools by wise men; for that wise men avoided the faults of fools, but that fools would not imitate the good examples of wise men.

-Plutarch (c. 46–120)

One reason the wise are wise is that they are excellent learners. They learn from good examples what to do and how to be, and from bad examples what not to do and how not to be. An important characteristic of sages is thus discernment. Sometimes fools appear wise. This is especially true of the worldly wise whose street smarts are not matched by good character.

An example is Gordon Gecko, the unscrupulous trader played by Michael Douglas in the hit movie of some years ago *Wall Street.* Because of his material success and smooth style, Gecko at first impresses the naive hero, a young man aching to make his fortune in the market. The young man's father cautions him against Gecko, but the son doesn't listen. Later he learns from his mistakes, but the lessons are costly and come almost too late.

The truly foolish are those who are unable to learn from their experiences. They exemplify the case where, in Jesus' parable, the seeds of personal growth fall on rocky or desert soil. No development is possible. Two sayings of the Buddha make this point: "If a fool can see his own folly, he in this at least is wise; but the fool who thinks he is wise, he indeed is the real fool," and, "If during the whole of his life a fool lives with a wise man, he never knows the path of wisdom as the spoon never knows the taste of the soup" (The Dhammapada). The two important ingredients are humility and consciousness. If we are humble, we will not think ourselves wise and will more easily be able to accept criticism and learn from our missteps. If we work on expanding our consciousness, moreover, we will be better able to heed warning signs and avoid making mistakes.

Discuss in your Wisdom Journal an example of when you have learned from a mistake or were able to avoid making one.

RETURN-ENGAGEMENT WISDOM

Keep coming back. It works!

-AN AFFIRMATION FREQUENTLY MADE AT THE END OF TWELVE STEP MEETINGS

I remember when my wife and I experienced our first visit to a hands-on healer. Simone has had lifelong digestive problems, chronic high blood pressure, knees that bother her, and the HMO doctor thinks she has incipient diabetes. As for me, I have carpal-tunnel syndrome in both hands and bursitis in my right shoulder, and three days after this visit to the healer, I had surgery scheduled for my cataract-clouded right eye. So, to quote my Grandma Ida, "Vat could it hoit?"

We heard about this healing church from our young friend Marni, who has been going there for about three years. In fact she assisted the minister in both our sessions. Now, Marni is the kind of person you would follow into a fire. She's extremely trustworthy. Further, there is no set rate for healing sessions. You just make a free-will donation.

Simone sent me in first. With eye surgery just ahead, this was a piece of cake. Reverend Aki, the minister of healing, a local Japanese American with a black ponytail, asked first what needs I brought. Then I lay back on an ordinary massage table. He put on some toning music that sounded like Tibetan chanting and left for five minutes while I relaxed. Then he began by holding my head and praying to "the Creator, Master Jesus, and the Holy Spirit to heal this brother from the ailments he has named." Marni, in the meantime, held my feet. During the treatment they moved their hands to different parts of my body while Aki "toned" in consort with the tape.

I felt very relaxed when it was over. Plus my bursitis pain has subsided and my right arm has become much more mobile. As for Simone, when she was finished, she glowed. "I will definitely come back," she told Marni and Aki. Time will tell whether the treatments work. For now, I am with Simone. I also will return.

Have you ever experienced bodywork or faith healing? If so, comment in your Wisdom Journal. If not, write why you would or wouldn't try it.

SHAMANIC WISDOM

The shaman's primary functions are . . . guiding the soul of a deceased person to its home in infernal or celestial realms or of journeying to those realms for the purpose of retrieving the soul of a sick person, which has either wandered off by itself or been stolen by the spirits while the patient was asleep.

-Dennis McKenna and Terence McKenna, *The Invisible Landscape*, 1975

In Martin Scorsese's film *Kundun*, which presents the early life of the Dalai Lama until his flight from Tibet, there is a sorcerer, or shaman, who appears several times. This figure, in a trance state, dances and shrieks in Halloween-like fashion. But apparently his counsel confirms the adolescent Dalai Lama's intuition that China will sweep his defenseless country, and that for Tibetan culture to survive, the young leader will have to lead a remnant to safety elsewhere.

Shaman is the generic term for spiritual practitioners in hunter-gatherer and tribal societies. Generally each small group had at least one and often two such specialists. They were the mediators between the everyday and the spirit worlds: the medicine men or women, the doctors, the psychologists, the magicians. Because of their access to invisible powers, shamans were generally at the center of their group and highly respected. Most writers distinguish between shamans and priests. Priests were experts in ritual who remained in the everyday world, but shamans entered the spirit world, sometimes doing battle there to cure the sick. For in contrast to the demon-possession theory of disease, shamanism holds that illness is caused by the temporary absence of the soul from the body. The shaman is literally the redeemer of lost souls.

The Yaqui Indian sorcerer Don Juan Matus, the main figure in many of Carlos Castaneda's books, is a modern-day representative of shamanism. Don Juan negotiates between this world and the world of power. For many of us who were young adults in the 1960s, Don Juan initiated us vicariously into his bipartite world as well. Some of us have been seeing double ever since.

Read Castaneda's Journey to Ixtlan, *then write your reaction in your Wisdom Journal.*

RETICENT WISDOM

Be wiser than other people, if you can, but do not tell them.

-Lord Chesterfield (1694–1773)

Known primarily for his letters to his son, Lord Chesterfield became a kind of literary Emily Post for eighteenth-century England. His advice has been must reading for generations of English gentlemen ever since.

A main theme is etiquette. Chesterfield insists that one refrain from calling attention to oneself by doing outlandish things or by not doing what is expected. One is to be visible in society, as it were, by being invisible. As in the Confucian cultures of China and especially Japan, moderation, politeness, and restraint are among the chief Chesterfieldian virtues. Ostentation, pretentiousness, and bragging, on the other hand, are definitely to be avoided.

In all times and places, wisdom is an esteemed quality that one should cultivate. Lord Chesterfield's England was no exception. Still, given the climate of eighteenth-century society in England and elsewhere in Europe, one is not surprised at the earl's advice to be wiser than others to the extent possible but to keep that fact to oneself. In a related statement, Chesterfield advised his son to "wear your learning, like your watch, in a private pocket: and do not pull it out and strike it, merely to show that you have one." Humility, reticence, and consideration for the likely effect on (if not for the feelings of) others are the watchwords.

We live in a time when it is okay to show up at the opera – though not the Academy Awards – in jeans. Chesterfield's starchy formality, like the bows and flourishes of the Rococo Age, is long gone from North American culture where, even in the eighteenth century, it was less in evidence than in Europe. Still, there is something to be said for not showing off. If a good wine needs no bush, we should reveal what wisdom we have by our actions, not our words. We should work on ourselves, attend to our own faults, and if we can't say something good about others, we should keep quiet. Lord Chesterfield had a point. Reticent wisdom is not without value.

Assess how discreet you are in your social interactions. Discuss your findings in your Wisdom Journal.

STUDS TERKEL'S WISDOM

Take it easy, but take it.

–Studs Terkel's tag line (by way of Woody Guthrie)

We all need heroes. Studs Terkel is one of mine. I first encountered him in 1955 on my first trip to our new hometown, Chicago. The legendary Richard J. Daley was mayor. Lake Michigan was resplendent. And there was Studs on radio station WFMT, which in those days broadcast about eight hours a day. Then, as now, the announcers were mainly men who all sounded alike–plummy baritones with the slightest trace of a "Chicawgah" accent. Then, as now, they correctly pronounced composers' names in a half dozen languages.

Studs was a whiskey baritone even in those days. He had already developed a signature radio voice. There was no mistaking where he was from, or what he was for. A lefty, a jazz guy, a history guy. Like Mike Royko and Hizzoner, Studs was a Chicago original.

I could never get enough of Studs's program. He would always select an interesting person–a folk singer like Pete Seeger, an activist like Dorothy Day–then ask the most stimulating questions. Of all the good interviewers, then and now, no one was quite like Studs. He knew his subjects' backgrounds and had read their books (Studs's interviewees were often happily shocked to see that his copy of their newly published work was dog-eared and marked up as if he'd owned it for years). He approached them with a warmth and enthusiasm that set them at ease and brought out their best, as if he were an old friend checking in. He used this same technique with "regular folks," resulting in a series of remarkable books that amount to an oral history of the twentieth century.

Decades later I met and talked with him twice. My junior-high daughter had written about Studs as an "Illinois institution" for the state history fair. I handed him her report. A week later Christine received a delightful handwritten letter from the man himself, and you can easily imagine how good that made her feel. Studs interviewed hundreds of interesting people. But for me he is among the most interesting of all.

Do you have a public person you look up to? Talk about him or her in your Wisdom Journal.

AMAZING-DAY WISDOM

i thank You God for most this amazing
day:for the leaping greenly spirits of trees
and a blue true dream of sky;and for everything
which is natural which is infinite which is yes

–E. E. CUMMINGS (1894–1962)

As I wake up to another beautiful day in Hawaii, to the green of bamboo shoots in front of blue sky, puffy white clouds, and emerald hills, I think of Cummings's exuberant poem of thanksgiving. My flu is reducing to a cold, and I slept the whole night through – a gift as I grow older. This is indeed the day the Lord has made, and I am grateful to be here to see it.

Cummings's poem continues, "(i who have died am alive again today)," and concludes, "(now the ears of my ears awake and / now the eyes of my eyes are opened)." Each night we die a little, and each day we are reborn. Death and resurrection, throwing off the body and taking on a new one, are as real as going to bed last night and getting up this morning. Today is filled with untold possibilities if I am alive and awake enough to realize them. And no one does come to the parent except through the child. For unless we become again as little children, we cannot enter the Kingdom of heaven. The door is too small for our large, blasé adult selves, and the windows, out of the question. That relationship of trust and surrender to the parentage we call God is the way, the truth, and the life.

The trees that seem rooted where they stand are alive, mobile, and willing to help our spirits move greenly, as theirs do. But it is up to us to ask. God is absolutely committed to our free will. Until we say yes, our meaning is no. Until we awaken, we remain asleep. God, I AM, is. The real question is, Will we be?

Take your bearings today. In your Wisdom Journal, assess where you are right now on your journey to wisdom.

ANTIBUREAUCRATIC WISDOM

Whenever his liquor begun to work, he most always went for the govment. This time he says:

"Call this a govment! why, just look at it and see what it's like. Here's the law a-standing ready to take a man's son away from him – a man's own son, which he has had all the trouble and all the anxiety and all the expense of raising. Yes, just as that man has got that son raised at last, and ready to go to work and begin to do suthin' for him *and give him a rest, the law up and goes for him. And they call* that *govment!"*

–MARK TWAIN (1835–1910), *THE ADVENTURES OF HUCKLEBERRY FINN*

Huck Finn's abusive, absentee drunkard of a father, Pap, is one of the great comic creations of American literature. He rails like an inebriated senator against government intervention in what he considers a private affair. His speech is funny because each of us, even today, can identify real-life people who make similar antigovernment speeches. Unfortunately what Pap stands for is not funny – being free to treat our children like property. The irony in Pap's case is that he has not raised Huck. He merely wants something for nothing – a servant, a slave, someone to support him so that he can continue his dissolute drinking life.

But while dismissing Pap, who wants to prohibit public officials from protecting his minor child from him, we can agree that government is many times part of the problem, not the solution. A frequent cause is the size of the bureaucracy. Here in Hawaii, which has the highest proportion of state workers to general population of any state in the union, bureaucracy is rampant. After all, every state employee needs something to do. So every petition, every request has to go through more committees, more individual officials, than in other states. As a result everything takes longer. From my perspective a lean government that does for us what we cannot or should not do for ourselves is appropriate. An inefficient, bloated bureaucracy is not.

Share in your Wisdom Journal your ideas about what constitutes a "wise government."

POETIC WISDOM

Everywhere we are told that our human resources are all to be used, that our civilization itself means the uses of everything it has – the inventions, the histories, every scrap of fact. But there is one kind of knowledge – infinitely precious, time-resistant more than monuments, here to be passed between the generations in any way it may be: never to be used. And that is poetry.

–Muriel Rukeyser, *The Life of Poetry*, 1949

My parents were not pleased by my decision to become a college English teacher. They were proud of my grades and academic honors, but I knew what they were thinking: "A Phi Beta Kappa from Yale! He could do better." As children of dirt-poor immigrants, survivors of the Great Depression, and sincere believers in the materialistic version of the American Dream, they couldn't understand my refusal to capitalize on my four-star education and enter a high-paying field.

My father would forever be mentioning some business associate who had "done well." He'd say, "You remember Mo Cohen? He's worth at least five million." "Wow!" I'd think to myself, "Someday I might be worth twenty thousand."

Where were my riches? Well, passed between the generations there was, for example, this William Wordsworth poem, which I had memorized in 1957 and still know today:

A slumber did my spirit seal;
I had no human fears:
She seemed a thing that could not feel
The touch of earthly years.

No motion has she now, no force;
She neither hears nor sees;
Rolled round in earth's diurnal course,
With rocks, and stones, and trees.

Even as a college student, I knew I would one day lose people I loved. Living presences would be no more. Then, like the poet, I would be forced to face the stonelike reality of death – but I would be comforted by his having visited that place first.

In your Wisdom Journal, write about a poem that is especially meaningful to you.

DOROTHY DAY'S WISDOM

The only answer to this life, to the loneliness we are all bound to feel, is community. The living together, working together, sharing together, loving God and loving our brother, and living close to him in community so we can show our love for Him.

–Dorothy Day (1897–1980), *The Long Loneliness*

Like her father, Dorothy Day was a journalist. Is this another example of *nomen est omen* (the name is ominous)? The English word *journalist* derives from the French word for day, *jour.* A "journal" is thus a daily newspaper or a diary. And, at the risk of riding this wave too far, journalists attempt to shed daylight on issues that have remained obscure.

Dorothy's father, to be sure, was a sports journalist. When she first got into the business in the early 1920s, however, she took a job as a reporter with the *New York Call,* a socialist newspaper. There she had her first (though by no means last) experience of social protest followed by time in jail. She converted to Catholicism as an adult, and when, in 1933, she met Peter Maurin, a Catholic social reformer from France, they co-founded the *Catholic Worker* newspaper. Dorothy continued to write for the *Catholic Worker* until her death forty-seven years later. Meanwhile she was midwife and leader of the Catholic Worker Movement, which endeavored to reach out to the poor, protest unfair labor practices, emphasize the importance of living close to the land, and practice pacifism. Today the *Catholic Worker* is still in print, and over one hundred Catholic Worker communities offer shelter, food, and social services to poor and homeless people around the United States.

What she primarily gained from her lifelong study of the Gospels, though, was the centrality of extended family, or "brotherhood." Until we understand that, through the parenthood of God, all human beings are our brothers and sisters and that this fact obligates us to act toward one another in certain ways, we will always be plagued by a dark night of the soul: what Dorothy referred to in the title of her autobiography as "the long loneliness."

How do you balance personal development and social reform in your life? Respond in your Wisdom Journal.

THE DIFFICULTY OF IMPARTING WISDOM

Every teacher knows how difficult it is to pass knowledge, as distinct from information, to students; hence, we give objective tests to determine how much information, rather than knowledge, they have acquired. As for imparting wisdom, it . . . has to do with personal chemistry and slow osmosis.

-Yi-fu Tuan

Gut Ding braucht Weile, the Germans say. "Anything of value takes time." The late Paul Goodman, author of *Growing Up Absurd,* was philosophically in tune with the social and political thrust of the 1960s. His last teaching assignment was in fact at the University of Hawaii's so-called Hippie College, where I also taught. Our students, Paul would say, wanted it all *now.* But correcting social and personal flaws is slow, painful work. The experiences of a lifetime convinced him that achieving something of value really did take sustained effort.

Some, of course, consider wisdom unteachable. You either have it or you don't. The wise arrive on the scene full of wisdom. Think of the twelve-year-old Jesus instructing the rabbis at the Temple. Or of George Lucas's Yoda, the all-knowing Jedi master who looks like he was born a full-blown sage. The process of growing up, according to this paradigm, merely frees one to communicate what he or she already knows.

I agree with Professor Tuan, a well-known geographer who has taught at major American universities. As one goes up the hierarchy from data to information to knowledge to wisdom, the task of teaching becomes more challenging. Idiot savants can be walking encyclopedias of data – sports or weather statistics, say. The average student, meanwhile, can memorize information such as the names of the states and their capitals. But when we get to knowledge and especially wisdom, the story changes. Here, in Shakespeare's phrase from *King Lear,* ripeness is all. Whether that ripeness comes from genes, former lives, experience in this life, good fortune in meeting the right teachers and mentors at the right time, or some combination, is a mystery, at least to me. Still, I obviously think wisdom can and should be learned, however difficult the task.

Write in your Wisdom Journal how you think wisdom can be acquired.

EXPERIENTIAL WISDOM

Histories make men wise.

–Francis Bacon (1561–1626)

Sir Francis Bacon was England's Renaissance man. He knew everything about everything, and wrote essays on almost everything he knew. Truth, death, revenge, adversity, marriage, the single life, atheism, travel, cunning, empire, fortune, law, travel, boldness, vicissitude, and gardening are just a sampling of his topics. For individuals unable to believe that a commoner from the country could have written Shakespeare's plays, Bacon, the urbane aristocrat, has often been named as the genius behind the quill.

He was also a king of one-liners. They often opened his essays. In "Of Gardens," for example, he begins, "God Almighty first planted a garden." In "Of Studies," his essay on the value of self-education, he favored series. Consider: "Reading maketh a full man, conference a ready man, and writing an exact man." To translate, by broad reading you will stock your mind with ideas, references, analogies, and arguments; by participating actively in conversations, you will learn to think on your feet and say the right thing at the right time; and by writing regularly, you will train yourself to pick the best words to convey what you mean. On the importance of studying different fields, he created the series from which today's lead quotation was drawn: "Histories make men wise; poets, witty; the mathematics, subtile; natural philosophy, deep; moral [philosophy], grave; logic and rhetoric, able to contend."

His point about history books and wisdom, clearly, is that we should learn from the mistakes of others. The proverb "Pride goeth before a fall" suggests an ordinary human dynamic. Milton illustrated this principle in his epic *Paradise Lost* through Satan's disobedience and his subsequent fall from heaven to hell. All the early novels – *Moll Flanders, Tom Jones,* and so on – were formally titled *The History of* . . . We can examine and learn from the role of cause and effect in fictional characters' lives too. Most important, of course, is to profit from our own triumphs and mistakes. This maxim might help: "Don't live in the past or lament it. Learn from it."

In your Wisdom Journal, discuss a situation in which you profited from "history."

FAMILY-COUNCIL WISDOM

Open covenants of peace, openly arrived at.

–President Woodrow Wilson (1856–1924),
point one of his Fourteen Points

We Americans are happy when we hear that countries around the world have traded in autocratic regimes for democracy. But when it comes to governance, charity really begins at home. And home, the nuclear family, is often the last bastion of dictatorship.

The watchword in the old days was, "Father knows best." The rationale was, "I pay, I say." Now this wasn't always bad. In my childhood my father would sometimes come home early on a sweltering Friday afternoon, tell us to pack up, and take us to Atlantic City for the weekend. Coming from our unair-conditioned house in the New York City suburbs, we would delight as the temperature dropped and the smell of salt in the air picked up as we neared our destination.

But sometimes the results were less pleasing. As a child you were told, not asked, what to do – like the time my parents urged me, at age fifteen, to get a summer job. Then when I secured one as a caddy at a New England resort, my mother arrived at my boarding school one day to say, "Your father and I have decided that you can't take that job." Can you imagine my teenaged frustration?

As a parent, alas, I duplicated both these top-down behaviors until a friend recommended Rudolf Dreikurs's book on family councils. From then on the four of us became a committee of the whole, attempting to resolve all family problems through the age-old process of give-and-take. I remember arriving in Vancouver, Canada, during our last family vacation in 1987. In the old days, I would have dictated our activities. This time we held a council meeting instead. Each person made a list of what they wanted to do. We then went around the table and arranged everyone's choices until our week was filled. Unlike past family trips, where sulks and screaming had been the rule, this vacation passed very harmoniously. Which proves the point: "Open covenants . . . openly arrived at" lead to peace.

In your Wisdom Journal, describe how decisions are made in your family.

FIGHTING WISDOM

We shall not flag or fail. We shall fight in France, we shall fight on the seas and oceans, we shall fight with growing confidence and growing strength in the air, we shall defend our island, whatever the cost may be, we shall fight on the beaches, we shall fight on the landing grounds, we shall fight in the fields and in the streets, we shall fight in the hills; we shall never surrender.

-SIR WINSTON CHURCHILL (1874–1965), JUNE 4, 1940

Though he was one of the greatest English rhetoricians, Winston Churchill had his work cut out for him in this speech made after Britain's crushing defeat at Dunkirk. The above lines, reiterating the phrase *we shall fight,* helped England survive the Battle of Britain and stem the tide of Nazi advance until America could enter the war. The speech also helped save Churchill's government and keep him at the helm during the critical days and months ahead.

World War II, as Studs Terkel, Tom Brokaw, and others have pointed out, was our last "good" war. Or at least so it seemed at the time and for a while afterward. Weren't the Nazis the incarnation of evil; Hitler, a living devil? Didn't the Japanese perpetrate a kind of minigenocide in Mongolia and kill thousands of innocent civilians in Shanghai, followed by their dastardly Sunday-morning attack on Pearl Harbor?

For someone who bases his philosophy on the 1960's slogan "Make love, not war," I have a hard time seeing any conflict as warranted. Yet there appear to be times when we must stand up and be counted. Avoiding conflict now may lead to broader conflict later, as when Churchill's predecessor Neville Chamberlain took Hitler at his word and predicted "peace in our times." Even if we achieve a world without war, there will always be disagreements impinging on our and our neighbors' right to life, liberty, and the pursuit of happiness. Appeasement or denial can't be acceptable alternatives in such situations. When mediation and arbitration fail, fighting may be the last, best option.

Do you believe in the concept of the "just war"? Respond in your Wisdom Journal.

GLOBAL-VILLAGE WISDOM

If we could shrink the earth's population to a village of precisely 100 people, with all the existing human ratios remaining the same, it would look like this. There would be 57 Asians, 21 Europeans, 14 from the Western Hemisphere (north and south), 8 Africans. Fifty-two would be female; 48 would be male. Seventy would be nonwhite; 30 white. Seventy would be non-Christian; 30 would be Christian. Eighty-nine would be heterosexual; eleven homosexual. Fifty-nine percent of the entire world's wealth would be in the hands of only six people, and all six would be citizens of the United States. Eighty would live in substandard housing. Seventy would be unable to read. Fifty would suffer from malnutrition; one would be near death, one near birth. One would have a college education, and one would own a computer. When one considers our world from such a compressed perspective, the need for both acceptance and understanding becomes glaringly apparent.

–Anonymous, from the Internet

Marshall McLuhan gave us the phrase *global village.* The corresponding picture was the "blue marble" seen from space, a perspective unavailable to us until the Apollo moon journeys. Meanwhile, Buckminster Fuller talked about Spaceship Earth. We were all riding around the solar system on a self-sufficient space vehicle. It contained food, water, a breathable atmosphere, life-sustaining temperatures, supplies, and a waste-control system to support its passengers in perpetuity so long as we did not overtax its carrying capacity through population increase or poor management.

Because we are all on this single interdependent spaceship, Fuller felt we needed to know how to live together peacefully and effectively. To that end he wrote his *Operating Manual for Spaceship Earth.* Perhaps someone should write a neighbors' guide to global living.

The above statistics indicate that the great masses of the planet are nonwhite, non-Christian, and poor. As the world becomes smaller, these inequities will destabilize our global society. Because, as wisdom suggests, prevention is the best cure, the sooner we help one another achieve inner and outer sufficiency, the better for all residents of the village.

Write freely for five minutes in your Wisdom Journal on what you think our global society will look like in 2100.

HEALING WISDOM

Jung spoke of the archetype called the wounded healer. I believe that each wound we suffer and eventually heal from is a soul-making experience with the potential to awaken our willingness to participate in the healing of the world.

-JOAN BORYSENKO, PHD, *FIRE IN THE SOUL*, 1993

Heal . . . hale . . . whole . . . holy. To heal is to make another sentient being healthy. "Hale and hardy" is the old-fashioned doublet for this state. Wholeness is a metaphor for good health, whether physical or mental. A house divided, Jesus tells us, cannot stand. The same holds for our bodies and minds. When germs invade us, we become ill. When we are beside ourselves, we may be possessed. Satan is legion; God is one. For Jung the goal of healing was psychic re-integration, restoring to wholeness a person who is "broken." Finally, when we are unbroken, all-of-a-piece, we become like God. And that wholeness is holy.

The world, which we sometimes refer to as the "whole world," is one in body as are we. It is also divided by its human inhabitants into ethnic groups and nation states that, unfortunately, have a history of not getting along. Military action has been a characteristic of every century. The planet is divided into north and south, more developed and less developed. There are areas of greater and lesser pollution. The Jewish tradition of *tikkun olam*, healing the world, is incumbent upon us all. For the earth is both mother and home. We need to respect our house, our lineage, and make sure our descendants have a place at least as good as ours to live.

Dr. Borysenko's main point, however, is that as we recover, we can become a source of recovery for others. Twelve Step sponsors are good examples. Having persevered in the program themselves, they can serve as role models and advisors to newer members. Many alcohol and drug counselors, by the same token, were once abusers of those substances themselves. From the sick and wounded, it seems, God can make doctors.

In your Wisdom Journal, list three things you are doing to heal the world.

ALCHEMICAL WISDOM

Throughout history, true alchemists, disdainful of wealth and worldly honours, have actively sought the Universal Medicine, the Panacea, which, ultimately sublimated, becomes the Fountain of Youth, the Elixir of Life and the Key to Immortality in both a spiritual and a mysterious physical sense. The Elixir would not only cure all ills by uprooting the causes of disease, but it would also rejuvenate and finally transmute the human body into an incorruptible "body of light."

–Stanislas Klossowski de Rola, *Alchemy: The Secret Art,* 1973

Alchemy fascinates us, like the mysterious practices of the Druids, the mythic power of Merlin, or the dark, crazy ministrations of Drs. Faust, Frankenstein, and Strangelove. It is a purposeful messing with the secrets of life, and it smacks of the demonic. The power source may just be real – and dangerous, like playing with fire.

Yet we also recall the story of Prometheus, the disobedient Titan who brought humanity the dangerous but useful gift of fire. Alchemy, after all, is the parent of three great sciences: chemistry (whose name comes from the older pursuit), metallurgy, and psychology. Experimenting with diverse materials, combining them under different temperatures and pressures, then recording the results may not have turned base metals into gold, but it certainly pioneered the scientific method. For in alchemical research, the emphasis was not so much on what the elders said but on what the individual discovered. Alchemy, in elevating experience over authority, helped launch the modern world. As Carl Jung has argued, alchemy implied the possibility of personal transformation, the promise of both psychotherapy and religion.

Working with power is always tricky. When we are successful, the danger of arrogance lurks. Eliphas Levi writes, "The Great Work [of alchemy] is . . . the creation of man by himself, that is to say, the full and entire conquest of his faculties and his future." By contrast, Jesus never considered himself a self-made person nor touted his personal power. When healing someone, he always gave credit to the Father or to the individual's belief. The ways of self-conquest and self-surrender diverge. Which we choose makes all the difference.

In your Wisdom Journal, write about the balance needed between personal power and surrender.

THE TALENT FOR WISDOM

When the wisest student hears about the Tao,
He follows it without ceasing
When the average student hears about it
He follows too, but not all of the time . . .
And when the poor student gets wind of it
he laughs at it like an idiot!
And if he didn't, then it wouldn't be the Tao!

-Lao Tzu (c. 604–531 b.c.e.), Tao Te Ching, translated by Kwok, Palmer, and Ramsay

Tao, pronounced "dow" in Mandarin, is the sound representation of the ideogram (concept-picture) for "road" or "path." It shows someone moving along, looking as they go. The character is used metaphorically for any doctrine or any intellectual way. The Chinese are a practical people, as the ideogram demonstrates. It is one thing to espouse a philosophy, but quite another when you actually set forth and act on your beliefs.

An agrarian people for thousands of years, the Chinese know about different soil types and their relative capacities to germinate seeds into fully mature crops. They also understand from long experience that patience is the first requisite of the good farmer. A Chinese proverb, quoted by Confucius, cautions against our pulling on young rice plants to make them grow faster. Natural processes have their own rhythms, which we disregard at our peril.

The wisest student is one who can correctly assess the value of something and act accordingly. Lao Tzu's philosophy is that we must all attune our daily activities to the Great Life Force of the Universe, the ultimate Way. The wisest among us will understand this message and immediately follow the path of Tao, much as some of Jesus' converts left whatever they were doing to follow him. Average students will more or less understand the value of the Way and react in kind. Foolish students, finally, will ridicule the Tao, and in so doing, will confirm that it is in fact what we should be pursuing. Whoever has ears, let them hear.

In your Wisdom Journal, spend five minutes writing freely about the Tao.

THE WISDOM HIERARCHY

Wisdom is integrated knowledge, information made super-useful by theory, which relates bits and fields of knowledge to each other, which in turn enables me to use the knowledge to do something. That's why wisdom is bound to cross the disciplinary barriers we set up to make the fields of knowledge manageable by the use of scientific method.

-HARLAN CLEVELAND, *THE KNOWLEDGE EXECUTIVE*, 1985

Hokusai, the eighteenth-century Japanese artist, created a famous series of prints called "One Hundred Views of Mount Fuji." Among the most famous is a picture of snow-capped Fuji glimpsed between two foam-capped waves. The eyes at first protest. Which is the mountain? Which are the waves? Indeed, from the artist's viewpoint, all three are quite similar. Fuji-San, as the Japanese call their sacred mountain, is a powerful entity. To get a true picture of something so complex and mysterious, a hundred views are not too many. Kurosawa's film *Rashomon* makes the same point. To come even close to what really happened in that crime story, we have to experience it from a number of different angles. Somewhere in the middle, we may find the truth.

This book provides 366 views of Mount Wisdom. Some are well grounded in the everyday and the practical. Others are aerial shots, abstract and theoretical. Today's view, clearly, is one of the latter. Harlan Cleveland – university dean and president, old China hand, former U.S. ambassador to NATO, author – has created a kind of wisdom hierarchy. At the low end he places *data,* which he considers "undigested observations." Next comes *information,* data "organized by others." Higher still lies *knowledge.* "Most knowledge," he writes, "is expertise – in a field, a subject, a science, a technology, a system of values, a form of social organization and authority." Highest of all, of course, is *wisdom,* "integrated knowledge" that we can use.

Now this may not be everyone's definition of wisdom. Though helpful, it is too intellectual and not practical enough for me. For contrast, my current definition is, "The capacity to make decisions that over time seem to help rather than harm self, others, and the world in which we live." What is your view?

In your Wisdom Journal, define wisdom *in three or four sentences.*

THE WISDOM OF THE BABEMBA

As I have loved you, so you are to love one another.

-JOHN 13:34

Here is another story from the Internet. Take it for what it is worth. According to my electronic informant, the Babemba, a South African tribe, follow this practice if someone has acted incorrectly or unjustly. The individual is placed in the center of the village. All work ceases as the entire village, including children, forms into a large circle around him or her. Then, for as long as it takes, each participant says something positive about the transgressor. Finally, when all the person's positive qualities and kindnesses have been recounted in detail – an activity which can last several days – the circle is disbanded and the village holds a feast to welcome the fully "chastised" and forgiven one back.

This ritual reminds me of several things. The first is a hippie technique known as "love-bombing." Basically, a group of people would saturate a particular individual, often an outspoken critic, with all kinds of positive statements along the lines of "I love you, man." Based on the Christian response of returning love for hate, it forms a stark contrast to the kind of shaming the Red Guard used on their enemies during the Chinese cultural revolution. There, supposed crimes against the people elicited vigorous public punishment, often with large groups of youth chastising a single older individual. I was also reminded of the Russian mystic G. I. Gurdjieff's practice of rewarding offenders against the group order with gifts of money. The greater the number of infractions, the larger the payment. Typically the offender was so shamed by being rewarded for something they themselves considered out of place that their behavior would change for the better.

Christianity is sometimes charged with being a Pollyannaish religion. How can one possibly do well in this world by giving away one's clothes, turning the other cheek, or returning love for hate? The example of the Babemba, whether or not they are Christian, suggests that Jesus' commandment to love may contain some practical wisdom after all.

In your Wisdom Journal, briefly share an example of the power of forgiveness.

U.N. WISDOM

WE THE PEOPLES OF THE UNITED NATIONS DETERMINED
to save succeeding generations from the scourge of war, which twice in our lifetime has brought untold sorrow to mankind, and to reaffirm faith in fundamental human rights, . . . and to establish conditions under which justice and respect for the obligations arising from treaties . . . can be maintained, and to promote social progress and better standards of life in larger freedom,
AND FOR THESE ENDS
to practise tolerance and live together in peace . . . , and to ensure . . . that armed force shall not be used, save in the common interest, and to employ international machinery for the . . . economic and social advancement of all peoples,
HAVE RESOLVED TO COMBINE OUR EFFORTS TO ACCOMPLISH THESE AIMS

–Preamble to the United Nations Charter, 1945

For some people, the U.N. Charter ranks with the *Communist Manifesto* as a diabolical document. After all, isn't the Communist Party theme song called "The Internationale"? The minute we shift even a little loyalty from red-white-and-blue to the U.N.'s blue-and-white, the fat is in the fire, they say. Everything previous generations have worked for will be lost.

Somehow I could never see what was bothering those people. I mean, what could be wrong with a world without war? A place where everyone's human rights are respected? Where promises between nations are kept? Where we all work together for the economic and social well-being of each? All this sounds remarkably like mainstream Jewish-Christian ethics to me. Like the Golden Rule in action. What could be wiser than that?

Discuss in your Wisdom Journal the promise and dangers of internationalism.

WISDOM FOR GROWING OLDER

I've been taught as a Christian how to die, . . . but I'm discovering I haven't been taught how to deal with old age – with the time before we die.

–Allan Emery, quoted by Billy Graham in *Just As I Am*, 1997

Our society worships youth. Many of the products marketed by Madison Avenue are supposed to make us look and feel younger. The point is, ours is not a Confucian culture. We do not place our elders on a pedestal. Given how busy we are, we are more likely to place them in a nursing home. Medicare, Social Security, and AARP discounts notwithstanding, no one wants to look, feel, or – above all – be old.

Mr. Emery may have been taught how to die or, as a Christian, how not to fear death. After all, Christianity holds that this life is a "vale of tears" and that the next life will be better for those who have been saved. Why be concerned? My sense, however, is that many of us know neither how to grow old gracefully nor how to die in peace. I suspect, moreover, that many Christians are included in this number.

Billy Graham writes that he never thought he would grow old. He believed he would take after his father and die young. Having reached age seventy-eight by the time he wrote his book *Just As I Am*, he felt he had a continuing responsibility to serve God as best he could, even if he could not be as active as in the past. The burdens of growing older – the physical infirmities, the decline in energy, the loss of friends, to borrow his examples – cannot be avoided. Yet the journey of life is more like a boat trip than a plane trip. The shifts in time zones and climates occur slowly, but occur they do. The best advice is to follow the Twelve Step slogan and live one day at a time. Plan, but be willing to make changes. Do things as time, energy, and funds allow, but recognize that not everything we once wanted to do is still doable. Realize that all is well.

In your Wisdom Journal, describe your ideal retirement.

THE WISDOM OF ACTIVE LEARNING

Tell me, and I'll forget. Show me, and I may not remember. Involve me, and I'll understand.

–A Native American saying

What do you remember from school? For my part, I don't remember what I remember. I obviously learned to read, write, and calculate. Also to understand some Latin and Spanish. After that, I don't know. School and college learning in my day was primarily a spectator sport. The teacher lectured. We listened and took notes. Exceptions were science classes, where we had occasional labs; or English and social studies, where we wrote papers or had combined essay and short-answer tests. But the concept was that the teacher explained, the student listened and learned.

Learning by doing was the domain of sports, scouts, social life, summer camps, arts activities, and clubs. Here we didn't have teachers but coaches, scoutmasters, counselors, sponsors, tutors, and each other. We learned to kick, throw, dribble, shoot, hit, run, fake, drive, putt, butterfly, backstroke, race dive, march, camp, hike, lindy, play clarinet, speak in front of groups, fingerspell, Charleston, make hospital corners, sing folk songs, and be away from home without crying. At boarding school we also learned to get along with a variety of peers by living with them, and in the 1950s, to clean our plate, be polite to elders, and become handy with brooms, dustpans, and mops.

In life, we learn by doing. Thanks to John Dewey and the Progressive Movement, this natural strategy is now being used in schools and colleges. Computer technology is helping students learn on their own through hundreds of interactive multimedia curricula. Service learning, where students assist in community projects, is becoming common; and school-to-work programs, based on the apprenticeship model, are being developed around the country. A NASA satellite, tracked by math and science students, gives them a new way to acquire knowledge and techniques in their fields. As a teacher, I believe telling and showing have their placc as educational strategies. But as the saying reminds us, experience is still the best teacher. Involve me, and I'll understand.

Pick three important skills of yours and, in your Wisdom Journal, describe how you acquired them.

THE WISDOM OF COMPLAINT-FREE LIVING

Do not complain about offenses perpetrated against you.

—Padre Pio (1860–1968)

When one of his disciples asked him for some guidelines for living, Father Grazio Forgione, the stigmatic later known as Padre Pio, offered a short list of six. The one quoted above was number two.

As sins go, complaining is clearly a misdemeanor, not a felony, venial rather than mortal. Along with gossip and criticizing others, it is something we do daily. The small-change of living, so to speak. But the change is dirty. We shouldn't eat or touch our eyes after handling it. We need always to wash our hands first.

To be honest, life can be frustrating. And complaining is one way to vent our frustrations. It is the verbal equivalent, in fact, of passing gas: a relief for the complainer, for whom it is a way to get something off the chest. But less so for those nearby. One of my father's favorite ways of describing the process continues the analogy. "Why are you bellyaching?" he would ask. A habitual complainer he would call a "bellyacher." "That Schwartz," he would say, "a real bellyacher!" Other members of our mainly Jewish circle, especially the older ones who would use Yiddish to convey information or opinions to our parents that my sister and I were not meant to hear, would use another term: *kvetscher.* Contemporary Jewish-American slang substitutes the shorter verb form for the noun. On Collins Avenue in Miami, you might hear, "That sister-in-law of mine, Zelda. What a *kvetsch!* All she does is complain, complain, complain!"

The irony, of course, is that in criticizing someone else for complaining, we become complainers ourselves. And even though the American slang "to bitch" suggests that *kvetschers* are from Venus rather than Mars, complaining is probably the most common shortcoming in people of all ages and both genders, at least in Western culture. Its very commonness can blind us to the habit and make it that much harder to break. Still, I agree with Padre Pio. It's a habit that should be broken.

Observe yourself for a day; then discuss in your Wisdom Journal how many times you actually complained.

COINCIDENTAL WISDOM

Coincidences are happening more and more frequently and . . . when they do, they strike us as beyond what would be expected by pure chance. They feel destined, as though our lives had been guided by some unexplained force. The experience induces a feeling of mystery and excitement and, as a result, we feel more alive.

–JAMES REDFIELD, *THE CELESTINE PROPHECY,* 1993

Whether or not there was an intensification of coincidences in the latter part of the twentieth century, I can't say. As a romantic with mystical tendencies, or vice versa, I would like to think so. But I can certainly agree with Redfield that experiencing a coincidence feels mysterious to the person in question.

In August 1973 I was in the process of moving from Germany back to the States to begin a new job that September in Chicago. My flight from Luxembourg ended in New York City. Rather than flying straight through, I decided to spend the weekend with my friend Victor. Sunday afternoon we joined an elderly Viennese friend, Francis, to eat a late brunch in Chinatown. Afterward Francis returned home. Victor and I decided to go to a famous Italian café in the East Village. Two tables away sat my graduate-school girlfriend, Jane Tompkins, whom I had not seen in six years. She happened to be in New York City from Philadelphia for the weekend to entertain friends from Italy. Later Victor and I calculated the probability of this meeting at well beyond a million to one. I felt the experience was an indication that I should stay in touch with Jane. Although it would be a few more years until we met again, we are now in regular contact and work together through Blue Sky Associates.

In Walt Whitman's "Leaves of Grass," he talks of grass as a "remembrancer" of the omnipresence of Spirit. For me, coincidences share something of that function. When I experience one, it seems to confirm that my life is more than random activity and that the universe has something in mind for me beyond my expectations.

Write in your Wisdom Journal about a coincidence and how it made you feel.

STUDIOUS WISDOM

What else therefore do we do when we study to be wise, except to concentrate our whole soul with all the ardor we can upon what we touch with our mind, and as it were place it there and fix it unshakeably; so that it may no longer enjoy privately what has entangled it in passing things, but freed from all influence of times or places may lay hold on that which is ever one and the same. For just as the soul is the whole life of the body, the happy life of the soul is God. While we do this, and until we have completed it, we are on the way.

–Saint Augustine of Hippo (354–430), "On Free Choice"

If you were planning a week-long workshop on "Enhancing Your Personal Wisdom," you could be forgiven for asking, "How do I use Saint Augustine's advice next Tuesday?" This is often the problem with abstract philosophical or theological language. How much easier to follow Thich Nhat Hanh's simple advice to breathe in and visualize a mountain, then breathe out and think, "I am solid." Or to practice centering prayer with the aid of a sacred word.

But it is always possible to troll in philosophical passages like this for meaning. This essay by Augustine is on free choice. Here he implies that we are each free to seek wisdom or not. There is no compulsion. However, if wisdom becomes our goal, we need to practice in everything we do. Jesus' advice that by seeking we shall surely find is appropriate here. Wisdom is all about us, but to gain eyes that see, we have, first, to look.

We must do our looking, however, in a way that will not merely entangle us in the web of difference. A banana is not a tomato. Yet both are fruits. A cosmic ray is not the morning newspaper. Yet both are made up of energy. A human being is not a gecko. Yet both are part of creation. Seeing God in or behind all things is both goal and path. To paraphrase Psalm 111, knowing the "here" of the Lord is the beginning of wisdom.

In your Wisdom Journal, describe a practical exercise you might use if you were giving a wisdom workshop.

THE WISDOM OF INCLUSIVE PRAYER

I thank you, Lord, for all the sins which I have not done, because you restrained me. I thank you for the sorrow I have felt for all the sins I have done. I thank you for all the people I have met, both friends and enemies. And I pray for them all, that they may all be your friends.

–MARGERY KEMPE (C. 1373–C. 1432)

When I was small, I practiced inclusive prayer, thanks to Florine, our African American housekeeper and my first spiritual guide. The simple prayer, which millions of children say each night before bed, goes: "Now I lay me down to sleep, I pray the Lord my soul to keep. If I should die before I wake, I pray the Lord my soul to take." Then I would add, "God bless Mommy, Daddy, Florine, my sister Natalie," anyone else I could think of, "and everyone."

The upside of this prayer was, by naming every last person and pet, I could stay up later and keep from having to face darkness and the room alone. The downside was that business about "if I should die before I wake." I mean, I was just a kid, and going to sleep alone was already scary enough. Even "lay me" had an edge because for the longest time, I thought it was a single word somehow related to being crippled. (In those days we often saw pictures of kids in iron lungs unable to even breathe on their own.)

So much of our all-too-humanness has to do with excluding others or even wishing them ill. In Paddy Chayefsky's play *The Tenth Man,* one character asks if there is a fitting curse for a hated mother-in-law. "Yes," another replies. "May your mother-in-law inherit a thousand-room mansion and die a horrible death in every room." By contrast, in Margery Kempe's little thanksgiving prayer, she follows Jesus' example and prays for both enemies and friends. She also thanks God, in effect, for her sins, because sinning can lead to remorse and a fresh start. In fact, everything we do or don't do can lead to God if we always include God as our friend.

In your Wisdom Journal, create a prayer of inclusion.

THE WISDOM OF LEADING FROM WITHIN

Identity doesn't depend on titles. It doesn't depend on degrees. It doesn't depend on functioning. It only depends . . . on the simple fact that I am a child of God, valued and treasured for what I am. When a leader knows that – the classroom is different, the hospital is different, and the office is different.

–PARKER J. PALMER, *LEADING FROM WITHIN*, 1990

Doing things from within is an important wisdom concept. When Parker Palmer, one of my mentors, agreed to host a meeting to help plan the national conference my colleagues and I intended to hold, I was delighted. Our topic was "education and the spirit." The title he suggested for the conference was "Teaching from Within." We all immediately agreed. It was perfect.

Doing anything from within is challenging, however. First we have to understand and feel the distinction between our deepest, truest self and our everyday self that can be influenced by ideas and emotions that take us away from who we really are. Gurdjieff's terms, *essence* and *personality*, are illustrative here. We also need to remember that not all spiritual forces are benign. Forces from the "dark side" can convincingly masquerade as angelic messengers. Only later, when the fruits of our words or actions become visible, do we sometimes have a better sense of "who was driving."

Still, as Parker suggests, leading from within begins, first of all, with the recognition on our part that others have their inner sources, their essences, also. They, too, are children of God. So, as supervisor or authority figure of any kind, we need to accept that the people "under" us may have ideas that are better, more productive, or less destructive than ours. Often there is more wisdom in asking than telling, listening than speaking. At the risk of seeming wishy-washy, we should always be willing to discard our solution or strategy in favor of someone else's. We don't know best just because we are the boss. Ultimately, leading from within means realizing that the ultimate within is not personal but cosmic, or, we just might say, God.

In your Wisdom Journal, describe someone you know who exemplifies leading from within.

THE WISDOM OF LIMITLESS MERCY

Let us not ruminate upon
the disagreeable scenes of the day. . . .
Mindful, Father,
of your infinite patience with us,
your infinite goodness,
we ask you to help us
never to harbour a single drop
of hatred, or resentment,
or bitterness
against anyone.
Fill us
with your limitless mercy.

-DOM HELDER CAMARA (1909–1999)

In the Judeo-Christian tradition, humanity is created just below the angels. One implication is that we are meant to act here on Earth in ways that correspond to life in heaven. Thus Thomas à Kempis wrote his *Imitation of Christ.* Obviously we cannot *be* Christ, but we can be Christlike. Or else why would Jesus have told his disciples–and, through them, us–to "go and do likewise"?

One of the hardest behaviors for us to resist has to be anger and the related desire for revenge. Life seems inherently unfair. If the so-called developed countries are made up of have-nots as well as haves, just consider the situation in materially less-well-off lands. In Rio de Janeiro on business in 1981, I visited with a Brazilian friend who lived in one of the many pastel high-rises dotting this beautiful city. Yet when I looked down from her apartment, I saw four cardboard walls, each about ten feet long, with no roof. There were thousands of such makeshift dwellings in Rio–exposing, not sheltering, their inhabitants. I was warned to protect myself from the thieves who lived in these *favelas.*

It is important for all of us to work for social justice. Poverty in the midst of wealth will always spark crime. As a Catholic archbishop, Dom Helder Camara himself had long been in the forefront of the battle for greater economic security in Brazil. Ultimately hatred must give way to love. Wisdom requires that we each cultivate in ourselves the limitless mercy of God.

Discuss in your Wisdom Journal how effective you are at forgiving and forgetting.

THE WISDOM OF LOVE

There is no difficulty that enough love will not conquer; no disease that enough love will not heal; no door that enough love will not open; no gulf that enough love will not bridge; no wall that enough love will not throw down; no sin that enough love will not redeem.

-EMMET FOX

As I write these daily meditations, I sometimes pause to reflect on whether I have left out some really important topic. With 366 opportunities, one should be able to hit almost everything at least once. So, when I was checking my files, I was virtually sure I would have to discard this quotation by the eminent commentator on the Sermon on the Mount. Love wisdom would certainly have been covered. Wrong! Where have I been? Of faith, hope, and love, Jesus tells us, love is the most important. So here I am, with months and months worth of daily essays done, and I am only now getting to love.

The Latin motto we English majors learn when studying Chaucer is *amor vincit omnia,* "love conquers all." These three words, in English or Latin, summarize Mr. Fox's more elaborately stated point. I remember Erich Segal's related comment, which has imprinted itself in our cultural memory, in his novel *Love Story,* "Love means never having to say you're sorry." I forget the context, but I suppose the sense is that in loving relationships, you show consideration by avoiding words or actions that upset the beloved. Then, of course, there is never a need to apologize.

Unfortunately I have all too often done or failed to do things that have hurt others. It happened again today. The persons in question are usually those I am closest to, both physically and emotionally. It is not enough to rationalize, as I do, that I am just following the Golden Rule – that I would not have been offended in their place. People are different. One takes offense where another wouldn't, and vice versa. For me, saying I am sorry and promising to be more sensitive in the future are love's way of keeping my relationships afloat – at least until I become more considerate.

Discuss in your Wisdom Journal how you maintain your loving relationships.

THE WISDOM OF QUESTIONING

The wise person questions the wisdom of others because they question their own; the foolish one, because it is different from their own.

-Leo Stein

On some other page of this book, you'll find a meditation called "The Wisdom of Not Questioning." Of course, having read this far, you won't be surprised to find an apparent contradiction within these pages. There are lots of them. We can view Mount Wisdom from more than one angle. It was Neils Bohr, the physicist, I believe, who said, "The opposite of truth is a lie, but the opposite of one great truth is another great truth." Or words to that effect. The problem with definitive, linear thinking is that it cannot fully describe a curvilinear universe. As the saying goes, God does not write in straight lines.

Balance is a main theme in this book. We can only walk, as Chairman Mao said, on two legs. If we use just one, we are no longer walking but hopping. Similarly we can only see fully with two eyes. If we close or lose the sight of one, we no longer have depth perception. In this regard William James advocated for a balance between belief and skepticism. The problem with those people who can be referred to as "true believers" is that they believe *uncritically* in something. Such become the lost souls of cults or extremist political groups. Then there are those who don't believe in anything, cynics who follow the Greek proverb "Remember to distrust." They are cursed to a life of broken relationships and bitterness.

Wisdom is knowing when to question and when to trust. Prudent questioning, moreover, begins with ourselves. Not everything we believe today will prove true tomorrow. Our ancestors perceived the world as flat. They were wrong. Disbelieving others just because their ideas differ from ours is narrow-mindedness. Accepting their ideas for the same reason is romanticism. Finding in all situations the right mix between trust and doubt is the way of the sage.

How good are you at balancing belief and skepticism? Respond in your Wisdom Journal.

THE WISDOM OF SEEING DOUBLE

I grew up in a double world, the small white clean Presbyterian American world of my parents and the big loving merry not-too-clean Chinese world, and there was no communication between them. When I was in the Chinese world I was Chinese, I spoke Chinese and behaved as a Chinese and ate as the Chinese did, and I shared their thoughts and feelings. When I was in the American world, I shut the door between.

–PEARL S. BUCK (1892–1973), *MY SEVERAL WORLDS*

I learned something about double vision when a fast-growing cataract caused me to undergo something called interocular lens replacement surgery in my right eye. The whole operation lasted forty minutes. I arrived at the hospital at 11:00 a.m. and was picked up at four. An immediate result was dramatic improvement in my right eye, from extreme nearsightedness to something like 20–40 vision. The problem was, my left eye – and the prescription for my eyeglasses – remained unchanged, by design, for five weeks. I could now drive without glasses for the first time in my life. But for the five weeks until I was permitted to get new glasses, I was seeing two different worlds at the same time, one clear and one fuzzy.

Pearl Buck, the daughter of missionaries serving in China, is among the great interpreters of China and the Orient to the West. She grew up in two distinct worlds. Each had a different view of reality. To live in one, she had to close off her view of the other, and vice versa. Eventually, though, she was able to see reality with even greater depth and acuity by drawing on her life in both.

My own experience as a Jew in a Gentile world, an American living daily in the German language, a humanities major working as an entrepreneur, and a Western intellectual committed to a contemplative path contains the same difficulties and advantages. What is sharp in one world is sometimes blurred in the other. What is *de rigueur* in one may be *verboten* in the other. But having these different perspectives helps me to see in depth and, I believe, to separate the merely cultural from the truly human.

Discuss in your Wisdom Journal how you achieve "double vision" in your life.

THE WISDOM OF SENECA FALLS

We hold these truths to be self-evident: that all men and women are created equal; that they are endowed by their Creator with certain inalienable rights; that among these are life, liberty, and the pursuit of happiness. . . .

The history of mankind is a history of repeated injuries and usurpations on the part of man toward woman, having in direct object the establishment of an absolute tyranny over her. . . .

He has usurped the prerogative of Jehovah himself, claiming it as his right to assign for her a sphere of action, when that belongs to her conscience and to her God.

He has endeavored, in every way that he could, to destroy her confidence in her own powers, to lessen her self-respect, and to make her willing to lead a dependent and abject life.

–"DECLARATION OF SENTIMENTS," SENECA FALLS CONVENTION, JULY 20, 1848

It is hard to admit that "mankind" has often been "mancruel" and that we men have long denied women their God-given equality. What was true 150 years ago remains true today. Certainly, thanks to the suffrage movement, aided by a few enlightened men, women now have the vote. Certainly, there are also women doctors, lawyers, jet pilots, CEOs. But in our minds and sometimes with our mouths, too many of us men continue to fight a rearguard action against gender equity. We cry, "It's just political correctness!"

Some of us refuse with pride to use "chairperson" or "chair." We insist on the generic "man" in everything. After all, we are the firstborn; women, an afterthought, the reason for our eviction from Eden. But as Gloria Steinem asks: "Would a man feel included in 'womankind'? Would he refer to himself as 'chairwoman,' 'Congresswoman,' or 'Mr. Mary Smith'? If a male student earned a 'Spinster of Arts' degree, . . . would he feel equal in academia?"

The Almighty found all creation good. So who are we to put down half of humankind? Isn't it time we get with the program?

In your Wisdom Journal, list three actions you could take, man or woman, to strengthen gender equity.

THE WISDOM OF THE NATURAL ARISTOCRACY

I agree with you that there is a natural aristocracy among men. The grounds of this are virtue and talents. . . . There is also an artificial aristocracy, founded on wealth and birth, without either virtue or talents. . . . The natural aristocracy I consider as the most precious gift of nature, for the instruction, the trusts, and the government of society. . . . In general they [the natural aristocrats] will elect the really good and wise. In some instances, wealth may corrupt, and birth blind them; but not in sufficient degree to endanger the society.

-THOMAS JEFFERSON (1743–1826)

Nearly two hundred years later, Jefferson's words may seem self-evident. Of course, we think. True aristocracy depends on who we are as individuals, not on our parentage or bank accounts. The concept is even recognized in England, where a hereditary class structure has existed for centuries. Signal achievement there can now be recognized by elevation to the peerage, as when members of the Beatles were knighted. In fairy tales, too, commoners, especially beautiful maidens, might suddenly find themselves the consorts of rulers. When the glass slipper fit, for example, Cinderella became a princess. And in Tibetan culture, the soul of the old Dalai Lama is reborn in the body of a child, whether from a high-born or a peasant family.

The basic principle of the natural aristocracy is founded in the idea, sometimes seen on bumper stickers, that "God don't make no junk!" Every child of God is, by that fact alone, an aristocrat, from the Greek *aristoi,* "the best." Yet we are not created equal, if by that we mean endowed with the same genes, intellectual or physical capacity, likelihood to live to a hundred, and so on. Nor, as the civil rights and feminist movements make clear, does every U.S. citizen have equal opportunities to achieve an excellent education, attractive living conditions, status, or wealth. Still, as our opportunities and self-esteem increase, the natural aristocracy of the human family will become less an ideal and more a reality.

List in your Wisdom Journal ten characteristics of a "true aristocrat."

THE WISDOM OF THE SUPERIOR PERSON

1. *To have little pride and envy*
2. *To have few desires and find satisfaction with simple things*
3. *To lack hypocrisy and deceit*
4. *To act with awareness of the consequences of one's actions*
5. *To be faithful to one's obligations*
6. *To be capable of friendship even while regarding all with impartiality*
7. *To look with pity and not anger upon those who live evilly*
8. *To allow others the victory, taking onto oneself the defeat*
9. *To differ from the multitude in every thought and action*
10. *To keep faithfully and without pride one's vows of chastity and piety*

–"THE TEN SIGNS OF A SUPERIOR MAN," PARAPHRASED FROM A TIBETAN BUDDHIST TEXT

Buddhism, the middle way between extreme asceticism and secularism, aims for release from suffering and for rebirth. So how can you tell whether someone is making progress? If she or he demonstrates qualities like the above ten.

But are they traits worth having? The first three make sense. Being proud, envious, hypocritical, and deceitful is hardly how we would want to be described. Living a simple life is the goal of many burdened by modern complexities. To govern our behavior by investing in actions likely to have good rather than bad outcomes is also wise. The issue is knowing which is which. Keeping our promises, maintaining long-term friendships, being impartial yet compassionate – all are no-brainers. But routinely ascribing victory to others and defeat to ourselves seems like false modesty; categorically differing from the multitude sounds undemocratic and biased; and the keeping of vows applies only to those who have taken such vows.

The lesson here is perhaps best expressed by the Twelve Step slogan "Take what you like and leave the rest." For the most part, wisdom transcends culture, but not always. We must each, finally, judge for ourselves.

In your Wisdom Journal, list seven characteristics of a "sage."

THE WISDOM TO DEVELOP SILENCE WITHIN

To preserve the silence within – amid all the noise. To remain open and quiet, a moist humus in the fertile darkness where the rain falls and the grain ripens – no matter how many tramp across the parade ground in whirling dust under an arid sky.

–Dag Hammarskjöld (1905–1961), *Markings*

Preserving inner stillness is the key to what the poet Rainer Maria Rilke called *Empfänglichkeit* (receptivity). Unless you are at home, you can't receive the special delivery being sent to you. And unless you learn to maintain inner stillness, you will never be at home.

The silence within, to use Hammarskjöld's phrase, does not require outward stillness, however. In fact, a person can refrain from speaking for hours and yet be noisy within. Novices in meditation practice are surprised to find how relentless their thinking mind is. They try to be silent, but the interior monologue rattles on, unobstructed. It takes time to become deeply quiet. Even techniques like mantras can take us only so far. Just as a child grows into the abilities to walk and talk, so we grow into our ability to be still. Patience is essential. The process has its own rhythm and cannot be rushed. We can only wait.

Yet once inner stillness is developed, its ability to germinate seeds seems totally separate from the events of our outer life. The weather may be arid and dusty or the rain falling in gusty torrents. Columns of soldiers may be marching across our parade ground. These factors have nothing to do with our inner situation. The Javanese saying "Outwardly active, inwardly quiet" captures the idea. We don't have to separate ourselves from the hectic pace of early twenty-first-century living *so long as* we have come to the point of creative quiet within. What we need to do is develop depth. In a storm the shallow water near the shore is churned up to its sandy bottom. But when the same storm visits its power on the deep ocean, only the water near the surface will be disturbed. The depths will remain as placid as before.

In your Wisdom Journal, describe someone you consider to be silent within.

WORKING WISDOM

Give me, dear Lord, a pure heart and a wise mind, that I may carry out my work according to your will. Save me from all false desires, from pride, greed, envy and anger, and let me accept joyfully every task you set before me. Let me seek to serve the poor, the sad and those unable to work. Help me to discern honestly my own gifts that I may do the things of which I am capable, and happily and humbly leave the rest to others. Above all, remind me constantly that I have nothing except what you give me, and can do nothing except what you enable me to do.

–JACOB BOEHME (1575–1624)

When Martin Luther translated the Bible into German, he hoped to make both the Scriptures and religion more broadly available. (Incidentally, Luther helped found compulsory public education, because most German speakers in his day were illiterate.) As a Catholic priest and Augustinian monk, however, he was careful to preserve the ordinary of the Mass (the parts that don't change) and to translate or create propers (the seasonal prayers of the Mass) for reading at the appointed times in church. Jacob Boehme, born ninety years after Luther, was a shoemaker from Saxony. The religious controversies of his day enraged him. He was Protestant, but nonetheless believed that the path to God lay not in protest and church reform but in contemplation. Boehme considered that anyone, by going within, could receive the sort of experiences described in the Bible and, incidentally, could write personal prayers.

Luther's reforming zeal helped usher in nationalism, individualism, democracy, and secularism. He introduced the Lutheran paradox, "Work as if everything depended on you; pray as if everything depended on God." A kind of balance was implied between God's responsibility and ours. Boehme, however, clearly takes the mystical position that everything depends on God and that one must therefore totally surrender to the divine will. Most important is that we discern our work and do it, serve others as Jesus served us, and acknowledge God as the source of all we have and do.

Discuss in your Wisdom Journal whether you side with Luther or Boehme and why.

HIERARCHICAL WISDOM

Even the wisdom of [the lowest order of] angels surpasses man's wisdom, for man is involved in the physical and the body's sense impressions; and man's physical sense impressions are on the lowest level of all.

This shows what kind of wisdom is proper to people who do their thinking on the basis of sense impressions, that is, people called "sense-oriented people." In fact, they are not involved in wisdom at all, only information.

It is different though with people whose thoughts are raised above sense impressions; and still more different with people whose more inward reaches are opened all the way into heaven's light.

—EMANUEL SWEDENBORG (1688–1772), *HEAVEN AND HELL*

Emanuel Swedenborg, Swedish mystic and mathematician, lived during a time when you could still be both and not be thought crazy. Swedenborg began his career as a scientist, and made contributions in chemistry, physics, biology, and mathematics. His mind had a practical turn too. In 1718, during a Swedish-Norwegian war, he invented a way of transporting boats over land. His method was so successful that the Swedish king knighted him. Beginning in 1745 he had a series of mystical visions, culminating in 1757 when he witnessed the Last Judgment. The ensuing new age, he claimed, required humanity henceforth to strive for direct union with God through love and wisdom. Then in 1787 a small group of English Swedenborgians established a new denomination, which exists to this day.

The mystical thrust of Swedenborgianism is democratic. We are all encouraged to strive for union with God. Still, as in other systems, there are hierarchies. The wisdom of the lowest angel is beyond what we humans can ever attain. But our possibilities can transcend mere information, the faux-wisdom of the sense-oriented, and reach clear to the light of God. Jacob's Ladder for Swedenborg was a ladder of wisdom.

Do you think wisdom is hierarchical? Respond in your Wisdom Journal.

INSPIRATIONAL WISDOM

The music of this opera [Madame Butterfly] *was dictated to me by God; I was merely instrumental in putting it on paper and communicating it to the public.*

–GIACOMO PUCCINI (1858–1924)

Where do ideas – artistic, musical, literary, scientific – come from? What is the source of inspiration? My daughter Marianna, who has a degree in art as well as two in English literature, provides a useful illustration. In 1995 we were looking for a logo for "Blue Sky Associates: Catalysts for Educational Change," the nonprofit consulting group several of us had started. Marianna sat quietly for a few minutes, then sketched part of the arc of the sun with rays of different lengths emanating from it. The partial sun was to be placed in the upper left-hand corner of the paper, with the rays flowing to the right. The color would be blue on a white background. The idea was simple and brilliant. To this day our logo elicits positive comments. When I asked Marianna how she came up with the idea, she answered, "It was what I saw after I got quiet."

Purposive thinking can lead to writer's cramp or a headache. Meditating (as in Marianna's case), doing sports, dancing, or watching an enjoyable movie, by contrast, clears the mind and makes a space for spirit to work. That, after all, is what *in-spiration* means, the in-flowing or in-dwelling of spirit. When we are too full of our ordinary self, we have no room for our deepest, God-connected self to function. Like an "empty" glass inverted in a bowl of water, no water can flow in because of the air pressure. Similarly artists of all kinds learn to get out of the way so that their creativity can enter and work.

Scientists find answers this way too. After dozens of failures, Edison discovered in a dream, another state where our ordinary selves with their censors are suspended, how to make a successful incandescent lightbulb. For my part I don't have a clue where the idea for this book came from. I just awoke one day, and there it was.

In your Wisdom Journal, write about the role inspiration plays in your life.

JUGGLING WISDOM

Imagine life as a game in which you are juggling some five balls in the air. You name them – work, family, health, friends and spirit – and you're keeping all of these in the air. You will soon understand that work is a rubber ball. If you drop it, it will bounce back. But the other four balls – family, health, friends and spirit – are made of glass. If you drop one of these, they will be irrevocably scuffed, marked, nicked, damaged or even shattered. They will never be the same. You must understand this and strive for balance in your life.

–Brian Dyson

Life may not be a cabaret, but it is certainly a juggling act. We all arrive on the scene to a family. Who and what it consists of varies greatly, from a traditional extended family to the impersonality of an orphanage. We may be received by an intact nuclear family as one of several children. We might be the child of a single mom or find ourselves in a blended family. Later on we may form families of our own. Again the possibilities are many. Whatever the case, family is something to which we must pay lifelong attention.

If we are lucky, we will acquire friends. Here in America we introduce someone we met two hours ago as "my friend so-and-so." My wife, born and raised in Germany, has much stricter standards. She just got off the phone from wishing a friend of forty-four years a happy sixtieth birthday. According to Simone, the ideal is to have a few close friends whom one cultivates and cares for throughout our lifetime.

By the nature of things, work gets the biggest piece of our energy and attention – often to the detriment of family, friends, health, and spirit. Yet, as Mr. Dyson implies, jobs come and go while the other areas of life are less forgiving. By choosing work and friends that make our spirit sing and by settling differences with family members, we will be taking important steps toward both good health and wisdom.

In your Wisdom Journal, discuss how you manage your juggling act.

BAHA'I WISDOM

It is our duty in this radiant century to investigate the essentials of divine religion, seek the realities underlying the oneness of the world of humanity, and discover the source of fellowship and agreement which will unite mankind in the heavenly bond of love. . . . For if we remain fettered and restricted by human inventions and dogmas, day by day the world of mankind will be degraded, day by day warfare and strife will increase and satanic forces converge toward the destruction of the human race.

–'ABDU'L-BAHA (1844–1921), ELDER SON OF BAHA'ULLAH

My parents moved from New York City to Chicago in the spring of 1955. I was a junior in a New Jersey boarding school at the time, and first visited our new home that May. A day or two after my arrival, we drove along Lake Michigan to visit friends in suburban Wilmette. Their house was easy to find. It came right after the Baha'i Temple.

The many-sided domed building was exquisite. I had never heard of the Baha'i faith. I decided to learn more. The philosophy impressed me. It was universalist to a fault. Besides Zoroaster, Baha'is consider the Buddha, Jesus, and Muhammad as divine manifestations. The stream of prophets was not sealed with Muhammad, as Muslims believe, but remained open as befits an almighty deity and changing human conditions. A Persian named Mirza Ali Mohammed announced, at the age of twenty-three, that an era was at hand when all religions would be united under one person. After Mirza's martyrdom six years later, Baha'ullah, one of his followers, took leadership, and today there are Baha'is in nearly every country. Their aims: an end to racial and religious prejudice, equality of the sexes, an international second language, and universal education, faith, and government.

Feeling the need for more ritual and greater mystical content, I never became a Baha'i. Still, I remain impressed with Baha'i architecture, universalism, and social programs. The rest of us could learn a thing or two from the Baha'is.

In your Wisdom Journal, list four or five goals you would like to see realized in the world by 2100.

PHILANTHROPRENEURIAL WISDOM

Government funds, charitable solicitations, and foundation grants have one thing in common: they represent somebody else's money. Nonprofits that rely on these sources shift limited dollars from one place to another, dividing the philanthropic pie rather than taking steps to create a bigger pie.

–BILL SHORE, *REVOLUTION OF THE HEART*, 1995

In 1997 my friend Loren and I created a monthly newsletter called "The Philanthropreneur." Our target audience was the nonprofit and government sectors. We believed that if nonprofit and government agencies could learn to be more entrepreneurial – to create funds, not just beg for them or get them through taxes – the results would be healthier for everyone.

We also perceived in the nonprofit world an imbalance between head and heart. Nonprofits were most often established because of some unmet need in the community – the need for a safe place for battered women and children, new homeless shelters, the nutritional needs of poor children. The founders of nonprofits were typically caring individuals, often professionals in a health or human-service field whose emphasis was on programming (the work of the heart), not administration or fund-raising (the work of the head). Such organizations often became dependent on erratic public funding or short-term foundation grants. How to become more self-sufficient?

We found dozens of cases in which such organizations found ways of doing well in order to do good. A university encouraged pharmacology professors to develop new drugs "on company time" and share the royalties. Other nonprofits found that affinity-group credit cards and long-distance services could provide percentages to help support their cause. A homeless charity found banks willing to donate distressed properties (which could be sold or developed) for a tax write-off. All of these are steps in the right direction.

Financially self-reliant nonprofits also provide a better example for their clientele. This, perhaps, is the aspect of philanthropreneurialism that holds the greatest benefit for the future.

In your Wisdom Journal, discuss how you might become a more effective "philanthropreneur" yourself.

PLAYING-HURT WISDOM

Most of the work of the world is done by people who don't feel particularly well that day.

–ELEANOR ROOSEVELT (1884–1962)

Someone sent this observation in to the "Sound and Spirit" refrigerator-saying contest. The idea was to share, in Ellen Kushner's phrase, the "words of wisdom that get you through a tough day." Ellen listed her favorites on the program's web site, where I found this one.

Our thresholds of pain differ. Aristotle's concept of virtue as the middle option between too much and too little makes sense as a model here. If every little owie lays us up, we'll never get anything done. But if we have a temperature of 103, it's a good idea to stay home, even on the day of a big presentation.

Sometimes when I am running, I feel a stitch in my side or a low-grade pain in one of my calves. Generally I'll slow down and ask my body for advice. Should I continue, but walk? Keep running, but at a slower pace? Carry on as before? Stop and go home? And, if I continue, should I go my planned distance? Whichever option I choose, if the pain goes away, I keep going. If I have decided to walk, I may switch to a jog. Then, if I have no reoccurrence of pain, I may speed up to a run. "Listen to your body" was the advice of the late running guru Jim Fixx. It generally gives good answers.

If we find ourselves not feeling particularly well on a regular basis, we should also pay attention. Most of us, alas, have too much to do and too little time. Feeling out of sorts on a regular basis may indicate that we are overdoing it and should ease up. Or perhaps it indicates that we are doing the wrong work and our inner selves are trying to register a complaint. The right response might be to stop, go on a weekend retreat, and ask for inner guidance. It's one thing to play through an owie. It's another to risk ruining our equipment by using it contrary to the Manufacturer's specifications.

How do you deal with "playing while hurt"? Respond in your Wisdom Journal.

RAT RACE WISDOM

The trouble with the rat race is that even if you win, you're still a rat.

–LILY TOMLIN

Yes, indeed. But it's even worse than that. The rat race is unwinnable. Rats are on a circular treadmill that leads nowhere. They are in a hell like that of Sisyphus, rolling his boulder up the hill only to have it roll back down. I recently experienced an endless loop like that on my computer. You keep trying and trying but you can never come to completion. Unless you have the sense to start over later or get help from an outsider, you will drive yourself crazy. So, conclusion one: It is foolish to try winning an unwinnable race.

If we forget the activity of a caged rat for a minute and think of the metaphorical race for worldly success, there is yet another reason why the race is unwinnable. Races have beginnings and ends. We talk about 100 meters, 400 meters, a mile, a marathon. But in this matter of worldly success, where is the end point? How much is enough? If we have one million dollars, we want two. If we have two, we want five. But think what we could do with a hundred million! Then, having achieved a hundred million, we conclude we've wasted our life chasing the Almighty Dollar. Our inner development is nil and our relationships unfulfilling. What now?

Lily Tomlin's great line leads me to another line of thought. The one race we are called on to win is the human race. We are here on Earth to learn what it means to be truly human, to fulfill our potential, to respect all other life, to live in accordance with the highest spiritual power. There is no shame in being a rat if you happen to be one. No one scolds pigs for eating like pigs or bulls for trashing china shops. What is out of place is for us to act like rats, pigs, or bulls.

On the other hand, my two cats live in commendable harmony. I aspire to their example in all my relationships.

How committed are you to the rat race? Respond in your Wisdom Journal.

SACRED PIPE WISDOM

Before we smoke [the sacred pipe], you must see how it is made and what it means. These four ribbons hanging here on the stem are the four quarters of the universe. . . .

But these four spirits are only one Spirit after all, and this eagle feather here is for that One, which is like a father, and also it is for the thoughts of men that should rise high as eagles do. Is not the sky a father and the earth a mother, and are not all living things with feet or wings or roots their children? And this hide upon the mouthpiece here . . . is for the earth, from whence we came and at whose breast we suck as babies all our lives. . . . And because it means all this, and more than any man can understand, the pipe is holy.

–JOHN G. NEIHARDT, *BLACK ELK SPEAKS*, 1932

During a 1990 flight to Japan, I sat just behind the business-class section. During the next nine hours, to my dismay, thick white clouds enveloped me. Although smoking had been banned on most domestic flights, airlines flying to Asia still permitted it in business class. They had to because cigarettes are an important part of Japanese business culture.

The pipe in Native American communities holds a revered place. As Black Elk states, this sacred instrument reunites us with our cosmic family. Think of the symbolism. Red willow bark, used as tobacco, is a gift of the Earth, our common mother. Fire turns it into smoke, an ethereal substance which returns to the Sky, our father. The communal rite of passing a single venerated pipe, while linking participants, reiterates that like all other life forms, we, too, are part matter, part spirit.

Further, all these parts, like the spirit of the different directions, form one whole, just as do the different parts within us, our communities, and the universe. Black Elk's pipe reminds us of the true meaning of *e pluribus unum.*

Using one *as your holy word, meditate for five minutes, then write freely in your Wisdom Journal.*

SELF-CARE WISDOM

There is a wisdom in this beyond the rules of physic. A man's own observation, what he finds good of and what he finds hurt of, is the best physic to preserve health.

–FRANCIS BACON (1561–1626)

In Bacon's day you couldn't simply make an appointment at your local HMO. We know from Shakespeare, of course, that there were physicians in the Elizabethan period. They administered physic–typically some form of herbal remedy. Hildegard of Bingen, the German abbess and mystic, was well known in twelfth-century Europe as a herbalist and healer. Shakespeare also spoke of doctors as "leeches." Now we can't say for sure whether he was casting aspersions on the cost of their services, but we do know that Elizabethans believed that imbalances in the four main bodily fluids affected the blood. So if you could get rid of the bad blood and allow for new, better-balanced blood to be produced, health might be restored. Doctors used leeches to draw out the old blood. Hence the name.

Still, in a time when people made their own soap, clothes, even shoes, the idea of being their own physician was not far-fetched. Folk cures and family remedies abounded. But Bacon, an early scientist and pragmatist, advised not to depend on external remedies, whether from doctors or neighborhood wisdom. We should see what works for us. If something makes us feel better, we should continue it. If not, we should try something else.

In an era of modern technological medicine and fairly universal health care, at least in more developed countries, we tend to call in the experts. Which is to say, we go to them, because home visits by doctors are a thing of the past. In so doing we have given away much of our freedom to heal ourselves. "In-tuition," as Gloria Steinem points out in her 1992 book *Revolution from Within,* means our inner capacity to teach ourselves. An important wisdom way is thus recovering an intuitive, reality-based sense of what is good for our bodies and what is not, and then to live accordingly.

How well do you listen to and talk with your body? Respond in your Wisdom Journal.

SHAKERTOWN WISDOM

I make the following declarations:

I am a world citizen. I commit myself to lead an ecologically sound life; to lead a life of creative simplicity and to share my personal wealth with the world's poor; to join with others in reshaping institutions in order to bring about a more just global society; to avoid the creation of products that cause harm; to care for my physical well-being, affirming that my body is a gift; to examine continually my relations with others; to personal renewal through prayer, meditation, and study; to responsible participation in a community of faith.

–Paraphrased from The Shakertown Pledge, 1973

It may be a gift to be simple, but no one said it would be easy. To think that I attended fifteen retreats at the actual restored Shaker village where this pledge was crafted, but did not find out about the pledge until doing research for this book! The Tibetans have their lists, we have ours. Perhaps East and West have met at last.

Shakertown was the right place to develop such a pledge. Although the last Shaker there died before World War I, the community at Pleasant Hill, Kentucky, was restored and is now an interpretive museum with a guest house, a restaurant, two gift shops, and conference facilities for small groups. The Shaker spirit of spare, functional beauty is palpable everywhere. The place even merited an essay by Thomas Merton in his *Mystics and Zen Masters.* Merton also took some exquisite photographs of the place in the 1960s – photos that provide such a clear sense of Shaker simplicity that they are almost as good as being there.

If the Shakertown Pledge were taken and followed by even a minority of the developed world's population, the impact in the new millennium would be, well, millennial. My sense is that whether we know it or not, we are all being moved in this direction. What do you think?

Which of the Shakertown commitments would you find the most difficult to implement and why? Respond in your Wisdom Journal.

SPELL-BREAKING WISDOM

The moment we find the true reason for some feeling that has an irrationally powerful hold over us, whether it has to do with body image or anything else, the spell is broken.

-Gloria Steinem, *Revolution from Within*, 1992

All education, the Swiss psychologist Jean Piaget once said, is discovery. So when we once hit on what is causing us trouble, it does seem to break the spell and allow us to move forward. I experience this phenomenon physically. For example, I get a particular headache that suggests an interior blockage. My meditation program includes a cleansing regimen that I then apply for five to ten minutes. During the process I am usually shown the cause. If not, it is essential that I ask myself why I have this physical symptom for no apparent reason. As soon as the reason reveals itself, the headache disappears – though the process does take energy and leaves me a little weak – and I can get on with my life.

In a recent *Unsolved Mysteries* program, a real-life exorcism was shown. Then a psychiatrist, who is also a professor at a prestigious medical school, stated in an interview that demon possession is an old-fashioned idea that should be discarded, and that persons receiving exorcisms would be better served by conventional psychiatric treatment. Not a surprising opinion, given the source.

My own spiritual practice since 1961, however, leads me to conclude that all kinds of spirits can and do possess us all the time. Often the culprits are not big-league demons, but conventional ideas, biases, or self-destructive beliefs that may, in time, prove just as effective in their negativity. Slow poison can still kill. Breaking spells and discovering how to become self-possessed are essential to wise living.

In your Wisdom Journal, describe an experience in which you "broke a spell" that was causing you trouble.

STEWARDSHIP WISDOM

In the Judeo-Christian tradition, the biblical concept of dominion is quite different from the concept of domination, and the difference is crucial. Specifically, followers of this tradition are charged with the duty of stewardship, because the same biblical passage that grants them "dominion" also requires them to "care for" the earth even as they "work" it. The requirement of stewardship and its grant of dominion are not in conflict; in recognizing the sacredness of creation, believers are called upon to remember that even as they "till" the earth they must also "keep" it.

–AL GORE, *EARTH IN THE BALANCE*, 1993

We moved to Hawaii in August of 1967. Thus, many of my experiences of the 1960s took place during my time teaching English at the university. Hawaii in those days seemed to be five years behind the U.S. mainland in everything. The first major campus protest didn't take place until 1968: a sit-in at the administration building over what we considered the illegal firing of a political science professor. Besides students, a sprinkling of faculty participated. Interestingly, many of us were idealistic, untenured assistant professors – the very ones with the most to lose. While the university president was our immediate target, the real "enemy" was the Board of Regents, political appointees whose concept of stewardship, we believed, had more to do with domination than dominion.

One of my friends at the time, a brilliant historian and former schoolteacher from Brooklyn, took an interest in crosscultural differences. Referring to the "dominion" section of Genesis (1:28), he pointed out how we in the Western world stab our food with forks and cut it with knives, while East Asians use wooden chopsticks and the nations of South and Southeast Asia traditionally eat with their hands. We were polluters who used the earth and its inhabitants however we wished. Those who ate with chopsticks and especially their hands showed greater respect for the environment.

Whether or not my friend's hypothesis holds, I have less trouble now with the dominion concept so long as we are talking about good, caring management. Domination, however, should never be confused with stewardship.

In your Wisdom Journal, discuss what you mean by "stewardship."

"BIG BOOK" WISDOM

I have gained the greatest thing accorded to any man, the love and understanding of a gracious God, who has lifted me from the alcoholic scrap-heap to a position of trust where I have been able to reap the rich rewards that come from showing a little love for others and from serving them as I can.

–FROM THE "BIG BOOK" OF *ALCOHOLICS ANONYMOUS*, 1976

The first edition of AA's "Big Book," as it is familiarly called, was born the same year I was, 1939. Subtitled "The Story of How Many Thousands of Men and Women Have Recovered from Alcoholism," the book contains several dozen first-person accounts of people's journey to alcoholic hell and back.

The first narrative, by Bill W., principal cofounder of AA, tells how he began drinking as a young soldier in World War I. Returning home, he started a promising career on Wall Street. Soon chronic drinking got in the way. Despite support from his wife and friends, many attempts to stop, and several hospitalizations, Bill seemed headed for early death. One day an old school friend and drinking buddy stopped by. Incredibly the friend had been sober for several months – the result of a religious conversion. Although he was at the end of his rope and willing to try anything, Bill was put off by the "God" talk. When his friend suggested that he choose his own conception of God, Bill's resistance collapsed. He entered the hospital for one last treatment and remained sober until his death in 1971. In the meantime he founded the Fellowship of Alcoholics Anonymous, which has helped millions of people build new lives.

My own spiritual guide, the late Muhammad Subuh, insisted that in spiritual affairs we simply tell our stories. People might then be moved to work on their own inner development. Twelve Step programs follow the same practice. A publishing phenomenon of our time, the *Chicken Soup for the Soul* books, share narratives with positive endings. Peer pressure is clearly powerful – for good or ill. If we choose our friends – and books – wisely, the results may pleasantly surprise us.

Scan a copy of the "Big Book" for thirty minutes; then write a brief reaction in your Wisdom Journal.

ARISTOTELIAN WISDOM

The term "wisdom" we apply in art to the greatest masters of the several arts. . . . But there are people whom we think wise generally. . . . Clearly this general wisdom will be the most complete of the forms of knowledge.

If so, then the wise man ought to know not only what follows from his first principles; he should know also the truth about these principles. Wisdom therefore will be a union of intuitive reason and scientific knowledge; it may be defined as the complete science of the loftiest matters.

–ARISTOTLE (384–322 B.C.E.), *NICOMACHEAN ETHICS*

The ancient Greeks gave the world both the terms and concepts *philosophy* and *philosopher*. In the language of Indonesia, a country and collection of cultures about as remote from classical Greece as you can get, the equivalents are *filsafat* and *filsuf*. The original terms mean "love of wisdom" and "lover of wisdom," respectively. Plato and his student Aristotle are considered the fathers of Western philosophy. Indeed, the common saying has it that all Western philosophy is but footnotes to Plato and Aristotle.

To be sure, Plato and Aristotle loved wisdom in different ways. Of the two, Plato was the more mystical and poetic, Aristotle the more rational and scientific. Borrowing some contemporary terminology, we might call Plato a philosopher of the right brain and Aristotle, one of the left brain.

From the above passage, it is clear that, for Aristotle, the wise person is not so much a sage who has learned to live the best possible life but a logician who both knows first principles and can accurately derive what follows from these principles. Aristotle's wise person, however, isn't simply a very bright and knowledgeable person; he or she combines intuition with science. One thinks of someone like Albert Einstein. And to be fair, in another part of the *Nicomachean Ethics*, Aristotle states, "Our idea of the truly good and wise man is that he bears all the chances of life with dignity and always does what is best in the circumstances."

In your Wisdom Journal, try your hand at constructing a "scientific" definition of wisdom.

COMPUTER WISDOM

BILL MOYERS: What about the argument that machines, like computers, dehumanize learning?

ISAAC ASIMOV: As a matter of fact, it's just the reverse. It's through this machine that for the first time, we'll be able to have a one-to-one relationship between information source and information consumer. . . . Everyone can have a teacher in the form of access to the gathered knowledge of the human species.

-BILL MOYERS, *A WORLD OF IDEAS,* 1989

One of my former bosses didn't own a computer, nor was there one in his office. A fast typist, he even eschewed electric typewriters, preferring to draft his memos on an old manual from his reporting days. (Now in retirement he has apparently made the switch.) I felt the same way for a while myself. For creative writing at least, I insisted on drafting my thoughts in pen on a legal pad. I believed inspiration would flow more freely that way. Once I became aware of such computer benefits as cutting and pasting, copying, and word counting, however, I changed my tune. You'll have to be the judge about its impact on inspiration in my writing.

The late Isaac Asimov, to be sure, was not talking about word processing. A true futurist, he saw – well before the Internet revolution – how computers could make the world's knowledge available to virtually everyone. Information technology, moreover, is perhaps the one area in society where power and sophistication continue to rise even as prices continue to fall. For what I paid for my Apple IIe with 64 kilobytes of memory fifteen years ago, I can now purchase a portable laptop device with a 300 megahertz processor and enough memory to store the entire *Encyclopaedia Britannica* and more. When it comes to computers, we can say with Robert Browning's Rabbi Ben Ezra, "Grow old along with me! / The best is yet to be."

Computer technology is not without its problems. As in other areas, the rich can get top-of-the-line while the poor must be satisfied with less, or even nothing at all. But it is wise to remember the potential while working to shape the best possible reality.

Discuss in your Wisdom Journal the potential benefits and drawbacks of the computer revolution.

THE LIMITS OF WORLDLY WISDOM

Be wisely worldly, be not worldly wise.

–FRANCIS QUARLES (1592–1644)

Practical wisdom has to do with knowing how to navigate safely through this world of rapids and rocks. I think of a worldly wise person as someone who has internalized all the cautionary proverbs. Remember to doubt. Keep one eye open. If a thief kisses you, count your teeth.

Speaking of teeth, the worldly wise brush theirs twice a day and go to the dentist twice a year. They also consult their brokers regularly, pay themselves first, and build a secure retirement that does not depend on the soundness of Social Security.

I don't mean to put people like this down. In fact I emulate them wherever I can. For example, I make sure to lock my briefcase in the trunk of my car *before* I arrive at my parking place. I remember to roll up my car windows and lock the doors. I am also careful to set the burglar alarm before leaving home, because Hawaii, with its Third World–like division between the well-to-do and the poor, has a high rate of break-ins.

But to be only worldly wise is not to be truly wise. We inhabit two realities – the physical and the spiritual. When you read and take to heart the good advice of a Ben Franklin or a Lord Chesterfield, you are attending to the former but probably not to the latter. To be "wisely worldly," as Francis Quarles recommends in his little epigram, is to take care of both inner and outer needs. For what's the sense of gaining the whole world, in Jesus' famous question, at the expense of our soul?

Remember to take the long view. Don't rush life away. Take time to be quiet. Ask yourself what you really want from life and whether that can be achieved through thrifty management. Consider whether you are prepared for death, others' and your own. Think if you are content to spend hours, even days, in your own company. Hardly an advocate of the spiritual, Chairman Mao said a wise thing when he reminded his countrymen to "walk on two legs."

How are you at balancing the material and the spiritual? Discuss this issue in your Wisdom Journal.

THE WISDOM OF MEANINGFULNESS

"Tut, tut, child," said the Duchess. "Everything's got a moral if only you can find it."

–LEWIS CARROLL, *ALICE'S ADVENTURES IN WONDERLAND*, 1865

A milestone on my continuing journey to wisdom was a little book by Dr. Viktor Frankl, *Man's Search for Meaning.* Despite the use of generic *man,* which suggests the work's vintage, this has to be one of the richest responses to the Holocaust ever written and a testimony to the unsinkable nature of the human spirit. I came across the book in my first year of college teaching, 1965.

For those of you unfamiliar with this memoir, let me sketch out its contents. Frankl, a young Viennese psychotherapist, was arrested one night by the Gestapo. He had just completed the manuscript of a book on healing through meaningfulness, what he referred to as "logotherapy." Even worse than what might happen to him, he thought, was the fact that his life's work would now be lost.

But Hitler's Final Solution didn't take Frankl's spirit into account. Satanic forces, fortunately, tend to underrate the divine. For on arriving at his camp, Frankl decided to test out his theory – that happiness flows from the meaningfulness of one's life and that misery flows from lack of meaning – by observing camp life. Through waving the wand of intentionality over the absurdity of the death camp, Frankl turned his time there into an experiment in learning. Even the Nazis could not keep him from transmuting the base metal of imprisonment in a concentration camp into gold. And this ability, he would comment later, kept him alive while others who were physically more fit soon lost hope and died.

Having survived internment, he went on to coach his clients to overcome life's difficulties by finding meaning in them. Viktor Frankl would have understood Ishmael's comment in Melville's *Moby Dick* that a whaling ship had been his Harvard and his Yale. For Frankl, ironically and blessedly, it had been Auschwitz.

How do you process experience? Above all, what do you do with setbacks? Are you able to make lemonade out of lemons? Respond to these questions in your Wisdom Journal.

PANTHEISTIC WISDOM

Not one of them who took up in his youth with the opinion that there were no gods, ever continued until old age faithful to his conviction.

–Plato (427–347 B.C.E.)

Plato wrote in another era. Society was closer to traditional cultures, where belief in tribal deities was a matter of course. Yet already, with growth of reliance on the human intellect, the absence of proof was becoming the proof of absence. The idea of the divine was not yet dead but had sustained its first body blow.

Plato's point re-emerged in the saying coined by American priest William Cummings in World War II, "There are no atheists in the foxholes." Fear of death is a powerful stimulus to belief in a higher power. Yet war, the deaths of innocents, fatal accidents, and the success of the unscrupulous counterbalance this fear and make it difficult, even impossible, for some people to believe in an all-powerful benevolent force that controls the universe.

My father was a case in point. He died with his ideological boots on, convinced that religion was for the shallow or fearful. Without recourse to the comfort of a belief in God, he faced the inevitability of his death with great courage and composure.

Belief can indeed be a challenging business. Take the title character of Euripides's tragedy *Hippolytus.* Hippolytus was devoted to Cynthia, virgin goddess of the hunt. He worshiped her and remained chaste. Aphrodite, goddess of love, was smitten with the young man. He resisted her temptations, so Aphrodite caused Phaedra, his stepmother, to fall in love with him. Hippolytus again resisted, and the distraught Phaedra committed suicide, leaving a note accusing Hippolytus of making advances to her and thus staining her honor. Believing the note, his father cursed Hippolytus, who soon after was dragged to death when a sea monster frightened his horses and he became tangled in his chariot's reins.

Tragedy results, Euripides' play suggests, from not respecting the full range of divine forces in our life or the world.

Write in your Wisdom Journal about your belief or lack of belief in higher powers. Are you happy with your present belief system?

CONVERSION WISDOM

From my childhood up, my mind had been full of objections against the doctrine of God's sovereignty. . . .

[One day] as I was walking, . . . there came into my mind so sweet a sense of the glorious majesty *and* grace *of God, that I know not how to express. . . .*

The appearance of every thing was altered. . . . God's excellency, his wisdom, his purity and love, seemed to appear in every thing; in the sun, moon, and stars; in the clouds, and blue sky; in the grass, flowers, trees; in the water, and all nature.

–JONATHAN EDWARDS (1703–1758), "PERSONAL NARRATIVE"

When people meet me, they assume I am Jewish. When I explain I am a Jewish Christian, some ask, "Are you a Jew for Jesus?" "No," I respond. "I am technically a Lutheran but consider myself a generic Christian." The next question goes something like, "Is your wife Christian, and is that why you converted?" This time I answer, "You're right about my wife but wrong about my conversion. It resulted from an experience."

September 1, 1966. Our first child, Marianna, was born. That same day my doctoral thesis was to be presented to the Yale faculty. Given the situation, I was granted a one-day extension. The next day, with the dissertation duly delivered, I was awaiting my 3:00 p.m. appointment with the Lutheran campus pastor. Simone and I had agreed to have our daughter baptized.

It was 2:40 p.m. As I was sitting alone in Dwight Chapel, a voice within me said, "Why don't you get baptized with your daughter?" I was taken aback. That was my last intention. The voice continued, "Take one of those books and look inside." I picked up a copy of the Book of Common Prayer and, opening it at random, turned to the order for adult baptism. Sobbing, I felt a weight fall from my back. It was 3:00 p.m., time to see Pastor Olson. On March 4, 1967, I was baptized with my infant daughter. And that is how I came to be a Christian.

If you have had a life-changing inner experience like this, describe it in your Wisdom Journal.

GRADUATE-SCHOOL WISDOM

When I talk about graduate school, try as I may, I can't keep the bitterness from creeping into my voice. . . .

In college I had worked out of aspiration and desire. . . . In graduate school the work turned into something else: a contest to see who could make the best impression on the professor, read the largest number of articles on a topic, come up with the most sophisticated reading of a text. An atmosphere of competitiveness, never spoken or named, per-meated the classes and the casual conversation.

–Jane Tompkins, *A Life in School*, 1996

I knew Jane Tompkins at Yale graduate school – in fact, we dated during our first year. We both faced the heart- and soul-wrenching rigors of our new life as PhD students. In Jane's case, she had her good undergraduate experience at Bryn Mawr to look back to – experience that made the dry bones of graduate study all the more unpalatable. In my case, I had been a Yale undergraduate in the very same department I was in as a graduate, and I had been a star. In the interim several things had happened. First, I had begun spiritual training. An immediate result was that the world of literature and culture stopped being my private high church. So when I returned to New Haven, several professors observed that I had lost a certain sharpness. Second, my new peer group was made up of the superstars from other distinguished undergraduate English programs around the country.

But Jane's main point is, I think, the main point. Graduate school was simply another professional training program like medical school or law school. It was about learning a craft as currently understood. We were being trained to think like English professors just as our peers were being molded to think like lawyers or physicians. It was no longer about loving literature and being formed by it. Love – and wisdom – had little to do with it. Graduate school was about gaining the world and losing your soul. Like Jane, I am still in recovery.

Almost everybody has had negative educational experiences. Write about one in your Wisdom Journal. What made it so bad?

WISDOM AND FOOLISHNESS

Basically, wisdom concerns how to live. It speaks of the nature of reality and how to live one's life in accord with reality. Central to it is the notion of a way or a path, indeed of two ways or paths: the wise way and the foolish way. Teachers of wisdom speak of these two ways, commending the one and warning of the consequences of following the other.

–MARCUS J. BORG, *MEETING JESUS AGAIN FOR THE FIRST TIME*, 1994

In my freshman year at college, I attended a talk by the famous Harvard psychologist B. F. Skinner. What I remember forty-three years later is his insistence that only positive stimuli and examples should be used to modify people's behavior. Positive, not negative, reinforcement was his theme. With so many of these daily reflections now written, I find that I have been a good Skinnerian. I have spoken almost exclusively of wisdom and have carefully avoided any reference to foolishness. Yet, as Marcus Borg points out in his excellent study of the historical Jesus, our greatest wisdom teachers have not been deterred by such concerns.

Consider Confucius. In his Analects he provides several dozen sayings contrasting the gentleman with small-minded persons. For example, "The superior man is satisfied and composed; the mean man is always full of distress." Serenity certainly seems more like a characteristic of wisdom than hysteria does. In the Dhammapada, comprising sayings attributed to the Buddha, a whole chapter is dedicated to "the fool." One of my favorites: "If during the whole of his life a fool lives with a wise man, he never knows the path of wisdom as the spoon never knows the taste of the soup."

For its part, the Judeo-Christian tradition has plenty to say about foolishness and wisdom. Proverbs, chapter 14, for instance, is a collection of paired contrasts: "A fool is too arrogant to make amends; / upright men know what reconciliation means" (14:9). Or, "A simple man believes every word he hears; a clever man understands the need for proof" (14:15). "Not it," after all, is a useful way to find "it."

In your Wisdom Journal, create two or three sayings contrasting wise and foolish behavior.

AMPHIBIAN WISDOM

Thus is man that great and true **amphibium,** *whose nature is disposed to live, not only like other creatures in diverse elements, but in divided and distinguished worlds . . . the one visible, the other invisible.*

-SIR THOMAS BROWNE, *RELIGIO MEDICI,* 1682

At the beach today, the warning flags at the lifeguard stations display the number 5. According to the key, five indicates strong riptides. I see only one person in the water, and he is more or less beached. But several gulls, with yogilike unflappability, are floating on the roiling waves. They are the same gulls that can glide for up to a minute without flapping their wings and can walk with some grace and speed on the sand.

Gulls go beyond the merely amphibian. They are triphibians, able to negotiate land, sea, and air. Gulls are a sort of triathlete. What would the President's Council on Fitness say if every American had that kind of ability?

At a minimum we each need to be able to deal in two worlds, the inner and the outer. Formal education prepares us primarily for work. Even the liberal arts seem to attend to basic skills for living successfully on the planet. But what about the inner world of the emotions? Concerns of attending to the sick and dying? Coping with living alone or in relationship? Facing our own physical decline and death? Who teaches these skills?

Traditional societies as well as Western civilization in some earlier stages assumed that we lived in several worlds at once and needed to be able to cope in all. Castaneda's Don Juan Matus, the Yaqui Indian sorcerer, spoke of the *nagual* and the *tonal.* I for one am pleased that more of my friends these days are volunteering at hospices, going to sweat lodges, doing vision quests, or participating in spiritual training of some kind. In a multilingual society like Switzerland, being monolingual won't do. In a multidimensional world like ours, attending to outer concerns while neglecting inner ones may land us in some dangerous riptides. It is not too soon to learn from the gulls.

What are you doing to become an "amphibian"? Should you be doing more? Discuss these questions in your Wisdom Journal.

APOCALYPTIC WISDOM

But about that day and hour no one knows, not even the angels in heaven, not even the Son; only the Father.

–MATTHEW 24:36

When it comes to the end of the world, we all like to play God. We all like to predict. Yesterday I was in the Angel Network's warehouse in Pearl City. Angel Network Charities, Inc., is a transitional housing program for homeless families here in Hawaii. I am the Network's fund-raiser.

Anyway, yesterday, as the warehouse manager, the marketing associate, and I were planning a "super blowout sale," one of our regular customers came up to buy spare parts. We stopped to chat with him. Soon the man said how glad he was to have found these particular items because he was preparing for the "troubles" that the year 2000 would unleash. Twenty-four hours later, Mae, my barber, asks in pidgin, "Say, Reynold, what you t'ink 'bout dis Y2K t'ing?" What worried her most was bank failure. If the banks went, she thought, everything else would follow.

Now the good news is, if you are reading this, January 1, 2000, will have come and gone, Saint Mary's Press will have been able to bring this book out as planned just after the turn of the century, and all is – if not well – at least no worse than in the last year beginning with a "19." I read recently that because Jesus was most likely born in 4 B.C.E., the real year 2000 already occurred four years ago.

I don't mean to make fun of people who sincerely worried about some impending worldwide disaster. But frankly, I doubt that God created thousand-year cycles. Had I been an adult in 1939, the year of my birth, I think I would have been more frightened for the world then than I am now. Anyway, each of us will experience the end of the world in our own death, so why all this hullabaloo about the Apocalypse now? As Jesus pointed out in the New Testament, God is a God of the living, not the dead.

Write in your Wisdom Journal about your feelings and beliefs as we reached the year 2000.

ARBOREAL WISDOM

There is, nevertheless, a certain respect, and a general duty of humanity, that ties us, not only to beasts that have life and sense, but even to trees and plants.

–MICHEL DE MONTAIGNE (1533–1592), "OF CRUELTY"

All right. I'll admit it. I am a tree hugger. Not in public, to be sure, but when alone, I like to hug trees. Once, as workshop leader, I even got a group of rural Minnesota Lutherans, including their pastor, to end a meditative outdoor walk by hugging the closest tree. Everyone complied. Later, though, no one wanted to talk about it, but the participants left the workshop happy and even invited me back. Garrison Keillor, take note.

What I experience from hugging trees is a sense of their strength and rectitude. They instinctively grow toward the sky. They also have long lives and the resilience to stand their ground, literally and figuratively, through all kinds of weather. Deep roots surely have something to do with it.

Once I asked for God to help me understand what it means to be of service. I visualized a field full of trees breathing in carbon dioxide and exhaling the oxygen needed by us mammals. They also offer shade to the earth, homes to arboreal animals, and beauty to those who can perceive it. And they do all this in silence.

Trees were an object of worship in pre-Christian Europe. They still are in some corners of the world – among the Dyaks of Borneo, for example. So when Saint Boniface (c. 675–754) was sent by the pope to Christianize the Germanic tribes, one of his principal acts was to chop down the Sacred Oak Tree. My wife, who grew up in Germany, is still attached to trees. She has planted one everywhere we have lived, and cried bitterly when the city of Saint Paul removed a tree near our house. Maybe my feeling for trees is ancestral too. After all, it was my people who thought up the Tree of Knowledge and the Tree of Life.

Write in your Wisdom Journal about how you feel toward trees. Or, if you are up to it, go hug a tree for at least ten seconds, then write about the experience.

ARCADIAN WISDOM

And this our life, exempt from public haunt,
Finds tongues in trees, books in the running brooks,
Sermons in stones, and good in every thing.

–William Shakespeare, *As You Like It,* II, i, 12–14

I am basically a city boy. It took the Boy Scouts, initially, to acquaint me with the outdoors. Summer camp reinforced what Scouts had started. But it was really the time spent hiking in New Hampshire, then sailing, that helped me find the Arcadian wisdom suggested by Shakespeare's lines.

At prep school I had an English teacher named Al Watson. Thanks to Al's efforts, I became a classical music fan, shifted my academic loyalties from science to English, and went to Yale. (He had graduated from Yale only a few years before I met him.) During short vacations like Thanksgiving, several of us would spend time with him at his cabin ("James Hill") near Mount Chocorua, New Hampshire.

Al Watson had something of the Pied Piper in him. In retrospect I am sure I chose Yale in large part because of the "magical mystery tour" of the campus he took several of us on one rainy, foggy evening in New Haven. Just the right ambiance for a hike through Yale's Gothic archways and secret tunnels. This was where I *had* to go.

In the New Hampshire cabin, fire blazing, he would give us each a small snifter of Drambuie and read us one of Poe's tales by candlelight. Then, huddled close together for protection against the unknown, we would take a midnight hike through the woods. Or by day we would read Robert Frost, mend a nearby wall, work up an appetite by splitting logs, and walk to Whitton Pond or the nearby quarry. It wasn't so much the moral lessons we learned as the conviction that there were numinous forces all around – friendly forces, on balance, but serious, powerful ones, not to be toyed with. Nature was a school, all right, but also a temple. Faulkner in "The Bear" was right. You didn't just learn from nature, but if you let it, it would transform you.

Write in your Wisdom Journal about a meaningful outdoor experience. What took place? What impact did it have on you?

ASSASSIN WISDOM

The afternoon knows what the morning never suspected.

–A Swedish proverb

Assassin wisdom – it sounds like a leap, but stay with me. I will begin with a particular type of assassin: Islam's *hashishin.* Founded in the late eleventh century, this extremist Shi'ite subsect then terrorized Persia and Asia Minor for 150 years. According to legend its members would drug themselves with hashish before murdering their enemies. Our word *assassin* comes from the Arabic for hashish-eaters. Still with me? Get ready for the leap.

The successors to this group comprise the modern Islamic sect called the Ismailis, better known in non-Islamic circles as the followers of the Agha Khan. Fifteen million strong – about the same number as the world Jewish population – Ismailis are found in the Middle East, India, Africa, Europe, and North America. Karim Agha Khan, their Harvard-educated leader, has his headquarters in Paris. The group owns half the island of Sardinia as well as some of the world's finest thoroughbred racehorses. Their minister of social affairs is a former president of Swarthmore College, a Caucasian American PhD. Ironically, the Ismailis, who began as the Shi'ite assassins of yore, are now the most peaceful proponents of Islam. You hardly ever hear about them. Their motto might as well be, "Make business, not holy war."

Karim Agha Khan has endowed two chairs in Islamic studies at his alma mater plus an annual prize for the year's best work of Islamic architecture. The Ismaili secretariat, as I understand it, will also provide venture capital to promising Ismaili business ventures. The owner of a rather good Indian restaurant in Vancouver told me he had received such an investment. Now that his business was prospering, the Ismaili venture-capital fund had even more money to invest.

Ismaili Islam has declared holy war against poverty, illiteracy, the inability to support oneself due to chronic illness, and other maladies. Apparently it has made significant inroads in all these areas. The sect has surely come a long way from its beginnings as the hashish-taking hitmen of Islam. Such is the leap of assassin wisdom.

History is full of surprises. In your Wisdom Journal, discuss something that started off badly for you but in the end yielded wonderful results.

CONFLICTING WISDOM?

The seeming truth which cunning times put on
To entrap the wisest.

-WILLIAM SHAKESPEARE, *THE MERCHANT OF VENICE*, III, II, 100

We moved back to New York City as I completed seventh grade. My parents did not want me to go to a New York City public school. Unfortunately all the private schools were filled. The solution turned out to be a boys' boarding school in central New Jersey. Although my seventh-grade marks had not been exceptional, I must have done well on the entrance exams. The admissions office said I could start in the fall as a freshman. The only catch was, I would need to take eighth-grade math and English in summer school and pass both with B's.

My strongest memory from that summer nearly fifty years ago was an English unit on proverbs with diametrically opposed meanings. "Look before you leap," but "He who hesitates is lost." "You are never too old to learn," but "You can't teach old dogs new tricks." "The pen is mightier than the sword," but "Actions speak louder than words." "Silence is golden," but "The squeaky wheel gets the grease."

Paradoxes of this kind have always intrigued me. Maybe the first proverb in the pair applied only to certain people at certain times, I thought, while the second applied to others in different circumstances. Some older individuals, for example, curious to their dying day, eagerly sign up for Elder Hostel programs. Others, however, remain set in their ways regardless of the benefits of change. Both proverbs on aging and learning seem to apply.

I later arrived at a solution. It's about circumstances. For example, some people seem to cogitate and plan forever, and when they do act–Hamlet comes to mind–they are too late. Spontaneous types, on the other hand, often don't wait long enough, launching some new project without sufficient forethought or research. When the scheme fails, only they are surprised. The trick is to know which piece of proverbial advice suits us in a particular situation, then to have the courage to put it into practice.

How do you deal with "good advice" from others that you know doesn't fit? Discuss an instance in your Wisdom Journal.

DAWN WISDOM

Don't go back to sleep.
The breeze at dawn
Has secrets to tell you.

–JALALUDDIN RUMI (1207–1273)

A few years ago, a friend and I climbed Honolulu's Diamond Head to see the sun rise. We were not alone. The cars waiting for the gates to open at 6:00 a.m. proved that. Yet the lingering darkness made us feel alone. Just the crater, the stars, and us.

You don't climb Diamond Head the way you do other mountains. Well, to be fair, Diamond Head isn't exactly a mountain. It's not even a hill. In its most famous aspect, it is a promontory, or headland. The ancient Hawaiians called it Leahi, meaning "fiery forehead," because of how it appears from the sea. In reality Diamond Head is a crater, one of a half dozen or so on the island of Oahu. Less than a thousand feet high from sea level, you climb it from the inside out. It's an easy climb.

The whole exercise takes about half an hour. If you start right after the gates open, it is still dark when you reach the top. The only tricky part is negotiating the tunnel that leads you to the outer lip. A flashlight here can prevent a sprained ankle. The U.S. Army installed pillboxes on the ocean side to defend against a possible Japanese attack in World War II. You emerge from one of these.

Looking *makai* (toward the ocean) you can make out the white foam of the breakers. But the real view is the lavalike flow of lights cascading down the residential valleys of the Ko'olau Mountains–Nu'uanu, Manoa, Palolo, and the rest. For this you must look *mauka* (toward the mountains).

My friend Sandra and I are both talkers. But from the moment we left the car, something told us to be quiet. Walking without speaking, we felt a palpable presence, a fullness in the stillness that surrounded us. A little breeze made it almost chilly, good weather for a light sweater. The darkness felt safe. In a half hour, the sun would rise.

Take a silent walk before dawn. When you come home, write about the experience in your Wisdom Journal.

DIVINE WISDOM WITHIN

The certain and absolute knowing that Your Divine presence and wisdom are within me saves me from taking a wrong turn in life. . . .

Thank you, God, for keeping me from wandering in the desert of confusion.

–"DAILY WORD," FOR APRIL 15, 1999

How appropriate that this sage advice occurs on the deadline for filing annual tax returns! Talk about confusion and wrong turns.

It contains another hard lesson for us moderns to learn. We either know it all, or, when our knowledge proves no match for hard realities, we know nothing. We then look to all sorts of outside sources for help. Bring on the doctors, the lawyers, the psychologists.

I remember when, during my student days in Germany, I came across this curious Latin phrase in a German history of medicine: *Vis medicatrix corporis.* The English translation would be something like "the curative powers of the body." According to the text – and this concept is familiar to our Christian Science and Science of Mind sisters and brothers – the human body has an innate ability to heal itself. The problem, the text continued, is that we either don't tap that power or, more likely, we get in its way. For example, when our body wants bed rest, we go for a run. Or when something inside tells us to stay home, we feel compelled to go to work, and rationalize, "I don't want the boss to yell at me."

My own spiritual guide, the late Muhammad Subuh, said that in olden times people would cheer themselves up by singing to themselves. Recently, when I am bummed out, I have begun forcing the corners of my mouth upward into something like a smile. I know it sounds hokey, but I have to report that shortly thereafter, my inner sun comes out and I am able to go my tranquil way. "Whistle a happy tune" may be more than just a random line from a show tune. Check it out.

Write in your Wisdom Journal about an experience in which you successfully tapped your inner wisdom to overcome a physical or emotional problem.

EARTH WISDOM

I do not see a delegation
For the Four-Footed.
I see no seat for the eagles.
We forget and we consider
Ourselves superior. . . .
And we stand somewhere between
The mountain and the Ant.
Somewhere and only there
As part and parcel
Of the Creation.

–CHIEF OREN LYONS, "CONSCIOUSNESS"

For the past few years, I have been doing foundation and fund-raising work in and around Indian country. I have evaluated grant requests on reservations or at tribally controlled colleges, and more recently I am raising funds for school curricula Buffy Sainte-Marie is developing "through Native American eyes."

My first significant encounter with an indigenous person, however, occurred in 1991. That summer I was fortunate to spend a weekend at a small conference with Chief Oren Lyons, faith-keeper for the Turtle Clan of the Onondaga Nation and spokesperson for the Six Nations Iroquois Confederacy. Oren's host was a close friend of mine, so I had the chance to get to know him better than I might have otherwise. By that summer Oren had already organized a loose confederation of the world's indigenous peoples, which he represented at the United Nations. Since the four-footed and the eagles couldn't argue their own needs, he endeavored to do so for them. He spoke quietly but with passion. His points were difficult to refute.

Earth wisdom begins with realizing that we are part of the natural world, not its owner. Lack of respect for the Earth has already resulted in the wholesale loss of plant and animal species and the degradation of air, land, and water. The world's Native traditions stand for living lightly on the Earth. Rather than spending all our efforts trying to "civilize" the Indians and other primal peoples, we would do well to learn from them, especially in this regard. The eagles and the four-footed will only benefit.

In your Wisdom Journal, assess your Earth-friendliness. What do you do that likely has a positive impact upon the natural world? In what ways might you improve?

THE WISDOM OF GRATITUDE

If the only prayer you say in your entire life is "Thank You," that would suffice.

–Meister Eckhart (1260?–?1327), translated by Matthew Fox

Requests are hot, thanks are cold. I spend hours crafting funding proposals. Still, when the checks come in, it takes me a mere five minutes to toss off a pro forma thank-you.

My relationship with God is similar. You'd think God was Santa Claus and I, some spoiled kid with an endless wish list. My plan in recent years has been to replace requests with thank-yous.

A few years ago, I was praying with a friend from Seattle. He owns a computer business and had been looking for some time for a knowledgeable associate. Our session took place one morning during a national meeting of the meditation group I belong to. He had asked if I would pray with him to help him find the right person.

Now the way I approach directive prayer is pretty straightforward. I get quiet, stand up, and ask out loud for God to give the guidance or help needed. I am as specific as possible. So in this case I said something like, "God, if it is your will, please help so-and-so receive the assistance he needs for his business in the near future." If I am sufficiently quiet, I may also receive guidance in an image, word, or phrase accompanied by a feeling. In this case I kept repeating "thank you." Afterward I told my friend that, based on what I had received, his problem had already been solved and he should be hearing something shortly. In the meantime he should just say "thank you."

That evening he came to me with this news: At lunch he had met a young man from Ohio. This individual had a master's degree in computer science plus relevant experience, and was planning to move to Seattle. He was looking for both a job and an initial place to live. Before the conference concluded, a deal had been struck, and the results are still positive.

Thank you.

For the coming week, every time you are about to petition for something, send God a thank-you instead. Note your experience in your Wisdom Journal.

ECUMENICAL WISDOM

In all of human history there has never been such an urgent need for ecumenical vitality – not in the narrow sense of Christian ecumenism but ecumenism of all humankind. We have at long last come to realize that we live in the oekumene, a global village inhabited not only by Christians but by people of other nations, other religions, other cultures.

–Choan-Seng Song, president, World Alliance of Reformed Churches, 1999

The Reverend Song, a Chinese American, presides over a fellowship of seventy million Christians in more than one hundred countries. Two-thirds live in Africa, Asia, and Latin America. Amid such diversity it is not surprising that the Reverend Song expresses such inclusive views, especially given that the church he heads comprises the modern successors to the intolerant Puritan church of Colonial New England. Early Quakers, for example, risked life and limb in the Puritan Massachusetts of the late seventeenth century.

Long ago, when the world's population was small and scattered and less mobile, most people lived amid others with similar appearance and beliefs. Inclusiveness was not an issue. Natural disasters, however, caused wholesale movements of peoples. Driven on by some of our baser human instincts, stronger groups would overrun their weaker neighbors, acquire land, take slaves, and mix their gene pool and culture with the defeated populace. Today few peoples remain isolated. We live in the global village.

This village nonetheless has neighborhoods, ghettoes, and gang fights. The ethnic hostilities between groups in the former Yugoslavia are a case in point. Unfortunately there are others. It will take many more leaders like the Reverend Song to help us understand that we belong to one family, live on one planet, exist in one universe, and have been formed by one Creator. The Bible instructs us that Satan is legion, many. Israel's Shema prayer declares that God, by contrast, is one. As residents of a single global village, we must find the wisdom to live together in harmony, creativity, and peace. Planetary survival requires it.

What does ecumenism mean to you? Write briefly on this topic in your Wisdom Journal.

FRANCISCAN WISDOM

Then St. Francis said: "Brother Wolf, I order you, in the name of the Lord Jesus Christ, to come with me now, without fear, into the town to make this peace pact in the name of the Lord."

And the wolf immediately began to walk along beside St. Francis, just like a very gentle lamb.

–From *The Little Flowers of St. Francis* (c. 1380)

Long before I read *The Little Flowers,* I had heard about Saint Francis of Assisi's ability to communicate with animals. I also knew that he would address them as close relatives, as brothers and sisters. This ability especially impressed me because on one occasion as a child, I had been attacked by an Irish setter while I was riding my bike, on another I had been bitten by a little dog in Germany, and on a third I had been thrown by a horse the year after college.

On another occasion I was leafletting for a gubernatorial candidate in Hawaii when a German shepherd came after me. It was midafternoon. No one was around. There was no place to run. Suddenly I felt as though I were twelve feet tall and had the capacity to kill that dog with my bare hands. I faced it, ready for action. The dog got within ten feet of me, stopped cold, and began to whimper. Then he backed away, still looking at me. He came at me again, but the same thing happened. It was as if he had hit an invisible wall. He ran away yelping and disappeared. I then seemed to shrink back to my normal size. I took a few breaths and went home.

My relationship with animals since then has been amicable. I speak with my cats, I like TV jungle shows, and I generally have high regard for animals. It impresses me how well our two cats get on. They play but never fight. They remind me of Mark Twain's famous remark: "Man is the Only Animal that Blushes. Or needs to."

How is your relationship with animals? Discuss it for a few minutes in your Wisdom Journal.

GULL WISDOM

Let go and let God.

-A slogan from the Twelve Step Program

One . . . two . . . three . . . forty-five. That's how many seconds the seagull I followed glided. It started out just in front of me, cruised up the beach about 150 yards, banked and came back about fifty yards, then landed before finally flapping its wings. During the entire flight, it would angle its body slightly to the left or right, perhaps to catch the air currents better. On one occasion it moved its talons as if grabbing air. What that motion was for, I have no idea.

The day before, my daughter Marianna had called. Her husband was stranded at LaGuardia Airport in New York City. His flight to the Twin Cities had been canceled, and she was concerned. Then, just before my gull walk, Marianna called again. "You'll never guess what happened, Dad. Harper booked a flight from Newark Airport. But he couldn't get to Newark, so he reserved space on a new flight from LaGuardia. This time the flight was oversold. No one wanted to give up their seat. Finally, when Northwest offered twelve hundred dollars in travel vouchers, Harper volunteered for a later flight. So now I'll be able to go with him on his next book-buying trip to London!"

In my experience all things really do come to those who wait. All things needful anyway. The French proverb is apt: "God visits us often, but usually we are not at home." We need to be more like gulls and less like hummingbirds. We have to learn to spread our wings and ride the thermals – making subtle movements as necessary to get where we are going. The currents are there. We just have to find and use them.

In your Wisdom Journal, describe an instance when impatience got in the way and caused you to mess something up. Then write about another occasion when you relaxed and things just seemed to flow. Lessons?

HEALTHY, WEALTHY, AND WISE?

For many men, the acquisition of wealth does not end their troubles, it only changes them.

–SENECA (4 B.C.E.?–65 C.E.)

If it were only a matter of early to bed, early to rise! Being healthy, wealthy, and wise at the same time is clearly a challenge, though it is one, I hasten to add, that I have not yet experienced firsthand.

In our materialistic culture, money is supposed to be the golden road to the good life. But while wealth can help us avoid worries about how to pay the bills, even that goal may elude us if, like the Great Gatsby, we live beyond our means. No amount of money will ever be enough if we routinely spend more than we make.

Wealth also attracts problems that less affluent people rarely have. No one marries you for your money, for instance, if you don't have money. A recent TV miniseries depicted the unhappy life of Doris Duke, heiress to the Duke tobacco fortune. The late J. Paul Getty, who at one point was the richest man in the world, wrote an essay entitled something like "It's Not Easy Being a Billionaire." Echoing the myth of King Midas, whose life was poisoned by the golden touch he wished for and got, Getty told how he could never have a trusting relationship. His concern was always that others were out for his money.

Riches don't guarantee good health either. King Hussein of Jordan, a wealthy and powerful man, could buy the best health care in the world. Yet all his affluence couldn't prevent his dying while still in his early sixties. Wisdom here is really understanding that wealth is not a one-way ticket to happiness. Contentment, if it comes at all, will come in spite of our wealth. As Seneca sagely noted two thousand years ago, being well-to-do does not end our troubles, it only changes them.

If you were wealthy, what would you do to avoid the sorts of problems that dogged Doris Duke and J. Paul Getty? Sketch out a strategy in your Wisdom Journal. If you are wealthy, write about how you are doing.

HERMETIC WISDOM

As above, so below.

-A principle of Hermetic philosophy

Gnosticism and esoteric thought in general are said to originate with the Egyptian god Thoth, known in the West as Hermes Trismegistus. This deity shared his secrets with chosen disciples. Alchemy and the Hermetic tradition of beliefs and practices are said to be the result.

One of the major Hermetic tenets is "as above, so below," or the doctrine of correspondence. If gods and goddesses struggle in their relationships, why shouldn't we? If they jockey for power among themselves, are we any different? If the Olympians live in beautiful palaces, why should earthly rulers settle for any less? If the god Hephaestos, the heavenly blacksmith, though incredibly strong and skillful, still had to work up a sweat to forge implements for his brother and sister deities, why should we be exempt from hard work? There is no free lunch in heaven; there is none here either.

When our ancestors looked at the night sky, the lights they saw seemed to be in motion. The sun and the moon were the main examples, but some of the stars – those we now call planets – moved also. Even the "fixed stars" twinkled. Everything from the largest creature to the smallest grew, changed, moved. Apparently solid structures like mountains eroded. The earth itself moved in quakes.

Or consider the related principle of eternal recurrence. The sun rises and sets each day. The moon goes through predictable phases. The seasons follow one another, year in and year out, with their cycles of birth, growth, death, and rebirth.

Correspondences are even to be found between the largest and smallest things. The ants, bees, and rabbits all have their families, their work, as do we and the gods. Electrons circle their nuclei just as planets do their sun. And forces of attraction and repulsion, engagement and flight, seem to pervade everything. As above, so below.

Can you think of other examples of the doctrine of correspondence? Write about one or more in your Wisdom Journal.

INEFFECTUAL WISDOM?

Nothing in human life is more to be lamented, than that a wise man should have so little influence.

–Herodotus (c. 484–c. 424 b.c.e.)

Herodotus was a historian. For the most part, he wrote about war. No wonder he had such a low regard for wisdom.

In the two and a half millennia since his day, there have been countless wars. A 1999 TV documentary on the images of the twentieth century was pervaded by footage of military violence. Often described in high-sounding phrases by nationalists and the writers of epics, wars are primarily about the power needs of their perpetrators. Those required to fight them and, increasingly, the noncombatants who get in the way are victims of someone else's values and decisions.

What has all the sage advice from the beginning of the world done to avert this needless expense of human life? Not much it seems. Moses received God's commandment not to kill. Then Joshua, his anointed successor, led the children of Israel on their authorized slaughter of the inhabitants of Jericho: men, women, and children. Jesus is known as the Prince of Peace. Yet for two thousand years, his official followers have left a trail of blood that could fill rivers. One need think only of the Inquisition or the First and Second World Wars, in which all the major combatant nations except Japan had Christian majorities.

In the Dhammapada, one of the principal Buddhist texts, the religion's founder is quoted as having said, "If you were truly aware of the fact of your own death, you would settle all your disputes peacefully." Yet one of the greatest slaughters of our time occurred in the killing fields of Cambodia, a country where virtually everyone is Buddhist.

The still, small voice of wisdom has had a hard time being heard above the din of battles it could not prevent. Yet someday humankind may finally hear that voice, heed it, and study war no more.

Describe in your Wisdom Journal an incident in which "the voice of wisdom" told you to do one thing and you did something else. What were the results? What did you learn?

INNATE WISDOM

Not by years but by disposition is wisdom acquired.

–Plautus (c. 254–184 b.c.e.)

"Older and wiser" is one of the most common English expressions pertaining to wisdom. We also speak of the "wise old owl." Somehow years bring with them the mantle of having learned a thing or two – of having traveled the world, lived through booms and busts, experienced enough good days as well as bad to have drawn some reasonably valid conclusions about life.

Of course, years of living might only bring bitterness and a distorted sense of reality. Like mistreated cats who apparently think all two-leggeds are sadists waiting to swing them by their tails, embittered people often make bad choices and give advice of only limited usefulness. By not trusting anyone, they forgo the opportunity to share life and love with others. Is theirs the kind of advice we need?

Those who saw the movie *Kundun,* about the childhood and adolescence of the present Dalai Lama, will remember how the little boy Kundun was discovered to be the reincarnation of the old Dalai Lama. Young in body and untrained in the ways of the world, he nonetheless had a soul that recognized and remembered objects that had belonged to him in his previous lifetime. These he could distinguish from other similar objects that had not belonged to the old Dalai Lama. As he grew older, he was privately schooled in the doctrines and practices of Tibetan Buddhism, and he had the inner capacity to respond to and modify what he learned.

With Saint Paul, I believe that human beings have a diversity of inner gifts. The capacity for wisdom, whether inherited or (as Buddhists believe) accumulated through many past lives, will differ from person to person. Yet by working on ourselves here and now, I am convinced that each of us can strengthen this capacity. The fact that you are reading this book suggests that you are already on this path. Best wishes for an enriching journey.

Reflect on important things you have known, really known, since childhood. Write for a few minutes in your Wisdom Journal about one or two such instances of innate understanding (or wisdom).

TAKE-YOUR-TIME WISDOM

Wisely and slow; they stumble that run fast.

–WILLIAM SHAKESPEARE, *ROMEO AND JULIET,* II, III, 94

If wisdom is about balance, then most of us in today's world need to slow down. Old people are remarkable for this ability. Okay, you say, but they do so only because their bodies force them to. But if you think about it, individuals who have reached or surpassed the biblical age of seventy know their time is limited and that if they don't take that Elder Hostel trip to China today, they may never have another chance. Yet for the most part, they live one day at a time, happy for a good night's sleep, a day without pain, the ability to get out of bed in the morning.

In this way many older people are wiser than us world-beaters. They know that the tortoise beats the hare every time, as Aesop told us millennia ago. They know that if they rush, they may fall. And if they fall, hip-replacement surgery may not be far behind. Better slow down.

As for those of us who are a generation or two their junior, we'd better slow down too, check our instructions, get out the map, and make sure we are not headed down the wrong road at fifteen miles per hour above the speed limit. No sense getting into an accident on our way to a false destination.

This is one piece of wisdom I find very difficult to assimilate. I seem to be swimming against a cultural riptide. My need to "do it all" sometimes overwhelms me. Perhaps the advice of Honolulu's lifeguards can help us in daily life also. You can't swim against a riptide, they tell you. So don't even try. Just relax and let it take you out to sea. Few riptides run farther than a hundred feet from land. Once the pull stops, swim several dozen strokes parallel to shore, because riptides average only thirty feet across. Then try swimming in. If you meet no further resistance, you have found a safe path.

Are you rushing your life away? Have you found some good techniques for slowing down? Write on this topic in your Wisdom Journal.

INCREMENTAL WISDOM

Little by little does the trick.

–AESOP, "THE CROW AND THE PITCHER," C. 550 B.C.E.

One of the official attractions of downtown Portland, Oregon, is Powell's Bookstore. An agglomeration of older and newer buildings, Powell's takes up an entire square city block. A walking tour of Portland begins at Powell's, though some never make the tour, preferring instead to get their exercise in the inner sanctums of the bookstore.

During one such walking tour through Powell's, I found a book on financial planning for teenagers and young adults. Written in snappy language by one of the editors of a money magazine, the book makes an astounding but apparently valid claim. If, beginning at age twenty-five, you regularly put five dollars a day into a passbook savings account, and the present, relatively low interest rates remain unchanged, by age sixty-five you will have amassed one million dollars. The magic of compound interest indeed! But also the miracle of little by little.

Aesop is a classic spokesperson for the twin virtues of incrementalism and consistency, or perseverance. The tortoise, as every child learns, beats the hare because "plodding wins the race." A few years ago, a book on how individuals can positively impact the environment offered fifty small personal changes that collectively would make a difference. Shutting off the water while brushing my teeth is something I now do. I have also appointed myself the chief marshal of the turning-off-the-lights police in our house. I reuse paper, too–for example, the clean side of first drafts of these pages become reminder notes and telephone message slips. Clearly, if many people did little things like this each day, the wholesale effect on Earth's resources would be significant.

Perhaps the most memorable example of the power of little repeated actions is dripping water eventually boring holes through rocks. Closer to home, a small water leak left unattended can end up costing a fortune. For better or worse, little by little certainly does do the trick.

In your Wisdom Journal, discuss some regular small activity that has had significant positive or negative consequences in your life.

THE WISDOM OF LISTENING

Having two ears and one tongue, we should listen twice as much as we speak.

–A Turkish proverb

When I was seven or eight, my parents started telling me (and others) I had "diarrhea of the mouth." My report cards, though generally good, concurred. It would be regularly noted under "Behavior" that I tended to talk too much in class. (One teacher back in the 1940s referred to it as "rattling." "Reynold rattles too much," she wrote.)

John Wayne impressed me. The strong, silent type. He spoke in monosyllables and short sentences. I spoke in polysyllables and paragraphs, even as a kid. I tried for a while to be like him. It was a joke. Like trying to hold back the ocean. The pressure to talk was just too great.

Now at age sixty, I am still a talker. If I were a football quarterback, I guess I'd always go long. Play-action passes would not be part of my repertoire. If I were silent for a whole day, people around me might have a spiritual experience. There might even be fear that the world were about to end.

Thanks to Al-Anon, I have learned to be a better listener. In that context the unwritten rule is never to interrupt, even if the person goes on and on. Don't ask questions. Don't finish their sentences for them. (I am still working on this last behavior.) One of the reasons twelve-step programs work so well may be that they provide one of the few places where a person really gets heard out.

Come to think of it, God must be the greatest listener of all time. Can you imagine the number of petitions, from this planet alone, going to God each day? Maybe that's what is meant when Muslims refer to the Deity as *el-Rahim,* the All-Merciful. Listening is an ultimate act of compassion. In fact, conversation may be the one area where it is more blessed to receive than to give.

Set aside a half day to fast from talking. Note in your Wisdom Journal the effects on yourself and others.

THE WISDOM OF DOING NOTHING

In the pursuit of learning one knows more every day; in the pursuit of the way one does less every day. One does less and less until one does nothing at all, and when one does nothing at all there is nothing that is undone.

–LAO TZU (C. 604–531 B.C.E.), TAO TE CHING, TRANSLATED BY D. C. LAU

It is said that the Catholic church is so big that sooner or later you will find every kind of believer. Well, China is so big – there are more Chinese in the world than Christians of *all* denominations – that it has room for both Confucius and Lao Tzu: one a social ethicist, the other a mystic and a master of paradox.

Confucius was definitely a historical figure. The jury is still out on Lao Tzu. Even his name sounds mythological, the characters meaning, literally, "old kid." Whereas Confucius advocated hard for study and unceasing enterprise, Lao Tzu's first principle was *wu-wei,* literally "don't do [anything]." My translation, based on Taoist literature, is "the fine art of leaving well enough alone."

Lao Tzu seemed to believe, like E. F. Schumacher and other twentieth-century exponents of simplicity, that less is more. When I first became a college dean, I was sent to a "new deans" workshop in Phoenix. One of the only things I remember is the advice that in nine cases out of ten brought to us for resolution, we should do nothing. These things usually settle themselves, the expert consultant stated. But if we involve ourselves at the outset, we will only get in the way of this natural resolution and probably end up making matters worse.

As a parent of thirty-three years, I think the Taoist advice is especially fitting. I remember lots of instances when I did get involved in situations with my kids that might have resolved themselves more easily and with much less "bloodshed" had I silently counted to ten and let nature take its course. Impatience is an enemy of good parenting, and no ally of wisdom either.

Can you recall an experience where you didn't get involved in something important to you and things worked out anyway? Write about it in your Wisdom Journal.

MOUNTAIN WISDOM

I will lift up mine eyes unto the hills, from whence cometh my help.

–Psalm 121:1, KJV

High places are holy in many traditions. Perhaps because of the perspective they afford. Perhaps because of the difficulty in reaching them. Perhaps because they stand above the flatlands of everyday life and really are closer to the stars.

I live on the skirts of a mountain whose name I do not know. On most mornings it is the first thing I see from my bedroom window. Sometimes fog or rain clouds obscure it. At all times it has a drapelike quality because of the way lava flowed down its side and congealed. In geologic time this mountain is a mere infant, with life span measured in tens of thousands of years, not millions.

During high school vacations, I climbed New Hampshire's Mount Chocorua several times. I remember puffing and panting to make the top. I also remember the elation of getting there and being rewarded by the view. What I mainly remember, though, is the feeling of having been on sacred ground.

In 1988 my wife and I visited Hawaii to celebrate our silver anniversary. We initially stayed in an oceanside cottage just below a dramatic cliff in an area called Waimanalo. Now Waimanalo is a place where many Hawaiians and part-Hawaiians still live. We arrived at night. There was no moon. On entering the cottage, I discovered my traveler's checks were gone. My wife advised me to look outside by the car. On reaching it I was suddenly aware of the mountain looming over me, as if inquiring why I had intruded in this place. I apologized in my mind, explained that we were former residents back to celebrate an important milestone, and requested permission to stay. Suddenly I was moved to reach down. There on the ground lay the pouch with my traveler's checks.

If you live near mountains, climb one solo and allow yourself to feel its strength. If not, find a picture of a mountain and meditate on it. Write the results of your experience in your Wisdom Journal.

DEATH, THE ALLY OF WISDOM

If I survive this life without dying, I shall be surprised.
—A saying of Mulla Nasrudin, Sufi sage

In a similar vein but much different tone, Castaneda's sorcerer Don Juan once advised Carlos to take death as his ally. At another time, when Carlos was complaining about his friend's bratty children in Los Angeles, Don Juan recommended that the teenagers be taken to the morgue and asked to touch a cadaver. That would cure them, Don Juan insisted.

Ours is a culture that avoids death like the plague. We may not live forever, but we don't want to be reminded. And it's not just us twentieth-century secular folks. Back in seventeenth-century France, La Rochefoucauld concluded (in moral maxim 25) that "neither the sun nor death can be looked at steadily." I for one start to panic after just five minutes of airborne turbulence. The old Latin tag comes to mind: *Timor mortis conturbat me.* "The fear of death throws me into disarray."

Yet much can be said for contemplating the inevitability of our death. Perhaps it, too, like the Old Testament's "fear of God," is the beginning of wisdom. Time may be a stream we go a-fishing in, as Thoreau said. But the stream does not go on forever. Yet that's the point. Death is the very thing that makes life precious. Thomas Mann said as much in his essay "In Praise of Transitoriness." The fact that our time is limited makes everything we do or don't do, say or don't say, meaningful. Life is about roads taken and rejected.

Maybe the best advice on this topic is the saying: "The past is history, the future's a mystery. All we have left is the present, and, as the word suggests, it's a gift." We'd best use it wisely.

Try this exercise in your Wisdom Journal. Complete the following: "Here lies [your name]. She (or he) ____________________." Based on this "epitaph," what might you do differently to live a better life?

NEIGHBORLY WISDOM

He that is void of wisdom despiseth his neighbour: but a man of understanding holdeth his peace.

–PROVERBS 11:12, KJV

The Book of Proverbs is perhaps the single best wisdom resource in print. The Dhammapada, or "Sayings of the Buddha," and the Analects of Confucius are also high on the list; perhaps it's a three-way tie. In any event, those interested in increasing their personal wisdom could do worse than reading a little from one of these texts each day.

Wisdom, these three books and many others imply, is about making right choices in our daily lives. Now a "right choice" can be determined by its longer-term results. Was your selection of spouse wise? Your choice of occupation? Your place or style of living? Well, are you still married? Are you happy in your work? Do you like where you live? Is your lifestyle landing you in bankruptcy court? Not that unwise choices can't have benefits. Poor decisions, so long as they are not fatal, can teach us a lot. True wisdom is as much about learning from our mistakes as about not making them in the first place.

When we judge our neighbors harshly, we typically see the speck in their eye while remaining unaware of the piece of wood in our own. We tend to project our faults with great generosity onto others. For example, as a loquacious person myself, I become impatient with and critical of other "talkers." If we are wise enough to know ourselves and human nature well, we will refrain from gossiping about or criticizing others. Like us, they have their reasons for being the way they are. Instead we might use that same energy and analytical ability to improve who and what we are. When it comes to bettering humanity, charity begins at home. Criticizing less and reflecting more will help us become good neighbors to ourselves as well as to others.

Monitor for one day the critical things you think and say about others. Reflect in your Wisdom Journal on what you have observed and what you would like to do about it.

THE WISDOM TO KNOW THE DIFFERENCE

God, grant me the serenity to accept the things I cannot change, the courage to change the things I can, and the wisdom to know the difference.

–The Serenity Prayer

I am blessed with several recovering alcoholics in my family. Blessed, not because they are alcoholics, but because they have been sober for some years and have built solid, responsible lives through participation in Alcoholics Anonymous.

In fact, I am twice blessed. Seven years ago I joined Al-Anon, a twelve-step program for friends and families of alcoholics. We practice the same program as AA members. The major difference is that we keep the focus on ourselves, not on the alcoholic in our lives. We learn to take our own inventories, not others', and acquire techniques for building up our own lives and for discovering–and recovering–who we really are.

The program has many tools. Among them are attending meetings, practicing the twelve steps and traditions, doing daily readings, hooking up with a sponsor (an established member who can serve as a coach), calling on other members for support, internalizing the slogans (easy does it, one day at a time, let go and let God, and so on), and practicing prayer and meditation.

Of all these, I suspect the most famous is probably the Serenity Prayer. It is printed on the medallions we receive to commemorate our time in the program. It is often used to open and close meetings.

Recently we took a visiting friend to the airport to return to Germany. As it happened her flight was canceled. Her English is minimal, so when she learned she would have to stay overnight in Los Angeles, she became hysterical. Though understandable, this reaction was not helpful. This is precisely the kind of situation that calls for the Serenity Prayer. Circumstances beyond one's control must be accepted. However, bad situations that can be changed should be. The real trick is knowing which is which. Therein lies wisdom, and serenity.

During the coming week, whenever you are in a tight spot, recite the Serenity Prayer to yourself. Write about the effects of this practice in your Wisdom Journal.

GOVERNMENTAL WISDOM

Smart public managers spend every penny of every line item, whether they need to or not. This explains why public organizations get so bloated: **our budget systems actually encourage every public manager to waste money.**

–David Osborne and Ted Gaebler, *Reinventing Government,* 1992

Here's one for the fans of the oxymoron. Wisdom in government? You've got to be kidding! In reality, of course, government, like all other human institutions, has its share of wise and foolish practices. The balance of powers set forth in the U.S. Constitution would be selected by many, I am sure, as an example of wisdom. And like former Sen. William Proxmire with his Golden Fleece Award, we could doubtless come up with lots of candidates for foolishness.

The example cited above from Osborne and Gaebler's 1992 book would be my personal favorite. I learned early in my twenty-year career as an academic administrator in public institutions to spend all my budget before the fiscal year ended. As a dean and academic vice president, I encouraged those reporting to me to do the same. After all, if we didn't spend all our allocations, maybe we didn't need that much. So April through June became a busy time for travel or the acquisition of that new computer system. Sometimes the workshops people attended seemed a bit removed from their areas of responsibility. Still, even the president wouldn't ask too many questions. After all, if one administrative area lost dollars, it was possible the whole institution would.

Osborne and Gaebler make the point that public administrators should be rewarded, not punished, for thrift. They give examples from around the country where the experiment has been tried and found successful. Working with an administrative team to do more with less presents a positive challenge. Actually achieving this goal generates a sense of accomplishment. Not that I am proposing that good programs be cut to the quick because of political or other external considerations. Rather, I am arguing that in government, as elsewhere, flexibility, not rigidity, is the way of wisdom.

In your Wisdom Journal, describe a foolish government practice and propose how the same purpose might be achieved more wisely.

CONFUCIAN WISDOM

The Master said, A gentleman can see a question from all sides without bias. The small man is biased and can see a question only from one side.

–CONFUCIUS, ANALECTS, TRANSLATED BY ARTHUR WALEY

Confucius, like many Chinese throughout history, spoke in proverbs. The four- and eight-character slogans of the People's Republic of China are also proverbial in form. One I learned in Chinese class – "Friendship first, competition second" – would be ritually intoned before sports matches, whereupon the teams would endeavor to blast each other out of the water.

Much of Confucian wisdom is based on the distinction between how a magnanimous person and a small-minded person typically act in various situations. For example, the "gentleman" follows the law; the "small man" looks for ways around it. The gentleman considers whether something is right; the small man asks if it will pay. The gentleman underpromises and overdelivers, while the small man, by implication, does just the opposite.

The Japanese proverb "You can't see the whole sky through a bamboo tube" suggests that the small-minded person's problem is limited vision. As you see, so you act. Jesus forever exhorted his audiences to use their eyes and ears more fully. He also asked God to forgive those who crucified him for not knowing what they were doing. Limited sight leads to or reinforces narrow-mindedness, which in turn fosters selfish, shortsighted, even criminal actions.

My riding teacher emphasized getting my head lower than the horse's if we were approaching a low-lying branch. The horse never calculates how much higher the rider's head is than its own. Unfortunately we often act like horses with regard to others who depend on us.

Generous vision, generous heart, generous action: These are the characteristics of Confucius's ideal person and are not far removed from those of the nineteenth-century's "Christian gentleman." The wisdom of Confucius is still good medicine in the twenty-first century.

In which areas are you broad-minded? In which, less so? How might you become more magnanimous across the board? Discuss these questions in your Wisdom Journal.

THE WISDOM OF GIVING AND RECEIVING

The sufi opens his hand to the universe
and gives away each instant, free.
Unlike someone who begs on the street for money to survive,
A dervish begs to give you his life.

-JALALUDDIN RUMI (1207–1273)

To keep myself off the streets, one of the things I do is raise money for homeless people. More specifically, I am part-time development director for a private nonprofit agency offering homeless people two years of transitional shelter. This organization helps to house, clothe, feed, and counsel such people while equipping them to support themselves.

From this experience I have learned that there are homeless and there are homeless. Not everyone on the streets is homeless, and not everyone in an apartment or house is accommodated. Even among those without an indoor place to live – which is a less daunting proposition in Hawaii, surely, than Minnesota – some still seem healthy-minded and optimistic enough to make it if given half a chance. Others seem dead on arrival – from alcohol, drugs, mental illness, or other causes. More than a hand up, they seem to need a miraculous laying on of hands.

A Portuguese friend once showed how the gesture to give and the gesture to receive are really the same. You put your hand out, palm up. If you have, you give. If you need, you receive. The essential attitude, I suppose, is being open. A clenched fist can neither give nor receive.

Inner content is what differentiates a Sufi from a beggar. A beggar simply needs. Having nothing, he or she feels like nothing. The Sufi, by contrast, receives in order to give, gives in order to receive. My own spiritual guide, himself from the Sufi tradition of Islamic spirituality, once said that wells that "give themselves away" stay pure from the new water that replenishes them, while boarded-up wells soon become polluted from the lack of replenishment and circulation.

Do you own your material possessions, or do they own you? How easy is it for you to give things away or receive things? Write in your Wisdom Journal about your generous and selfish sides.

HEALTHY WISDOM

There's no joy even in beautiful Wisdom, unless one have holy Health.

–SIMONIDES OF CEOS (C. 556–C. 468 B.C.E.)

As my eighty-one-year-old father lay dying of multiple myeloma (bone-marrow cancer), he was blessed to retain his mind. He was able to ask good questions and give good, if short, answers. He was also proud of the fact that when his doctor quizzed him on the current and recent U.S. presidents, he could respond correctly. Yet in those last weeks, my father was unable to laugh or smile. With life and health rapidly deserting him, he found little in his life to celebrate.

My father was not a practitioner of any religion. If he believed in a higher power, he never shared that information with me. He was more of a noble Roman, stoically "facing the inevitable," as he put it. I can't say whether or not people of strong religious faith, as they approach death, can laugh or smile. I should ask our pastor. For myself, I am not smiling much today, down as I am with a touch of the flu.

In short, Simonides seems to have a point. (Check out the length of his life, by the way, from the numbers after his name, above. He was blessed, presumably, with a sufficiency of "holy Health," for he lived to be eighty-seven – a stellar accomplishment 2,500 years ago.) The ability to feel joy must be anchored in reasonably good health. The psychologist Abraham Maslow's "hierarchy of needs" likewise begins with satisfying the basics of food, shelter, clothing, and health. So-called peak experiences come at the top, not the bottom, of his schematic pyramid.

The gift of life provides us with the chance to cultivate and strengthen our innate wisdom. Good health is a special blessing in this pursuit. Yet we should not forget how people with significant disabilities – Helen Keller, Beethoven, and Stephen Hawking come to mind – have sometimes found the ability to transmute the base metal of their physical lives into the pure gold of creativity and wisdom.

In your Wisdom Journal, write about a bout of illness you have had. What wisdom, if any, were you able to glean from it?

PRAGMATIC WISDOM

Speak of the moderns without contempt, and of the ancients without idolatry; judge them all by their merits, but not by their age.

–FROM A LETTER BY LORD CHESTERFIELD TO HIS SON, 1748

In Chesterfield's day the battle raged between supporters of the classical Greek and Roman writers and supporters of the modern "greats" such as Dante, Cervantes, and Shakespeare. These "culture wars," to borrow a current term, could turn ugly. Although fought mainly on paper, they sometimes erupted in *Shakespeare in Love*–type fist fights.

A similar intellectual battle developed in the eighteenth century between the ancient Greek concept of degeneration from Golden to Silver to Bronze to Iron Ages and the then-contemporary idea of progress. Many in earlier periods, and some now, consider that humankind's best days are well behind us, whether in a biblical Eden, a sunken Atlantis or Lemuria, T'ang Dynasty China, Pericles's Athens, Ashoka's India, Cicero's Rome, the Italian Renaissance, Elizabethan England, or the era of the American founding fathers.

Realistically, of course, there was good and bad back then. There is good and bad now. In terms of material culture, we are far better off today. Many diseases have been conquered, we have greater civil rights, and goods and services are distributed more equitably. But we've also got polluted air and water, disappearing species, the splitting of the nuclear family–not to mention the atom, and the widespread loss of belief in a positive spiritual reality. As for wisdom, the ancients had no monopoly on it, just as we have no monopoly on foolishness.

There have been pragmatists throughout time. Jesus advised judging trees by their fruit. That's pragmatism. Chesterfield similarly counseled his son to evaluate writers based on merit, not pedigree, whether ancient or modern. If America's primary gift to world music has been jazz, its main contribution to philosophy has been pragmatism. William James used to talk about "the cash value of ideas." For my money, assessing a concept–or something pragmatic, like a diet–by its proven benefits is not a bad way to go.

Do you judge something based on its conformity to principles or on its benefits? Discuss this question in your Wisdom Journal.

THE WISDOM OF IMMEDIACY

Asked to explain a difficult* étude*, Schumann sat down and played it a second time.

–GEORGE STEINER, *REAL PRESENCES,* 1989

An *étude* is a piece of music written specifically to exercise and improve a musician's playing technique. When nineteenth-century composer Robert Schumann "explained" the étude by playing it again, he recognized that secondhand experience – talk *about* the piece – is far inferior to the immediacy of hearing or playing it.

Children have a ravenous appetite for immediate experience, evidenced by the common childhood refrain, "I can do it myself!" Children might well listen to Schumann play an étude, but their musical education really begins when they climb up on the piano bench and start banging on the keys themselves. Through immediacy they may gain a respect for how difficult it is to do something well; they may also learn the need to study, or to do études, in the first place.

George Steiner goes on to suggest that immediacy is key to our understanding of literature and the arts. The best critique of a play may just be an actor's interpretation of it, for unlike an "objective" critic or scholar, an actor's critique is characterized by answerability – she or he is responsible to the text and to the audience. Every time actors go on stage, they put themselves on the line with their critical interpretation.

Our lives are more fully lived when we involve ourselves directly in some creative activity, whether it be writing, painting, singing, dancing, cooking, gardening. We need to do something that puts us into the thick of creativity. Interested in Shakespeare's *Othello*? Rather than study the play alone, gather a group of friends and read it out loud. We need to encourage ourselves and those around us to stop relying on others – teachers, critics, television pundits – to form our understanding of the world, whether in relation to the arts, politics, or any other facet of modern life. In the 1960s and 1970s, we were encouraged to "get it." In the 1980s and 1990s, we were told "Go for it" and "Just do it." In the new era – or in any era – it is unlikely we will come to understand much of anything if we don't give new activities a firsthand try.

In your Wisdom Journal, write about a breakthrough you have had by way of direct involvement in something new.

REFORMATION WISDOM

Ecclesia semper est reformanda.
The Church must be in a continuous process of reformation.

–Martin Luther (1483–1546)

You may find it odd that I am addressing this topic in a book published by a Catholic press. In fact, I shall not talk about Lutheranism or the Protestant Reformation at all, except in passing. My interest is rather the wisdom of what industry now calls "continuous improvement." Products and services are never as good, cheap, or useful as they might be. How can they be bettered so that more will be sold and more consumers fully satisfied? Good answers to these questions will generate more sales.

In education we refer to the analogous process as "lifelong learning." A German proverb counsels, "We grow all too soon old and all too late smart." So the more we endeavor to learn and the longer we keep at it, the better for us and those around us.

When climbing mountains, we are not there until we are there. Rest stops are only interim destinations. Even the peak is but a way station to the descent and another day of climbing. In life every experience is both complete in itself and a new chance for learning. One-time mistakes are one of God's greatest gifts to humanity. And if Hindus and Buddhists are correct about reincarnation, we have more than one lifetime to become wise through and through.

Re-forming ourselves, learning from our mistakes in this life, is a choice always before us. It is prudent to do our best here and now (and that would remain so even if reincarnation were a proven fact). Given free will, reformation is strongly recommended but never required. Luther's statement about ongoing church reform is profoundly wise. Alas, once he and his church decided they had gotten it right, reformation was continued by others who established churches and sects of their own.

Change is often frightening. Yet as nature continues to evolve, we are called to a life of ongoing movement and improvement. Whether we accept or reject that call is up to us.

How well do you learn from your mistakes? Recount one or two examples in your Wisdom Journal to illustrate your success.

RELATIONSHIP WISDOM

God has given us enough wisdom to make improvements in our relations.

–Mikhail S. Gorbachev

Mr. Gorbachev was most likely talking about relations between nations, such as those old Cold War foes, the United States and the Soviet Union, when he made the statement above For most of us, however, improved relations, like charity, begin at home. If divorce statistics are any guide, the *other* cold war is alive, well, and heating up.

Actually, improved relations begin even closer to home than we might think. They need to occur where Jesus said the Kingdom of heaven is located: within. If God in the monotheistic religions is one, Satan is legion – many. More often than not, we are unwittingly members of the devil's party, at least to the extent that we are divided within and not a unified whole. We are ambivalent. We want to say yes, but we say no. We think it better to be cautious, yet we follow the crowd. We feel we should take a risk, but we don't have the courage of our convictions. As a result we chastise ourselves for things done or left undone. Whatever we end up doing, part of us remains dissatisfied.

"Loving" our neighbor as ourselves thus puts our neighbor at risk. For at times we can't stand ourselves. Our neighbor, in consequence, becomes the target of our self-dissatisfied thoughts, words, or deeds. So if the goal is improved relations, the place to begin is within. Religion, counseling, self-help programs, support groups, and spiritual training all have something to offer. So does job counseling – nothing causes frustration and unhappiness like working in a job that fails to suit our talents and interests.

Alcoholics Anonymous advises newly sober members not to date, or above all enter a serious relationship, until they have been working their program for at least a year. This principle applies to the rest of us. Until we gain a measure of internal integration, our chances for maintaining healthy relationships with others are slim.

Describe in your Wisdom Journal how you are working to improve relations within yourself. What progress can you note over the last year or so?

SABBATH WISDOM

Some keep the Sabbath going to church;
I keep it staying at home,
With a bobolink for a chorister,
And an orchard for a dome. . . .

God preaches, – a noted clergyman, –
And the sermon is never long;
So instead of getting to heaven at last,
I'm going all along!

–Emily Dickinson (1830–1886)

My wife and I are regular churchgoers, and have been since our kids were in elementary school. In our case the ritual of Sunday church started the summer of 1978. Prior to that time, we had attended only sporadically, mainly on major holidays.

We were asked to be sponsors at the baptism of our friends' five-year-old son, Michael. These friends were not churchgoers. Once inside the chapel, Michael became wild and refused to settle down. We sponsors ended up having to hold him throughout the service. It occurred to my wife and me that if we expected our daughters to be confirmed – they had both been baptized as infants – we had better start attending church ourselves. We found a liberal Lutheran church near our home, joined the choir, and have been regulars ever since. We appreciate many aspects of institutional church life, from the services themselves to adult study groups to men's and women's groups.

But to tell the truth, I agree with Emily Dickinson that God's house is bigger than any formal place of worship. Not everyone who follows the rules of his or her religion necessarily keeps the Sabbath in a real sense, while some who never set foot inside houses of worship live in intimacy with God. There is no easy way to tell.

God's world, I believe, is much more inclusive than ours. Who forbids a sunset or a rainbow on grounds of some formal affiliation? Capitalists and communists alike may listen to a nightingale without visas or special permits. God seems very willing to meet individuals where they are. The God who sent Christ is that kind of God.

Write in your Wisdom Journal about a religious or spiritual experience you've had in nature. Explain why it was meaningful for you. What does this say about your "religiosity"?

SAILING WISDOM

Hoist up saile while gale doth last,
Tide and wind stay no man's pleasure.

-ROBERT SOUTHWELL (1561–1595), "ST. PETER'S COMPLAINT"

The year was 1956. The place, North Star Camp in Hayward, Wisconsin. I had been hired as a junior swimming counselor. Having just graduated from high school at age sixteen, I was too young to be a senior counselor.

During the first day of pre-camp, the owner called three of us junior swimming counselors to the office. The junior sailing counselor would not be coming. Did any of us know how to sail? None did. I had been a passenger on a sailboat once on Long Island Sound. "Okay, Feldman. You're the new junior sailing counselor. Take the next five days and learn to sail. Next week you'll be teaching sailing."

The oldest campers were only a year younger than me, and some had been sailing for five or six summers. A few even had boats of their own back home. And I would be teaching *them!* Fortunately decent winds lasted all week, and the senior sailing counselor proved a good teacher. Before the campers arrived, I learned that a "sheet" wasn't a sail, and "hiking" didn't mean a three-mile walk. I also discovered that you couldn't simply point the nose–that is, "bow"–of the boat in the direction you wanted to go and sail there. Given the physics involved, you could never sail directly into the wind. Getting from here to there sometimes required "tacking," or sailing crosswind in zigzags. Occasionally you could take the wind from behind, spread your sails, and "run free." You had to be careful, though, in case the "boom" suddenly "jibed."

That summer was my first teaching job. I sailed and sailed and sailed –in sunfish, sailing canoes, small sloops, and the camp's e-class scow. I learned that God is in the wind. You can do much with skill, but not everything. You can't have speed, safety, and direction all at the same time. You need to choose how much of each you want. Above all, the wind comes first: No wind, no ride.

Have you ever sailed? Hang gliding, skydiving, or flying a motorless plane will work too. Comment on the experience in your Wisdom Journal.

SECRET WISDOM

The secret things belong unto the LORD our God.
–DEUTERONOMY 29:29, KJV

In 1970 Simone and I acquired an unusual friend, Madame Farida. She came to us in an unusual way too. While visiting Hawaii from Jakarta, Indonesia, she wanted to be put in touch with Hawaiian *kahuna* (spiritual specialists). So she asked the Indonesian professor at the University, Dr. Soenyono. Because Javanese are too polite not to respond to a request, he said, "Call Dr. Feldman." Now I am about as far from a *kahuna* as you can get. But because my spiritual teacher was himself Javanese – a fact that has intrigued every Indonesian I've ever met – I was the best resource Soenyono could come up with.

Farida was a great character, half gypsy, half bureaucrat. She favored saris over her own ethnic dress or Western clothes. Besides Indonesian and her colorful English, she spoke Dutch, German, and Japanese. Often she would speak several languages at once. Back home she was a palmist of renown, and on one occasion was nearly jailed by Sukarno for reading certain lines in his hand.

Farida was on a lifelong quest. She would speak of it in whispers. Or else, looking you intently in the eye, she would say in a dramatic voice something like, "Reinhold, those *kahuna* have . . . the secret of life."

As my colleagues and I plan our World Wisdom Gathering, a bringing together of several thousand individuals and organizations in Hawaii in early 2001 to share their wisdom on wisdom, we have encountered understandable reluctance on the part of indigenous peoples to make their wisdom available to outsiders. To quote what a Maori woman e-mailed: "We First Nations people have lost so much to others that we wish to preserve this one last thing, our secret knowledge, for ourselves and our children. After all, if we give it away, others will just make money with it, and we'll have nothing left." On the other hand, the world now needs wisdom from all possible sources. So perhaps we can learn to share without diminishing one another's light. Indeed, as more tapers are lit, we can, together, illuminate the world.

Write in your Wisdom Journal how you think one should approach the accessing of "secret wisdom."

WISDOM IS AS WISDOM DOES

Two Hasids were discussing their weekend plans. One said, "I intend to visit the great rabbi in Lvov." "To hear his words of wisdom?" his friend inquired. "No, to see how he ties his shoes."

–ADAPTED FROM MARTIN BUBER'S *TALES OF THE HASIDIM*

Beauty is as beauty does. The same holds for wisdom. Talking a good game is relatively easy. When I went to college, we called it "a snow job." In fact, some of us thought college was all about learning to do bigger and better snow jobs – on parents, on girlfriends, on future employers. Impress them, we believed, and as surely as day followed night, we would get our way.

Great wisdom, the first Hasid in our anecdote implies, manifests in the small change of daily living. We are as we do, not as we say. Buckminster Fuller, known for his long, abstract speeches, wrote a brief, easily understood poem entitled "God Is a Verb." *Natura naturans* was how Renaissance writers put this thought in Latin: "Nature naturing."

But this brings up an issue. If we are faithful to who we are and really do our thing, then who we are will affect what we do. A Javanese proverb makes this point succinctly: "Carpenters can't build tables better than themselves." If we separate the word *wisdom* after the first letter, we get *w-isdom.* In other words, wisdom does as wisdom is. So to act wisely, we have to become wise – or wiser. And to do the right thing most of the time, wisdom has to be dominant within our being. The trick is learning how to become wiser. I hope this book has been giving you some tips.

Personal transformation – the journey from our smaller, more foolish self to our larger, wiser self – is a prime motive of all the world's religious and spiritual traditions. The late Varindra Tarzie Vittachi of UNICEF liked to say, "Any conversation not about human transformation is mere gossip." "Working on ourselves" is a phrase often heard in spiritual circles. The secular equivalent is "self-improvement."

Who is the wisest person you know? Describe this individual in your Wisdom Journal. What makes her or him wise? How might you apply some of this person's way of living to your own life?

SIMPLE GIFTS

When the solution is simple, God is answering. . . . Things should be as simple as possible, but not any simpler.

–ALBERT EINSTEIN (1879–1955)

We live in an age of complexity. Consequently we are taught that knowledge, sophistication, and subtlety are good. When I was age twenty, a newly minted Yale graduate, I was at the height of my sophistication. Inside, though, I aimed the sharply honed weapons of critical analysis at all and sundry. Sophistication in my case was a first cousin to arrogance, and the family resemblance was striking.

Graduate school cured me of my smugness. As an undergraduate I had been a star. Yale graduate school was another matter. My new colleagues knew as much as I did – or more. I remember one significant incident during my first year in the PhD program. It happened to be November 6, my birthday, when I attended a lecture by Dr. René Wellek, who at the time was Sterling Professor of Comparative Literature. In a brilliant performance, he demonstrated a broad as well as deep knowledge of the languages and literatures of a half dozen countries. I walked home through the damp November rain to the third-floor apartment I shared with two other grad students. They were out. I realized with depressing clarity that I would never know as much as Professor Wellek nor be able to give a lecture like the one I had just heard. In that mood I opened the window and put one leg out, with the intention to jump. Obviously I didn't. In fact, I made it through graduate school and got my doctorate five years later. But that incident marked the end of my intellectual snobbery and the beginning of a process of simplification that has continued to this day.

When all the gifts are counted, one of the greatest, surely, will be simplicity. "Old and wise" is the English cliché. But I'd rather equate wisdom with simplicity. Per Einstein, "Things should be as simple as possible, but not any simpler."

Do you live as simply as possible? Write in your Wisdom Journal for about ten minutes on how you might simplify yourself or your life.

THE WISDOM OF SOLOMON

My [child], if you take my words to heart
and lay up my commands in your mind,
giving your attention to wisdom
and your mind to understanding, . . .
then you will understand the fear of the LORD
and attain to the knowledge of God;
for the LORD bestows wisdom
and teaches knowledge and understanding.

–PROVERBS 2:1–6

What is wisdom? "Knowledge of what is true or right coupled with good judgment," says one dictionary. Another adds that this good judgment is about "action." The Anglo-Saxon roots are *wis* and *deman:* to make judgments ("to deem" in modern English) based on knowledge or understanding (*wissen;* "to know" in modern German).

Solomon's famous judgment about which of two women had really mothered an infant, as narrated in 1 Kings, chapter 3, exemplifies wisdom in this sense. Two women, prostitutes living in the same house, asked the king to settle their dispute. One asserted that the other had suffocated her child by accident while asleep. On waking she allegedly substituted her dead infant for the living child of her house-mate. The second woman denied the charge. The living child was hers.

Solomon called for a sword, commanded that the child be cut in half, and ruled that each woman be given an equal share. One of them demanded her half. The other protested, "Give the whole child to her!" Solomon reasoned that the real mother would prefer losing a living child to receiving half a dead one. So he gave the child to the woman who had protested. The Bible comments, "All [Israel] . . . stood in awe [of the king], for they saw that he had the wisdom of God within him to administer justice" (1 Kings 3:28). Later, of course, we learn that Solomon had 700 wives and 300 concubines (1 Kings, chapter 11), and that he got into trouble with God over one wife in particular. We thus wonder just how wise he really was. Still, there you have it: the wisdom of Solomon.

What do you think wisdom is? Write down your own definition in your Wisdom Journal and refer to it from time to time as you go through this book.

SOUL WISDOM

When you have shut your doors, and darkened your room, remember never to say that you are alone, for you are not alone; but God is within, and your genius is within, – and what need have they of light to see what you are doing?

–EPICTETUS (C. 55–C. 135)

An abiding theological question is the immanence or transcendence of divinity. Is God out there or in here?

Some traditions, like Deism, reduce God to a distant creator, a kind of absentee parent who started life, then left it to its own devices. The usual metaphor in Deism is God as clockmaker. Divinity built the universe and its inhabitants like a large, complex clock. Once going, it continues to run according to its own mechanism (natural law) until, if not rewound, it stops.

Traditions like Judaism and Islam posit a more involved deity, yet one still very much out there. Jehovah and Allah create, guide, lay down rules for, and punish or reward their creatures. Mystical traditions, on the other hand, understand God as a force that pervades the universe and lives within each creature. According to mystics, human beings need to become aware of and eventually attain union with the God within. Mystical paths contain techniques for attaining this goal.

Unfortunately the "inner" and "outer" aspects of religion have historically had a somewhat tense relationship. Established communities, based on broadly accepted and sanctioned tenets of faith, are understandably concerned by mystical freelancers. A Muslim mystic, El Hallaj, lost his life at the hands of orthodox believers for uttering in a state of rapture *"Ana ul-Haq"* (I am the Truth). For in Islam *Truth* is one of the Ninety-Nine Names of God, and the chief sin for Muslims is making anyone or anything equivalent to Allah.

As in most matters, the middle way seems best. God is both out there – the Supreme Other – and in here – the Deepest, Truest Self. To follow the ethical tenets of one's faith is a good idea. Meanwhile, to live in accordance with the promptings of God from within will assure, as the song suggests, that we will never walk alone.

What is your experience of living in the presence of God? Describe it in your Wisdom Journal.

WISDOM AND THE WILL

Though the will to do good is there, the deed is not. The good which I want to do, I fail to do; but what I do is the wrong which is against my will.

–Romans 7:18–19

If it were easy to do whatever we wanted, then we would all be rich and famous, not to mention intelligent, attractive, popular, healthy, long-lived, productive, and happy. Our best intentions often never get realized. New Year's resolutions routinely lie scattered on the ground. A friend of mine quips, "If you'd like to make God laugh, tell God your plans."

Plato apparently thought that to *do* the right thing, all you needed was to *know* what that thing was. Yet if that is so, why do so many people continue to smoke when the surgeon general's warning adorns every pack of cigarettes? In the next line of his letter to the Romans, Saint Paul writes, "And if what I do is against my will, clearly it is no longer I who am the agent, but sin that has its lodging in me."

Although it may be possible for us to become wiser, the way is less than easy. A recent "guru" story goes: A New Yorker decides she must know the meaning of life. So she sells everything and undertakes an expensive trip to the Himalayas to meet with the Great Sage. After cooling her heels for several weeks in a small village, she is finally guided to the great man's cave. "O Great Sage," she begins. "I have only one question. Please, Great One, tell me. What is the meaning of life?" After an interminable pause, the Great Sage says, "Life is just a bowl of cherries." "What?!" she nearly screams. "I have given up everything, made this difficult journey, waited around in your godforsaken village, and now you tell me, 'Life is just a bowl of cherries'?" "You mean, it is *not* just a bowl of cherries?" comes the reply.

Write in your Wisdom Journal about an instance in your life when, despite your best efforts, things just went wrong. Now write what you learned from that experience.

THE WISDOM OF PERCEPTION

Happy are your eyes because they see, and your ears because they hear! Many prophets and saints, I tell you, desired to see what you now see, yet never saw it; to hear what you hear, yet never heard it.

–Matthew 13:16–17

We see what we see. But we also see what we are. To a great extent, the eye is the I. Animals know this, for they look us in the eye. They are aware that this is where we live.

We all see the same reality, people say. But do we? When my father, age eighty-one, was in his final days, he saw dead relatives in his hospital room. They talked with him. He answered in Yiddish. My sister, there at the time, didn't see or hear anything except my father. He was hallucinating, she explained to me later. But why should she trust her perception more than his?

"I can't see it" is another way of saying "I don't get it," or "I don't understand." "I hear you" means the opposite. Our pastor once pointed out that by taking the sentence "God is nowhere" and adding one space, you come up with "God is now here." The letters are exactly the same. The meaning is diametrically opposed. Everything depends on how we see things.

Some famous figures of antiquity had to lose their sight in order to understand. Samson and Saul of Tarsus are notable examples from the Judeo-Christian tradition; Tiresias and Oedipus, from classical Greece. Sometimes it is necessary to look away in order to see. This happens to me regularly with crossword puzzles. When I can't find the right word, I set the puzzle aside. When I return, the solution is obvious. In this minor example of amazing grace, I was blind but now I see.

In matters of greater import, unless the necessary wisdom is inside us, we will look but not see, listen but not understand. Perception, finally, is as much spiritual as physical.

Discuss in your Wisdom Journal an example of seeing something in a new light. What conclusions do you draw?

EDITORIAL WISDOM

Even the best writer has to erase.

–A Spanish saying

Tell me about it! And I'm far from the best writer. At least the computer makes things easier now. In the old days of cut and paste, we *really* had to cut and paste. We English majors at Yale, moreover, were given so many writing assignments that there was virtually no time to edit. Writing and editing thus became a single combined activity. No wonder people got writer's block.

During the 1960s and 1970s, research in composition showed that it was advisable to separate the acts of writing and editing. The former went best when allowed to flow. In consequence, college composition teachers began to assign free-writing exercises. "Don't worry about grammar, punctuation, and spelling," teachers would instruct their shocked students. "Just write down your thoughts as they come. You'll be able to edit and polish later."

Actually, the research makes sense. We write from the creative right side of the brain but edit from the logical left side. Not that editors can't be creative when looking for a solution to an editorial problem. Still, their job is basically to criticize what someone else has written, then make improvements.

The Hippocratic Code prohibits us from operating on ourselves. Only action-movie superheroes stranded a thousand miles from the nearest trauma center wield the scalpel on themselves. Mostly, though, we have to function as our own editors. The best strategy is to put our work aside for a few days or even weeks before reviewing it. Then we come to it as if someone else had been the author. If this is not possible, even a few hours will give us some critical distance. In the editing mode, we should try to place ourselves in the shoes of our readers. Will they understand what we are writing? Will they know the acronyms, the historical references? Is our vocabulary too technical, too simple? Are our sentences too long or short? This book is being edited by professionals, so here's hoping they have answered such questions to your satisfaction.

In your Wisdom Journal, discuss how you write and edit your own work.

BITE-YOUR-TONGUE WISDOM

It's so simple to be wise. Just think of something stupid to say and then don't say it.

–Sam Levenson

Unlike Moses, I have never been slow of tongue. It is a matter of record which of us is the prophet. I have been in many situations in which I should have recalled the Portuguese proverb "Fish die by their mouths." But the issue for me isn't the trouble I get into by saying the wrong thing. It is, rather, the hurt I give.

Back in Scarsdale, in seventh grade, my last year in public school, I had a girlfriend named Linda. She was a bright girl who lived in another, posher part of town. I specifically remember her teaching me to dance swing at a party in her basement – something which has stood me in good stead throughout a lifetime of dancing.

Linda had a prominent aquiline nose. But this was the year I dropped out of Hebrew School, and I was not a fan of anything that reminded me of Jewishness, my own or others'. Fact was, I was something of a Jewish anti-Semite, a sickness that did not abate until my experience visiting Dachau during my junior year abroad. Another fact was, I had thought of stupid things to say about Linda's nose, and I had said them. Sam Levenson, a fine comedian, had it right – it would have been so simple to be wise.

Once on a trip back to Scarsdale from New York City, where we were then living, one of my old classmates mentioned that Linda had had a nose job. Apparently some of my unkind remarks had gotten back to her, and she was so miserable that her parents had finally authorized this expensive elective surgery. I never saw her after that. For nearly fifty years, I have carried the memory of this experience with me, however, and – like the gift of dance – she has also given me a touchstone that has kept me, at least sometimes, from saying hurtful things. As Muhammad Subuh, my late spiritual guide, used to say, "Persons who have made progress in developing themselves will correct their mistakes *before* making them." I will look for Linda and apologize if I find her.

How are you at biting your tongue? Are you proficient, or do you need work? If it's the latter, what are your plans for improvement? Write for ten minutes in your Wisdom Journal.

THE WISDOM OF SELF-NEGATION

"Our kingdom go" is the necessary and unavoidable corollary of "Thy kingdom come." For the more there is of self, the less there is of God.

—Aldous Huxley (1894–1963), *The Perennial Philosophy*

I still remember the experiment from science class. Mr. Reed, our teacher, turned an empty glass upside down in a basin of water. Even though he pushed the glass down, the water somehow could not fill it up. The reason was no less profound for being elementary. The glass was *not* empty. So long as air molecules filled the top part of the inverted glass, there was simply no place for the water. No room in the inn. The air had to be leaked out before the water could replace it.

Similarly, so long as we are full of ourselves, by which I mean our limited, everyday selves, there is no room for anything else. It's like preparing what we are going to say while someone else is speaking. By concentrating on our own thoughts, we can't take in those of the speaker. We may hear the words, but we are not able to attend to them.

This physicslike principle is the reason so many mystical traditions emphasize the *via negativa,* or path of purification. By practicing the various disciplines, from fasts to vigils, from meditation to contemplation, we clean our spiritual house and little by little become available to receive instructions and guidance from our higher self. Our inner ears must likewise be opened to hear the "still, small voice." Our will also undergoes purification so that we are eventually able to follow the guidance we receive. Then we can say with Jesus, "Not my will but thy will be done," and we can turn our inner promptings into reality.

Surrender is a hard word for us in the West. Yet in turning our will and our lives over to God, we allow our Higher Power to enter, awaken, and train us to realize our highest possibilities. That is the promise of the way of self-negation.

Have you ever practiced some form of self-negation? If so, discuss the experience and results in your Wisdom Journal.

THE WISDOM OF SLOWING DOWN

The world is too much with us, late and soon,
Getting and spending, we lay waste our powers:
Little we see in Nature that is ours;
We have given our hearts away, a sordid boon!

–William Wordsworth (1770–1850),
"The World Is Too Much with Us"

At my boarding school back in the 1950s, boys got points for their various extracurricular activities. If you captained a team or edited the yearbook, you got bonus points for leadership. At Prize Day, as the assistant headmaster intoned the names of the runners-up, I wondered if I might be among them. Guess not. Then turning to me, Mr. Roman said my name, adding: "This prize normally goes to seniors. This year our winner is a junior. Mr. Feldman, please come forward."

My mother always wondered why I could never slow down. I was a classic case of "What makes Sammy run?" What, indeed! I always needed to achieve, to be first. This mania continued on to college. I graduated, four years after entering, with a host of honors. The greatest "achievement" of my schooldays, however, was getting 100 percent from the Baptist minister who taught the required religion course at my prep school. How unchristian was my rejoicing at having beaten the Christian boys in learning about their own religion!

Now, at the age of sixty, I have discovered that I am pretty good at *il dólce far' niènte,* the sweet art of doing nothing. The problem is, I don't do it nearly enough. Here we live in Hawaii, a place that people scrimp and save for all their lives to visit once for a week or two. Moreover, we are a fifteen-minute drive from one of the world's top beaches. Yet it takes Simone's tactical nagging to get us there at least twice a month, and then, typically, for only an hour.

My goal this year is finally to slow down. I intend to pursue it vigorously!

Inventory your activity level. Is it too high? If not, how do you keep to a reasonable pace? If so, list in your Wisdom Journal three things you'll do this year to slow down.

THE WISDOM OF SUFFICIENCY

Remember this, – that very little is needed to make a happy life.

–Marcus Aurelius (121–180)

So far I have spared you one of my most bothersome character defects: I love to pun. Well, I can resist no longer. When it comes to the issue of sufficiency, the wisdom is all French. *Un oeuf* is *un oeuf!*

If Marcus Aurelius is right, happiness consists in having few wants. The fewer the wants, the more likely they can be fulfilled. Wishing for the moon requires being an astronaut. And even NASA isn't sending folks there these days.

My friend and mentor, the late Varindra Tarzie Vittachi of UNICEF, used to tell of his first major assignment as a journalist for the *Ceylon Times*. World War II had just ended. British Ceylon was on its way to becoming independent Sri Lanka. Through the good offices of his wife's father, a Ceylonese official in India, the young journalist wangled the opportunity to interview the Mahatma Gandhi. For that occasion Vittachi constructed this question: "Gandhiji, now that we in Asia are about to become free, what advice would you give us?" Gandhi paused, his face purpling in reflection, as Vittachi put it. Then Gandhi turned to Vittachi and said: "Decrease your wants. Fulfill your needs."

That's the trick, of course. Figuring out the few things needful and sloughing off all the rest. Learning to pack and travel light. The more desires we stuff into our knapsacks, the more likely we are to throw out our backs. Yet surrounded by great material abundance, we find it hard to be satisfied with just a few things. As my kids like to say, we are high-maintenance people.

According to Diogenes Laertes, who lived one hundred years after the Emperor Marcus Aurelius, Socrates made the point this way: "Those who want the fewest things are nearest to the gods." How close are we?

Do you travel lightly through the desire patch of life? What three things might you do to decrease your wants and fulfill your needs? Confide these ideas to your Wisdom Journal and let them germinate.

THE WISDOM OF DEATH AS REBIRTH

In the span extending from infancy to old age we are ripening for another birth. Another beginning awaits us, another status. . . . That day which you dread as the end is your birth into eternity.

–Seneca (4 B.C.E.?–65 C.E.)

Janus was the Roman god of beginnings and endings. Depicted with two faces, he looked to both past and future. I remember the thrill when I first understood that while *graduation* means moving on, that other Latin-derived word, *commencement,* means starting. Here was a Janus-like ritual of completion that was also a new beginning. "My end is my beginning" was the motto of an early American flag, with the mystic serpent forming a perfect circle, its tail in its mouth. "The king is dead, long live the king!"

As the chronological likelihood of my death approaches, I take solace in Seneca's insight. From spirit to body we come. From body to spirit we go. From the spiritual to the material. From the material back to the spiritual. Dust to dust. But also, breath to breath.

My Sri Lankan friend Varindra told me that his grandmother started every story she ever told in the same way, "Brahma breathes in, Brahma breathes out." Then she would continue, "Once there was a princess . . ."

Now as to whether there is nothing after physical death, or a new physical life of some kind (reincarnation), or a sort of undifferentiated spiritual existence as when a raindrop rejoins the ocean, or an eternal spiritual life of reward or punishment, I suppose each of us will just have to wait to find out. Frankly, I feel least inclined to the eternal-reward-or-eternal-punishment scenario. Nothingness at the end also doesn't sit right with my intuition, though I prefer it to the heaven-or-hell model. Even though it is not what I was brought up with, some kind of reincarnation makes the most sense to me, like a mastery-education approach where you keep at your learning task until you get it right. Time will tell whether my inclination, intuition, or logical sense is most accurate. But I'm in no hurry to reach that graduation. Or commencement.

What do you think will happen after death? Sit quietly for five minutes, then write freely on this topic in your Wisdom Journal.

UNEXPECTED WISDOM

. . . For those who fear
God, He (ever) prepares
A way out,
And He provides for him
From (sources) he never
Could imagine.

–The Koran, Sura lxv, 2–3

I learned this lesson in 1958 as an exchange student in Germany. Between semesters another American student and I did some traveling. Our last stop was Munich.

On a dreary autumn day, Douglas and I caught the local to the nearby village of Dachau. The German government had not yet erected the memorial museum on the site of the death camp. In fact, after arriving we had no idea how to find it and didn't want to ask the locals. After wandering around in the bone-chilling drizzle, we stumbled on a U.S. military compound. "This way," the M.P. said. "It's right here on post."

Incredibly, Douglas and I were the only visitors there that afternoon. At one point, alone, I encountered two pizza-style ovens that had been left intact, their doors wide open. Spontaneously I put my right index finger through the grate and, with the retrieved ash or rust, drew a capital "J" on the back of my left hand. Talkative as I am, I somehow failed to share the experience with Douglas.

The next day, on the express back to Heidelberg, two leather-coated men in their forties joined us in our compartment. They asked us about ourselves. Douglas answered first, saying he was an American exchange student of German ancestry. "I'm an American exchange student, too," I said, "but my ancestors were all Jewish." They began to protest their ignorance of the camps. But I didn't care about them. You see, I had carefully hidden my Jewishness during my four previous months in Germany–afraid of how people might react. In fact, I had generally been ashamed of being a Jew even in the States, where there had been no Holocaust. Suddenly I remembered the day before. I knew. The six million had not died totally in vain. This was their gift to me. I never again denied my Jewish identity.

In your Wisdom Journal, write about how a significant problem was resolved in a way beyond your expectations.

THE WISDOM OF COMPARTMENTALIZING

When climbing, don't look up or down. Just concentrate on where to place your next step.

–Advice given to novice climbers

President Clinton, like a good climber, had a way of concentrating on his next step. I recall when the U.S. Senate was close to its decision on whether to remove Clinton from office. There was the president, presenting his budget on TV, making speeches, shaking the hands of well-wishers, even looking relaxed and happy with his wife who, for her part, looked happy too.

The word often used to describe Clinton's ability to keep working, living, eating, and sleeping despite being waist deep in investigations and scandal was *compartmentalization.* Like the *Titanic,* whose many airtight compartments were supposed to render it unsinkable, Mr. Clinton seemed able to detach himself from the difficulties of the moment and concentrate on his job. And he had more success than the famous ship.

My father was no Bill Clinton, but he did have some of this ability. For example, he could lose himself in a book. I remember my mother's nightly routine: "Jack. Jack! It's midnight. Put that book away. You can read some more tomorrow." No answer. "Jack!!!" Still no answer. As she shuffled off, defeated again, a sincere-sounding "Wha?" came from the general direction of my father's chair. He hadn't heard a thing. Or take his work. As a commodities broker, he dealt with millions each day. Yet he never brought his work home. I asked him once how he did it. "Easy, Kid," he said in his New York accent. "It's all just telephone numbers to me." He was a regular yogi of the Board of Trade.

While I don't condone the actions that got President Clinton into trouble, I can compartmentalize enough myself to appreciate the good things he did for the country. After all, in this imperfect world, no one is perfect, especially our leaders. Next to such biblical paragons as Kings David and Solomon, whose misdeeds included murder and adultery, President Clinton comes across like the Eagle Scout he once was. I can also appreciate his ability–and my father's–to concentrate on the matter at hand. I hope to become a better compartmentalizer myself.

Assess your compartmentalizing skills in your Wisdom Journal.

THE WISDOM OF GROWING OLD GRACEFULLY

To know how to grow old is the master work of wisdom, and one of the most difficult chapters in the great art of living.

–Henri-Frédéric Amiel (1821–1881)

Growing old, assuming our life is prolonged to old age, is not optional. Whether or not we grow old gracefully is. Science may help us retain our health. Art, however, is required for us to know how best to use the life and health that we have.

As in most things, our attitude is key. I was lucky. Because I skipped the eighth grade, I was always younger than my peers. This was doubly true in my boarding school, because boys often elected to repeat a grade on entering to give themselves a better chance of being accepted by a top college. As a result I was two, even three, years younger than my classmates. Thus to this day, I always feel younger than everybody else. I sound young on the telephone too. Now in my sixtieth year, I am occasionally asked by car-rental agents if I am over twenty-five, old enough to rent. My daughters, now both adults, report that when they lived at home and I answered the phone, their boyfriends would ask, "Who's the dude?" They knew the girls had no brother. So when Marianna or Christine would say, "My dad," the boyfriends would reply, "Yeah. Sure."

Fortunately my hair has now turned white, so the checkout clerks at supermarkets routinely ask if I need help out to the car. I am also sometimes offered senior discounts on things. All is not lost.

In his essay on aging, Cicero, senator and moralist during Rome's Golden Age, wrote, "For as I like a young man in whom there is something of the old, so I like an old man in whom there is something of the young; and he who follows this maxim, in body will possibly be an old man, but he will never be an old man in his mind." As Cicero suggests, growing old gracefully means staying young inside.

Write in your Wisdom Journal about how your last big birthday felt. How are you coping with the prospect of getting older?

WARRIOR WISDOM

"The hardest thing in the world is to assume the mood of a warrior," he said. "It is of no use to be sad and complain and feel justified in doing so, believing that someone is always doing something to us. Nobody is doing anything to anybody, much less to a warrior."

–DON JUAN'S ADVICE TO CARLOS IN CASTANEDA'S *JOURNEY TO IXTLAN*, 1972

Those of us who became college teachers in the 1960s were a liberal crew with an antimilitary bias. Being just the right age for Vietnam, we looked for ways to avoid participating in that war. We didn't want to kill or be killed. Let the dominoes fall, we thought. We'd go to Canada.

I was married and had a daughter by September 1966, and was a college teacher to boot, so I was given a deferment. When illustrating the literary term *oxymoron*, a paradoxical phrase, in Intro to Poetry, however, I couldn't resist the smart-aleck example then making the rounds: "military intelligence." Now there was an oxymoron – ha, ha, ha!

In 1972–73, while teaching English for the University of Maryland on military bases in Germany, I began to see military personnel for the human beings they had always been. Some are still friends. I learned that in many rural towns, especially in the South and Southwest, military service was the golden road to free education, world travel, and a life beyond pumping gas down the street.

Military wisdom is all about courage, discipline, preparedness, and understanding one's opponents. The word *strategy* is derived from the Greek for "general." The term represents the art and science of achieving military objectives. True – sometimes these objectives would be achieved through organized violence. (I still prefer the military as a deterrent, not as an active force.) But through observing professional soldiers, reading the Bhagavad-Gita (in which Arjuna, a principle character, is a warrior), and learning with Carlos from Don Juan about the impeccability of the warrior, I began to see how "military wisdom" might not be the contradiction in terms it at first seemed to be.

Have you ever been in the military? The Scouts? Some other regimented group? Discuss in your Wisdom Journal what wisdom you derived from this experience.

WISDOM AND MUTABILITY

At high tide fish eat ants; at low tide ants eat fish.

–A THAI PROVERB

In Chicago, where I lived for twenty years, people would say: "If you don't like the weather, just wait. It will change." This principle was an article of faith in the Middle Ages. We were all – individuals, families, cities, kingdoms – on a great wheel of fortune. If we happened to be on top now, just wait. But the same held true if we happened to be on the bottom. Every dog would have its day, over and over again, as well as its night. Pride went before a fall, but by the same token, humility preceded a rise.

This theory of perpetual oscillation between extremes complements the two classical conceptions of history: degeneration from an Edenic Golden Age through Silver and Bronze to an Age of Iron and the more recent idea of progress, whether linear or of the two-steps-forward-one-step-back variety.

In a universe that seems averse to stasis, "just wait" is a useful strategy for living. It also helps one to deal with occasional bouts of envy or greed.

The valedictorian of my prep-school graduating class was a nice guy. I generally came in second or third to him academically. Regardless of what I did, he maintained his edge. Whether he was smarter or worked harder or both, I'll never know. His pace was just too fast. After prep school we both attended Yale. I stayed on for graduate school, but he went on to law school at Harvard or Columbia. Years later, at our twenty-fifth reunion, I saw him for the first time since senior year. He was still handsome, friendly, and unaffected by his success as a Wall Street lawyer.

A few years later, I read an announcement of his death in our school alumni magazine. No details were given. I found his number and called his widow. After giving my condolences, I learned that he had died in a freak accident while on a barge trip through England's canals. Failing to notice an oncoming low bridge, he was struck and killed on the spot. How quickly things can change! I was ashamed of my envy.

Write for ten minutes in your Wisdom Journal about an experience you have had with the wheel of fortune.

THE WISDOM OF FAILURE

For the pure scientist, a failed experiment is no failure at all but a vital step toward learning the truth.

–Parker J. Palmer, *The Active Life*, 1991

In our success-oriented culture, failure can be a fate worse than death. One remembers the stories of exmillionaires throwing themselves from Wall Street windows after losing fortunes in the 1929 stock market crash. How can there be wisdom in failure?

John Holt, author of *Why Children Fail*, liked to play Twenty Questions in elementary-school classrooms he would visit. For those of you not yet of a certain age, Twenty Questions was a radio game show in which celebrity panelists tried to find the identity of something in twenty questions or less. The only clue was whether the target was animal, mineral, or vegetable. So Holt would say to the children, "I am thinking of a number between one and 1,000." First question, "Is it between one and 500?" "No," responded Holt. "Aw," said the disappointed children. Their first answer had been wasted. Or so they thought.

However, Holt went on to explain to them that a "No" answer was just as useful as a "Yes." In both cases the field was narrowed by fifty percent. But because our society equates "Yes" with being correct, the elementary-school children were already unable to see the usefulness of their "mistake."

Through failures we can build a pathway to success. Failed businesses help us to see what needs to be done better to achieve profits. Failed relationships, if properly understood, can equip us for making healthier choices next time. Jobs that don't work out can give us insight into our true talents and enable us to know the sort of work that will be best for us. In my case academic administration was something I learned to do. That I got fired from two administrative positions, while not altogether my fault, nevertheless helped me to understand that this sort of work was not my calling. My belief is that our Higher Power guides us with "No" as well as "Yes." Wisdom is knowing that failure is often the springboard to success.

In your Wisdom Journal, discuss a "failure" that ended up helping you to a better life.

THE WISDOM OF IMPECCABILITY

"You should learn to live the impeccable life of a warrior."

–DON JUAN'S ADVICE TO CARLOS IN CASTANEDA'S *JOURNEY TO IXTLAN*, 1972

When World War II ended, my future wife, Simone, was nearly fourteen. With her mother and older sister, she had fled from the oncoming Russian front in her native East Prussia, then the remotest part of the German Reich. The three women arrived in Munich during an air raid. They had only the clothes on their backs, some baby things, and a few photo albums. They spent their first night in a bomb shelter. They were lucky to be alive.

Simone is no friend of war. Yet I think Carlos Castaneda's mentor, the Yaqui Indian sorcerer Don Juan Matus, would have found her an "impeccable warrior." In 1950 she was attending secretarial school by day and working at the village movie theater by night. She sold tickets, ushered, changed reels, and cleaned up after shows. The job didn't pay much, but work was scarce at the time. One evening she left her new leather wallet in the projection booth. When she returned, it was gone. A gift, the wallet had contained forty marks, a lot of money in those days, plus irreplaceable family photos. She cried and prayed. The wallet and money were one thing. But the pictures!

Two weeks later the wallet was recovered in a nearby hotel men's room. Only the money was missing. Simone was elated. Not long after that, while cleaning the theater, she found another wallet, this one bulging with bills plus an ID card. The owner was quickly located. The next evening a well-dressed man approached Simone just before the show. "Excuse me, Fräulein. I understand that you found my wallet. The officer also told me that yours was recently taken and that you lost forty marks. If you don't mind, I'd like to give you these forty marks for finding mine." Don Juan might have commented that the universe had approved of Simone's impeccability.

In your Wisdom Journal, describe an occasion when you acted "impeccably." What was the outcome? How did you feel?

THE WISDOM OF DENIAL?

... Why should [the young] know their fate,
Since sorrow never comes too late,
And happiness too swiftly flies?
Thought would disturb their paradise.
No more; where ignorance is bliss,
'Tis folly to be wise.

–Thomas Gray (1716–1771),
"On a Distant Prospect of Eton College"

In these well-known lines, English poet Thomas Gray is using *wisdom* as a synonym for *knowledge*. The reason is obvious. *Wise* rhymes with *paradise*. Where youthful ignorance is bliss, he is saying, it is foolish for young people to know too much about life.

Another formal consideration is also at work. The larger poem, of which these lines are a part, is technically an elegy. Elegies express nostalgia for the past, in this case represented by youth's Eden-like time (in the poet's view) at Eton College. (Note that even the two words *Eton* and *Eden* sound alike.) Gray's point seems to be that burdening the mind of young people with thoughts of life's difficulties, illness, old age, and death would do them a disservice. They will find out soon enough for themselves.

But is denying these realities really wise? Isn't it better to tell young people the truth? Not to sour youth on life, but to vaccinate them against unrealistic expectations and the resulting disappointments.

I can see advantages and disadvantages to both approaches. Perhaps it is an individual matter, depending upon the young person's temperament. As a prep-school graduate myself, I do think Gray romanticizes boarding-school life. In my recollection it was less than blissful.

There is certainly something to be said, of course, for not taking away the magic of belief in Santa Claus too early, but allowing it to fall away on its own. On the other hand, a twenty-year-old who still believes in the elf's existence would be a candidate for therapy. I also think of my cats, who don't get stressed about a trip to the vet until they are in the car. Why disturb them before it is necessary?

What is your take on when and how to enlighten children about the realities of life? Discuss it briefly in your Wisdom Journal.

THE WISDOM OF DYING IN PEACE

The more we have made our lives meaningful, the less we will regret at the time of death. The way we feel when we come to die is thus very much dependent on the way we have lived.

–His Holiness the Dalai Lama, *The Joy of Living and Dying in Peace*, 1997

The theme of death is important to me these days. In fact, as I write, I am in Miami for my mother's funeral. She died ten days ago at age ninety-five.

I remember my father's death twelve years earlier. Six days after his eighty-first birthday, he died of bone-marrow cancer. As a child my father had been force-fed orthodox Judaism by his mother, the daughter of a scribe. When his father left his mother for an extended separation, Father, then fifteen and the oldest of three sons, began supporting the family but stopped attending synagogue. From then on the hassles, but also the consolations, of religion, belonged to others, never to him. For a variety of reasons, I became religious, while my sister, like our father, remained secular.

My mother was a caring sister and good friend. Had she been born later and in other circumstances, she might have become a social worker. Instead she was a housewife who loved shopping and who, in later life, helped raise my widowed sister's three children. In her early eighties, her short-term memory started to go, and by the age of ninety, she was in the grips of senile dementia. On a positive note, her personal intensity, characteristic of her middle years, also left her, to be replaced by a playful side. After a week in the hospital, she fell asleep for the last time, without tubes, in the hospice unit.

The older I get, the better job my parents seem to have done–in parenting and in living. Both died relatively peaceful, effortless deaths. I pray the same for myself and others I know.

How are you preparing for death? What impact does its inevitability have on your life choices? Respond to these questions in your Wisdom Journal.

THE WISDOM OF FASTING

If . . . the individual comprehends the real meaning of fasting and, through the observation of his own heart, ascertains its place and value in the journey on the road to the hereafter, he will not fail to find out where the welfare of his heart lies.

–Al-Ghazzali, "The Mysteries of Fasting," c. 1100

As I write these words, it is midway through the Ramadan fast. My ethnic and religious backgrounds notwithstanding, I have attempted this fast some twenty-five times since 1970. That first time, while I was on staff at Hawaii's East-West Center, I was supported by Muslim fellow fasters from Indonesia, Malaysia, and Pakistan. It was a bit like doing the marathon with a group of running mates. I remember headaches, spaciness, and lots of looking at my watch for the magic hour of break-fast to arrive. There was also the awkwardness of going to lunch meetings, not eating, then having to explain.

For those unfamiliar with Ramadan fasting, one does not eat, drink, or smoke between dawn and dusk for a lunar month. Ramadan commemorates the time the Prophet Muhammad first received the Koran. Muslims believe the heavens are especially open during this month and that the fast – an annual requirement – is an excellent way for strengthening one's connection. The hardest part, however, is the "inner" fast. No gossiping, criticizing, "looking at wrong things," or getting angry for a whole month. Now there's a fast!

For those raised in a culture of instant gratification, fasting may seem like a ritual created by sadists for masochists. I can only say that the practice has borne many fruits for me. Last year, for example, was a financial roller coaster. A few months after Ramadan, my two major consulting accounts were withdrawn. Rather than freaking out, I was still sufficiently enveloped in quietness to approach my situation creatively. Things are now back on track. Many religious traditions include opportunities to fast. Based on my experience, I am convinced of the wisdom of fasting, not just for the hereafter but for the here and now.

Have you ever fasted? If not, take a day-long sabbatical from anger or critical remarks. Describe the experience in your Wisdom Journal.

THE WISDOM OF SPEAKING FROM WITHIN

The more we receive in silent prayer, the more we can give in our active life. We need silence to be able to touch souls. The essential thing is not what we say, but what God says to us and through us.

-MOTHER TERESA OF CALCUTTA, *A GIFT FOR GOD,* 1975

According to an old tradition, when we speak our best, it is not our ordinary self speaking but the divine element within us. This is the literal meaning of *inspiration* (being filled with the spirit) and *enthusiasm* (having the god-force, *theos,* within).

When we speak from this place, our listeners are rapt–caught up in spirit–and moved. Consider the disciples on Pentecost, filled with the Spirit, empowered to proclaim the risen Jesus in many foreign tongues. The Holy Spirit, *ta hagia ta pneuma,* is a wind that blows where it wishes and takes all things with it. An African American spiritual suggests one result of such an experience: "Every time I feel the Spirit moving in my heart, I will pray." Coming forth from that experience, we ought not be surprised to hear inspired speech.

About to be sent on his historic mission to pharaoh, Moses complained to God that he, Moses, was "slow of tongue." God counseled him not to worry, for He, the Lord, would do the talking. All Moses had to do was show up. Jesus similarly advised the disciples not to be concerned about what to say on their mission trips, because the Spirit would give them the right words. Or, in shamanic cultures, spirit-guides possess the adepts, enabling them to give messages of prophecy or healing.

I have experienced something like this on two occasions. Once as I was addressing a psychology class at a university in Jakarta about an East-West Center project and on another occasion during a professional lecture in Saint Paul. In both cases I talked freely, as if from an invisible script another had prepared, while observing both myself and the audience. These were perhaps the most effective talks I have ever given.

Have you ever felt inspired while speaking publicly or privately? Recount the experience in your Wisdom Journal.

STEROID WISDOM

I ran against a Prejudice
That quite cut off the view.

–Charlotte Perkins Stetson Gilman (1860–1935),
"The Obstacle"

Early in my sophomore year at Yale, I woke up one night with a sharp pain in my chest. It was the first of several times I thought I was dying. My roommate, Terry Reilly, got up, called a cab, and accompanied me to the Yale infirmary. I was not dying, but had fallen victim to the Asian flu. It was autumn 1957. There was a nationwide epidemic. Colleges had been hit especially hard.

In my case, according to Dr. Nixon's diagnosis, the disease had been complicated by pneumonia and a touch of pleurisy. Apparently I had inherited my paternal grandmother's weak lungs. She had contracted tuberculosis as a teenager, but was now in her mid-eighties, which was good news for me. (She lived to be ninety-four.)

My various lung diseases could be controlled by round-the-clock doses of penicillin. But I had a scary reaction to the wonder drug. My whole body swelled up, I itched as if I were one giant mosquito bite, and I had trouble breathing. The cure proved worse than the disease. A worried Dr. Nixon showed up with a mean-looking syringe. "Cortisone," he said. "Anything," I wheezed. "Just help me breathe." Later the syringe held ACTH, another wonder drug, to undo the damage of the first. A day or two later, out of danger, I could breathe normally. I spent the rest of the term recovering.

Not surprisingly I have maintained a lifelong prejudice against drugs. I'll become a veritable pincushion for acupuncture needles before getting a prescription filled. Recently, though, I told my HMO doctor I was fed up with my bursitis, with having to cry out every time I took off my undershirt. "Well," she said, "There's always the cortisone shot." "Isn't cortisone a steroid?" I countered. She said, "You're not trying out for the Olympics, are you?" "Okay, Doc," I capitulated, "you win. This is the place in my right shoulder." Two days later, for the first time in ten years, I was pain-free.

In your Wisdom Journal, write about some prejudice you have overcome.

THE WISDOM OF EQUANIMITY

Whoever yields himself to joy, forgetful of his former poverty, is very unwise, for he forgets also that pure reverence for the Lord which fears to lose grace already given. Nor is he wise who, in trouble and adversity, yields to despair, and fails to put his trust in Me.

–THOMAS À KEMPIS (1379–1471), *THE IMITATION OF CHRIST*

In one of the *Apu* movies by Bengali director Satyajit Ray, a young Brahmin dives into a lake and just floats. The camera remains on the youth ten seconds, twenty seconds. No movement. That image of the floating Brahmin stayed in my mind for years. Then one day I read in a classical Hindu text (the *Apastamba Dharma Sutra*) that a Brahmin should not "sport in the water whilst bathing; / let him swim motionless like a stick." Water, a symbol for the Great Life Force of Brahman, will carry us if we learn to relax and float.

In many traditions equanimity – not swinging too high in good times nor too low in bad – is the ideal. In Thomas à Kempis's *Imitation of Christ*, we are advised not to yield to either extreme. Instead we are to trust that whatever befalls us is part of God's plan. If we have done our best and things are still not right, our job is to accept what is and move on.

What a difficult lesson! I have known from my teen years that this is the best way to live. My spiritual path since age twenty-one has been in part to help me moderate my mood swings. Still, developing good mental hygiene does not come easily.

The middle way is subtle. To be sure, equanimity does not require giving up fun. And living a life of puritanical rigor or animal seriousness may have negative effects on mental and spiritual health. For biochemical reasons, lots of laughter and aerobic exercise do wonders. A diet of dancing, tennis, or volleyball, for example, is one of the best ways to stay on an even keel. Also, getting enough sleep. Not a bad way to sail!

In your Wisdom Journal, discuss how you maintain your serenity. Write about what you learned from the last time you lost your cool.

GRAY-FLANNEL WISDOM

"Geronimo!" a lot of the men used to yell as they jumped, trying to sound fierce as hell. Tom used to yell it too when it was expected of him, but what he was really thinking, with a curiously comforting air of detachment, was "It doesn't really matter." And then, just as Tom went through the door into the prop blast, the second part of the charm had always come to him: "Here goes nothing." And when the parachute had opened, . . . the third part of his incantation had always come to him: "It will be interesting to see what happens."

–SLOAN WILSON, *THE MAN IN THE GRAY FLANNEL SUIT*, 1955

The mind is like flypaper. It traps ideas, images, and phrases that suit our needs. I read Sloan Wilson's postwar novel on my trip to Germany. All I recall of the novel now is the protagonist's routine as a paratrooper during World War II – a routine that would also help him negotiate the career obstacle course after the war.

I cannot speak as a paratrooper, but I feel that the nihilism of the first two sentences of the incantation is not winning. I would hate to think that what I do or don't do is irrelevant to myself, those around me, or my community. While my daily actions are not all-important – whose are? – they are certainly not "nothing." Acts, committed or omitted, do matter. Ask a single mom who is still awaiting last month's child-support check. Think about the parent who boxed his kid's ear so hard the child had a hearing problem ever after. Or, for a positive example, consider the dad who kept from yelling at his daughter who had just totaled the family car, making it possible for her to ask his advice five years later on a serious relationship problem.

The third statement is more promising. Curiosity may have killed a few cats, but it does facilitate our putting one foot in front of the other. If nothing else, it helps us understand the effects that come from certain causes. For instance, people who show love never seem at a loss for friends.

In fairness, even the first two statements are not totally foolish. By scaling down our expectations, we keep from setting ourselves up for disappointment.

Do you have some words you live by? In your Wisdom Journal, write about how they help you get through life.

HISTORICAL WISDOM

BILL MOYERS: Do you see any evidence that we really take away lessons from the library, from the past, that make us different, that cause us to change course before we hit the iceberg?

VARTAN GREGORIAN: I absolutely do. But whether we're willing to change course or not – that's different.

-BILL MOYERS, *A WORLD OF IDEAS,* 1989

Was it George Santayana who said, "Those unwilling to learn the lessons of the past are doomed to repeat them"? If so, Bartlett's let me down. It is a memorable statement. I heard it enough times in college, and rightly so. That is what college is for, at least in part: to acquaint us contemporary provincials with some of the earlier scenes and actors in the great tragicomedy of human existence.

We attempt, individually, to learn from the past and from others by reading biography and personal journals. James Boswell (1740–1795), considered the most famous literary journal-keeper in English, used his, he said, to adjust his character as milady used her mirror to adjust her toilet. And Dr. Samuel Johnson, the subject of Boswell's famous biography, told Boswell that biography was his favorite type of book. By studying the lives of others, he said, he could draw lessons for his own.

Historians provide us with the same kind of perspective on a larger scale. Another eighteenth-century Englishman, Edward Gibbon, attempted in his three-volume treatment to tease out the moral causes of the decline and fall of Rome. A twentieth-century compatriot, Arnold Toynbee, studied the life cycles of civilizations in general. Have we improved as individuals or peoples over time? Have we individually or collectively learned from the past? Or are we like Napoleon III, about whom historian A. J. P. Taylor commented, "Like most of those who study history, he learned from the mistakes of the past how to make new ones"? The jury is still out. But I hope we never stop trying.

What is the major lesson you think people in the twenty-first century should draw from the twentieth? Why? Sketch out an answer in your Wisdom Journal.

INNER-WEATHER WISDOM

. . . Tree, I have seen you taken and tossed,
And if you have seen me when I slept,
You have seen me when I was taken and swept
And all but lost.

That day she put our heads together,
Fate had her imagination about her,
Your head so much concerned with outer,
Mine with inner, weather.

–Robert Frost (1874–1963), "Tree at My Window"

Robert Frost had a way of saying profound things in the simple, spare, folksy language of his native New England. This particular poem is about loneliness and companionship. Each of us is blown about by our own thoughts and feelings. Things rise up in us from who knows where. During the daytime we can suppress or divert these unwelcome visitors. We can pursue long-term strategies like meditation, prayer, or the mental-hygiene techniques of the Twelve Step program to help us negotiate the sometimes rough weather of our inner life. We may even be able to change our inner content. Yet when we are asleep, all bets are off. Suddenly we are an airplane loaded with passengers and cargo that may not make it off the ground before the runway ends.

Like trees in a storm, we are blown and tossed. Life is like that. There are windy days – and nights. Even occasional gales and hurricanes. Yet as the Vietnamese Buddhist monk Thich Nhat Hanh observes, while the smaller leaves and branches of a tree are moved by the wind, its trunk remains firm – a phenomenon caused by the trunk's greater size and weight combined with the stability provided by an extensive root system.

By seeing the relationship between himself and the tree outside his window, the poet is no longer alone. By witnessing how the tree weathers storm after storm, he gains a new perspective. He, too, can somehow get through the inner storms of life. And so can we.

How do you deal with the inner windstorms that occasionally visit you? In your Wisdom Journal, write about the techniques you use.

LAUGHING WISDOM

I call no man wise until he has made the progress from the wisdom of knowledge to the wisdom of foolishness, and become a laughing philosopher, feeling first life's tragedy and then life's comedy. For we must weep before we can laugh. Out of sadness comes the awakening and out of the awakening comes the laughter of the philosopher, with kindliness and tolerance to boot.

–LIN YUTANG, *THE IMPORTANCE OF LIVING*, 1937

In my spiritual practice, the founder would test our progress by asking us questions and inviting us to respond spontaneously, without volition or thought. He would do this during periodic world tours when he would visit larger centers. Two years after my initiation, undertaken by several of his disciples, I had my first occasion to meet this gentleman. The place was New York City, the year was 1963. I was twenty-three years old.

After giving a talk on aspects of the spiritual practice, he asked four or five of us to come forward to test our progress. There were hundreds in the audience, but because work had kept me from attending a just-concluded two-week world congress and seminar, I decided to volunteer. One of his questions was, "Can you sing?" Now this did not mean coming out with "You Are My Sunshine" or some other tune memorized in childhood; a song had to arise by itself from within us. We all came out with a different single tone that sounded like "hoo." Our leader chuckled, then said, "The question was not, 'Can you make the sound of a boat?' but 'Can you sing?'" Now everyone laughed, including the five of us.

Later he tested whether we could cry and laugh in that same spontaneous way. I discovered I could cry, but laughing was another matter. It took until 1981 before I could manifest the inner capacity to laugh. So my experience dovetails with Lin Yutang's description. Laughter may well be one of the later gifts on the path of spiritual development.

Sit quietly. Now try to laugh. Discuss this experience in your Wisdom Journal.

LEGISLATIVE WISDOM

O God, the fountain of wisdom, whose statutes are good and gracious and whose law is truth: We beseech thee so to guide and bless the Legislature of this State, that it may ordain for our governance only such things as please thee, to the glory of thy Name and the welfare of the people; through Jesus Christ, thy Son, our Lord. Amen.

–PRAYER FOR A STATE LEGISLATURE, *BOOK OF COMMON PRAYER*, 1789

The Elizabethan cadences of Thomas Cranmer (1489–1556), the first Anglican Archbishop of Canterbury, survived our Revolution and are found in this first Episcopal prayer book in America. The initial *Book of Common Prayer*, published by Cranmer in 1549, contained translations or adaptations of the Latin texts then in use by the Catholic church. Although the terminology and content soon became more Protestant, all later versions have retained the organlike word flow that makes this book an accepted landmark of English prose.

American, of course, is the reference to state legislatures. True democratic deliberative bodies did not exist in Cranmer's day. The above prayer highlights one aspect of the separation between church and state in our country. While a particular religion is not to be established, as in England, and while the state is to remain secular, different faiths are free to invoke the deity to aid and guide government. Lord knows, with the vying interests of their constituents, the people's representatives have always needed as much help as they can get, secular or sacred.

In the religious view, God is the source of all wisdom, and God's statutes, based on truth, are universally beneficial. The same does not generally hold for human regulations. So if legislators were granted the wisdom of creating laws in accordance with divine law, the people, religious adherents believe, would be well served.

Taking the long view or considering the big picture characterizes the best public representatives in our secular republic. Given our all-too-human nature, however, prayer for wise governance is still a good idea.

What is your view of "legislative wisdom"? In your Wisdom Journal, briefly discuss what you think sage governance would entail.

LIFELONG WISDOM

Wisdom is not a product of schooling but of the lifelong attempt to acquire it.

–Albert Einstein (1879–1955)

As a teacher I always have trouble with statements like this. After all, I once taught a course called "The Literature of Wisdom." You can say, I suppose, that formal education is not where wisdom should be taught. It is enough if schools instill basic intellectual skills, transmit cultural values, and prepare one for a vocation. In fact, you might say that wisdom is unteachable, even unlearnable. At best, wisdom may be caught, not taught. Look at the hard time Jesus had with what our pastor likes to call the "duh-sciples." There they were, first-row witnesses to his miracles. They were even empowered to do some of their own during his lifetime. He, meanwhile, was perhaps the greatest teacher in human history. Yet they never seemed fully to believe in him or comprehend who he was.

For anyone who has had a hard time in school, it is heartening to learn that geniuses like Einstein and Edison either dropped out or were kicked out of school. In traditional schools teachers represent the power and authority of the older generation and its ideas. All talk about Socratic method notwithstanding, teachers of this kind know what's what, and it's the student's job not to question them but to accept and learn what they offer up as truth. They form a kind of secular missionary corps. Their pupils are underaged heathens who must be civilized. In this model, students are not encouraged to present divergent ideas or to tap their native wisdom.

Fortunately each of us also attends the larger private school of life. It continues as long as we do, tuition is free, and special admission programs are unnecessary. We all get individualized tutoring at no extra cost, and every class has a required lab. According to one theory, we have to retake courses until we master the material. It is a cause for hope that no less a personage than Albert Einstein thought attendance in this school might eventually help us to become wise.

In your Wisdom Journal, discuss how the School of Hard Knocks has produced a measure of wisdom in your life.

LOST-AND-FOUND WISDOM

A wise man never loses anything if he have himself.

-Michel de Montaigne (1533–1592)

The prayer hot line really heats up when we can't find something important. In my case it would be an object like the daily calendar in which I note consulting hours worked, or last year's IRS Form 1040 needed for a loan application, or – God forbid! – my wallet. What makes matters worse is that I generally discover an item is missing just when it is needed and there is no time to look. Our hectic lifestyle makes losing things hazardous to our health and the health of those around us. In our moment of frustration, the easy thing is to blame the individual closest at hand, typically a loved one, for having used and not returned or even having thrown away the object in question.

I routinely consider my wife to be the great misplacer of items in our family. She practically has Saint Anthony, the patron of those who have lost things, on retainer. "Papa, have you seen my HMO card? I gave it to you last time, remember?" We are leaving for the doctor in five minutes. "I always give it back to you right away," I respond. Fortunately I keep a spare card for her, so this doesn't need to escalate into World War III.

In reality I probably misplace things as often as she does. It is hard to be objective when assessing blame. Blaming is an area in which I am trying to improve. For even if I do misplace things less frequently, I tend to go ballistic when I do – I use bad language and I even blame God, when in reality I simply failed, say, to refile the document. Nowadays I can stay calm by thinking, "I guess it's just moved." Also, on the prevention side, I try to return things to their place more regularly. Finally, I attempt to help my wife when she can't find something and refrain from blaming her for things I can't find. Things generally turn up when you are not frantically searching for them, so why risk losing yourself over some material object gone AWOL?

Discuss in your Wisdom Journal how you handle misplacing things.

MAINLAND WISDOM

No man is an island, entire of itself; every man is a piece of the continent, a part of the main; if a clod be washed away by the sea, Europe is the less, as well as if a promontory were, as well as if a manor of thy friends or of thine own were; any man's death diminishes me, because I am involved in mankind; and therefore never send to know for whom the bell tolls; it tolls for thee.

-JOHN DONNE (1572–1631)

Here in Hawaii we know about islands. Our state, a far-flung miniarchipelago stretching a thousand miles or more, consists of very little land. We are among the smallest of the fifty states. Even the "Big Island" is but a pebble in a vast sea. We also know about mainlands. Most of us hail from one, North American or Asian. When capitalized, the term refers to the continental United States. You might ask someone, "Where's George?" and get the answer, "He's on the Mainland."

The John Donne excerpt quoted above ranks with the Twenty-third Psalm, the Sermon on the Mount, and Hamlet's "To Be or Not to Be" soliloquy as one of the most famous passages in English. At least two subsequent book titles derive from it. As memorable as the language is, however, the sentiment expressed is even more important.

As human beings we seem to be separate individuals, islands preempted by our personal needs and locked up in our own heads. But the act of procreation itself shows that this is not so. Even artificial insemination requires a sperm donor and a host of medical specialists. The Y2K scare also made it clear that every person and company is dependent on a large network of others just to function. Really *knowing* that each of us is part of the whole, members of the human family, coparticipants in the ecosystem, interdependent neighbors of the plants and animals, and citizens of the world will one day make holocausts and ethnic cleansings, gang violence and abuse things of the past. May we take John Donne's words to heart.

Do you consider yourself a world citizen? Why? Why not? Respond in your Wisdom Journal.

WISECRACK WISDOM

My good friend Jacques Monod spoke often of the randomness of the cosmos. He believed everything in existence occurred by pure chance with the possible exception of his breakfast, which he felt certain was made by his housekeeper.

–Woody Allen, "My Speech to the Graduates"

Woody Allen is famous for many reasons, but here I am focusing on his ability to take a huge, mysterious topic like the "randomness of the cosmos" and turn it into a belly laugh.

Allen is not alone in this ability, of course. Countless comedians and satirists have paved humor's way down through the centuries, and I believe we are the better for it. Wisecracks and comedy, whether in daily conversation or professional entertainment, remind us to laugh at life once in a while. Perhaps more important, though, they sometimes cause us to see ourselves and the world from new angles, which is more often to our benefit than to our detriment.

Woody Allen's humor has that definite Jewish zing. It's like the fragrance and crunch of a real pickle-barrel pickle – you either know it or you don't. I'm sure I identify with it because I grew up as a Jew in New York, exposed to a long line of Jewish humorists. Among my favorites, I recall Sam Levenson, the schoolteacher-comic, a gentleman among Jewish stand-ups in TV's black-and-white past. More recent avatars – Gilda Radner, Jerry Seinfeld, Fran Drescher, and Adam Sandler, to name a few – have plenty of the old flavor too. There's cleverness, self-deprecation, the unexpected, and always, just beneath the surface, a hint of the presence of evil. As Tevye says in *Fiddler on the Roof,* the reason Orthodox Jewish men keep their hats on even in the house is they never know when they'll have to leave in a hurry. Typical of our gallows humor is the saying, "If the rich could pay the poor to die for them, the poor could make a nice living."

That being said, I should not stereotype – not all Jews are sharp-tongued wisecrackers. But I like to think I'm capable of the occasional zinger. My humor is at its best when the joke is on myself or the cosmos rather than on someone else, and when it helps me to lighten up or to see things from a new perspective.

What role does humor play in your life? Write in your Wisdom Journal about a funny, enlightening moment you have experienced.

PRAYER WISDOM

There will always be prayers in public schools – as long as there are final exams to take.

–B. Norman Frisch, quoted in *Practical Proverbs and Wacky Wit*, 1996

I was good at school. As a high school student, I attended an American Baptist boarding school. No objection to prayer there, but then I looked forward to final exams and usually did very well on them. So I can't recall ever having prayed before them. On the other hand, I did pray before swim meets. As my team's third starter in my event, I usually asked for at least a third. Mostly I came in fourth or fifth. My prayers were regular enough, just not efficacious.

As an adult I pray more frequently. Come to think of it, I still pray before my current exercise of choice: walking or running. I usually ask God to protect my body, with special emphasis on knees, legs, feet, and back. I remember to warm up and cool down, though, because I don't consider prayer a substitute for doing my part. Maybe that was the problem with my swimming prayers at prep school. Maybe I never trained hard enough. Maybe I didn't have the right stuff to begin with. Maybe God answers some of our prayers by not answering them, at least not in accordance with our expectations.

A friend of mine, recently experiencing hard times, told me of a breakthrough she was proud of. She had prayed for what she considered positive outcomes to several situations. Then, right after offering her prayers, she spontaneously added, "God, please give me the strength and understanding to accept whatever way you want these situations to end." She surrendered her own desires and expectations to God's will. Then, for the first time since her hard times had begun, she felt a new sense of freedom and lightness. Several days later both situations turned out exactly as she had hoped. She sat on the floor of her apartment and wept. All God wanted, it seemed, was for her to let go.

In your Wisdom Journal, discuss your prayer life.

NOMINAL WISDOM

Each child is named at birth, but it is understood that as a person develops, the birth name will be outgrown, and the individuals will select for themselves a more appropriate greeting. Hopefully one's name will change several times in a lifetime as wisdom, creativity and purpose also become more clearly defined with time.

–Marlo Morgan, *Mutant Message Down Under*, 1991

Our younger daughter's name is Christine Jacqueline Feldman. In elementary school she was Tina. In middle school she became Chris for a while. Then in high school she announced she wanted henceforth to be called Christine. Nowadays at the travel agency where she works, she is Jacqueline, because the manager is Christie. In the meantime her stage name as a rock musician is Christine Darling.

There are many traditions, such as the Australian Aboriginal one described above, that involve names. Numerous cultures require different names for children and adults. Names sometimes signify new assignments. In the Bible Abram becomes Abraham, Sarai becomes Sarah, Simon becomes Peter, Saul becomes Paul, and so on. Members of religious orders often take new names. Orthodox Jews change the names of sickly children to fool the Angel of Death. Japanese, Chinese, Hungarians, and Bavarians, by putting last names first, give pride of place to the family. Job seekers are advised that repeating an interviewer's name may help them land a position. On the other hand, if you meet a casual acquaintance who remembers and uses your name while you have forgotten and don't use theirs, well, guess who is one up on whom?

The first chapter of Laurence Sterne's classic eighteenth-century novel *Tristram Shandy* explains how the hero's life was ruined by having been saddled with the sad-sounding first name "Tristram." My own spiritual guide offered the practice of giving followers new first names that, presumably, were more in accord with their inner natures. Every time these name were repeated would thus be like a prayer for the individuals to become their real selves. I recall the Latin motto *nomen est omen.* "The name is full of numinous power."

In your Wisdom Journal, discuss how you feel about your name.

MOLEHILL WISDOM

One way to get high blood pressure is to go mountain climbing over molehills.

-Earl Wilson

In the Twelve Step program are two relevant slogans: How important is it? and Take it easy. Making mountains out of molehills, then climbing them, can be funny – in other people. A comic blowing a gasket over something trivial gets an easy laugh. It's not so funny, of course, when we are the one with smoke coming out of our ears.

In thirty-five years of marriage, I have blown a number of gaskets over my wife's punctuality, or lack thereof. I often play the German card, with lines like, "Aren't Germans supposed to be punctual?" Or: "Now I know why the Allies won the War. The Wehrmacht could never show up for battle on time, so we won by default." She, on the other hand, is much more forgiving of my peccadilloes. Also, my friends point out that I have a tendency to arrive late for things myself, even when I attend alone.

With borderline high blood pressure, I have good reason to chill out. Can't you just see it? "Author of book on wisdom dies of stroke because his wife was ten minutes late leaving for party." How important is it really? And if arriving on time is such an important concern for me and I know she will be late, why not tell her the event starts a half hour before it does? That way she can get ready at her pace, I can stay calm, and we'll still arrive when we are supposed to.

Time-management gurus like to point out how items marked "urgent" are not always important or, contrarily, how important items are not always urgent. An acquaintance of mine just lost her twenty-year-old son in a freak fishing accident. That's important *and* urgent. If I have any sense, I'll lock up my mountain climbing boots and refuse to take them out for any hill under a thousand feet.

How are you at keeping your cool in the face of minor-league irritations? Write about it in your Wisdom Journal.

MONEY WISDOM

Having money in the bank gives one a sense of Buddhistic calm.

-AYN RAND (1905–1982)

Money is usually overrated. We live in a money-oriented culture. Yet as the Beatles' song reminds us, it can't buy us love.

But people like me tend to underrate money. As a student of the humanities, and a religious one to boot, I put money way down on my list of values. In my case, moreover, I had an early prejudice against money. First, my father was a businessman. Dinner-table discussions often turned on how much – in dollar terms – someone was worth. I tended to value people based on things like how nice, interesting, or funny they were. Once, I was instructed to be on my best behavior because Dad was bringing Mr. So-and-So, a wealthy associate, home for dinner. When he arrived, however, he turned out to be just another boring adult.

Second, our family was Jewish. Early on I learned that Jews were supposed to be interested only in money. Well, it did seem that way at our house. So I took a private vow that money wasn't going to be a big deal for me when I grew up. Later, when my family made sure I got the best "Gentile" education money could buy, I felt pressure to go into business or a high-paying profession like medicine or law. How disappointed my parents were when their son the doctor chose to operate on nineteenth-century American fiction! They were always convinced I could have done better.

Now, at the age of sixty, I am content that I did not enter a career for which I had no interest or talent, just for the sake of making money. On the other hand, I do regret that I haven't been a better steward of what I did make. I had both the discipline and the knowledge, but my prejudice blinded me to the importance. Money, as the saying goes, can't buy happiness, but it can rent it. Or as the great Joe Louis once said, "I don't like money, actually, but it quiets my nerves." A more balanced view of money would have served me and my family better.

Discuss your attitude toward money in your Wisdom Journal.

NEAR-DEATH WISDOM

I felt a surge of energy. It was almost as if I felt a pop or release inside me, and my spirit was suddenly drawn out through my chest and pulled upward, as if by a giant magnet. My first impression was that I was free. . . . I was above the bed, hovering near the ceiling. . . . I turned and saw a body lying on the bed. . . . I knew at once that it was lifeless. And then I recognized that it was my own.

–BETTY J. EADIE, *EMBRACED BY THE LIGHT,* 1992

I first became aware of near-death experiences in 1974 when I heard a tape-recorded speech by Dr. Ian Stevenson, a physician who had had an out-of-body experience during World War II. Later, after recovering from his injuries, Stevenson learned that he had been pronounced clinically dead for several minutes, but had been revived.

Some years after that, a book by another physician, Dr. Raymond Moody, appeared. In *Life After Life* Dr. Moody studied a number of near-death cases. Moody looked at the similarities that ranged across many of the cases: the consciousness leaving the body, hovering above it, recognizing it but feeling detached; being moved rapidly through a dark tunnel; coming to a welcoming figure of light at the end of the tunnel; undergoing a life review; seeing dead friends and relatives in a beautiful landscape across a barrier like a river; being told one couldn't cross over but had to return to complete some task; and then feeling the pain upon re-entering one's body.

My own father, a week before he died, reported having started going through a tunnel but getting stuck midway. He was unaware of Moody's work. What the process of dying is really like and whether we will consciously experience an afterlife is something each of us can only know for certain in due course.

Meanwhile, the stories of near-death survivors offer us comfort and hope, not only about the process of dying but about what comes next as well.

Have you had an experience that gives you insight into what dying might be like? Sketch it out in your Wisdom Journal.

NONJUDGMENTAL WISDOM

Men of true wisdom and goodness are contented to take persons and things as they are, without complaining of their imperfections, or attempting to amend them. They can see a fault in a friend, a relation, or an acquaintance, without ever mentioning it to the parties themselves, or to any others, and this often without lessening their affection.

–Henry Fielding (1707–1754), *The History of Tom Jones: A Foundling*

Fielding's "comic epic in prose" is filled with characters and situations that teach us about wisdom and folly. Squire Allworthy is the book's touchstone for virtue, generosity, and good sense. Since encountering him in my sophomore year, I have met some Squire Allworthys in real life. For whatever reasons, all of them grew up in or were members of the United Methodist Church. One I was fortunate to have as my boss for a time. Another was my senior-year prep-school roommate. A third almost became the governor of South Dakota. Not a scientific sample, I know, but an interesting coincidence nevertheless.

A characteristic of all three was to know and incorporate into their behavior an attitude of acceptance. I never saw them "take someone down," whether to that person's face or, worse, behind the person's back. People are people, was their view, and no one is perfect. They understood that we are all sinners and so have no right to carp at others' shortcomings. They took seriously Jesus' metaphor about the mote and the beam, or the Old Testament warning, quoted by Paul (in Romans 12:19) that "to [God] belongeth vengeance, and recompence" (Deuteronomy 32:35, KJV).

One of my character defects has been a tendency to criticize others. This was enhanced by my father's example and abetted by my learning the use of teasing as a pedagogical device. In learning critical thinking at Yale, I found I could articulate what was wrong with others, or their poetry, in a prioritized list replete with technical terms. Years of spiritual training fortunately have helped me to become less judgmental. But Squire Allworthy's example still lies out ahead.

In your Wisdom Journal, assess how well you reserve judgment of others.

PASTORAL WISDOM

The Lord opened unto me that being bred at Oxford or Cambridge was not enough to fit and qualify men to be ministers of Christ.

–GEORGE FOX (1624–1691)

Pendulums do swing back and forth. The first ministers of the Christian church, with the notable exception of Saint Paul, were simple people, fishermen and the like. But the time came when the public and church officials began to call for an "educated clergy." Oxford and Cambridge Universities began as monasteries. Monks, more than priests, represented the lettered and learned class of medieval Christendom. After the Reformation the Anglican church preferred its clergy to be university bred, and the Puritans who colonized New England shared that preference. Both Harvard and Yale were founded as places where, in the words of the Puritan clergyman Cotton Mather, "a succession of a learned and able ministry might be educated."

George Fox, founder of the Religious Society of Friends, was a mystic. He understood that revelation, to be transformative, could not be a secondhand experience. With externally acquired knowledge, he believed, we see through a glass darkly. Things "opened unto" us in our understanding, however, we can see clearly. Come to think of it, where did Jesus study? He was brought up as a carpenter's son, yet at the age of twelve, he was teaching the rabbis in the Temple. His learning seemed to come through experiences such as his forty-day fast in the desert. What university degree certified him to both speak and act with authority? Similarly the Prophet Muhammad was an illiterate camel driver. Yet one of the world's treasures, the Koran, was received and later dictated by him, and he founded Islam. What institution qualified him for this task?

As a triple graduate from Yale, I am certainly grateful for my formal education. Yet I agree with George Fox that transformative education about God has to come from God. Pastoral wisdom is realizing that book learning alone is not sufficient to qualify one to lead God's people toward their Creator.

Write in your Wisdom Journal about your spiritual formation.

PERSONAL-DEVELOPMENT WISDOM

I have frequently seen people become neurotic when they content themselves with inadequate or wrong answers to the questions of life. . . . Such people are usually confined within too narrow a spiritual horizon. . . . If they are enabled to develop into more spacious personalities, the neurosis generally disappears. For that reason the idea of development was always of the highest importance to me.

–C. G. Jung (1875–1961), *Memories, Dreams, Reflections*

In the old *Mission Impossible* TV series, the hero would go to a preselected place, switch on a cleverly hidden tape recorder, and an authoritative voice would describe "this mission, if you choose to accept it," and so on. The voice would always conclude, "This tape will self-destruct in five seconds." Then the Mission Impossible team would be off to right another of the world's wrongs in a mere sixty minutes (if you count the commercials).

A basic tenet of those who believe in reincarnation is that life on Earth is a school of personal development. Souls put on bodies to gain, one by one, the basic understandings required for the journey back to God. Each rebirth is equivalent to moving up a grade, though we sometimes repeat a grade or have to be put back. When we finally learn all things needful, we graduate. Reaching that level is known as Enlightenment. Having achieved Enlightenment, the soul may move on to further spheres of experience.

Carl Gustav Jung, the son of a Protestant pastor in Switzerland, was at one time Freud's heir apparent to lead the Freudian School of Psychoanalysis. The two men broke over the issue of neurosis. For Freud, neurosis was caused by unresolved conflicts between personal, often sexual, drives and social mores. For Jung, neurosis was a sign that individuals were contenting themselves with "inadequate answers to the questions of life." In both cases the main issue was the mission impossible of successful personal development. For both, neurosis warned of blockage, and needed to be treated for growth to occur.

Write freely for ten minutes in your Wisdom Journal on where you think you are in your own personal development.

PHILANTHROPIC WISDOM

Philanthropy is commendable, but it must not cause the philanthropist to overlook the circumstances of economic injustice which make philanthropy necessary.

–MARTIN LUTHER KING JR. (1929–1968)

In 1969, while working for the University of Hawaii, I was in the midst of a job interview at the East-West Center when the local Students for a Democratic Society staged a sit-in. At the time the Center was still a federal institution, so it was the closest thing in Hawaii to a federal office; and it was right on the University campus, so it was an obvious target for SDS. The SDS head, who served with me on the University's student-faculty relations committee, was a smart, articulate kid. As I was leaving, he said, "Hey, Reynold, do you really want to work for people like this?"

John's point was like the Reverend King's. The center was giving free education, travel, room, and board to Asia's future leaders. It had been created in response to the Soviet Union's Lumumba Friendship University in Moscow. Each institution clearly hoped to win influential friends through the gift of education and the Trojan horse of acculturation. Meanwhile our government – and the Soviets – supported the dictatorships running many of the students' countries of origin. My SDS friend thought it better, in classic Marxian terms, to "heighten the contradictions." A little charity around the edges helped drain some frustration while keeping the old warlords in power. Better not to invite the students, he believed, unless the goal was to radicalize them.

Philanthropy is a complex matter. Do you give or don't you? Will your gift solve a problem or only alleviate symptoms? Will it truly help or only deepen a sense of entitlement while sapping initiative? Donor organizations face these issues daily. The foundations I have worked for think of themselves as booster rockets, launching a new project perhaps, but not as the main engine. Philanthropic wisdom has to do with finding the balance between immediate assistance and long-term empowerment.

Write in your Wisdom Journal how you determine whether to give to an approaching beggar.

WISDOM AS PANACEA?

The only medicine for suffering, crime, and all the other woes of mankind is wisdom.

—THOMAS H. HUXLEY (1825–1895), *SCIENCE AND EDUCATION*

Because I am writing this book on wisdom, I am tempted to frame Huxley's statement and hang it above my computer. Still, a part of wisdom has to be knowing that there are no silver bullets. Or if there are, their primary function is to kill vampires. Or is that werewolves? In any case, wisdom is no silver bullet.

What about this statement in Ecclesiastes, which is part of the Bible's "wisdom literature"?

> *And I gave my heart to know wisdom, and to know madness and folly: I perceived that this also is vexation of spirit. For in much wisdom is much grief: and he that increaseth knowledge increaseth sorrow. (1:17–18)*

So who's right—Huxley or Solomon? Both—and neither. I am reminded of a story my friend Victor likes to tell. Two rabbinical students are arguing over a point of doctrine. Unable to reach a conclusion, they seek out the most famous rabbi in their district. First one, then the other, states his case. After each presentation the rabbi says, "You're right." Another well-known scholar, listening to the exchange, interjects, "My dear Moishe, how can both Shmuel and Hymie be right when they are taking opposite sides?" Rabbi Moishe replies, "You know, Jakov, you've got a point too!"

In *Survival of the Wisest,* Jonas Salk writes that evolution is now calling for a critical mass of human beings with the capacity to make life-affirming decisions. Global survival may depend on it. Yet to say that "wisdom is the only medicine," as Huxley does, is an exaggeration. On the other hand, how much credence can we give the statement of Solomon, someone who finds "all things . . . wearisome" (Ecclesiastes 1:8)? The truth, as usual, lies somewhere in between.

In what ways might wisdom improve the human condition? Write on this topic for ten minutes in your Wisdom Journal.

THE WISDOM OF AGNOSTICISM

It is a contradiction in terms and ideas to call anything a revelation that comes to us at second-hand, either verbally or in writing. Revelation is necessarily limited to the first communication.

–THOMAS PAINE (1737–1809), *THE AGE OF REASON*

The wisdom of *agnosticism?* Those of you who have been reading in this book may be surprised by this title. After all, I am pretty clearly a "believer." But it is only common sense to believe no more than one knows from experience. I for one would have been a flat-earther in the days before Columbus. My older daughter recently got an M.A. from the University of Saint Thomas in Saint Paul. The namesakes of these places, both saints of the church, could not believe without proof. They were from Missouri, so to speak: "Show me, Lord."

I am not condemning belief based in authority. But I do become concerned when I hear the line, "How do I know? The Bible tells me so." The Bible can be dangerous in the wrong hands. Even the devil can cite the Scriptures and, in tempting Jesus, does. It is a complex, contradictory collection of books. One of the Ten Commandments enjoins us not to kill. Not many chapters later, the Children of Israel, with Jehovah at their side, are happily killing or enslaving the population of the Promised Land. Which Bible do we believe?

Sometimes holding a smaller belief prevents us from gaining a larger one. If an Ultimate Power exists, it will certainly not be put out of business by my, or anyone else's, wavering belief. If God wishes to reveal "Himself" to me, he can't do that so long as I hold on to secondhand notions about who "He" is. So long as agnostics are open to learning from their experience, however, God may prove a great believer in them.

Do you believe in God? Is it the God of Sunday School or an entity you have come to know through daily living? Write in your Wisdom Journal about what "God" is like for you.

UNIVERSAL WISDOM

In every head is some wisdom.

–AN AFRICAN PROVERB

Spring 1990 was an eventful time for me. I lost my job as university vice president, my mother-in-law died, and I began planning a course called "The Literature of Wisdom." It was to be about increasing one's personal wisdom through reading, discussing, and reflecting on selections from world literature. By the time we moved to Hawaii in the fall of 1996, it had been offered twelve times.

Class met one night per week, three hours at a time, for fourteen weeks. The first session invariably consisted of self-introductions, a sharing of individual definitions of wisdom, and an orientation to the course. We spent at least twenty minutes learning one another's names. The last class was always a potluck party at my house, where we shared not only our dishes but read aloud our take-home finals – letters to our fellow class participants. The questions never changed: (1) What are three things I got out of this course? (2) What do I think wisdom is now? (3) What am I sure wisdom is not? (4) What are three things I intend to do after this course to become a wiser person? (5) What final thoughts would I like to share?

In between we looked at a variety of works, ranging from ancient to modern, literary to popular and New Age. We always spent the second session on proverbial wisdom. Another continuing and very popular assignment was to write a one-page letter in which we gave someone else advice for living "the good life." Everyone also did a class journal and final group project.

The most impressive thing to me was how much natural wisdom existed in each of us. God truly makes no junk. The other big learning was how a few weeks' attention to common course materials in a safe environment could forge a powerful sense of community. When we held hands in the final wisdom circle, there were always some tears. Learning wisdom together, we had come home.

In your Wisdom Journal, spend ten minutes writing yourself a letter on how to live more wisely.

SELF-HELP WISDOM

The gods help them that help themselves.

–Aesop, "Hercules and the Waggoner," c. 550 b.c.e.

This is a saying we Americans love. We are, after all, a society of rugged individualists. Entrepreneurship and innovation are our life's blood. The growth in the number of small businesses in the late 1980s, coupled with the increase in productivity of large businesses, has launched the longest period of prosperity in our nation's history. We like to help ourselves – to figure out what's wrong with our bodies, minds, spirits, or pocketbooks. We then install a regimen to help us do better. These regimens, if we can stick to them, often work.

Benjamin Franklin had a program for successful living. Basically you spend one week concentrating on one of thirteen virtues. You observe how you are doing in such areas as silence, industry, or moderation. Then you move on to the next. You go through four cycles each year – assessing and improving your practice of each virtue. This program presumably helped Franklin, the tenth child of a relatively poor, obscure Bostonian, become one of the most affluent, illustrious individuals in the Colonies. He could retire early from self-employment – two other American ideals – and devote himself entirely to public service (a third). His civic good works include, among others, the founding of the American Philosophical Society, our first learned association; the establishment of the Pennsylvania Hospital, our first medical center; and the creation of the University of Pennsylvania, the world's first institution of higher learning based on secular principles. Not bad results for a self-help program! And these examples come from a long list that also includes founding the U.S. Postal Service and the U.S. Mint.

As a person who has had trouble keeping weight off, I can testify that not every self-help program is effective for everyone. To borrow a saying from the Twelve Step community, you have to work your program. Some programs, moreover, may work only for their founders – financially. Or there may be negative side effects. Still, much can be said for self-help programs that work. Which ones work, however, we must find out for ourselves.

Describe a success or failure you have had with a self-help program. What lessons do you draw from this experience?

THE FOOLISHNESS OF USING FORCE

Force without wisdom falls of its own weight.

-Horace (65–8 B.C.E.)

I was psychologically and physically abusive to our older daughter. As a child she was demanding and difficult. Usually busy with too many things, I had a low tolerance for her (in my opinion) unreasonable behavior. Although I remember receiving only one or two spankings from my own parents, I followed the precept of "spare the rod and spoil the child" with this daughter.

On the psychological side, I used teasing and sarcasm to try to "shape her up." The same techniques my favorite prep-school teacher had used on me–successfully, I thought–I applied to her, not as an adolescent but as an elementary-school student. What might have been good pedagogy for me was, in hindsight, inappropriate parental discipline for a child her age. What she no doubt got from my unreasonable behavior toward her was that I was mean and didn't love her.

As a child I was teased and bullied by some of the older or cooler kids. By the time I was eleven or twelve, at camp for instance, I began to bully younger or less cool kids myself–not a pleasant character trait to remember now.

When my older daughter was still a toddler, I recall spanking her for her willful crying. We were staying with friends in Santa Monica. I can still see how shocked and disturbed the young wife, our hostess, was by my action. Finally, when our daughter was twelve and I had punished her for some infraction, I promised that I would never hit her again. I have kept this vow. I have also made amends to her for my shameful behavior and can only pray that her adult life will not be traumatized by my bullying her as a child.

"Force without wisdom falls of its own weight." Thank goodness. But the costs until then are sometimes too high.

Reflect in the privacy of your Wisdom Journal on some action that was less than wise, especially with regard to using psychological or physical force. What steps might you take now to rectify this behavior?

WISDOM AND WONDER

When I heard the learn'd astronomer,
When the proofs, the figures, were ranged in columns
before me,
When I was shown the charts and diagrams, to add, divide,
and measure them,
When I sitting heard the astronomer where he lectured
with much applause in the lecture-room,
How soon unaccountable I became tired and sick,
Till rising and gliding out I wander'd off by myself,
In the mystical moist night-air, and from time to time,
Look'd up in perfect silence at the stars.

-WALT WHITMAN (1819–1892),
"WHEN I HEARD THE LEARN'D ASTRONOMER"

When I was in elementary school, one of my favorite radio programs was "The Answer Man." People from around the country would send in questions like "Why is the sky blue?" or "Do ulcers really come from worry?" Research would be done, and a voice, sounding like the voice of God, would let us know what was what.

But then there was Walt Whitman, a cultural *refusnik* if ever there was one. Yes, the distinguished astronomer in the poem presents an abundance of facts and figures about the heavens. But the poet soon becomes "tired and sick." (Cultural *refusniks* won't even word their clichés correctly.) Once outside, freed from the stultifying atmosphere of charts and diagrams, alone in the *mystical* "moist night-air," he looks up "in perfect silence," free of the imperfections of human speech, at the stars.

Harlan Cleveland, I think it was, constructed a kind of wisdom hierarchy, beginning with *noise.* After that came *signal, data, information, knowledge, understanding,* and *wisdom.* Whitman uses the "learn'd astronomer" as a foil for the person wise enough to consider the stars a source of wonder, not just data or information. For me, though, scientific knowledge and mystical experience are not necessarily opposites. The Answer Man's answers can lead to new questions, and all roads can lead to wonder–and wisdom.

Where is the wisdom in science for you? What about in nature? Note your responses in your Wisdom Journal.

SWAMI WISDOM

By their fruits ye shall know them.

–MATTHEW 7:20, KJV

A former colleague of mine did her doctorate in religious studies at the University of Minnesota. Her dissertation recounted the growth of non-Western spiritual groups in the Twin Cities. Virtually all the founding figures had been "holy men from the East." A few were American-born Caucasians. I don't recall any women.

My friend interviewed members of these organizations, most based in Hinduism, Buddhism, and Islam. In one particular case, in an organization that enjoined restraint from bodily pleasures, she encountered a pattern of sexual exploitation on the part of the swami – a case of do-as-I-say-not-as-I-do. Of course, the dynamic of extremism breeding extreme responses is nothing new. Nor is it limited to the Exotic East. Somerset Maugham chronicled a similar scenario concerning a Christian missionary in the short story "Rain." One question is whether the perpetrator in Minnesota was a wolf in sheep's clothing or the victim of his own strictures.

With the Jonestown and Waco incidents in mind, we are well advised to exercise caution in getting our wisdom from self-declared gurus. The lives we save may be our own, or those of our children. On the other hand, the continuing existence of non-Western spiritual training centers in most cities of the Western world suggests that people have been finding something of value there for themselves. My own experience of nearly forty years with a spiritual guide from an Eastern tradition has been nonexploitative and positive. I advise those who feel drawn to a "nontraditional" spiritual discipline to use common sense. Interview older and newer followers, assess whether there are fees and decide if they are reasonable. Size up the leader by what he or she says *and* does. Also, nowadays it is possible to get spiritual training in the Christian context in centering prayer or Christian meditation groups. For Jews, meditation is sometimes practiced as part of Reform services, and there are groups that study the mysticism of the Kabbalah and the Hasidim. In all cases remember: By their fruits you shall know them.

Can you share in your Wisdom Journal a good or bad experience with a spiritual teacher? What lessons did you learn?

GURU WISDOM

Gladly would he learn and gladly teach.

–GEOFFREY CHAUCER (1343–1400), DESCRIBING ONE OF THE PILGRIMS IN *THE CANTERBURY TALES*

In the Literature of Wisdom course I created in 1990, teaching and learning activities seemed to emerge naturally. Once I asked the students to point to the teacher. Most of them pointed to me. Because we were at an adult-oriented nontraditional university, a few remembered their orientation course and pointed to each other as well. I then asked them to try again and be more creative. This time more pointed to each other, about half pointed to themselves, a few pointed up, one pointed down, and I (joining in) pointed all around.

The "point" is that the more effective we are as learners, the more "teachers" we will find. Everyone and everything can educate. The kingdom of learning is within and all around.

The Hindu saying is pertinent: When the disciple is ready, the guru will appear. Now *guru* is no more – but also no less – than the Sanskrit word for *teacher.* In India today there are cooking gurus, marching gurus, singing gurus, even grammar gurus. At a gathering at the Unversity of Hawaii in 1971, I remember Ravi Shankar, the Indian sitar virtuoso, talking about his guru. He was referring to his sitar teacher.

The first time I walked into a classroom as the official teacher, I was twenty-five. A young man, maybe nineteen years old, sat at one of the student desks. Class would begin in fifteen minutes. When I plopped my books onto the teacher's desk, he looked up and said: "Hey kid, I wouldn't do that. The teacher won't like it." "But I'm the teacher," I replied. "Oh yeah. What's your name?" I told him. He looked doubtful. Then he said, "Can I see your draft card?"

One of the Javanese names for God is *Mahaguru,* Great Teacher. If God is everywhere, then that which can teach us must be everywhere too: Our official teachers, but also our family, friends, lovers, pets, experiences, even strangers we meet on airplanes. Most of all, our great teacher is ourselves. If we look inside, we'll find most of the answers we need.

Write in your Wisdom Journal about a learning experience mediated by someone or something other than an official teacher.

INSTRUCTIONAL WISDOM

He waves his hand when we try to explain why we're here. "I know why you're here! White Man came to this country and forgot his original Instructions. We have never forgotten our Instructions. So you're here looking for the Instructions you lost."

–MATHEW KING, LAKOTA ELDER, IN *WISDOMKEEPERS*, BY HARVEY ARDEN AND STEVE WALL

When you saw today's title, I bet you thought I would be talking about something academic. After all, I am by profession a college teacher; and I *have* been to more than one workshop with the word *instructional* in the title.

My friend Hamilton Camp, a character actor and folksinger, always reminds me of another sort of instruction. He does this German spy-movie shtick whenever he sees me, maybe because I have a German wife. Anyway, the routine, with full German accent, goes something like this: "Herr Feldmann! You vill go to Barcelona. There you vill find a certain Feldmann. He vill haf inshtructions."

The instructions Mathew King is speaking about, of course, are spiritual ones. What are we supposed to be doing as individuals? As a society? How are we supposed to organize our lives? Traditional societies lived with and by their traditions. Young people came to learn and honor these traditions through rites of passage. "Where there is no vision, the people perish," Proverbs 29:18 (KJV) advises. Native American young people attended sweat lodges, fasted, prayed, and went on vision quests. Spending one or more nights alone in the wilderness with only a blanket and their thoughts, questers would receive instructions, later to be shared with the medicine people of the tribe. These formative experiences would provide spiritual and material direction for the rest of the individuals' lives.

Where is our vision as a people? Where and how do we as individuals find our instructions about who we are meant to be? My computer has a user's manual 199 pages long. Where is the user's manual for myself? How can I learn *my* instructions?

Quietly pray to the God of your understanding for guidance, and then write freely in your Wisdom Journal a set of "instructions" for your life.

MIRACULOUS WISDOM

There is no order of difficulty in miracles. . . . All expressions of love are maximal.

Miracles as such do not matter. The only thing that matters is their Source, Which is far beyond evaluation.

Miracles occur naturally as expressions of love.

Miracles are habits, and should be involuntary.

Miracles are everyone's right, but purification is necessary first.

-FOUNDATION FOR INNER PEACE, *A COURSE IN MIRACLES*, 1975

I remember reading this book on publication. What impressed me most was how it came about: It was received in automatic writing by a Jewish psychology professor at Columbia. Not that Jewish people are somehow so intellectually inclined that automatic writing lies outside their ken. Exclude Jewish members and many of the leaders of New Age movements would disappear. But what really interested me as a Jewish Christian was the frequency of references to Christ and Christianity. This was a very distinctive Jewish psychology professor.

In the course itself, I did not find much new or surprising. It reiterated the basic spiritual premise that we are born with everything we need to live full spiritual lives. The problem is that we somehow lose sight of this fact and end up being selfish when we should be generous, driven by material things when we should be led by spirit. Principle seven of the Fifty Principles of Miracles, with which the course begins, makes it clear that although "miracles are everyone's right, . . . purification is necessary first." By studying the course, participants are set free to perform daily miracles, not of conjuring but of love.

I have been a guest at two course meetings, but I have not taken the course myself. Everyone I know who has taken it speaks positively of the experience. Group members read passages from the course text and workbook. Individuals then relate what they have heard to their lives, or ask others to interpret a particular statement. My conclusion: Any practice that can regularly bring diverse people together all over the world to enhance their inner growth must be a wisdom way worth considering.

In your Wisdom Journal, discuss your experiences with the miraculous.

ANNE FRANK'S WISDOM

People who have a religion should be glad, for not everyone has the gift of believing in heavenly things. You don't necessarily even have to be afraid of punishment after death; purgatory, hell, and heaven are things that a lot of people can't accept, but still a religion, it doesn't matter which, keeps a person on the right path. . . . How noble and good everyone could be if, every evening before falling asleep, they were to recall to their minds the events of the whole day and consider exactly what has been good and bad. Then, without realizing it, you try to improve yourself at the start of each new day; of course, you achieve quite a lot in the course of time.

–ANNE FRANK (1929–1944), *THE DIARY OF A YOUNG GIRL*

Anne wrote this in her diary on July 6, 1944. Four weeks later the Gestapo broke into the Frank family's hideout. A month later Anne was on her way to Auschwitz. She had just turned fifteen.

An old soul, Anne already knew that religion is not something you do but something you receive. She also knew that real religion is based on love, not fear. God is not some sadistic manipulator, forcing us to be good or else. During her short life, however, she had observed how rules sometimes help keep people on "the right path." She also intuited that true faith is the True Faith. God reaches out as any parent to all "His" children. Still, those not yet graced with belief are only nominally "believers" despite their religious affiliation. As the French proverb observes, "God often visits us, but most of the time we are not at home." Being at home when God arrives is one way of describing faith.

In lieu of evening prayer, Anne suggests a Ben Franklin–type inventory of our daily actions. Armed with such reflections, we would naturally work to do better the next day. Just imagine the results, she writes, if everyone would follow this practice. Thanks for your message, Sister Anne. You achieved a lot in your brief time here. We are working to catch up.

Write in your Wisdom Journal about your evening prayer regimen.

PRUDENTIAL WISDOM

Never drive faster than your guardian angel can fly.

–From a bumper sticker

In 1992 a colleague and I published a collection of proverbs entitled *A World Treasury of Folk Wisdom.* A year earlier, when pitching the book to potential publishers, we presented 100 categories, from Adversity through Youth and Age. In our proposal we included an introductory essay, two sample proverbs per category, and – to show the depth of our collection – about eighty proverbs on Caution and Care.

You might get the impression that we had thousands of proverbs ready for selection. In time we would. But at that moment we had barely several hundred. We didn't want to do too much work without a publishing contract in hand. Our "starter file" was rich, however, in cautionary sayings. So rich, in fact, that we created categories like Appearance and Reality, Balance and Moderation, Basic Truths, Conduct of Life, Discretion, Prudence, and Vigilance – just to take advantage of our wealth. For the reality is that many proverbs, perhaps most, counsel prudence. Just think about it: Look before you leap. A stitch in time saves nine. Or the personal favorite of my late mother: It's as easy to fall in love with a rich girl as a poor girl. (I disappointed her on that score.)

My co-compiler and I were excited to find this cautionary vein to be fairly universal. Consider some sayings. First, from Korea: *If you kick a stone in anger, you'll hurt your own foot.* From West Africa we learn, *The teeth that laugh are also those that bite.* Or – still in the dental mode, from the Yiddish – *If a thief kisses you, count your teeth.* I especially appreciate this piece of advice from Mexico about pulling down the shades: *Love is blind but not the neighbors.*

The world is full of dangers and curves in the road. Caution is advised. The twentieth century has blessed us in many ways, but it has also made some of the eternal verities more pertinent than ever. So as you drive along in this new century and millennium, please take care not to go faster than your guardian angel can fly.

Here's a homemade proverb: You can outwait the devil but you can't outrun him. Create an original proverb and discuss in your Wisdom Journal why it contains useful advice.

THE TRADITION OF INNER WISDOM

If you do not find the Wisdom and Mystery of life within yourself, you surely will never find it without.

–From the "Charge of the Goddess," quoted in *Virgin, Mother, Crone,* by Donna Wilshire

In nineteenth-century novels, the way to recover from a deep disappointment was to travel abroad. This idea was expressed in the phrase "to get away from it all." When Satan, in Milton's *Paradise Lost,* was able to free himself from hell, the place, he discovered that the hell of his defeat by God's armies continued to burn inside. "Myself am hell," he said in a famous line.

When I was eighteen, I left the United States for the first time on my own. I had been selected as one of six Yale-Heidelberg exchange students for academic year 1958–59. Although I had lived away from home for significant periods since age eleven, this trip was to be different. Spending a year on my own as an American Jew in Germany thirteen years after the end of World War II was not the same as being away at school in New Jersey or Connecticut. In many respects those twelve months comprised the richest year of my life. I learned among other things that in Germany, just as in the States, there were people I liked, people I didn't like, and many toward whom I had no particular feeling. Intellectually, of course, I already knew that people are people. But now I learned this reality from experience.

Today I believe that wisdom is an attribute of the human soul. The God-part within each of us already knows the answers to the key questions. It knows, for example, that people everywhere are people regardless of outer distinctions. Small children are in touch with this inner knowing and have no problem playing with other children who may be from another country or culture. But soon we are socialized to play only with certain kids. If we are lucky, our inner knowing one day reasserts itself and we throw off the shackles of these limiting beliefs.

Write in your Wisdom Journal how you have overcome some limiting belief, or describe how you feel when someone close to you displays racial or other prejudice.

THE WISDOM OF ACCEPTING THE INEVITABLE

The wise person never refuses anything to necessity.

–Publilius Syrus, Maxim 540, c. 42 B.C.E.

The trick, of course, is to know what necessity is. Some things are obvious: to eat, to sleep, to earn a living. Others seem optional, but may in fact be required: to learn, to have fun, to take responsibility for the preservation of life on Earth, to prepare for death.

For me, the best way to learn what is necessary is to act as if nothing is. Soon the basic needs will assert themselves. Life is a grand experiment. We are called on to keep careful lab notes and to profit by our observations.

My mother lived to be ninety-five. When her twin sister, Helen, died at eighty-seven, my sister, Natalie, and I were advised that Mother could go soon too. She was slender till the end and fairly healthy physically. In her mid-eighties, however, her mind began to fail. I had accepted the inevitability of her death. When her final illness came, I was prepared.

Natalie had done a heroic job of caring for Mother. It wasn't easy. Mother would take too many pills or spit out the ones she was supposed to take when Natalie wasn't looking. She would wander off at times. Natalie had to watch her like a hawk.

My mother and sister lived in southeastern Florida. I was thousands of miles away in Hawaii. As Mother lay dying, she was attended to by Natalie and her daughter Leslie. I called Leslie's cell phone. Leslie was in Mother's hospital room. I could hear Mother moaning in the background. Leslie held the phone to Mother's ear and I said, "Good-bye, Mother. I love you. Thank you for being a good mother. Feel free to leave whenever you're ready. People are waiting to take care of you when you arrive." Apparently I said the right thing because she immediately stopped moaning, relaxed, and fell asleep. Twenty-six hours later she died.

Facing the inevitability of a parent's death, and knowing the right thing to say or do before he or she passes, seem also to belong to the art of wise living.

Write in your Wisdom Journal about going through the experience of a close friend's or relative's death.

THE WISDOM OF LIFELONG LEARNING

I grow old learning something new every day.

-Solon (c. 630–c. 560 b.c.e.)

The Germans have a related saying: *Man lernt nie aus.* The sense is, you can never stop learning because you'll never know enough. As a university dean in Chicago in the 1970s and 1980s, I was in charge of "continuing education." With the rapid changes in technology and the job market, individuals need to constantly update their skills. Many licensed professionals – registered nurses come to mind – are required to have a certain amount of course work each year in order to retain their licenses. For their part universities need the extra income supplied by continuing students. So, done well, continuing-education programs supply something valuable to both institutions and students.

Less formally, we human beings may be described as "learning animals." Not that other animals don't or can't learn. My wife taught our older cat, now fourteen, first to go on a leash, then to heel. (Well, to the extent that even the most learning-crazy cat will ever heel.)

Life throws us all kinds of pitches. To prepare for and swing at every ball as if it would come low and fast over the outside corner would be foolish. Being prepared for a variety of contingencies seems just plain smart. And learning continuously from experience what those contingencies might be is a big part of lifelong learning.

I am a great fan of Richard Bolles's book *The Three Boxes of Life.* In it Bolles talks about the linear pattern many of us find ourselves living: youth for learning, the middle years for earning, and the later (retirement) years for leisure. He recommends that we interweave the three strands of learning, work (productive activity), and leisure throughout our lives, so that, to paraphrase Emily Dickinson's line (see October 7), rather than getting to heaven at last, we are going all along. Sage advice it seems to me.

What kind of learner are you? Write freely in your Wisdom Journal about what you now do – and what you might do – to learn something new every day.

THE PERSON OF STEADY WISDOM

One who is not disturbed in mind even amidst the threefold miseries or elated when there is happiness, and who is free from attachment, fear and anger, is called a sage of steady mind.

In the material world, one who is unaffected by whatever good or evil he may obtain, neither praising it nor despising it, is firmly fixed in perfect knowledge.

One who restrains his senses, keeping them under full control, and fixes his consciousness upon Me, is known as a man of steady intelligence.

–Bhagavad-Gita, 2:56–57,61; Prabhupada translation

When I graduated from college in 1960, *meditate* to me meant "thinking hard about something." My image was Rodin's great sculpture "The Thinker." Sitting bent over, his head supported by his hand, invisible smoke coming out of his ears.

The next year I met Kasi, a South Indian Brahmin working on a doctorate in accounting. He helped me understand that the sculpture I should have had in mind was the contemplative Buddha. Kasi also introduced me to Indian classical music–"You listen as if it comes from inside, not outside"–and took me to the Vivekananda Vedanta Center, not three blocks from my family's apartment.

I remember sitting in that quiet room on Elm Street, trying to do nothing. It was always easier when Swami Vishwananda came in and began to intone in Sanskrit. Later he would translate in his Indian-accented bass, "Bring us from the unreal to the Real." I definitely got something from that.

Soon I learned about the classical Hindu concept of the wise person, whose mood swings avoided both manic and depressive. As a tortoise draws in its legs, so the person of steady wisdom withdraws into the quiet shell of meditation, learning to act without attachment to the results.

Sit quietly. Concentrate on your breath. Don't attend to your thoughts. After twenty minutes return to normal consciousness. Comment on the experience in your Wisdom Journal.

THE WISDOM OF DANCING

"What came over you to make you dance like that?"
"What could I do, boss? My joy was choking me. I had to find some outlet. And what sort of outlet? Words? Pff!"

–Nikos Kazantzakis, *Zorba the Greek*, 1952

My only memory of Viola Wolf's Dance School in Manhattan is that I didn't want to go. My parents were hopeful that I'd meet some nice people my age. We were new in the city, and Viola Wolf was famous for bringing together Jewish teenagers from the better New York families and teaching them to dance. We would learn the social graces along the way. Obedient, I went.

The experience must not have been too traumatic, however, because I looked forward to my next round of formal dancing lessons. The place was the Palm Beach Biltmore during our family's Christmas vacation. I was fifteen – a seasoned prep-school sophisticate. The theme was Latin dancing, the year 1954, and pre-Castro Cuba was little more than 150 miles away. The husband-wife team, questionably Latin, took turns leading me or being led. They were good teachers, and I, an apt student. The music was irresistible. I was the youngest student, and I won a prize. I felt I had arrived at a new plateau of self-confidence. Life was good.

Since then I have experienced three or four other formal dance classes, from a few hours learning a folk dance at a professional conference to eight weeks of couples' ballroom instruction in a church basement. My favorites are a Greek line dance, Samba, and free-form rock-n-roll. Even now I can lose myself in the whir of motion. Daily concerns seem to evaporate. By the time I leave, I am soaking wet, stone sober, and happy.

Like Zorba I am convinced that dancing is required by the soul. Here in Hawaii sacred hula is enjoying a comeback, and last year several local Sufis demonstrated how dervishes whirl. For my part, posthumous thanks to my parents for forcing me to go to Viola Wolf's and paying for those lessons in Florida. Dancing has been an ongoing source of wisdom for me.

Do you like to dance? Write freely for a few minutes in your Wisdom Journal about your experience with dancing.

THE WISDOM IN DIFFERENCE

Vive la différence!
–A FRENCH SAYING

Difference is bad. Difference is frightening. Think of "aliens." As a rule they are bad, frightening, different. In Minnesota, when you want to criticize something without losing your "Minnesota nice," you say, "Gee, that's different." Come to think of it, the aliens in the movie *Contact* were pretty savvy to come to Jodie Foster's character as her father. After all, he was familiar to her, not at all scary, not at all different.

So where is the wisdom in difference? To start with, difference allows one to get outside the box of accustomed ways of thinking and doing. I experienced this dynamic when, at age eleven, my parents sent me to boarding school. Everything was different. I now shared rooms with roommates, ate institutional food, and was expected to make my bed and clean my room each day. The work program had me policing the grounds and mopping bathrooms every day but Sunday. Not only that, but I encountered my first Thais, Chinese, and Venezuelans, among others. I found that some of these foreigners became my closest friends. When I came home for my first vacation, I said "Yes, Sir," "No, Ma'am," made my bed without being asked, and ate everything on my plate. To his dying day, my father considered sending me to that boarding school the best investment he'd ever made.

Later, as an exchange student in Germany, the field of difference for me became even more charged. I learned a great deal about myself and my country. I also found certain aspects of German life superior to the way things were back home: outdoor cafés, removable shower heads (not yet available in the States), and higher-resolution TV. My French friend Lestari used to say this was precisely the meaning of *"Vive la différence!"* Difference was as often good as bad. But if you cordoned yourself off from it, you'd never find out. I agree. Long live difference!

Reflect on the first person from another country or another racial or ethnic group that you came to know well. Write in your Wisdom Journal on what this relationship has meant to your development.

ASIAN WISDOM

We of the West still hold instinctively to the prejudice that our world and our civilization are the "whole world" and that we have a mission to lead all others to the particular cultural goals we have set for ourselves. But the world is bigger than we have imagined, and its new directions are not always those that we ourselves have envisaged. . . . But times are changing. . . . At such a time it is vitally necessary for the West to understand the traditional thought of the great Asian cultures: China, India, and Japan. This is necessary not only for specialists, but for every educated person in the West.

-THOMAS MERTON (1915–1968)

Father Merton will prove to be one of the prophets of the 1960s. It took courage for him, a Trappist monk and ordained priest, to publish thoughts like these at a time when cultural and religious chauvinism were still in the ascendant. Not that intellectual and spiritual provincialism is dead. But at least official leaders now agree with Merton and echo his position.

Consider this statement by Pope John Paul II to a Japanese audience in 1981. (The Holy Father was speaking in Tokyo.) "You are the heirs and keepers of an ancient wisdom. This wisdom in Japan and in the Orient has inspired high degrees of moral life. It has taught you to venerate the pure, transparent, and honest heart. It has inspired you to discover the divine presence in every creature, and especially in every human being."

Imitation, the saying goes, is the sincerest form of flattery. I would put the thought somewhat differently. Becoming your student's student is the greatest form of respect. As teachers, adults, members of a developed nation, practitioners of a religion some not only consider best but feel called to spread to all humankind, we are well advised to absent ourselves a while from the authoritative role and learn from the wisdom of those different from ourselves. Who knows how we might grow if we allow ourselves to hear the secrets God has whispered to others.

In your Wisdom Journal, discuss the non-Western influence that has meant the most to you personally.

MONASTIC WISDOM

One of the first things I noticed on my longer retreats, when I was with the monks in choir four or five times a day for a week or more, was how like an exercise class the liturgy seemed. It was sometimes difficult to rise early for morning office; at other times during the day it seemed tedious to be going back to church, but knowing that the others would be there made all the difference. Once there, the benefits were tangible, and I usually wondered how I could have wished to be anywhere else. When I compared all this to an aerobics class, a monk said, "That's exactly right."

–KATHLEEN NORRIS, *DAKOTA: A SPIRITUAL GEOGRAPHY,* 1993

I have always wanted to go on a Catholic spiritual retreat. The closest I've come was, on one occasion, participating in the all-night Easter Vigil at the Franciscan Sisters' convent in Bloomington, Minnesota, and on another, singing in the Vespers Antiphonal with the Dominican Sisters in Columbus, Ohio.

Joe Engelberg, my Jewish Quaker friend in Lexington, Kentucky, went on regular retreats at the Trappist monastery in Gethsemane, Kentucky, Thomas Merton's monastic home. We used to talk about going there together one year. Joe was a quiet person, a happy combination, no doubt, of his basic personality plus years of Quaker formation. As for me, an addictive talker at times – my business partner uses the adjective *prolix* – being silent for twenty-four hours would produce a spiritual experience for someone! Whatever the reason, the Gethsemane plan never came to fruition.

Reading Father Merton's or Kathleen Norris's writings provides a taste of the work required and the aerobic-type "high" resulting from monastic observances. Yet *high* is probably the wrong word. It must be more like the contentment of a person able to let go and let God on a regular basis. Yesterday in a talk I attended, the speaker defined a saint as someone who daily subordinates his or her will to God's. Monastic living strikes me as a support group to attain this goal.

Have you ever attended a spiritual retreat? Would you like to? Write in your Wisdom Journal about what you experienced or what you anticipate.

CROSSCULTURAL WISDOM

Most Americans . . . are not conscious of the elaborate patterning of behavior which prescribes our handling of time, our spatial relationships, our attitudes toward work, play, and learning. In addition to what we say with our verbal language we are constantly communicating our real feelings in our silent language – the language of behavior. Sometimes this is correctly interpreted by other nationalities, but more often it is not.

-EDWARD T. HALL, *THE SILENT LANGUAGE*, 1959

The Silent Language appeared on my horizon in the late 1960s, soon after my arrival as a new assistant professor of English at the University of Hawaii. I was fresh – in every sense of the word – from New York City, where I had spent the first two years of my career teaching at Queens College, the City University of New York.

At Queens it had never been a problem getting students to talk in class. The problem was more likely to be how to keep things under control. I was at home in this culture in which we speak freely regardless of our knowledge base. But with two-thirds of its population from Asian or Pacific roots, Hawaii was another matter. We *Haole* (Caucasian) faculty, by far the majority, would worry about our taciturn students. "How do you get them to talk?" we asked each other in hopes of finding a surefire recipe. Or else we would say something like, "I just got this incredible midterm from a young Filipina who hasn't opened her mouth all semester. Who would have thought she had it in her?"

Professor Hall's analysis helped me understand the strong Confucian influence that kept even Americanized students of East Asian and related backgrounds from risking loss of face by "going public" with positions that might be insufficiently considered. We later found that by putting students together in "buzz groups," they were able to speak up. Reporters would share with the class what anonymous group members had concluded. As a humanities professor, I am convinced that all human beings have many important things in common. When it comes to communication between cultures, however, experience suggests that Dr. Hall really knows what he is talking about.

In your Wisdom Journal, discuss a crosscultural misunderstanding you have had.

EXPLORATORY WISDOM

Twenty years from now you will be more disappointed by the things that you didn't do than by the ones you did do. So throw off the bowlines. Sail away from the safe harbor. Catch the trade winds in your sails. Explore. Dream. Discover.

-Mark Twain (1835–1910)

Nowadays we encourage each other to "go for it!" Otherwise we'll have to wait till we are old to wear purple, go barefoot, or visit China. In the 1960s Ram Dass encouraged us to "do it now!" For now, as Eastern traditions caution, is the only time we have for certain. Say "I'm sorry" *now.* Say "I love you" *now.* Handle that difficult family or business situation *now.* Later may be too late. There may be no later.

Before getting too morbid, I want to take a different tack. Twain's advice is not just about personal initiative. It could be the credo of every scientist who ever left the safe haven of accepted truth and struck out for undiscovered countries of the mind. Galileo is the classic example. Having the chutzpah to assert that the earth might circle the sun in opposition to the belief of his day got him into trouble with the church. If Aristotle and the church fathers believed all heavenly bodies circled the earth, who was Galileo to assert otherwise? Why should calculations based on looking through a telescope be more persuasive than received tradition bolstered by the proof of following the sun across the daytime sky?

Lord Tennyson (1809–1892) may have been the source of Twain's sailing metaphor. In his poem "Ulysses," he draws on the legend that Ulysses was the first explorer to look for land in the Eastern Atlantic:

. . . Come, my friends
'Tis not too late to seek a newer world.
. . . For my purpose holds
To sail beyond the sunset, and the baths
Of all the western stars, until I die.

Like Ulysses, scientists continue to sail beyond the sunset to seek a new world.

Write in your Wisdom Journal about your willingness to shed old views for new ones. How flexible are you?

FASHIONABLE WISDOM

The philosophies of one age have become the absurdities of the next, and the foolishness of yesterday has become the wisdom of tomorrow.

–Sir William Osler (1849–1919), in *Montreal Medical Journal*

Back in the 1960s, Thomas Kuhn helped many of us understand periodic changes like this in the sciences. His term *paradigm shift* became a phrase heard at teach-ins and cocktail parties. Societies, too, we came to believe, went through upheavals and reversals in what they accepted as truth.

As a science-fiction fan, I have always been fascinated by the Holodeck in *Star Trek*. As many of you will recall, the Holodeck uses futuristic, still-fictional holographic technology to enable starship crew members to take minivacations without ever leaving their home in space. The would-be vacationer selects a fantasy much as we would pick out a video, gives the command, and then (alone or with friends) "travels" to a distant planet to sunbathe on a tropical beach or get caught up in a Wild West shoot-out.

Paradigms in real life shift less dramatically. People here and there begin seeing things differently. Architecture and music change, as do ways of thinking and feeling. When these changes reach a critical mass, what were the Middle Ages "suddenly" become the Renaissance. Here, at the beginning of a new century, millennium, and astrological age, I believe we are going through a similar shift in consciousness. Belief in science and cognitive thinking as our highest instruments, the nation-state as the optimal political unit, and secularism as the appropriate stance for rational people will be repudiated by Western culture by the time our grandchildren retire. All these ideas will be considered the benighted, or at least limited, habits of mind of the last dark age, superseded by a greater balance between heart and mind, a deep planetary consciousness, and a rebirth of personal spirituality. Who knows but that life will have been found elsewhere and that contact will have been made with sentient beings from other planets or dimensions? Leonardo's airships became reality. Why not UFOs?

In your Wisdom Journal, write about a single major difference you foresee for life in 2050. What implications, if any, does your vision have for how we live today?

IMMODERATE WISDOM

Excess on occasion is exhilarating. It prevents moderation from acquiring the deadening effect of a habit.

-W. Somerset Maugham (1874–1965)

The Ancient Greeks advocated the Golden Mean. Buddhism prizes the Middle Way. But Somerset Maugham makes the point that excessive moderation is also excessive. You *can* have too much of a good thing.

I prefer the Chinese concept of the ever-dynamic balancing act called Yin and Yang. True moderation is the result of the interaction of extremes, not their avoidance. Our puritanical culture assumes that by staying away from the manic, we will keep ourselves safe from depression. This prescription is as foolish as not having fun in order to avoid being sad. Nathaniel Hawthorne's novels and short stories show how gloomy Puritan New Englanders in the Colonial period were. Excessive moderation not only dulls, it deadens.

A good extreme once in a while is healthy for body and soul. Think of staying up really late on New Year's Eve, going out on a special occasion to a really good but really expensive restaurant, dancing until dawn, or treating yourself to that dream vacation. The occasional extreme is to a life of moderation what the Sabbath is to the rest of the week. On six days thou shalt watch thy step and live moderately, but on the seventh thou shalt let out the stops, take risks, and go all out to have fun.

The first time I bought a car, the salesperson asked if I intended to use the car primarily for local driving. I said that I did. "Well, just make sure you go for a spin on the expressway two or three times a month," he advised. "That way you'll keep your engine running smoothly." Many of us know this truth with regard to our own lives. As a result we balance hard work with hard play, activity with leisure. But in case we don't, we should remember that when it comes to living moderately, we should do so with moderation.

Can you kick up your heels every now and then and really go all out? Discuss in your Wisdom Journal how good you are at living life to the fullest.

LAISSEZ-FAIRE WISDOM

Live and let live.

–A common English saying

One of my favorite books, *The Best of Bits and Pieces,* states that "much wisdom can be crowded into but four words." Examples include "This too shall pass," "Still waters run deep," "Nothing succeeds like success," "Let sleeping dogs lie," and "Live and let live."

We all have a stake in the behavior of others. The burglar-alarm business, to name just one, depends on our consideration that we cannot trust some neighbors to respect our property or person. City, state, and federal government likewise intervene in our lives by circumscribing what we may or may not do. Penalties for illegal behavior are established by our representatives to keep people, to the extent possible, in line.

Parents, too, attempt to shape their children's behavior through positive and negative means. On the positive side, stories instill a sense of right and wrong action. "The Little Engine That Could" helps us learn the benefits of perseverance. "The Boy Who Cried Wolf" teaches the dangers of exaggeration. Real-life role models help as well, be they public figures or people encountered in everyday life. We can also reward children for their good deeds. On the negative side, children may be psychologically or physically punished for infractions of family rules.

The philosophy of "live and let live" is based on the assumption that people are born with an inherent guidance system. If left to their own devices, this view holds, people will come to understand where their self-interest really lies and act accordingly. An example is how drivers give way until it is safe to cross an intersection where the traffic lights have malfunctioned. Political differences can be calibrated according to our relative preference for intervention and behavioral control versus letting people follow their lights. I tend to take a middle position, because I see where there is a time and place for both rules and the well-established philosophy of live and let live.

How do you sort out the relative importance of letting people follow their lights versus the need for social control? Discuss the topic briefly in your Wisdom Journal.

UTOPIAN WISDOM

Utopus had heard that before his arrival the inhabitants had been continually quarreling among themselves. . . . From the very beginning, therefore, . . . he especially ordained that it should be lawful for every man to follow the religion of his choice, that each might strive to bring others over to his own, provided that he quietly and modestly supported his own by reasons nor bitterly demolished all others if his persuasions were not successful nor used any violence and refrained from abuse.

–SAINT THOMAS MORE (1478–1535), *UTOPIA*

The English word *utopia* derives from two Greek terms that together mean "no place." Indeed, the religious tolerance More proposed in his five-hundred-year-old classic was not widespread in his own day. Christianity, once a persecuted faith itself, had become the religion of Europe. In the name of the Prince of Peace, who forgave his own murderers from the cross, believers now thought nothing of capturing and martyring Jews on Good Friday. "Kill the Christ killers" was their watchword. To be fair, religious intolerance is limited neither to Christianity nor to former times. Mutual hatred between Hindus and Muslims in India or Buddhists and Hindus in Sri Lanka is a well-known cause of violence. Even within the same religion fatal animosities exist, as between Catholics and Protestants in Northern Ireland or Sunni and Shi'ite Muslims in Iran.

In matters of religion, said the Prophet Muhammad, let there be no use of force. Jesus, while imploring his listeners to understand what he was saying, knew they had to have the ears to hear. Even his miracles were not enough for some. Belief is a gift. It cannot be commanded.

The good news is, with two steps forward and one back, the world is slowly catching up with Saint Thomas More's vision. In more and more countries, religious freedom has become the law of the land. People may now worship the god of their choice or none at all. Religious affiliation is no longer a criterion for public office or private leadership. Perhaps utopia may be someplace after all.

In your Wisdom Journal, briefly discuss another feature you would have in your utopia.

OLDER AND WISER?

Elders who are sitting see farther than children who are standing.

–A Nigerian proverb

"Older and wiser" is a common turn of phrase in English. We are so committed to the notion that wisdom correlates with time-on-planet that we become angry when encountering the contrary. We vent our frustration in such phrases as "old enough to know better," "second childhood," and "there's no fool like an old fool."

The logic is straightforward. The longer we live, the more experiences we have. The more experiences we have, the more we have learned – or should have learned – from those experiences. Darwin's special theory of evolution takes this idea and applies it to flora and fauna. Animals and plants over generations develop features that help them adapt to a changing environment. In this regard we can say successful species are "older and wiser" than predecessors that would not be viable on the earth as it is today.

The process is similar in manufacturing. My last Honda was made in 1986. My present one is a 1994. The latter maintains what worked in the older model, but has excellent new features too – a footrest for my left foot, a small vanity mirror in the driver side sunshield, and a pull-out change drawer lined with Velcro to keep the coins from jingling. My dealer informed me that Honda takes owner feedback seriously and is committed to making improvements small and large from year to year.

Naturally, wisdom doesn't always correlate with age. When the twelve-year-old Jesus stayed behind in Jerusalem to discuss theology with the rabbis at the Temple, his parents were baffled at the boy's reply that he had been going about his Father's business (Luke 2:49). Yet in general the examined life yields understanding, and elders, though sitting, can often see farther than children who are on their feet.

Do you find wisdom accruing in your life with the passage of time? What about in the lives of others you know? Reflect on these questions in your Wisdom Journal.

LIVING WISELY, DYING WISELY

I have seen children and adults reach the state in which their soma and psyche are in harmony. It is these dying people whose lives end serenely with a sense of fulfillment and meaning. . . . I believe that it is the dying patient's right to expect others to help him reach as complete a life as he possibly can while he enters the terminal stage of living.

–ELISABETH KÜBLER-ROSS, *LIVING WITH DEATH AND DYING*, 1981

As the year draws to an end, thoughts of endings and new beginnings arise by themselves. The world is one year older, and so are we. Neither one of us will be here forever, but the world, despite our best efforts, will certainly outlast us. Dr. Elisabeth Kübler-Ross, the great Swiss pioneer of studies in death and dying, finds from her experience that when body and mind have reached a balance, individuals can die in peace. If someone has begun the dying process, it behooves the individual's friends and family to assist them in attaining that balance.

Tibetan culture, being Buddhist, believes in multiple lives with an in-between time called *bardo*. In the introduction to his translation of *The Tibetan Book of the Dead*, a handbook on dying well, Dr. Robert A. F. Thurman, an expert on Buddhism at Columbia University, explains: "Tibetans . . . have credible accounts by enlightened voyagers who have gone through the between experience consciously, preserved the memory, and reported their experiences. . . . Tibetans act on this Buddhist perspective in a practical manner, using their lifetimes to educate themselves to understand the world and to prepare for death and future lives by improving their ethical actions, emotional habits, and critical insight."

Those of you reading this book are fortunate. You have already chosen to invest time and energy in wisdom. At a deep level, wisdom means accepting the inevitability of our own death and using that consciousness to foster a healthy spiritual-material balance – the kind that allows us to die serenely and to be ready for whatever comes next.

In your Wisdom Journal, write your three highest priorities for the coming year.

THE RELATIVITY OF WISDOM

Divine folly is wiser than the wisdom of man, and divine weakness stronger than man's strength.

–1 CORINTHIANS 1:25

Adjectives come in three degrees: absolute, comparative, and superlative. So with regard to wisdom, grammar requires that some are wise, others wiser, and one individual (or group) wisest. If we limit ourselves to human beings and talk about wealth instead of wisdom, we can list out the world's fifty richest people in dollar terms. We can then say that these fifty individuals are wealthy, that number 48, for example, is wealthier than number 49, and that number 1 is wealthiest of all.

For better or worse, wisdom is a softer value than wealth. (Naturally, there are nonfinancial ways of being rich. Still, one can resort to dollar measures to arrive at some sort of acceptable ranking.) But when it comes to wisdom, how does one rate the Dalai Lama, say, against Mother Teresa, Gandhi against Einstein, Jesus against the Buddha? Or, for that matter, Florine, the wonderful African American woman who raised me, against my mother, who taught Florine to read and write?

One tradition, coming from the judgment of Solomon, relates wisdom to the quality of the decisions one makes. If two judges, say, made 100 decisions each over a period of ten years, an expert panel of attorneys and peers might be able to rate which judge, on average, made the better decisions and determine the wiser of the two.

If we talk about individuals, it should be possible to distinguish, at the extremes, between the wiser and the more foolish. It is heartening as well as humbling to know that no one of us will ever be all-wise. That attribute, like other perfections, belongs to the Divine. As our largest planet, Jupiter, is dwarfed by even the smallest of the visible stars, so do humankind's wisest persons pale when placed next to the perfect wisdom of God.

Do a "wisdom audit" on yourself. Which characteristics are "wise"? Which are "foolish"? In your Wisdom Journal, advise yourself on how you might improve just one characteristic.

THE WISDOM OF STEADINESS

Jesus Christ the same yesterday, and today, and for ever.

-Hebrews 13:8, KJV

My prep-school marching song began, "Steady old Peddie is marching along. / Her sons are loyal ever." I don't know how the administration has altered the text since Peddie became coed, but it's pretty clear that *steady* was as much a child of rhyme as reason. I'll grant you that the school has been in business since 1864. Thanks, moreover, to the generosity of one of its most illustrious and wealthiest "sons," the Hon. Walter J. Annenberg, Peddie boasts an endowment approaching 200 million dollars. The school is the envy of colleges three and four times its size. *Steady* and *old*, indeed!

Well, I've been around since 1939, the grandchild of Eastern European immigrants. Don't ask me about my net worth. My riches are definitely where thieves don't steal and moths don't corrode. As for steadiness, this is one virtue I wish I had more of.

I pride myself on keeping promises. For example, I am pretty much on schedule with this book. Or, here in Hawaii where many people are months behind in their rent, I make sure to pay my rent a few days early. Even if I have to borrow the money because of a cash-flow situation, I still get my check to the landlord on time.

Despite all this conspicuous promise keeping, the pile of letters in my inbox often waits till Christmas to get answered. I feel like the person who routinely carries too many books. Some get dropped, and the back occasionally goes out. I manage to put too many promises out there ever to get fulfilled in a timely way. Being overcommitted leaves me with negative discretionary time and energy. And God has shown no signs of creating a fifty-hour day.

So the time has come to assess and restructure. I am all for steadiness, doing a few things well and on time, and having a discretionary hour for myself that isn't stolen from five pending obligations. This may require fairly radical surgery.

How steady are you as you march along in life? Discuss this topic briefly in your Wisdom Journal.

PRINCELY WISDOM

The first and most important objective is the instruction of the prince in the matter of ruling wisely during times of peace. . . .

Authority is gained by the following varied characteristics: in the first place wisdom, then integrity, self-restraint, seriousness, and alertness.

–DESIDERIUS ERASMUS (1466?–1536), *THE EDUCATION OF A CHRISTIAN PRINCE*

Desiderius Erasmus, Dutch writer, scholar, humanist, and Catholic priest, was a contemporary of the Italian historian, statesman, and political philosopher Niccolò Machiavelli. Among other works, both wrote books for princes.

Of the two, Machiavelli's *The Prince* is the more famous by far. In it the author advised heads of Italian city-states, and by implication other heads of state, on how to retain power. He also suggested to those out of power how they might get it. His key strategy seems to be: Do whatever it takes, whether legal or illegal. Just make sure you don't get caught. For his efforts the adjective *Machiavellian* has entered the English language. Its meaning, according to Webster, is "unscrupulously cunning or devious."

Erasmus accepted the institution of divine-right kings. As a student of history, however, he saw how those who inherited their thrones were often unable to govern responsibly or effectively. Though nominally Christian, these monarchs seemed primarily to put their own interests first, to the detriment of their people. To remedy this situation, Erasmus wrote *The Education of a Christian Prince.* His point was straightforward: A good ruler will gain the love and respect of his subjects by loving, respecting, and acting responsibly toward them. In order to do this, the young prince will have to be raised to become a strong Christian. Good character coupled with wisdom will assure a productive reign. Finally, a wise ruler will understand that universal education is essential, because "nothing is more important to a prince than to have the best possible subjects."

Rulers, including today's managers, can be wise, foolish, or – like King Solomon – both. Machiavelli wished to train them to be clever. Erasmus hoped to educate them to be wise.

Write in your Wisdom Journal about the best boss you have ever had. In what respects was he or she wise?

THE WISDOM OF FREE WILL

God created things which had free will. That means creatures which can go either wrong or right. . . . If a thing is free to be good it is also free to be bad. . . . Why, then, did God give them free will? Because free will, though it makes evil possible, is also the only thing that makes possible any love or goodness or joy worth having. A world of automata – of creatures that worked like machines – would hardly be worth creating.

–C. S. Lewis (1898–1963), *Mere Christianity*

My wife had a firsthand encounter with evil. As a child of fourteen, she sat in a stalled train in East Prussia in January 1945. As the Russian guns moved closer, she looked out the window and saw all the people in danger of losing their lives. If the cold didn't do them in, the advancing Red Army would. How could it be the will of an almighty, all-good God, she asked herself, to have wars? Then a voice inside her said, very quietly: "It is not God's will to have wars. God did not create this war. Human beings did."

The Judeo-Christian tradition talks about sin. All of us have a dual nature. We are capable of perpetrating acts of good and evil. Original Sin, in the Christian tradition, biases us toward choosing evil or, at least, never fully embracing the good. Saint Paul complains that the good he wishes to do he fails to do, but the evil act he intends not to do, he ends up doing. Islam teaches that the true Holy War takes place in our hearts, between our higher and our lower forces. To win means to be able, finally, to surrender our fallible human will to the will of Allah.

The conjoined issues of good and evil, free will, and divine creation have perplexed human beings for eons. The answer C. S. Lewis gives and the one my wife received in her experience toward the end of World War II are probably as close as we human beings can come to fully understanding this puzzle.

Why do you think the world contains evil? Respond in your Wisdom Journal.

MOTHERING WISDOM

Although great strides have been made in the fields of child psychology and development, every woman should remember that we have the intuitive radar to know exactly how to listen to our children, what to say to our children, and how to love our children. Parenting classes and books can be helpful, but their main purpose should be to serve as tools by which we are put in touch with our natural wisdom, not directed away from it. Good parenting is not intellectual as much as emotional and intuitive.

-MARIANNE WILLIAMSON, *A WOMAN'S WORTH,* 1993

The classical view is that we human beings arrive as little *tabulae rasae,* blank slates. Our parents, pastors, teachers, and culture write in our instructions. A second more organic but less pleasant classical view is that we are born little savages needing to be civilized, like wild horses that must be broken and tamed. The Freudian model, a variant of this last belief, proposes that the emotionally mature adult is the successful product of the struggle between a person's instincts (the id) and the rules and regulations of society (the superego).

Marianne Williamson favors the romantic view. As she writes elsewhere in *A Woman's Worth,* children have their own personhood that their parents, to whom they are entrusted, should cultivate and not smother. The claims of our souls should be stronger than those of society. For we are not formless putty to be molded. Rather, we arrive as complete human beings, albeit small ones, who must be protected and nourished so that we can grow into our unique adult selves.

Further, mothers, by remembering that society has attempted to smother or restrict their own uniqueness, should form the first line of defense in protecting the individuality of their children. Outside expertise can be helpful in childrearing. But too often it substitutes for a mother's instincts while decreasing her self-reliance. Experts can draw on their own experiences, and science often has useful things to say. On balance, though, I agree with Williamson. Human beings are children of God – a fact that mothers – and fathers – forget at their peril.

In your Wisdom Journal, describe good and bad examples of mothering.

CHRISTMAS WISDOM

Christmas is not a date. It is a state of mind.

–MARY ELLEN CHASE (1887–1973)

Christmas is an annual reminder to Christians of God's gift to us of Himself. In celebration we practice giving ourselves to one another. The resulting Christmas presents symbolize the Christian ethic that it is more blessed to give than to receive.

Yet as David Grayson (1870–1945) concludes, we may expect too much of Christmas Day: "We try to crowd into it the long arrears of kindliness and humanity of the whole year." The point is rather to give of our abundance each and every day.

"What if I have no abundance?" you ask. If we limit giving to store-bought presents, that may certainly be an issue. Fortunately we can share whatever we do have, including who we are. We may give of our time and energy as well. Being there for another person can make every day Christmas. My friend Marni, an avid surfer, takes her ninety-year-old grandmother in for medical treatments whether the surf is up or not. My friend Jessica does all kinds of chores for her shut-in friend, Charley. A growing number of people I know volunteer at hospice, where they listen as dying people tell about what was important to them during their lives or what their major concerns are as they face death.

Even if we are talking about material gifts, the issue really is the spirit involved, not the price tag. Elementary-school children with no money create all kinds of presents, from personally designed plates to clothespin memo holders, that their parents treasure for decades. The Japanese, who are mainly Buddhists, never fail to bring *omiyage*, little household gifts, to people they are visiting. Indonesians, who are Muslims, do the same thing with their *oleh-oleh*.

Christmas reminds Christians and non-Christians alike that it is the nature of Divinity to give. If God came down at Christmas, as a beautiful Christmas anthem says, the Holy Spirit comforts and assists us year-round, twenty-four hours a day. As God's creatures and children, we are called upon, so far as we can, to do likewise.

Merry Christmas!

Reflect on and then write in your Wisdom Journal about your philosophy and practice of giving.

THE WISDOM OF ACCEPTANCE

Freedom consists in making the best of what we have, our parentage, our physical nature and mental gifts. Every kind of capacity, every form of vocation, if rightly used, will lead us to the centre.

–Radhakrishnan, *The Hindu View of Life*

America is known as the land of opportunity. People continue to immigrate here and make something of their lives. A recent "Parade Magazine" featured a Mexican American family. The father and mother had crossed into the United States illegally some years ago. In an amnesty they became citizens. They never earned much, but through determination and hard work, they made sure that all their many children graduated from college. One became a priest, another a physician, two others correctional workers, and so on. Each one made it into the middle class.

Yet America is also a country where we are tempted to act rich and famous even if we are not. A name change can create a Gatsby from a Gatz. Plastic surgery can help one marry up, get a better job, or pass for something one is not. Credit cards can even give one the temporary illusion of "having it all" – until the bills start coming in.

The concept of acceptance is not often invoked. There is wisdom, surely, in having high goals, working hard, and giving life one's best shot. Equally, there is a kind of quietism, a quitting before one has truly started, that is pathological. A friend of mine in college, during a rough time, said he decided to "give up for Lent."

Radhakrishnan, the philosopher who became president of India, is right, it seems to me. Our genetic make-up, the time and place of our birth, and the quality of the parenting we receive are all limiting factors over which we have no control. Yet only by accepting these limitations can we become all we have the potential to be. Acceptance is the magic road from the margins of ourselves to the center.

Think about something in your background or make-up that has always been a problem for you. Now write down three positive things in your Wisdom Journal about this feature or characteristic. You may be surprised.

SCRIPTURAL WISDOM

Remember that from early childhood you have been familiar with the sacred writings which have power to make you wise. . . . Every inspired scripture has its use for teaching the truth and refuting error, or for reformation of manners and discipline in right living, so that the man who belongs to God may be efficient and equipped for good work of every kind.

–2 Timothy 3:15–17

Soon after moving to Hawaii in 1967, my family and I began attending Church of the Crossroads, a United Church of Christ congregation near the university. The minister, a charismatic preacher with strong left-wing leanings that kept him in controversy, happened to be the brother of a longtime family friend. The services were rarely boring.

One of the many features of Crossroads was the reading of the Scriptures. Whereas most churches have Old and New Testament readings, a selection from the Psalms, and the Gospel reading, Crossroads had Old Testament, New Testament, and *Now* Testament. The concept was very 1960s, but it still makes sense to me today.

If this book of reflections is about anything, it is the universality of wisdom. God created everything. Therefore everything contains its maker's signature. And the signature of God is *Wisdom.* As Jesus so often said, we need only the eyes to see and the ears to hear. Wisdom is within each of us. It is thus within our neighbors, even our enemies.

What then is "Scripture"? For me, whatever leads me closer to God and God's will for my life on a daily basis is Scripture. It need not be Jewish or Christian. It need not even be something I understand with my conscious mind. Recently, for example, I heard the Koran recited in Arabic. My body began swaying ever so slightly, and I knew God was close. Nor need it be religious. The poetry of Rilke, Matthias Claudius, and the early Wordsworth form part of my Scripture. So do the "Big Book" from Alcoholics Anonymous, Frankl's *Man's Search for Meaning,* and Gibran's *The Prophet.* What about for you?

In your Wisdom Journal, talk about a few nonbiblical works that comprise your Scripture.

PHENOMENAL WISDOM

In the year 1141, . . . when I was forty-two years and seven months of age, a fiery light, flashing intensely, came from the open vault of heaven and poured through my whole brain. Like a flame that is hot without burning it kindled all my heart. . . . And suddenly I could understand what such books as the Old and New Testament actually set forth.

–HILDEGARD OF BINGEN (1098–1179)

In 1996 John Travolta starred in a movie called *Phenomenon.* He played an ordinary small-town auto mechanic who, while walking down Main Street late one night, experienced a ball of fire falling out of the sky and entering his head. Subsequently he attained superhuman powers of body, mind, and spirit. His incredible brain activity was demonstrated by EEG, CAT scans, and other lab tests. The only problem was that his new powers were literally burning him up. His phenomenal life was over almost before it had begun.

Saint Hildegard fared better. She lived to be eighty-one, a very old age for those days. Not only that, but in a time when the glass ceiling was lower and stronger, she became abbess of a convent and founded a second one, and she was an author, theologian, musician, painter, herbalist, healer, chef, spiritual director, administrator, mystic, and political mediator. In fact, she was the favored "diplomat" of Frederick Barbarossa, the Holy Roman Emperor.

My own spiritual guide, Muhammad Subuh, was born in Java in 1901 and died on his birthday eighty-six years later. One summer night in 1925, he went out to clear his head before turning in. Suddenly the sky became bright. Looking up he saw a ball of light like the daytime sun. Only this "sun," descending rapidly, entered his head. His whole body shook. He went home expecting to die. Instead, over the next three years, he received a series of spontaneous exercises that became the basis for the spiritual training he passed on to followers in eighty countries.

Have you ever experienced something outside your understanding of the "normal"? If so, write about it in the privacy of your Wisdom Journal.

NIGHT WISDOM

In night there is counsel.

–An ancient Greek proverb

Proverbs are funny. Sometimes you get them right away. Sometimes you struggle for years to find their meaning. This one I got right away, so I was surprised when my college students in Minnesota had a hard time.

The obvious, maybe superficial, meaning can be gotten from the saying's American equivalent: "Sleep on it." In other words, if you are facing a dilemma, don't try to force a decision. Turn to other matters instead. Let the arguments and counterarguments drain from your memory. Then, like a nugget of gold left in the prospector's pan, you may find an answer that satisfies. A variant on this technique is what the British mathematician and philosopher John Bennett referred to as "reflection." By this he meant just the opposite of thinking about an issue. His advice: Every time you get what you think is the solution, push it away, reflect it back to its source. If you keep getting the same indication, he believed, chances are it was correct.

Daytime is when we use our left brain to organize our lives and make decisions. It is the domain of the sun, of yang. Night, however, is the domain of the moon, of yin. It is the time that we relax. We fall asleep and give ourselves over to the mysterious world of intuition and dreams. According to some psychologists, dreaming is the process whereby the mind cleanses and renews itself as well as massages problems until they yield solutions. After dozens of unsuccessful tries at creating the lightbulb, Edison got his answer one night in a dream.

So, the real meaning of this proverb is that we have another wisdom resource within us besides our logical thinking mind. It is better accessed by surrender than by force. Just as our computers have much more capacity than most of us will ever use, so it is with our minds. In night there really is counsel – we just have to learn to listen.

Discuss in your Wisdom Journal how you use intuition and other "nighttime" techniques to solve problems.

MILLENNIUM-HYMN WISDOM

Through the darkness of the ages,
Through the sorrows of the days,
Strength of weary generations,
Lifting hearts in hope and praise.
Light in darkness, joy in sorrow,
Presence to allay all fears,
Jesus, You have kept Your promise,
Faithful through 2,000 years.

–HILLARY JOLLY, WINNER OF THE MILLENNIUM HYMN COMPETITION, ENGLAND

You may wonder where I find my quotations. More often than not, they find me – through family, business associates, or friends. As I near completion of this reader, I am aware that there are thousands of statements I have missed. I apologize if I have omitted one of your favorites. Please send it to me, with full attribution, to our web site: *www.worldwisdomproject.org.* We'll gladly share it with others on our Wisdom Resources page.

Today's quotation came to me courtesy of my wife. She found it in a Christian magazine. According to the article, the verse was written by Hillary Jolly, a fifty-two-year-old church cleaning woman in England. Besides her job, she cares for her mentally ill daughter and is an amateur poet. When she heard about the Millennium Hymn Contest, she set to work – and won. Her hymn was performed before the Royal Family and others in Saint Paul's Cathedral, London, on January 2, 2000, the first Sunday of that august year. Her entry won over those submitted by professional hymn writers and poets.

Despite her last name, Hillary Jolly's life has been anything but easy. Yet the fact that she has worked, supported herself and her child, cared for her daughter, and transformed her suffering into prize-winning verse provides testimony to the power of faith. As I read her story, I was reminded of the two anonymous working-class English women who wrote the best-selling devotional *God Calling.* The wisdom in both cases is straightforward. God will help us overcome any adversity. We must simply believe.

In your Wisdom Journal, share an instance when your faith helped you through a difficult time.

COMMENCEMENT WISDOM

In my end is my beginning.

–A MOTTO OF MARY STUART, QUEEN OF SCOTS (1542–1587)

Commencement, any high-school graduate can tell you, is a word that looks two ways. During my student days, I thought of it as denoting the end of a course of study, a recognition that someone had completed all requirements for a degree and was ready to move on. The word itself, of course, has to do with beginnings. New beginnings. The familiar expression says it all: "Today is the first day of the rest of your life."

Commencement wisdom is knowing that God makes everything new and that we, as cocreators, have the opportunity each moment to begin again as well. Yesterday I may have *graduated,* a word that means no more but no less than "having taken a step." Where there's life, there's movement. But today I am called on to graduate again. We have to keep on keeping on.

It helps to celebrate the successful completion of each day or, in this case, each year. It is also sensible to break up life into a series of present opportunities. This strategy is contained in the Twelve Step slogan "One day at a time." Letting bygones be bygones, starting afresh, celebrating the accomplishment of having reached this new day, this new year, is a formula for wise living. If a single college graduation can equip one for a lifetime of productive activity, think of the self-confidence that will flow from a lifetime of daily commencements.

So, as you graduate from the year just concluding, reflect on what you have learned. May the new year give you 365 (or 366) daily chances to live a wiser life. If you have found a few techniques to help you along the way, this book will have served its purpose.

Happy New Year!

Spend an hour leafing through your Wisdom Journal. Then do a five-minute relaxation exercise. Sit quietly and focus on your breathing. Let the thoughts and images come and go. When you are finished, do one more Wisdom Journal exercise. Write three things you intend to do in the coming year to live more wisely. Bon voyage on your journey to wisdom!

A FAREWELL TO THE READER

A Visit to Sophie's House

We carry with us every story we have ever heard and every story we have ever lived. . . . We carry most of those stories unread, as it were, until we have grown the capacity or readiness to read them. When that happens they may come back to us filled with a previously unsuspected meaning. It is almost as if we have been collecting pieces of a greater wisdom, sometimes over many years without knowing.

-Rachel Naomi Remen, MD, *Kitchen Table Wisdom*, 1996

Dear Reader,

I have one more story to tell. A few years ago, I was spending a day doing foundation site visits in rural Minnesota. My appointment schedule left me with four hours to kill. As usual I went to a local café instead of a fast-food franchise just outside town. As I ate lunch, I noticed something strange. Across the street was a small, white cottage amid the stores. My server, a woman in her late fifties, noticed my quizzical expression. "That's Sophie's house," she said. "She's the Methodist minister's widow. Lived there for years. Folks, especially the young people, like to visit her. She's everyone's grandma, seems."

On a lark I bought a box of After Eight mints and knocked on Sophie's door. A tall, white-haired woman with the bluest eyes greeted me as if she had been expecting me. For the next two hours, over tea and homemade apple pie, we had an extraordinary conversation. I told her about my life and dreams. She listened with a faint smile. Then she spoke. She seemed to know things about me that even I only half knew. While it would be too much to pass on everything she said, I want to share her last words to me: "Reynold, you have been studying important things all your life, it seems. Now you have to write your book. It may take a while, but you'll do it. Remember, though. God has put wisdom into each of his children. If you can remind your readers of that, you'll have done God's work."

After that I thanked her, we hugged, and I left for my appointment. I hope, dear reader, that I have followed Sophie's advice.

With Aloha from Hawaii,
Reynold Feldman
Kane'ohe, O'ahu, June 22, 1999

AUTHOR'S ACKNOWLEDGMENTS

No one writes a book alone. This is not a truism so much as the simple truth, especially in the case of this book. Think of it. Every daily reflection begins with a quotation: sometimes short–a one-liner or a proverb–frequently an extended statement. In either case, other people's thoughts are what provoked my thinking and writing. They formed the paper cones that I stuck into the cotton candy machine. No paper cones, no cotton candy.

Even after I completed the introduction and a sampler, some publisher had to buy the idea. Two of my colleagues, Dr. John Lawry and Sr. Helene Zimmerman, recommended Saint Mary's Press. So, imagine how delighted I was when they offered me a contract. Special thanks to former senior editor Carl Koch for his enthusiasm and to Michael Wilt, the editor who worked on the project and who has the gift of sounding more like me sometimes than I do myself. Michael was invariably able to take a pretty good reflection and make it sing, or zing, depending on the circumstances. Not only that, but he can count better than I can. After I was sure I had sent in the right number of daily reflections, he called and asked, very diplomatically, if I couldn't write just a few more. Thank you, Michael, for your wonderful work.

While I am on the subject of Saint Mary's Press, I should express my gratitude to Pamela Johnson, the Press's publicist, even though much of her work will begin after I have written these words. Still, we are off to a good start.

Special thanks are due to some special people. I think first of my friend and "coach," Dr. Loren Ekroth, who never stopped with advice, almost always good and useful, but went on to provide some of the best lead quotations in the book. I am also grateful to my colleagues in the World Wisdom Project–Marni Suu Reynolds and Jessica Woodrow–who sat patiently while I read them my latest creation. The same is true for Faith Feldman, our goddaughter, who, while living with us, would ask me to read what I'd written on a particular day.

In the book you have met many of my teachers, formal and informal. Whether *Wisdom* would have been possible with out Florine Tolson Bond, Al Watson, Alec Witherspoon, Dick Sewall, Jane Tompkins,

Muhammad Subuh, Varindra Tarzie Vittachi, Sr. Eileen Rice, Jonas Salk, Rahayu Martohudoyo, Sr. Joan Tuberty, Parker Palmer, and Doug Olson in my life is questionable. Frankly I doubt it.

Finally, I owe an unpayable debt of gratitude to my children—Marianna Levine, her husband Harper, and Christine Feldman—who were enthusiastic from the first. No one, however, has been more supportive than my wife, Simone Zimmermann Feldman. She has gone through thick and thin with me for thirty-six years and, along with the kids, knows the limits of my wisdom better than anyone else. If you find some things in this book that are wise, she will know just where to point you for the source.

ACKNOWLEDGMENTS (CONTINUED FROM COPYRIGHT PAGE)

The scriptural quotations marked KJV are from the King James' Version of the Bible.

All other scriptural quotations are from the New English Bible with the Apocrypha. Copyright © 1970 by the Oxford University Press and Cambridge University Press. All rights reserved.

The poetry by Emily Dickinson on pages 140, 201, and 292 is from *The Poems of Emily Dickinson*, edited by Ralph W. Franklin (Cambridge, MA: The Belknap Press of Harvard University Press, 1979). Copyright © 1951, 1955, 1979 by the President and Fellows of Harvard College. Reprinted by permission of the publishers and the Trustees of Amherst College.

The poetry by E. E. Cummings on page 207 is from *Complete Poems: 1913–1962*, by E. E. Cummings (New York: Harcourt Brace Jovanovich, Publishers, 1980), page 663. Copyright © renewed 1979 by Nancy T. Andrews. Permission applied for.